The AGE of UTOPIA

Christendom from the Renaissance to the Russian Revolution

John Strickland

PARADISE AND UTOPIA

The Rise and Fall of What the West Once Was

VOLUME 3

ANCIENT FAITH PUBLISHING ✠ CHESTERTON, INDIANA

The Age of Utopia: Christendom from the Renaissance to the Russian Revolution

Volume Three of Paradise and Utopia: The Rise and Fall of What the West Once Was

Published by:
Ancient Faith Publishing
A Division of Ancient Faith Ministries
P.O. Box 748
Chesterton, IN 46304

ISBN: 978-1-955890-05-2

Library of Congress Control Number: 2021945295

Printed in the United States of America

Contents

Beside the divine garden from which I have been driven away, I will build a New Eden for myself which I will populate with mine own kind. I will station the invisible sentinel Progress at its entrance, and place a flaming sword into his hands. And he will say to God, "Thou shalt not enter here!"

Jules-Antoine Castagnary, 1858

PROLOGUE

At the Summit of Mount Ventoux

WITH ONE FINAL LURCH, FRANCESCO Petrarch hoisted himself up onto the summit of Mount Ventoux in southern France. There he stood as if in triumph. He had struggled all day to reach the peak, taking numerous breaks as he fought his way up six thousand feet of mountainside. The battle had been worth it. Now, stretching out below him in all directions, lay the glorious civilization of the West.

He was no conqueror, but he could not resist bringing to mind the martial image of the famous Philip of Macedon. That king—the father of Alexander the Great—had once ascended another mountain to survey his spoils. The lands that lay at Petrarch's feet may not have been his possession in a political sense, but they represented a cultural inheritance to which he, the greatest scholar of his generation, intended to lay claim. A sensation of intellectual mastery surged within him as he gazed across the welcoming landscape.

It was exhilarating. To the northeast rose the Alps, encased in their glaciers above a vast plane of low-lying clouds. To the west, the Rhone River wandered through the bucolic countryside of Provence until it merged with the Mediterranean, whose surf-splashed shores were just visible through the haze of the southern horizon. Regretfully, Petrarch could not see what his heart most desired to see: the borderlands of his native Italy. But he knew where to look. There beyond the eastern horizon lay the land his family had once inhabited before political misfortune forced them into exile. Such a recollection only stirred the longing that would drive his future work and the fame it promised.

Taking it all in, the young scholar was overwhelmed with inspiration. His reflex was to reach into a knapsack for the book he had packed for brief snatches of edification during rest stops. After all, in addition to being one of history's first recreational mountaineers, Petrarch was a self-proclaimed and inveterate bookworm. The volume in question was Augustine's *Confessions,* and what he now read in its pages, according to an account he later gave, would change his life forever. In doing so it would also change Christendom, a civilization with a supporting culture that had long directed its members toward the heavenly transformation of the world.

PETRARCH'S ASCENT OF MOUNT VENTOUX—THE first ever recorded—occurred in 1336. The fourteenth century that framed it was a period of acute uncertainty for the West. The scholar was himself a product of this uncertainty, and he more than any other contemporary provided a creative resolution to it.

Petrarch had been born in exile, the son of an Italian political refugee who, along with the poet Dante, had been forced to flee his native city of Florence. As a child, Petrarch never had a real home, and he would never have one as an adult. He would always consider himself a "pilgrim everywhere" (*peregrinus ubique*), attached to no place on earth.

Petrarch came of age while his father was serving at the papal court in Avignon, France. The papacy had moved away from Rome due in part to the volatile political climate of Italy. More than that, however, the king of France now sought control over the Roman Catholic Church's highest office and insisted it reside closer to his own court. King Philip the Fair (r. 1285–1314) had only a few decades earlier ordered the abduction of Pope Boniface VIII (r. 1294–1303), whose papal bull *Unum Sanctum* contained the most provocative assertion of papal supremacy ever made: "It is necessary for salvation that every human being be subject to the Roman Pontiff." Brutally beaten by

Philip's agents, the pope subsequently died in humiliation just nine months before Petrarch's birth. The new papal headquarters, while renowned for their opulence and culture (Petrarch developed his lifelong love of learning there), symbolized a civilization in confusion.

So did the great university system that Petrarch entered after leaving Avignon as a young man. He entered the West's most prestigious school of law, that of the University of Bologna, and there was immersed in the discipline of learning known as scholasticism. Less than a century had elapsed since scholasticism's most famous advocate, Thomas Aquinas (d. 1274), had used the philosophy of Aristotle as the intellectual framework for nearly all knowledge about God, man, and the cosmos. The study of law in particular had been thoroughly integrated into the scholastic system, producing a uniform body of canon law that regulated everything from papal authority to the practice of penance.

But change was in the air. By the middle of the fourteenth century, a rebellion against the systematic confidence of scholasticism was launched by William of Occam (d. 1347), whose philosophical method of "nominalism" rejected universal truths in favor of a knowledge of particulars. Petrarch may have felt these winds of change even within the conservative atmosphere of Bologna. In any event, he abruptly departed the university after losing respect for scholasticism. Moving from one town to another, he spent the remainder of his life advancing a new intellectual movement that came to be known, in the century following his death, as humanism.

The goal of humanism was to restore to man his full potential for life in this world. For Petrarch, the culture of the West had long downgraded what was once the glorious status of the human being within God's creation. He saw the preeminence of Aristotelianism as a cause of this, for it assigned to the world a universal and unchanging order that, in Petrarch's judgment, stifled personal spiritual growth. Especially pernicious was the scholastic approach to knowledge that was based on Aristotle, in which acquisition of the truth appeared limited to rational cognition and rote memorization. Knowledge, Petrarch believed, must be transformative. Its only legitimate purpose is to stir the will toward a desire for moral and spiritual reform.

"It is better to will the good," he famously wrote, "than to know the truth."[1] Ironically, it was pagan philosophers like Plato and pagan orators like Cicero, he claimed—not Christian theologians like Aquinas—who could restore to Christendom its imperative toward transformation.

But for Petrarch there was more to the fourteenth-century crisis of values than this. The problem was not simply opposing Platonism to Aristotelianism, or Ciceronian rhetoric to Thomistic metaphysics. Below the surface of his revolt against scholasticism was a perception that Western culture had become trapped within a labyrinth of pessimism about the condition of man. This insight runs through many of his writings. He himself was far from immune to such pessimism. Repeatedly he returns to the fact that as a young man he fell in love with a married woman named Laura, though he was never able to consummate his lustful desire. Beyond romance, he was also driven by a passion for celebrity that he recognized as vanity.

Pessimism about his futile attachments to the world was most prominent in an imaginary dialogue between himself and Augustine, entitled *The Private Conflict of My Thoughts*.[2] The title of the work is significant, for as the earliest prominent humanist he was torn in two by despair about his salvation and the desire to experience spiritual transformation in this life. In this work he complains relentlessly about "all the miseries of the human condition." Everything in this world, he declares, is tainted by mortality and therefore a source of "loathing and contempt."[3] But he delights in the world and cannot put his love for it aside. The only reasonable path through life, his saintly interlocutor advises, consists of a ceaseless meditation on death.

A DIFFERENT CULTURE WAS TO be found in the East, beyond the limits of the Italian horizon for which Petrarch longed from his vantage point on Mount Ventoux. Eastern Christendom had not followed the West in the

---

1 Petrarch, *On His Own Ignorance and That of Many Others*, in *The Renaissance Philosophy of Man*, ed. Ernst Cassirer, Paul Oskar Kristeller, and John Herman Randall (Chicago: University of Chicago, 1948), 47–133.

2 The work is often abbreviated as *Secretum*.

3 Petrarch, *Secretum*, trans. J. G. Nichols (Richmond, England: Oneworld Classics, 2010), 61.

introduction of papal supremacy or scholastic theology. Its piety had not been infected by the same pessimism about the human condition. Following the Great Schism of 1054, Byzantium, Russia, and other Orthodox lands had preserved traditional Christianity's experience of the kingdom of heaven in this world. Petrarch seems to have known little about it, but Eastern Christendom possessed something that can be called a culture of paradise.

Its most illustrative expression in the fourteenth century was a movement known as hesychasm. This movement was articulated by an Athonite theologian named Gregory Palamas (d. 1359), who had spent his youth not in the libraries of Italy and France but in the monasteries of Byzantium. From Mount Athos, he looked down on landscapes as breathtaking as those Petrarch saw, but he did so with very different eyes. Drawing on the ascetical tradition of an intensive "prayer of the heart" rooted in the teachings of the ancient desert fathers, hesychasm claimed that even now, in this world, man can experience the kingdom of heaven. Gregory spoke of this experience as the consequence of the Incarnation, by which divinity was joined to humanity in the person of Jesus Christ. Those baptized into His sacramental body, the Church, experienced a transformation comparable to that longed for by Petrarch back in the West. The difference was that they did so in the present age, not merely after the miserable struggle in this world had spent itself. Through the divine "energies" of God, Christians could enjoy the immediate experience of paradise even now, in a cosmos transfigured by the divine presence. Life within the Church became an opportunity for continuous transformation. The entire human person—body and soul—participated in divinity through liturgical worship and the sacrament of the Eucharist.

Gregory was vehemently opposed by a monk from southern Italy named Barlaam (d. 1348). The latter came to Constantinople with the intention of bringing an end to the Great Schism. He placed his hopes in Platonist philosophy, which, in its rejection of man's ability to know God directly, offered a kind of liberating agnosticism to the advocates of church reunion. In the absence of sure knowledge of God, Barlaam argued, Roman Catholics and Orthodox could simply dismiss many of the objections that lay at the root of their division. But there was more to Barlaam's Platonist theology than

Barlaam of Calabria

this. He extended it to claim that the hesychasts' doctrine of divine energies, though grounded in the Incarnation, violated a radical distinction that must be maintained between spirit and matter. The human body was little more than a prison house for the soul, as Plato had demonstrated, and only the soul was capable of spiritual transformation.

In 1341 a council at Constantinople confirmed hesychasm as Orthodox doctrine, and Barlaam was forced to return to Italy. Humiliated by the experience, he converted to Roman Catholicism. He also became acquainted with Petrarch. The two scholars formed a lasting friendship, based especially on their mutual love for pagan literature. Petrarch was eager to read the Greek classics, and Barlaam agreed to tutor him. In this way Petrarch obtained treatises by Plato and even helped set in motion the first-ever translation of Homer into Latin.

Their days of collaboration did not last long, but the exchange reinforced two important and interrelated convictions already forming in Petrarch. The first was that because of His transcendence, God is fundamentally unknowable by man. The Platonist Barlaam had rejected the claim of the hesychasts about man's participation in the divine energies. Petrarch seems to have embraced this view, observing that man's unbridgeable distance from heaven leaves him in a state of perpetual misery. "In this life," he lamented,

> *it is impossible to know God in His fullness; . . . knowledge sometimes makes us miserable—as does that knowledge the demons have, who tremble below in*

> *hell before Him they have learned to know.*[4]

The cultivation of an ardent love of God could assuage what was otherwise demonic despair about God's impending judgment. But it was a love that could be consummated with its divine object only after death, not in this world.

The second conviction growing in Petrarch's mind was that without the ability to know God in this world, man's experience of transformation here could be only *secular*, that is, "of this age." It could not be heavenly. This was the origin of secular humanism, a belief that the natural, spiritually untransformed world provides the means of human fulfillment. It was a belief radically at odds with traditional Christianity, and it would forever alter the character of Christendom.

WHICH BRINGS US BACK TO the lofty summit of Mount Ventoux. After scanning the physical horizons of the West stretching out beneath him, Petrarch opened his copy of the *Confessions*. He did so at a random point, imitating Augustine's own famous method of spiritual discernment through spontaneous reading. Just as the saint had once chanced on a passage from Romans about righteousness, Petrarch now read the following:

> *And men go to admire the high mountains, the vast floods of the sea, the huge streams of the rivers, the circumference of the ocean, and the revolutions of the stars—and desert themselves.*[5]

According to Petrarch, this statement completely altered the experience of ascending Mount Ventoux.

To be sure, he did not dismiss as irrelevant the glory of the natural world (something Augustine would have been inclined to do). In fact, his later writings would celebrate what in Latin was known as the *saeculum*, the world in

---

4 Petrarch, *On His Own Ignorance*.

5 The passage read by Augustine and recorded in his *Confessions* was Romans 13:13–14.

its spiritually untransformed condition. But the excerpt from the *Confessions* led him to separate such a secularized world from the inner life of spiritual transformation. The tendency was uniquely Augustinian in its psychological intensity. It was also dualistic, and Petrarch was consciously drawn toward Augustine because of the latter's heightened distinction between body and spirit. A psychologically defined intellect, freed from a corrupted body and its impressionable senses, would never "desert itself" but would instead pursue virtue. And it would do so subjectively, as an expression of its autonomy.[6]

The sun was now setting on the western horizon, and the time had come to descend the mountain. Petrarch, upon finishing his brief reading, fell into complete silence for the remainder of the journey. His companions wondered at what had transpired in his soul, but he said nothing to them. As darkness descended, so did he, until finally, upon arrival at his lodge, he recorded his impressions in a letter to his father confessor. Throughout the remainder of his life he would return to these notes, expanding and enhancing them with the insights of old age.

And for this reason the letter documenting Petrarch's ascent of Mount Ventoux marks the birth of secular humanism. Its Augustinian conviction that the world is separated from the spiritual life of man departed fundamentally from the anthropology and cosmology of traditional Christianity. Since the time of Pentecost, the Church had cultivated a *heavenly* transformation of the world through man's communion with God. A world thus sanctified had been an antechamber to paradise.

Now a new age was beginning. The West, separated from Eastern Christendom and estranged from its hesychastic values, began a process of desanctification or desecration. It began to direct its members toward a *secular* transformation of the world. This was the beginning of an age of utopia.

---

6 Alexander Lee has argued that Petrarch's Augustinianism when writing the ascent was based on the theologian's early writings, which assigned more autonomy to the human will than his more mature and famous writings against the Pelagians. Alexander Lee, *Petrarch and St. Augustine: Classical Scholarship, Christian Theology, and the Origins of the Renaissance in Italy* (Leiden: Brill, 2012), 61.

PART I

The Desecration of the World

CHAPTER ONE

Fathering Humanism

CHRISTENDOM REACHED A FATEFUL TURNING point during the fourteenth century. Since its dawn at Pentecost, the civilization had directed its members toward the heavenly transformation of the world. In 1054, however, a parting of the ways occurred when first Rome and then Constantinople excommunicated one another. This Great Schism created two cultural poles, one in the East and one in the West. Each shared in the cultural heritage of the first millennium. But each developed a very different approach to the transformational imperative.

In the East, the Orthodox Church largely preserved the culture of old Christendom. Its principal states, Byzantium and Russia, experienced many historical disruptions—especially in the form of pagan invasions from Asia—but their continuity with the past assured a vital adherence to Christendom's core value, the manifestation in the world of the kingdom of heaven or paradise.

In the West, the Roman Catholic Church formed what can be called a new Christendom. At first it continued to share with the East in the paradisiacal heritage of the first millennium. However, as the Great Division advanced beyond the eleventh century, advocates of papal supremacy introduced reforms that altered traditional Christianity. From Italy in the south to Britain in the north, and from Spain in the west to the Poland in the east, a Papal Reformation institutionalized "reform for the better," and these reforms brought profound change. The culture of the West—and the civilization it supported—was therefore gradually realigned with a reformational form of Christianity.

And as this happened, the culture of the West began to lose its hold on paradise. Temple architecture changed. Departing from an anagogical representation of heaven on earth, the new Gothic style dematerialized the cosmos and projected heaven into an increasingly cerebral and remote "afterlife." Iconography no longer proclaimed the objective presence of Christ among men but was reduced to stimulating largely subjective and guilt-directed emotions. Monastics were as much concerned with staffing universities and inquisitions as with revealing the mystical kingdom of heaven. And the laity, once a partner with the clergy in the sanctification of the world, was becoming a passive witness to a mounting clericalism.

Pessimism was in the air, and many within the new Christendom were stifled by it. One of these was Francesco Petrarch. Catching his breath with difficulty, this most reflective of Westerners clung to what remained of the transformational imperative. But instead of following its ancient orientation toward the kingdom of heaven, he recalibrated it to a mode of life known as the *saeculum*. Losing sight of paradise, he began to grope his way toward utopia.

A Disfigured Culture

PETRARCH'S GENERATION INHERITED A CULTURAL disposition claiming that because of Adam's banishment from paradise, the entire human race would not taste of its fruits again until the Second Coming. This was more than a doctrine of the Fall, which traditional Christianity had always held. It was a pessimistic denial of the presence in this world of the kingdom of heaven.

This disposition was drawn largely from the doctrines of Augustinianism. In the fifth century, Augustine (d. 430) had found it necessary to emphasize man's extreme degradation as a result of the Fall, to which he notoriously

Francesco Petrarch

assigned a guilt that was universal for the entire human race. His motivation was to counter the heresy of Pelagianism, which regarded man as capable of autonomously willing his own salvation within the life of the Church. Augustine insisted that only through a divinely bestowed prevenient grace could an individual human being will his salvation. This idea created a sharp distinction between divine grace and human nature. The effect, recorded by less nuanced Latin fathers in the centuries that followed, was that humanity was fundamentally estranged from paradise in this world. Following the Great Division, this pessimistic vision of man increasingly disfigured the culture of the new Christendom.

The old Christendom had long cultivated an optimistic vision of humanity that arose from what can be called a *metamorphocentric* or "transformation-centered" piety. At its heart was a transformational imperative. The kingdom of heaven revealed by the gospel was the measure by which life in the world was to be lived and organized. The world was therefore constantly in a process of heavenly transformation under the influence of the Church. This created a paradisiacal culture that manifested the kingdom of heaven in ways too numerous to summarize.[1]

A lone example will have to suffice in describing this culture. It relates

1 For an account of Christendom's paradisiacal culture, see *The Age of Paradise*.

to the way Christians sanctified space and time in their use of temple architecture—often called *anagogy*. The physical space occupied by Christians as they assembled together in worship was "oriented," that is, it was directed toward paradise, which church tradition located symbolically in the east (*oriens* in Latin).[2] During both the Divine Liturgy and the Mass, the clergy brought the consecrated Eucharist to worshippers from the altar located at the easternmost part of a church building. The architectural orientation of Christian temples thus represented the transcendent God's immanence on earth. Through it, man entered an experience of heaven on earth and a participation in divinity. The world became the antechamber of paradise.

However, during the eleventh century the transformational imperative became altered in the West. The papacy that emerged from the Great Schism of 1054 introduced a logic of what was considered "reform for the better." Its goals were the subjection of the world to the values that guided the Papal Reformation. Among these was a political subjugation of the state to the papacy and a cultural subversion of marriage, which, though normative for the laity, was now prohibited among the spiritually superior clergy.

Scholasticism began more and more to circumscribe the sacramental terms of divine participation. With the establishment of a doctrine of purgatory, heavenly immanence gave way to an understanding of salvation that projected paradise to a point in time far beyond this age when, perhaps thousands of "years" hence, God's implacable wrath would finally be assuaged through the harrowing process of postmortem punishment. Theologians beginning with Anselm of Canterbury (d. 1109)—known as "the last of the fathers and the first of the scholastics"—presented human salvation not as the process of deification, of becoming ever more filled with the life of God, but as a one-time release from an impending punishment at the hands of an offended God who demanded satisfaction for man's offenses.

The best one could do under these cultural circumstances was to embrace

2 Ironically, in Rome itself the most famous basilicas—those dedicated to St. John at the Lateran and to St. Peter at the Vatican—were not oriented. But many in the West were, especially under the influence of the East, where the practice appears to have originated.

a *stavrocentric* (or "cross-centered") piety in which one's sense of guilt for causing Jesus' death was mollified through a cathartic meditation on His suffering. Anselm himself set the example by writing a series of prayers about his meditations on the Crucifixion. Naturalistic statuary representing the Last Judgment placed at the entrance portals of Gothic cathedrals, as well as graphic images of the "dance of death," elaborated the stavrocentric experience. And if blindness or visual insensitivity dulled the anxiety about salvation such images were intended to produce, hymns like the *Dies irae* ("Day of Wrath") provided disquieting compensation. Under such cultural circumstances the penitential piety of Western culture became, as Petrarch would lament, overwhelmingly pessimistic.

Yet it need not have been so. Traditional Christianity had long offered the sinner a path toward reconciliation with God that was metamorphocentric rather than stavrocentric. Paradise was as near as the believer's capacity for a truly transformational experience of repentance. From the beginning of His ministry, Christ had called on His followers to repent, "for the kingdom of heaven is at hand" (Matt. 3:2). For more than a millennium, penitential practices had centered on heartfelt confession. The Greek word for "sin" (*amartia*) in the New Testament means "missing of the mark," that is, failing to be what God made one to be. Repentance was not merely a juridical listing of offenses or a cathartic act of self-loathing. It was a "change of heart" (*metanoia*), a resolve to turn away from the darkness of sin toward a God who, like the father in the parable of the prodigal son, watches lovingly for the sinner's return and, on seeing him, rushes to welcome him back into the joy of communion (Luke 15:11–32). Sacramental confession arose to provide the penitent with exactly this experience of heavenly transformation.

But three centuries after the Great Division, penitents like Petrarch found little in Western piety to encourage them. Most troubling was the system of penances that was now associated with the practice of confession. They were often perfunctory. In 1350, for instance, a pilgrimage was organized in Rome by decree of the pope, who had recently begun to claim the exclusive power of dissolving penitential "obligations" by virtue of being the earthly substitute or "vicar" of Christ. This Roman jubilee—the first since the time of Boniface VIII—brought Petrarch and thousands of other penitents to the city's holy places with the promise of release from what many expected to be thousands of years of horrendous suffering in purgatory.

The new Christendom's penitential system was often experienced as external to the needs of the penitent. It was based on new patterns of canon law that codified sin and the penances that negated it. The system could be overwhelmingly legalistic and for some authorities was centered not on the penitent but on his clerical confessor. It was concerned more with divine satisfaction than with human transformation.

Petrarch and others might therefore have looked eastward toward Byzantium, or (however unlikely) even toward Russia. There the paradisiacal culture was flourishing, even if the political system of each was mortally threatened by, respectively, Turks and Mongols. But after three centuries of schism, the West knew almost nothing of Eastern Christendom. And what they did know repelled them because it was filtered through a cultural prejudice that stretched back in time to Charlemagne. Abortive contacts like those of Barlaam (discussed in the prologue above) only reinforced a prejudice—promoted actively by the papacy—that the Orthodox Church was an obstacle to Christian civilization.

Historical misconceptions and fallacies proved difficult to correct. At the time of excommunication, for instance, Rome asserted the Greeks had "altered" the Nicene Creed because they did not include the *filioque* (the clause about the Holy Spirit that states He proceeds from the Father "and the Son"). In fact, the Orthodox had refused to change the Creed by adding a canonically forbidden clause to it. Rome also asserted the Greeks had "deviated" from ancient ecclesiology because they did not recognize the supremacy of the pope over all Christians on earth. In fact, the Orthodox had refused to change the ancient tradition that recognized in all bishops an equality and brotherhood of jurisdiction.

The East proved resolute in its adherence to traditional Christianity, but in one of the great ironies of history, this only appeared as intransigence to the innovative West. For their part, Roman Catholic critics of the Orthodox after 1054 were blinded by a cloud of historical ignorance and reformist zeal.

But within this cloud they felt divinely vindicated by the speed with which Constantinople fell to their armies during the Fourth Crusade, and by the vulnerability of the Orthodox to unremitting invasions from the pagan east.

For centuries to come, therefore, the new Christendom of the West would look condescendingly on the old Christendom of the East, seeing it at the worst of times as an enemy, or, when conflicts eased, as a kind of crazed younger sister who deserved condescending sympathy and a guiding hand toward westernization.

Left without Orthodoxy's exalted vision of man, the West therefore fell increasingly under the influence of a brilliant but one-sided Augustinianism in the centuries following the Great Division. And under such circumstances the West was increasingly subject to the curse of anthropological pessimism.

This was articulated by one of the Papal Reformation's most consequential pontiffs. Innocent III (r. 1198–1216) was renowned for advancing the role of canon law in defining Roman Catholicism. He also launched crusades that resulted in the suppression of the Albigensian heresy and in the conquest of Orthodox Constantinople. Under his authority, the Fourth Lateran Council assembled in 1215 to consolidate changes that had come to transform Western Christendom since the Great Schism. This council is considered the high-water mark of the reform movement, codifying bans on clerical marriage and establishing for the laity a rule of annual sacramental confession. Innocent went further than any previous advocates of papal supremacy by claiming to be the "Vicar of Christ."

Prior to his election as pope, Innocent wrote a treatise entitled *On Contempt for the World*, the subtitle of which was *On the Misery of the Human Condition.* It makes for painful reading, as assuredly it did for contemporaries who still enjoyed fading contact with the old Christendom. The treatise is an unrelenting anathema against the creation. Particularly disparaging is its account of the origins of human life. "Let me elaborate this point," he asserts in its opening sections (sensing, perhaps, that no one really wanted him to do so):

> *Man has been formed of dust, clay, ashes, and a thing far more vile, of filthy sperm. Man has been conceived in the desire of the flesh, in the heat of sensual*

> *lust, in the foul stench of wantonness. He was born to labor, to fear, to sufferings and, most miserable of all, to death. His evil doings offend God, offend his neighbor, offend himself. He defiles his good name, contaminates his person, violates his conscience through his shameful acts. His vanity prompts him to neglect what is most important, most necessary and most useful. Accordingly, he is destined to become the fuel of the everlasting, eternally painful hellfire; the food of voracious, consuming worms. His destiny is to be a putrid mass that eternally emits a most horrible stench.*[3]

Innocent's unconditional disdain for divinely established sexual intercourse can be traced to earlier statements of Western monastic reformers such as Odo of Cluny. It was Augustinian in that even relations between husband and wife were considered inherently sinful because they were tainted by concupiscence, that is, a desire for something distinct from God.

Because of his role in the conquest and forced conversion of Constantinople at the hands of the crusaders, Innocent had done much to stamp the Great Division indelibly upon the character of reformational Christianity. His treatise is evidence of the disfiguration of Western culture that resulted. It bears the marks of Augustine's doctrine of original guilt, to which Eastern fathers had never subscribed. According to this doctrine, mankind was guilty of the Fall of Adam and Eve, and through the act of procreation every human being deserved eternal punishment in hell. "O heavy necessity and unhappy condition," Innocent laments, "before we sinned, sin already had taken possession of us; before we were capable of doing evil we already had become evil."[4]

So miserable is the human condition in this view that this leading architect of the new Christendom speculates that when Jesus wept in response to those mourning the death of Lazarus, He did so not from compassion for their experience of death, but from the thought that Lazarus, soon to

3 *Two Views of Man*, trans. and ed. Bernard Muchland (New York: Frederick Ungar Publishing, 1966), 4.

4 Ibid, 7.

be raised, "was about to return to the miseries of life."[5]

Remarkably, Pope Innocent's treatise became the thirteenth-century equivalent of a best seller. It was translated into the vernacular for popular consumption, and hundreds of copies remain today from its unusually wide scope of distribution. Like the fifteenth-century *Imitation of Christ*, with which it shares much in common, *On Contempt for the World* helped establish a deeply pessimistic view of the human condition in the West.

Petrarch's Agony

FRANCESCO PETRARCH (d. 1374) PROVIDED ONE of the most eloquent reactions to the disfigurement of the new Christendom. He discovered a way of navigating around its cultural pessimism. But in doing so, the conqueror of Mount Ventoux spent his life in a state of exhausting and unresolved inner division.

On the one hand, Petrarch was a passionate lover of the world and of man's place within it. Not even his close friend and contemporary Boccaccio, author of the delightful collection of tales called the *Decameron*, could match his interest in topics like youthful desire, political intrigue, and the charms of nature. Petrarch's learning came not only from a keen skill in observation but from the insights of Roman pagandom. Everything he did, every impression he formed, was related to the adventures told by Virgil and the histories recorded by Livy. Petrarch scoured the monasteries of Italy, Germany, and France in search of reading material from the ancients, buying everything he could get his hands on and even discovering forgotten works by Cicero. As we have seen, he longed for the day when the Greek classics would also be available to him in Latin translation, since learning to read them in the original under the tutelage of Barlaam had proved abortive. The pagan culture of antiquity was for Petrarch the West's most valuable literary asset because, in his judgment, it did more to reveal the meaning of human life in this world than any other body of literature, especially that of fourteenth-century Western Christendom. For this reason, Petrarch became an advocate of the

5 Ibid, 26.

"study of the humanities" (*studia humanitatis*). He became, according to both his immediate followers and modern historians, the "father of humanism."

Yet for all his love for the culture of pagandom, Petrarch was a devout son of the Roman Catholic Church. In fact, as we shall see, it was precisely his identification with the reformational Christianity of the new Christendom that turned him toward secular humanism. In this great irony is contained the key to understanding the subsequent history of the West and the crisis of its culture in modern times.

It is not coincidental that the one book Petrarch chose to carry to the mountaintop in 1336 was the *Confessions*. Augustine offered him companionship on that day and seemingly every day that followed during the first humanist's long and prolific life. The first book he ever acquired, in fact, was a copy of Augustine's *City of God*. And only in his old age, just before death, did he lovingly surrender to a young friend that very copy of the *Confessions* that he had always kept within easy reach. Commenting on the book's "handy pocket size," he recalled fondly to its recipient how, during a lifetime of travels, "by constant use hand and book became so inseparable that they seemed to grow together."[6]

In light of his great influence on the father of humanism, it is tempting to look on Augustine as a sort of grandfather of utopianism. Such a view is not fanciful. It is supported by an examination of Petrarch's most profound work, the *Secretum*. Here Augustine is assigned the authority of a spiritual father to whom the author makes an imaginary and heartrending confession.

In the dialogue Petrarch admits, for instance, to a lifelong struggle with lust. He speaks directly of a young married woman named Laura with whom (at her insistence, not his) he never consummated his desire.[7] In the back-

---

6 *Letters from Petrarch*, ed. and trans. Morris Bishop (Bloomington: Indiana University, 1966), 292.

7 The young woman was featured in Petrarch's most famous poems, the *Canzoniere*, which became a prototype for modern romantic poetry. Following Dante's famous use in the *Divine Comedy* and the *New Life* of Beatrice, another beautiful maiden observed chastely from a distance, Petrarch used Laura to explore his most exalted feelings of youth. In doing so both he and Dante were

ground, however, are other turbulent affairs. These resulted in the father of humanism becoming the father of children as well, though it was a paternity he proved far less eager to advertise.[8]

Augustine

What is more, he also confesses to a vanity that seems to have ruled almost every relationship with other people. Petrarch's letters are mostly free of the contempt that would characterize post-Romantic writers later in the age of utopia (humility, after all, was still considered one of Christendom's principal virtues). But the letters exude a sense of indignation at the current state of culture and the intellectual leadership responsible for it. Vanity, he admits, has driven his creative work from his earliest years, and he is possessed by a mania for literary fame. This, he notes, drove him to seek and then obtain public coronation as poet laureate at Rome in 1341.

---

drawing upon the Western literary convention of chivalry.

8 The illegitimate conception of his son Giovanni occurred in Avignon only months after Petrarch returned from Mount Ventoux. Petrarch's retreat to the rural town of Vaucluse the following year was made in an effort to escape responsibility for the boy, whom he mostly scorned. Giovanni died from the plague in 1361. Petrarch's second known offspring, Francesca, enjoyed a much better relationship with her father. Unlike the idealized Laura celebrated in Petrach's poetry, the identity of the mother or mothers of his children remained unspoken and will therefore never be known.

As his spiritual father, the imaginary Augustine engages Petrarch readily on these and other shortcomings. Most notably, he urges the poet to overcome earthly passions by a continuous meditation on death. Reminding Petrarch of the impression made by the *Confessions* as he stood on the heights of Mount Ventoux, Augustine alludes to the undue influence of pagan classics by declaring, "You would sooner abandon yourself than those books of yours." He then continues,

> *Come back to yourself. This is where we started from: think of your death which, without realizing it, you are approaching. Tear away the veils of darkness, and fix your eyes on death. Let no day or night go by without thinking of your last hour. Everything which passes before your eyes or comes into your mind should be seen in the light of this.*[9]

Regardless of how well they characterized the patristic wisdom of the real Augustine, such words were consistent with the monastic wisdom of the ancient Church. They were certainly expressive of a form of piety that had recently emerged within the new Christendom.

But what served ascetics living in monastic seclusion was not necessarily what served the laity living in society. By contrast, John Chrysostom and other fathers in the old Christendom had addressed the laity with less emphasis on the vanity of earthly things and more on the capacity of the world to offer Christians opportunities for sanctification. Perhaps the most important of these was holy matrimony, which even ascetics like Anthony of Egypt recognized as equal to monasticism in its potential for heavenly transformation. As a result of the Papal Reformation, however, the fourteenth-century West no longer held such a paradisiacal view of married life.[10]

The severe counsel of Petrarch's imaginary confessor was not limited to philosophical reflections on mortality. Augustine is likewise made to threaten the poet with the prospect of eternal punishment for frittering his

---

9 Petrarch, *Secretum*, 121.

10 The place of marriage in the West after the Great Division is discussed in *The Age of Division*, 83–84.

life away on the enjoyment of the world's vain potential. He tells of the horrifying and implacable "anger of a God Who will never be appeased" without repentance.[11] He becomes for Petrarch a sort of superego, attacking with irrefutable theological conviction any basis for living life abundantly and joyfully in this world. The effect is utterly debilitating for Petrarch. "You pile up so many miseries and necessities," he cries out at one point in the dialogue, "that I am almost sorry I was born a human being."[12]

Petrarch allows Augustine to point out that he is suffering from what the desert fathers of old named *acedia*, or spiritual despondency. All other sorrows in life bring at least some level of pleasure, he observes, "however delusory." But "in this sadness, on the other hand, all is cruel and wretched and horrible, the way to despair is always open, and everything conspires to drive unhappy souls to their destruction." Under its effects, Petrarch confesses to an experience "not of light and life, but infernal night and the semblance of bitter death. And (what is the worst of all miseries) I feed on my tears and grief, with a sort of dark pleasure, so that it is only with great reluctance that I can tear myself away from them."

In modern times such a condition would be called depression. For Petrarch it was crushing. And "add to that my loathing and contempt for the human condition," he concludes, "and you will see that I can hardly be other than gloomy."[13]

A man with Petrarch's sensitivity and talent could not remain in such a state forever. In fact, it was he who was bold enough to issue the first criticism of the illustrious Pope Innocent's morbid treatise. His response took the form of a dialogue between Reason and Sorrow contained in a larger work entitled *Remedies for Fortune Fair and Foul.* Entitled "Sadness and Misery," the dialogue represents a turning point in one of the most important streams of contemporary Western culture. For more than three centuries, the human condition in this world had become sunk in a morass of degradation and futility. This had been Petrarch's initial conclusion in the *Secretum,*

---

11 Ibid, 27.

12 Ibid, 51.

13 Ibid, 60–62.

when an imaginary Augustine urged him toward an unremitting contemplation of death. Such advice reverberates through the *Remedies*. "The whole work," wrote one biographer, "demands a constant negative: no man happy before death, and no man happy except in death."[14]

Nevertheless, as Petrarch reached the end of his emotionally tormented life, he began to speak in a new key. "Sadness and Misery" alludes to Innocent's treatise by defining its topic as "the misery of the human condition," which, the author notes, "some have bewailed in whole big tomes."[15]

Petrarch suggests a totally different approach to the question. On the one hand, he asserts somewhat indignantly that there exist "many things which make this life happy and pleasant, although, if I am not mistaken, no one has written about them." He summarizes the many earthly dignities of man, moving eventually to those that are heavenly. And as he does this, for a moment he speaks the language of the old Christendom:

> *And what surpasses all dignity, not only human but angelic, humanity itself is so conjoined to divinity that He who was God is become man, and likewise one in number He begins to be, perfectly containing two natures in himself, God and man, so that He makes man God, having been made man out of ineffable God, and the humility [of God] is the highest happiness and glory of man.*[16]

Here Petrarch embraces something like the West's lost doctrine of deification. He does not elaborate it, however, and he certainly does not allude to any of the Greek fathers as authorities in defining it.

Indeed, the old Christendom's paradisiacal solution to spiritual despondency now gives way to a utopian one. For the father of humanism, misery is no longer the condition of *acedia* described by traditional asceticism, to be

14 J. H. Whitfield, *Petrarch and the Renascence* (New York: Russell and Russell, 1965), 55.

15 Petrarch, *Remedies for Fortune Fair and Foul*, vol. 2, trans. with commentary by Conrad H. Rawski (Bloomington: Indiana University, 1991), 224.

16 Ibid., 225. The translation I use here is that found in Charles Trinkaus, *In Our Image and Likeness: Humanity and Divinity in Italian Humanist Thought*, vol. 1 (Chicago: University of Chicago, 1970), 191.

cured by detachment from the world. For Petrarch, according to one historian, "mortal misery is now seen not merely as a well-deserved spiritual trial, but as a psychological condition requiring a remedy."[17] And it is man, not God, who is the source of healing.

With Petrarch we see the earliest appearance of a system of beliefs and values in the West that certainly deserves the name of "humanism." It began to displace traditional Christianity as the source of Christendom's culture. But to understand how this occurred, it is necessary to explore an element of humanism known as the "secular."

Retreat to the Saeculum

THE TWENTIETH-CENTURY SOCIOLOGIST MAX WEBER once characterized the modern condition as one of "disenchantment." By this he meant the loss of an experience of life in the world in which anything heavenly participates. All experiences of transcendence have ceased. An atheist himself, he was simply observing with more insight than most the outcome of secular humanism during the age of utopia.

To an historian more sympathetic to the ancient culture of Christendom, the same condition might just as well be called desecration. For the process in question was in fact one of desacralization, of the negation of what was once a world filled with an experience of the divine presence. It was rather like declaring a liturgical building such as a church void of sanctity. Such has, indeed, occurred on a large scale since Weber's time. The twentieth century is rife with instances of church buildings being desecrated. From the Soviet Union to the United States, countless churches once dedicated to framing Christendom's experience of heavenly immanence have been demolished or converted into anything from scientific museums to sports palaces to gourmet restaurants and nightclubs. Christendom, like these former churches, has become "secular."

To understand how the secularization of the world began, it is necessary

---

17 George W. McClure, *Sorrow and Consolation in Italian Humanism* (Princeton: Princeton University, 1990), 57.

to understand the effects of the Papal Reformation. Many historians attribute the initial displacement of Christianity and the origins of modernity to the rise of humanism. As we saw earlier in this chapter, the infusion of pagan culture after the fourteenth century did indeed have a debilitating effect on Christian culture. But so did the intense anthropological pessimism that caused the turn to pagandom in the first place. In fact, long before Petrarch decided to flee the sanctified though imaginary confessional of the *Secretum*, Western Christendom had already prepared a non-sanctified space for him and other humanists to occupy.

This space was known as the *saeculum*. The Latin word for it was a translation of the Greek word for "age" (*aeon*). In the New Testament the word related to the experience of time in this world prior to the Incarnation, which at one point Paul called a mystery that had been hidden for "ages" (Col. 1:26). As such saeculum related to the kind of earthly time the Greeks called *kronos*, and which they distinguished from the heavenly presence in time known as *kairos*. It was Augustine who first used saeculum as a concept of an earthly experience untransformed by the kingdom of heaven, what eventually would be known in English as the "secular."

According to the historian Robert Markus, Augustine originally seems to have embraced traditional Christianity's sanctifying cosmology. Grounded in the doctrine of the Incarnation, Christianity viewed the world as the creation of a loving God who filled the world with His presence. Such a cosmology was unitary in the sense that it believed the eschatological kingdom of heaven had penetrated the world and no longer remained aloof from it. The experience of pagandom's mass conversion to Christianity in the wake of Constantine's conversion bolstered such optimism, and Augustine, like Eusebius of Caesarea a century earlier, believed the world would continue to experience heavenly immanence until the end of time. At one point in his early ministry as bishop, for instance, he celebrated the fact that "the whole world has become a choir praising Christ."[18]

But the collapse of the Roman Empire in the West early in the fifth

18 Robert A. Markus, *Saeculum: History and Society in the Theology of Augustine* (Cambridge: Cambridge University, 1970), 30.

century forced Augustine to reconsider such optimism and the affirmation of the world that went with it. He had watched as the barbarians first conquered Rome and then advanced inexorably toward his own helpless city of Hippo. In the words of Markus, he came to the conclusion that "the christianisation of the Roman Empire is as accidental to the history of salvation as it is reversible."[19]

Instead of the optimistic unitary cosmology he had inherited, the north African bishop now laid out a dualistic and pessimistic one. The Incarnation remained for him the turning point in history, but even so the world would remain basically corrupt until the end of time. It should be noted that this did not mean Augustine became a millenarian. He held no expectations of an imminent Parousia, though as we shall see this would become a strong force among some of his intellectual heirs. Rejecting both a sacred world filled with the presence of heaven and a profane world awaiting the impending Second Coming of Christ, then, he considered the world in which the Church lived out her history to be neither good nor bad, neither sacred nor profane. It was simply neutral. It was "secular."

Such a cosmology was new. As Markus noted, "the sacred and the profane were both familiar in antiquity; but until it was imported by [Augustinian] Christianity, there was no notion of the 'secular' in the ancient world. The word and the concept are both alien to Greco-Roman religion."[20]

They are also alien, it can be added, to traditional Christianity. The early Church was confronted by a world that often persecuted her, and she certainly made clear distinctions between the things of God and the things of men. Tertullian (d. 220), the intellectual forefather of Augustine in north Africa, had scornfully contrasted the two, asking, "What has Athens to do with Jerusalem?"

However, it is a mistake to assume that Christians therefore looked on their surroundings as invariably profane, assigning holiness only to their catacomb assemblies. In fact, long before the conversion of Constantine,

---

19 Ibid., 54.

20 Robert A. Markus, *Christianity and the Secular* (Notre Dame, IN: University of Notre Dame, 2006), 4.

the most evangelically minded of them expressed a strong affirmation of the world insofar as they interacted with it. After all, God had declared creation to be "very good," and through the life of the Church He now filled it with the light of the gospel. Christians measured their prayers by the universe's cycles of time, believing creatures on earth and the stars of heaven participated mystically in worship. They treasured the physical remains of the martyrs, placing them in sanctuaries for veneration. They engaged the pagans around them, whether at home or in the arena. Pagan husbands were gently converted by Christian wives, and pagan persecutors were often abruptly converted by the faith, hope, and charity of Christian victims of Roman blood sport. Even when put to death for their faith, early Christians like Ignatius of Antioch experienced a divine love for the world in its spiritually transformed state.[21]

Contrary to many historical accounts, then, when Eusebius of Caesarea in the time of Constantine elaborated the most affirmative vision of the world to date, he was not inventing it out of the ether. He was drawing on three centuries of reflection on the meaning of the Incarnation.

Only in the fifth century did a variant cosmology appear, and it did so in the West under the influence of Augustine. Like his other innovative views, the concept of the saeculum was elaborated as a defense of traditional Christianity. Among the holy bishop's many efforts to defend the faith was a struggle he waged against the Donatist heresy, which claimed that a small group of Christian ascetics that had separated themselves from the world were the eschatological fulfillment of salvation history. Against this claim he insisted that the Church on earth is in fact a mixture of the saved and the damned. Only at the end of time will the sanctity of her faithful be truly revealed. In the meantime her composition at any point in history is necessarily ambiguous. And if the Christian community's sanctity is ambiguous, even more so is the world around it.

Augustine's concept of the saeculum was necessarily pessimistic. This is not to say that it was the result of an indifference to cosmic sanctification.

---

21 For an account of the early Church's affirmative cosmology and its role in evangelization, see *Age of Paradise*, chapters 1–2.

The bishop always hoped for more of that. Rather, it was the result of a conviction, born from both polemics against the Donatists and the catastrophe of Christian Rome's fall, that the world could never fully accommodate the kingdom of heaven.

Such a cosmology served the Church in maintaining a spiritually healthy distance between heaven and the world in which she lived, something Markus called an "eschatological gap." And indeed, long after the time of Augustine, the degeneration of Christian society in the West was met with clear-minded resistance by the clergy. The greatest test came during the tenth century, when a proprietary system of church governance arose in which a worldly laity dominated monasticism and the papacy. Because it viewed the world dualistically, Augustinianism provided the clergy with a means of filling the gap, of setting spiritual ideals against the given realities of the proprietary system. The result was a reformation that soon broke out of the monasteries and entered the papal headquarters in Rome. From there it projected reform throughout the Church in the West, and it soon demanded the subjugation of all Christendom. This, more than any other immediate cause, is what resulted in Rome's excommunication from a defiantly traditional Orthodox Church in 1054.[22]

The Papal Reformation that was both cause and consequence of the Great Division was an assertion of the sacred against the profane within the sphere of the saeculum. Launched by Pope Leo IX (r. 1049–1054), its leadership bifurcated society by secularizing it. Two opposing spiritual classes—the clergy and the laity—were made more distinct than ever before. In every case the former banished the latter to the realm of the saeculum. Cardinal Humbert (d. 1061), for instance, elevated the clergy over the laity by dividing the state from the papacy. Peter Damian (d. 1072) did the same by demanding clerical celibacy as a superior alternative to lay matrimony. And in consolidating the Papal Reformation itself through administrative and canonical measures, Pope Gregory VII (r. 1073–1085) subjugated a "secular" laity to a "religious" clergy. Indeed, "the church" now became a term denoting a clerical hierarchy emanating from the power of the papacy as much as it

---

22 *Age of Division*, chapter 1.

meant what it had in traditional Christianity—the entire body of the faithful in Christ. To this day the term is commonly misused in this way within the media of a post-Christian Christendom, as if the old Christendom had never existed.

The transformational imperative was put to new use. On the one hand, it provoked a confrontation with practices such as the sale of clerical offices that clearly deviated from traditional Christianity. On the other hand, it institutionalized this confrontation so that a new legalism began to replace personal repentance. In both cases, transformation was reduced to reformation. The longing for paradise gave way to conformity with institutionalized sanctity.

The changes this brought were as divisive as they were ambitious. The West was rent between church and state, between clergy and laity, between heaven and earth. In time, even the clergy themselves were divided by gradations of secularity. Those priests involved with pastoral responsibilities among the laity within parishes came to be designated *secular,* while those who joined one of the newly created monastic orders were known as *regular,* or simply *religious.* The result of this was that most of Western Christendom was consigned to the "secular." The very word was now opposed in its connotations to clergy, who, in contrast to the laity, were understood to live lives dedicated to acquiring the kingdom of heaven. This conceptual bifurcation of the West led to a cognitive separation of earth from heaven, reflecting like few other polarities the consequences of Christendom's age of division.

Severed from the Orthodox Church, the new Christendom became isolated and tragically self-sufficient. According to Markus,

> *Western Christendom was enabled to close in on itself. Its estrangement from the Eastern churches was compounded by the loss of North Africa to Islam. The see of Rome was left without rival in Western Europe. Consolidating its authority over Western Christendom from the eleventh century, it no longer had, in its isolation, anything to learn, was no longer exposed to the fruitful tensions which had in the ancient Church secured some give-and-take between major centres of ecclesiastical authority, each with its own tradition. The*

> *Roman see assumed near-absolute authority over an increasingly consolidated hierarchical Church, as did that Church over the secular world around it. In becoming the unchallenged mistress of Western Europe, the [Roman Catholic] Church became dangerously identified with a culture and a social order more constricting than ever, for it now inhabited a more homogeneous world largely of its own making.*[23]

As the process of secularization advanced beyond the eleventh century, the transformational imperative was directed away from paradise toward the experience of continuous reformation.

This was a decided step toward the "not yet" eschatology of utopia. In his book *A Secular Age*, Charles Taylor has noted the "very long-lasting bent of European culture toward Reform, in the widest sense. I mean by this," he adds,

> *the attempt by elites to make over society, and the life and practices of non-elites, so as to conform to what the elites identify as higher standards. This is a remarkable fact. I don't pretend to have an explanation for it, but I offer it as a fact, that ever since the [Gregorian] Reform of the eleventh century, there were recurrent attempts to raise the standards of mass practice. At first, these were religious reforms; they attempted to raise the whole body of the clergy, and later even the mass of the laity, to the higher standard of devotion and pious life which was largely defined by the best of monastic and clerical practice. . . . The idea begins slowly to arise, developing through stages over several centuries, of a world here and now in which no compromises need to be made with any alternative principle.*[24]

In the wake of the Papal Reformation, then, Western Christendom became restless. New hopes and expectations for the future began to appear.

The atmosphere was what another historian, alluding to the vision of

---

23 Ibid., 89–90.

24 Charles Taylor, *A Secular Age* (Cambridge, MA: Harvard University, 2007), 242–43.

Russian Communism, characterized as "permanent revolution."[25] Under such conditions, the perception of a pattern of progress in history began to appear, displacing the traditional view that the world had reached its fulfillment in the Incarnation. An example of one who perceived this pattern is Anselm of Havelberg (d. 1158). Writing a century after the Papal Reformation, he noted the "waves of innovation" that were emanating from it. A tripartite sequence of earthly improvement was beginning to appear in the historical record, graduating from "good" (*bona*) to "better" (*meliora*) and finally, he hoped, to "best" (*optima*). Anselm's point of view is doubly interesting because he was closely engaged in discussions with the Orthodox about the role of papal supremacy in causing the Great Division. He could use his progressive view of history to argue that such a doctrine, though absent in the first millennium, was nevertheless useful in raising Christendom to a more advanced level in his time. For him the Orthodox were, by contrast, unprogressive.

The new historical optimism found its most influential expression in Joachim of Fiore (d. 1202). He formulated a tripartite vision of world history culminating in a creative age of the Holy Spirit. This vision was also an example of the uniquely Western conception of history that issued from the Papal Reformation. Indeed, as it was elaborated by the Franciscans—one of the newly formed monastic orders dedicated to defending papal supremacy—this view came to include a prophecy about an "angelic pope" who would establish a final age of earthly perfection. The appeal of such a view rested on a claim that the Incarnation was not the fulfillment of God's presence in the world, but that a greater act of heavenly immanence was yet to come. The reformation launched by the papacy in the eleventh century was thus seen as the beginning of a process that would bring the Incarnation to its fulfillment only in the future.

For the first time, Christendom was finding it difficult to experience the kingdom of heaven in this age. For many in the West, the transformational imperative could be satisfied only in anticipation. Paradise was fading, and

---

25 Henri Daniel-Rops, *Cathedral and Crusade: Studies of the Medieval Church* (New York: Dutton, 1957), 119.

men like Petrarch were beginning to seek an alternative by looking forward in time to a perfect society that lay just beyond the horizon.

An Experiment in Utopia

SO PETRARCH TURNED FROM THE new Christendom to an alternative civilization with a supporting culture he and later humanists could respect: Roman pagandom. Particularly attractive was the civic culture of ancient Rome, which encouraged both individual and political transformation. At the individual level Petrarch found Cicero, the great Stoic philosopher whose letters inspired a personal striving worthy in his mind of Christianity. In fact, Petrarch was fond of recalling how it was the Roman orator's work *Hortensius* that led a still-pagan Augustine to Christianity. Cicero was also a famous defender of all that was great in the political order of the Roman Republic. Beyond Petrarch's favorite writer, pagan Rome produced what seemed to be innumerable examples of men seeking reform for the better in their own lives and those of fellow citizens.

Like a zealous proselyte, Petrarch juxtaposed the optimism of Roman pagandom against the pessimism of the new Christendom. He became indignant. His frustrated desire for transformation was directed especially toward the papal court, which he knew so well because of his many years living at Avignon. He was not a critic of papal supremacy, but he was convinced that a sharp decline in spiritual life had occurred as a result of what many called the papacy's Babylonian Captivity far from Rome. He therefore petitioned regularly for its return to the city of Saint Peter.

But the need for change did not end with this. Rome was in the hands of warring aristocratic factions, and beyond it Italy was divided into mutually exclusive city-states. Even more egregious than an exiled papacy or divided Italy, though, was the degenerate culture of the West. It had become incapable of living up to the transformational imperative.

Suddenly, however, the usually pessimistic father of humanism was filled with hope. In 1343, a young but brilliant notary arrived in Avignon from Rome as the head of a delegation to petition Pope Clement VI to return

Cola di Rienzo

to the city of Saint Peter. His name was Cola di Rienzo, and he promised to bring Petrarch's hopes to fulfillment in one of Christendom's earliest experiments in utopianism.

Rienzo's greatest talent was his oratory, which won over just about everyone with whom he spoke—at least initially. On this occasion it certainly won over Petrarch. The poet became a friend to the Roman statesman, and the two engaged in rapt conversation about "the present decadence and ruin of the divine Republic"—by which they meant not the kingdom of heaven but the state of ancient Rome.[26] They commiserated about how great culture had been before the rise of Christendom, and how the golden age of art and statecraft might be restored. It is no surprise, then, that Petrarch was delighted to learn four years later that his friend had seized power in modern Rome in order to recatechize it with the values of pagandom.

This is not to say that the Rienzo revolution in Rome—the first of two, as it turned out—was purely secular. It was in fact self-consciously Christian, at least in a modern, reformational sense. A key is the day on which it was launched in 1347: Pentecost, the feast of the Holy Spirit. This was not coincidental, for the dictator had imbibed heavily of the millennialism of the Joachimites. As we noted above, the mystic and his Franciscan followers believed history was divided into three ages corresponding to the Holy Trinity. The final age, that of the Holy Spirit, would commence under the reign of an "angelic pope."

---

26 Morris Bishop, *Petrarch and His World* (Bloomington: Indiana University, 1963), 257.

Such a charismatic figure had briefly come and gone during the strange pontificate of Celestine V (r. 1294), but the radical wing of the Franciscan order had been keeping hopes alive during the decades since. The Joachimite movement was, in fact, an example of despair over the cultural desiccation of a new Christendom divided from the old, of a civilization with a supporting culture that was failing to direct its members toward the heavenly transformation of the world. The unfulfilled longing for a reign of the Holy Spirit under which the West would "finally" taste of the kingdom of heaven—more or less what Eastern Christendom had quietly been continuing to do since the Great Division—was the unintended outcome of the uniquely Western Papal Reformation. So, on the day of Pentecost Rienzo acted to fulfill the longing.

On the one hand, he prefigured the Russian Revolution by promising relief for the poor and the suppression of the nobility. His would be a proto-socialist utopia. On the other hand, it would be emphatically reformational. For instance, he ordered all citizens to receive the Eucharist at least once a year on pain of losing their property. But perhaps the most remarkable feature of Rienzo's brief dictatorship was its use of symbolic pageantry. This too resembled in certain ways what would come in the twentieth century, and the age of utopia, as we shall see in the final chapter, reached its culmination in the cult of Vladimir Lenin. Making his headquarters the vacant Lateran Palace (the absent pope had no use for it), he appropriated the adjoining cathedral as a stage for enacting rituals of messianic rule. One was immersion in the same font in which Roman legend claimed Emperor Constantine had been baptized. Indeed, a rudimentary cult of personality was instituted, and a propaganda machine began to compare Rienzo to Jesus Christ. As in the one great revolution that preceded Russia's, that of eighteenth-century France, a new calendar replaced the one used by the Church for centuries. Instead of measuring time from the Incarnation, it marked the years beginning with the advent of Rienzo's dictatorship.

Indeed, the Rienzo Revolution was a harbinger of the future. The leader himself spoke frequently of creating a utopian commonwealth, what he called the *buono stato* ("good state").[27] In a certain sense it was the West's

27 Ronald G. Musto, *Apocalypse in Rome: Cola di Rienzo and the Politics of the New*

first modern revolution. Christendom had seen as many political upheavals as any civilization. The palace coups of Byzantium were perhaps the most frequent and loathsome. But never had the overthrow of government been so ideological, so driven by a vision of justice and a plan for progress. One historian even characterized it as "strangely proto-Fascist."[28]

And as Rienzo's revolutionary vision expanded, the dictator naturally considered the need for intellectual support. For this he turned to his friend and fellow visionary in Avignon. Petrarch was apparently invited to come to Rome to serve as a sort of minister of enlightenment. Given the humanist's independence of mind, it might seem that the idea was a complete nonstarter. But it was not. The poet had received the news of Rienzo's coup d'etat with joy, sending a hastily written letter to his old friend that hailed him as an advocate of liberty, a sword of vengeance against the unjust, and a messenger from heaven. Even if he must die a martyr's death, Petrarch urged, Rienzo had been chosen by fortune to begin the transformation of the world.

Petrarch made haste for Rome but failed to reach it before a counterrevolution of nobles overthrew Rienzo. Fleeing the city, the former dictator would wander for years in exile, as Vladimir Lenin did after the failed insurgency of 1905, which served as a "dress rehearsal" for the Russian Revolution. Both visionaries, in fact, fled to the Alps. But whereas the Bolshevik would settle in Geneva to resume his study of the scientific predictions of Karl Marx, the fourteenth-century millennialist found refuge in a remote monastery where he could return to studying the prophecies of Joachim of Fiore.

Eventually, Rienzo was captured and condemned by the inquisition. He was then brought to Avignon. There Petrarch eagerly awaited his arrival and at once offered renewed support for the effort to build utopia. "In this man," Petrarch lamented in a letter to a friend,

> *I had reposed my last hope of Italian liberty. . . . So much did I hope from him that now, when all hope is lost, I grieve all the more. And now I admit that,*

Age (Berkeley: University of California, 2003), 130.

28 Bishop, *Petrarch and His World*, 261.

whatever may be the outcome, I can't help admiring his beginnings.[1]

If there is anything to be regretted, the father of humanism reflects, it is that Rienzo did not persevere against the counter-revolution and eliminate its leadership with a merciless purge.

Rienzo's end would soon come, but not, as it turns out, at the hands of the inquisition. With Pope Clement VI's sudden death, the condemned revolutionary was unexpectedly pardoned and just as unpredictably sent back to Rome as the new pope's ambassador. But upon entering the city in 1354, he reverted to his old ways. He once again declared himself the leader of the oppressed and raised a new revolt against the nobility. This time, however, very few were prepared to follow him. Surrounded by a mob, he was dragged to the Capitoline Hill—once the site of the pagan Temple of Jupiter Optimus, ancient Rome's most revered place of worship—and there ceremonially stabbed to death. His body was hung upside down in public, as if in anticipation of his twentieth-century Fascist successor Benito Mussolini. There it hung for days, looking, according to one eyewitness, "like a giant buffalo or cow in the slaughterhouse."[2] The body was later burned to ashes and thrown into the Tiber.

Petrarch outlived his utopian alter ego by two decades. He never repented of encouraging the revolution that caused the deaths of not only Rienzo but countless nobles and commoners. He seems actually to have regretted that the revolution had not gone further. For him, the culture of Christendom was in need of totally new values, and political violence was a legitimate means of instituting them.

Yet the experience of utopia in the fourteenth century would not come through revolution. For that, the new Christendom would have to transmute reformational Christianity into revolutionary ideology.

For now, humanists would learn to work within the existing system to advance the secular transformation of the world.

---

1 *Letters from Petrarch*, 116.

2 Musto, *Apocalypse in Rome*, 345.

CHAPTER TWO

The Font of Pagandom

MORE THAN A HUNDRED YEARS ago, the Swiss historian Jacob Burkhardt famously recounted the rise of humanism in Italy during the fifteenth century. In doing so he lodged an important word in the cultural vocabulary of the West. That word is *renaissance* (French for "rebirth").[3] The author was as much a product of the event he narrated as its historian, for he unselfconsciously celebrated its secular preoccupations. For him, the Renaissance was the dawn of modern culture. By the twentieth century, it came to be seen as the turning point in history after which Christianity was progressively displaced by secular humanism. This became the dominant narrative learned by undergraduates throughout the standardized curriculum of the university systems of Europe and America.

It is only correct to a degree. As I argued in *The Age of Division*, the eleventh-century Papal Reformation was an even more formative event in the rise and fall of what the West once was. It released forces that fundamentally altered the character of Christianity, and these were what eventually gave rise to the Renaissance. Chief among these forces were anthropological pessimism and cosmological contempt. They provoked the turn toward

3 The first to use the word for the historical event was Jules Michelet earlier in the nineteenth century.

pagandom that Petrarch, in his creative agony, did more than any to promote. The result, as we have seen, was secular humanism. It became at once the balm but also the pathology of the new Christendom.

Therefore, if something was "reborn" during the fifteenth century, it was not pagandom. That civilization could not be revived. Too many centuries had passed during which its cruelest and most obnoxious values—from infanticide to sexual degradation—had been permanently repudiated. This fact has recently been emphasized by Tom Holland, whose book *Dominion* shows how very irretrievable were the values of classical antiquity after the rise of Christianity.[4] The Renaissance was a rebirth not of pagandom but of Christendom.

Burkhardt reported what he considered the dawn of modernity. What he witnessed, in fact, was more like the end of a solar eclipse. For five centuries, cultural pessimism had progressively benighted Christendom's western landscape. Daybreak had occurred long before, at Pentecost, and the paradisiacal culture it cast across the world had only been interrupted in the West since the eleventh century. But the optimism that now filled the eyes of Petrarch and his successors was discolored by an element not present in the first millennium. Secular humanism distorted the paradisiacal values it was designed to recover. It was a counterfeit of traditional Christianity.

This can be seen in the baptismal vocabulary appropriated to advance the humanist agenda. Much was drawn from the Gospel of Saint John. Petrarch, for instance, called to mind the first chapter when speaking of the "darkness" that overshadowed the culture of his time. Georgio Vasari alluded in a history of contemporary Italian painting to the third chapter's exchange between Jesus and Nicodemus about being "born again."

It was in the font of pagandom, then, that Western Christendom was rebaptized. A withered culture of paradise went into the font, and a vigorous but radically changed culture of utopia sprang forth.

---

4 Tom Holland, *Dominion: How the Christian Revolution Remade the World* (New York: Basic Books, 2019).

The School of Platonism

IN CHAPTER ONE WE OBSERVED how Petrarch, agonizing over the pessimistic state of contemporary Christian culture, retreated to the saeculum for relief. By doing this, he opened up a hitherto untapped resource for fulfilling the transformational imperative. A problem immediately presented itself, however. Because Christendom was a civilization directed toward the heavenly transformation of the world, a purely immanent culture—that is, one without any transcendent source of inspiration—would never be stable within it. This problem was not a passing one. It would in fact haunt Christendom throughout a six-century age of utopia.

At the inception of this age, then, humanists were in search of a transcendent anchor for the culture they were aligning with the saeculum. It obviously could not be traditional Christianity, for the gospel recognized no innate value in a spiritually untransformed cosmos. Nor would the intellectual system of reformational Christianity provide stability. Scholasticism, with its Aristotelian underpinnings, did not so much open the heavens to man as set the boundaries by which he must live while in this world.

Scholasticism was based on an institution, not an idea. The university or "school" from which it derived its name had displaced the monastery and the temple as the center of man's knowledge of heaven. It was one of many items in the cultural baggage used to supply the train of papal reform. During the first millennium, theology had been the work of bishops or monks living in seclusion, and that theology had found its way into the sacramental liturgy of the local parish church. But during the eleventh century, theology became a professional discipline for which academic degrees such as the doctorate were invented and awarded. The theologian ceased to be, in Gregory the Theologian's words, "one who prays." Instead, he became one who thinks. Scholasticism institutionalized learning much as did the university system of the twentieth-century West. And if the latter became known for a lack of spiritual creativity and tendency toward speech codes, scholasticism tended to place learning in a straitjacket of presuppositions and procedures.

For the scholastics, these were provided by Aristotle, whose formerly unknown works flooded the West during the twelfth century in direct relationship to the expansion of the universities. Aristotelianism emphasized the role of logic in reaching conclusions, and the result of his influence was the rationalization of Western theology. Aristotle also presented the cosmos as an order that never changed, created by a remote deity impersonally known as the "unmovable mover." The goal of man was to comprehend the order of things and accommodate himself to it rather than transforming it.

In its Christianized scholastic form, such a cosmology appealed strongly to advocates of the Papal Reformation, who claimed an eternal order of clerical supremacy over a world in which moral law could be rationally determined and codified. Aristotelianism provided the philosophical framework onto which Thomas Aquinas (d. 1274) fastened his famous *Summa theologica* ("summation of theology"), building a theological edifice at the center of Roman Catholic Christendom around which no subsequent theologian could easily pass.

Only in the fourteenth century did cracks in this edifice begin to appear. The main cause was a movement known as nominalism. An offshoot of scholasticism, it emphasized only the particular experiences of this world and regarded theological claims about God and salvation with skepticism. The ambitious statements about the metaphysical order of things made by the scholastics were now greatly qualified. Natural reason could comprehend with certainty only things that were apparent and real, and knowledge of heaven could be based only on faith. Nominalism would influence the theology of Protestant reformers such as Luther. However, the totally abstract cerebral puzzles of nominalist theologians were far removed from the personal transformation for which Petrarch and his successors longed. Scholasticism, with its nominalist offshoot, seemed to be the unassailable basis of Western thought.

Until, that is, the humanists came on the scene. Petrarch as always was the first to challenge scholasticism and the reign of Aristotle that lay behind it. That challenge was issued in the name of Plato, whose vision of heavenly ideals provided a means toward earthly transcendence. We have seen how Petrarch obtained a partial education in Platonism from Barlaam. In fact, his last substantial work was a defense of Plato against a group of scholastics who regarded any criticism of Aristotelianism as a form of doctrinal heresy. Petrarch's advocacy was that of a man searching desperately for a transcendent anchor to which the secular transformation of the world might be attached. Nevertheless, by the time of his death, Platonism remained mostly inaccessible in the West.

Then, during the century that followed—known in Italian as the *quattrocento* or "fourteen-hundreds"—a wave of Greek scholars came to the West and injected Platonism into its febrile intellectual bloodstream. The first to do so was Manuel Chrysoloras (d. 1415). One day in Constantinople he received a flattering letter from the chancellor of Florence, Coluccio Salutati (a humanist scholar in his own right and follower of Petrarch), begging him to come and teach the language of Homer to the Italians. But he was only the first to do so. Many Greeks traveled to Italy during the quattrocento, facilitating a cross-cultural exchange the scale of which had not been seen since the Byzantine papacy of the eighth century. Unlike that earlier wave of Eastern influence in the West, however, this one was not generated by a zeal for traditional Christianity. Many of the Greeks who now came were predisposed to interpret the impending collapse of Byzantium as a judgment against the Orthodox Church.

Such was the attitude of the cohort that accompanied Emperor John VIII to Florence in 1439 to participate in an abortive council of reunion. John was desperate for military assistance, and he selected scholars whose doctrinal adaptability he could trust. One was Ecumenical Patriarch Joseph II, who composed a statement confessing the Roman Catholic faith but died before it could be accepted. Another was Metropolitan Isidore of Moscow, a Greek who established deferential relations with the papacy and as a result emerged from the council as a Roman Catholic cardinal.[5] Even more accommodating was Metropolitan Bessarion of Nicaea, who came to Italy as a disgruntled Orthodox Neoplatonist and left, like Isidore, a Roman Catholic cardinal.[6]

---

5 Isidore would return to Russia but was immediately imprisoned for his betrayal of Orthodoxy. He eventually escaped, and in 1452 it was he who stood in Hagia Sophia on behalf of the pope to proclaim the union treaty only months before the fall of Constantinople to the Turks.

6 Eventually settling in Rome, he became a patron of humanism and was even considered a candidate for the papacy.

Emperor John VIII, from the Medici Chapel, Florence

Only one of the Greek scholars, in fact, remained faithful to Orthodoxy. Metropolitan Mark of Ephesus was a hesychast. Like others, he was eager to see a reunion of East and West. But unlike others, he insisted that it be achieved on the basis of doctrinal integrity. Much of what had become the Roman Catholic faith he attributed to effects of the Papal Reformation. In particular, he rejected papal supremacy and purgatory, both of which had become doctrines fundamental to the new Christendom. Both were introduced after the mutual excommunications of 1054, he noted, and neither was attested widely in the Orthodox Catholic Church before that date.

Mark's Eastern colleagues had little investment in such a point of view, however, and eventually it was Bessarion who proclaimed their acceptance of Roman Catholicism before the pope and emperor at the conclusion of the council. Among all the Greeks, only Mark refused to sign. But his act was decisive in subverting the council's authority in the East. Sullenly, the Greek delegation returned to Constantinople to find their apostasy publicly condemned by the populace. Mark's resistance was thus ultimately vindicated, and the hesychast became known as a "pillar of Orthodoxy." The Council of Florence came to naught.

But its afterlife in the West was formative. One of the Greek participants declined to return to a politically doomed Constantinople, preferring the comforts and opportunities of Italy. His name was George Plethon (d. 1454). He lingered in Florence, basking in its humanism and enjoying the status of an intellectual celebrity who refused to align himself with any ecclesiastical authority. Prior to the council, back in Byzantium, he had become a celebrated fountainhead of Platonism, counting among his students not only Bessarion but Mark of Ephesus. The outcome of Plethon's infatuation with Plato (after whom he adopted his like-sounding surname), had it been foreseen, would have made both men cringe. For at the end of his life he became an advocate for the restoration of classical paganism. Retiring to the town of Mistras, he ultimately renounced Christianity and called on the Greeks to return to their ancient pantheon in the face of the final Muslim onslaught.

But for now, Plethon was accosted by humanists with itching ears who sought, as had Petrarch, a philosophical alternative to Aristotelianism. Always looking for a way to use scholarship for political advantage, Florence's oligarchical ruler Cosimo de Medici (r. 1434–1464) scooped him up and commissioned him to lecture on the superiority of Plato over Aristotle. Based on Plethon's teaching, Cosimo founded a Platonic Academy. There, a generation of intellectual resistance to Aristotle—and, by association, scholasticism—came into existence.

It could not have done so without the political ambition of Cosimo. Head of Italy's most lucrative bank, he oversaw a commercial empire that extended throughout the West. Its most important client was the papacy, whose financial portfolio had expanded vastly since returning from Avignon soon after the death of Petrarch. Cosimo used his influence to attain power in Florence and then to enhance it with lavish endowments to the arts.

One example was the Medici Palace he built at the heart of the city. For its chapel he commissioned murals of the Three Wise Men. Audaciously, he had his son and heir Lorenzo the Magnificent depicted as one of the Magi, with himself depicted as an attendant. Cosimo had been instrumental in persuading the pope to host the Council of Florence in his city, and he used that event as another allusion in his prestige-enhancing chapel. Accordingly, the faces of Byzantine Emperor John and Ecumenical Patriarch Joseph appear on the two remaining Magi. The "iconography" of the chapel was, therefore, far more a celebration of Cosimo's power than a representation of sacred history.

The Platonic Academy mentioned above was established in the city with a similar aim. To its leadership, Cosimo appointed the humanist Marsilio Ficino (d. 1499) and commissioned him to produce the first Latin translation of Plato's collected works. This was a major achievement whose impact on the future direction of the West cannot be underestimated. However, Ficino was not merely a translator. He was also an advocate for a totally new way of conceiving the human condition.

From Adam to Prometheus

A FELLOW COUNTRYMAN OF FICINO named Giannozzo Manetti (d. 1459) was one of the earliest to apply this perspective. As popular as Petrarch's "remedy book" had proven to be, the dialogue on human misery contained within it was not direct or prominent enough to challenge the West's prevailing cult of pessimism. Manetti, inspired by the infusion of Platonist thought from the East, became the first to write a formal refutation of Pope Innocent's *Misery of the Human Condition* (which we discussed in chapter one).

Though of Florentine origin, Manetti wrote while living in Naples as a guest of its ruler. King Alfonso V of Aragon (r. 1416–1458) was then fighting a war of expansion into Italy and had made the Mediterranean seaport his territorial stronghold. Like other Italian potentates, he considered patronage of scholarship an important sign of his political legitimacy. In fact, it was he that commissioned Lorenzo Valla at about this time to undertake a study of the *Donation of Constantine*, used since the Great Schism to justify papal claims of supremacy against not only Constantinople but also political rivals in the West. The resulting work permanently discredited the *Donation* by revealing it to be an audacious hoax. Since Alfonso was at war with the papacy for control of central Italy, Valla's scholarship proved ideologically invaluable.

In the case of Manetti, the king was seeking a writer who would ennoble his territorial ambitions at the expense of the papacy. Alfonso had recently commissioned another humanist scholar named Bartolome Facio to write a treatise on the dignity of man, but to his chagrin, when the work appeared it was dedicated not to him but to his illustrious enemy Pope Nicholas V. Manetti's commission was a second effort to celebrate Alfonso's reign through literary patronage.

The ambitious king was not disappointed. What emerged from *On the Dignity and Excellence of Man* was a completely new anthropological vision. "I thought it important to refute," Manetti writes, "what has been written by many ancient and modern writers on the goodness of death and the misery of human life. What they wrote is somewhat repugnant."[7] Perhaps to satisfy his royal patron, he even criticizes Pope Nicholas's famous predecessor Innocent by name.

Manetti's vision centers on what can be called *homo faber*, man as the creator and fashioner of his own destiny. The innovation went beyond a mere celebration of man as "the image of God" (*imago Dei*), the characterization proclaimed in Genesis about Adam and dear to the patristic anthropology of the old Christendom. To be sure, man was this. But he was more. He possessed the power to create on his own terms. Manetti remarks that it is no wonder the ancient pagans made their gods in the image of man, endowed as he was with the virtues of beauty, intelligence, creativity, and power. He was particularly fascinated with the classical myth of Prometheus, in which man, created by the rebellious titan, was endowed with the power to generate civilization independently of the gods. The image of Prometheus would grow ever more mesmerizing as the emerging age of utopia advanced, beckoning humanists toward that ultimate act of self-determination, political rebellion.

Manetti's defense of human dignity was echoed back in his native Florence. There at the Platonic Academy Ficino went even further in breaking from the legacy of Pope Innocent. In a work entitled *Platonic Theology*, the disciple of Plethon sought to demonstrate how Platonism was, like the New Testament, divinely inspired. Following Plato, he claims that man occupies a midpoint in the creation between God and matter, and that it is man's honored role to mediate between the two. Building on Manetti's praise of homo faber, Ficino asserts that man not only practices the "industrial arts," but exercises a divine creativity within the cosmic chain of being. "Universal providence is proper to God who is the universal cause," he declares.

> *Therefore man who universally provides for all things living and not living is a certain god. He is the god without doubt of the animals since he uses all of them, rules them, and teaches some of them. He is established also as god of the elements since he inhabits and cultivates them all. He is, finally, the god of*

7 *Two Views of Man*, 63.

> *all materials since he handles all, and turns and changes them. Anyone who dominates the body in so many and such great things and acts as the vicar of immortal God is without doubt immortal.*[8]

For Ficino, man acquires through his creativity a kind of deification. But in contrast to the teachings of hesychasm, this is presented as an innate, natural condition resulting from the created order of things and not, as Orthodox theologians like Gregory Palamas had insisted, through dependence on the transcendent Trinity. Such creativity was essentially promethean.

Ficino's Platonist model of human deification becomes particularly interesting when discussing the art of statecraft. Eastern Christendom had long held to a cosmology that claimed Christian rulers serve the Church in her ministry of manifesting the kingdom of heaven on earth. Ficino, breaking from the cosmological contempt of Innocent and other Augustinian theologians of the West, now returns to a fulsomely affirmative view of government for its own sake. He asserts that "man alone so abounds in perfection that he rules himself first, which no beasts do, then governs his family, administers the state, rules peoples and commands the entire world." Here, however, the paradisiacal vision of the old Christendom is absent. Man is once again considered in a state of individual isolation from the incarnate God. "Born for ruling," Ficino claims, he is like Prometheus in being "entirely impatient of servitude."[9]

Ficino was a thoroughgoing Platonist and as such disdained the material creation. This included the human body. The immaterial soul was for him the only truly worthy part of a human being. "For if the mind," he writes,

> *lifts itself as much higher for the sake of contemplating spiritual things as it removes itself farther from corporeal things, if the supreme end which the intelligence can attain is the very substance of God, it follows that then at length the mind is able to draw near the divine substance, when it will be totally alienated from mortal senses. Therefore the soul, freed from the*

8 Quoted in Trinkaus, *Image and Likeness*, vol. 2, 484.
9 Ibid.

> *chains of this body, and departing in purity, does in a certain mode become God.*[10]

Again, it is clear that this prominent humanist was, in restoring dignity to the human condition, groping toward a doctrine of deification. We noted in chapter one how Petrarch had done something similar. Suffering the effects of three centuries of division from the Orthodox Church, however, humanists were often blind to—or by theological formation unconcerned with—the paradisiacal culture of the old Christendom.

This is the tragedy of humanism's origin, for in the East hesychasm had long defined the goal of human life as the glorious participation of both body and soul in the divine energies of an incarnate God. According to traditional Christianity, the New Adam, Jesus Christ, had assumed both a human body and a human soul. Platonism was a paltry substitute, for it denied the value of the body and grossly misrepresented the sanctification of the soul. But such was the result of the Great Division. It had ensured that the only thing a quattrocento philosopher like Ficino really knew about the East was mediated through the demoralized and distorted fantasies of the "Second Plato," the neopagan George Plethon.

Yet it was Ficino's Platonism that would guide the work of the most influential Italian humanist, Pico della Mirandola.

By now, Florence had become a new Athens for Western culture. Under Cosimo's son Lorenzo the Magnificent (r. 1469–1492), the Medici continued to patronize scholarship and art on a grand scale. But even their financial resources had limits. As a result, scholars and artists fanned out across the peninsula seeking new markets for their creative work. The most illustrious market was to be found in Rome, where a series of "Renaissance popes" competed with other Italian potentates to patronize the new culture.

The Avignon departure had been followed by the Papal Schism, when two and then three canonically elected popes rivaled each other for the status of true head of the Roman Catholic Church. Only after this crisis had been resolved was the papacy able to begin the process of reconsolidating its

10 Quoted in Trinkaus, *Image and Likeness*, vol. 2, 487–88.

leadership, which it did in part by asserting political, territorial, and military claims not made since the height of the Papal Reformation. The reconstruction of Rome became a symbol of papal recovery.

Pope Nicholas V (r. 1447–1455) set the standard for his successors by rebuilding the city after a century of neglect. At the top of his list was the relocation of the papal court from the dilapidated Lateran Palace, headquarters of Rienzo's short-lived government, to the Vatican on the opposite side of the Tiber River. A plan was devised to completely rebuild Saint Peter's Basilica there, but funding issues prevented it from being realized before the pope's death. In the meantime, Sixtus IV (r. 1471–1484) adorned the Vatican with a new church named, in the spirit of the age, after himself. The site of future papal convocations, the Sistine Chapel would be decorated by Michelangelo with some of modern Christendom's most famous murals.

The Renaissance papacy was known for more than its building projects. Rome also became a center of scholarship as the popes struggled to reassert intellectual leadership. With their wealth and influence, they attracted a flood of literary aspirants to the city. Humanists like Leonardo Bruni, Poggio Bracholini, and Lorenzo Valla all earned their livings at the papal court.

The Florentine Lapo da Castiglionchio (d. 1438) was less fortunate. He tried unsuccessfully to obtain entrée to the papal court and in doing so wrote a study of its moral character. It is a strange work, filled with salacious accounts of revelry and fornication by the clergy and their underage male attendants. The charges were by no means unique. In his memoirs, even Pius II (r. 1458–1464) described in detail the gluttony and promiscuity of his court. One cardinal remodeled his Vatican apartments to include pornographic images on the ceilings, and by the end of the quattrocento, accounts of debauchery by the popes themselves were commonplace.

One such account described the weekly regime of Alexander VI (r. 1492–1503) as a cycle of feasting and fornication, "after which," a contemporary drily observed, "he would vomit."[11] In a period of profligate extremes, it was Alexander who earned the greatest infamy. Himself the beneficiary of

11 Quoted in Alexander Lee, *The Ugly Renaissance: Sex, Greed, Violence, and Depravity in an Age of Beauty* (New York: Anchor Books, 2013), 256.

endemic nepotism, he sealed his election as Vicar of Christ through a campaign of unabashed bribery. Never interested in piety, he made the Vatican a staging ground for bullfights and dances. War and the territorial expansion of the Papal States made up his vision of ministry. He sired five known children by a variety of mistresses, with son Cesare Borgia being the most like his father. The byword of corruption for posterity, Borgia more than doubled the number of children born of illegitimate relationships (eleven) and warred his way to glory so successfully as to earn the glowing admiration of the amoral political commentator Niccolò Machiavelli. Yet as such praise suggests, there was a paradoxical admiration for the Renaissance popes as patrons of culture.

Not all contemporaries were complacent about the new culture. Erasmus of Rotterdam (d. 1536), for instance, wrote a satirical dialogue on the arrogant efforts of the late Pope Julius II first to force and then to bribe his way into heaven. Even more emphatic were the objections of a Dominican friar named Girolamo Savonarola (d. 1498). Seizing power in Florence as a prophet, he attacked the Medici system and the clergy who acquiesced to it. Humanism was to him an abomination that deserved harsh judgment. Most abhorrent was the new, naturalistic art it inspired. Savonarola's public "bonfires of the vanities" consumed a great many of the most modern of the city's famous paintings. But his influence was brief. Overthrown and executed, he was a prophet speaking before his time. It would be Calvinist Protestants who would eventually destroy religious art on an even greater scale during the century that followed.

Nevertheless, the papacy's rich patronage of arts and letters won the admiration of many humanists. As we have seen, several obtained key positions at the papal court. Lapo da Castiglionchio's exposé helps explain this paradox. It presents courtly splendor as the necessary means of elevating the church hierarchy, enabling it to establish Christianity solidly in the world. A little later in the century, Valla would write a treatise attacking the monastic practices of poverty, chastity, and obedience, seeing them all as violations of human dignity.[12] With the same humanist values, Lapo argues that the

12 See Lorenzo Valla, *The Profession of the Religious and Selections from the*

papal court and the civilization it inspires needs for its very legitimacy luxury and opulence. He even goes so far as to subvert traditional Christianity's vision of Jesus' poverty. "One should draw back a bit from that ancient severity and energy of Christ," he suggests at one point, "and add something new."[13] Humanism was transforming Western Christendom into something very new indeed.

The papacy's endorsement of the new culture, then, had a magnetic effect on humanists. The most famous among them was the young philosopher Giovanni Pico della Mirandola (d. 1494), a student of Ficino and even more original than his teacher, if such was possible, in his vision of the dignity of man. Like many other Florentines, Pico was drawn toward Rome as to the center of what he understood a truly new Christendom to be. He knew nothing of the old Christendom, it seems, though he did master the Greek language. The sources he knew were Neoplatonist philosophers like Plethon and disgruntled Orthodox bishops like Bessarion. They were not the writings of Eastern Christian fathers like Basil the Great, Maximos the Confessor, or Gregory Palamas.

Interestingly, in addition to his training in Neoplatonism, Pico had mastered the Jewish Kabbala, Islam, Zoroastrianism, and the magical treatises of an ancient writer named Hermes Trismegistus. It was from the latter that an occult tradition known as hermeticism sprang. Building on the work of Ficino, Pico hoped to discover what mystics like him called a *prisca theologia*, an archaic deposit of religious truth that preceded the revelation of the Old Covenant—to say nothing of Christianity itself.

With this dizzying syncretism, Pico composed a treatise entitled *Nine Hundred Theses* touching on every aspect of religion. He organized a symposium in Rome in 1487 to debate the theses. The plan was as utopian as the revolution of Rienzo. In his youthful idealism (he was but twenty-four at the time), he convinced himself that he had discovered the key to proving

---

Falsely-Believed and Forged Donation of Constantine, ed. and trans. Olga Zorzi Pugliese (Toronto: Centre for Reformation and Renaissance Studies, 1994).

13 Quoted in Christopher S. Celenza, *Renaissance Humanism and the Papal Curia: Lapo da Castiglionchio the Younger's De curiae commodis* (Ann Arbor: University of Michigan, 1999), 75.

the divinity of Jesus Christ. He even offered to pay the travel expenses of any scholar who would venture to Rome to listen. For the occasion, he composed a short treatise known as the *Oration on the Dignity of Man*. To his profound disappointment, the symposium never occurred. Getting wind of the strange event, Pope Innocent VIII ordered its suspension and an investigation of the *Theses*. Not surprisingly, several were declared heretical. Only the *Oration* survived, to be taken up by subsequent humanists and celebrated as the quattrocento's greatest statement of human dignity.

The *Oration*'s most striking argument is that man is not the intermediary between God and creation, as Neoplatonists like Ficino had claimed. Instead, man is completely free of God and creation. He is *autonomous* (from the Greek for "self-ruled"). All other creatures would by contrast be *heteronomous*, that is, "ruled by another." But true dignity, as Valla had indicated in his repudiation of monastic obedience, requires liberation from the rule of all others. For Pico, man is free to stand proudly alone, like Prometheus, to create his own destiny.

This exhilarating idea is developed in Pico's account of the creation of Adam. He has God tell the first man that the latter is free to choose any course of life he wishes, for like the Creator he belongs to no fixed reality in the cosmos.

> *"We have given you, O Adam, no visage proper to yourself, nor any endowment properly your own, in order that whatever place, whatever form, whatever gifts you may, with premeditation, select, these same you may have and possess through your own judgment and decision. The nature of all other creatures is defined and restricted within laws which We have laid down; you, by contrast, impeded by no such restrictions, may, by your own free will, to whose custody We have assigned you, trace for yourself the lineaments of your own nature. I have placed you at the very center of the world, so that from that vantage point you may with greater ease glance round about you on all that the world contains. We have made you a creature neither of heaven nor of earth, neither mortal nor immortal, in order that you may, as the free and proud shaper of your own being, fashion yourself in the form you may prefer.*

> *It will be in your power to descend to the lower, brutish forms of life; you will be able, through your own decision, to rise again to the superior orders whose life is divine."*[14]

Pico—like Ficino, Manetti, and Petrarch—was self-consciously a Christian. But by advancing humanism's project to liberate the West from the pessimistic culture inherited from the Great Division, he reached the conclusion that man was no longer what God had made him to be. Man was not Adam but Prometheus. In the words of the Renaissance historian Paul Oskar Kristeller, man was "outside the hierarchy" of creation.[15] He had become autonomous.

The only commandment he was called on to obey was to trace for himself "the lineaments of his own nature"—that is, to recreate himself and the world he was called to rule.

And to do that he needed to recreate his image.

The End of Iconography

THE TIME HAD COME FOR man to reevaluate Western depictions of the human image. For once it was not Petrarch who led the way. His close friend and literary collaborator Boccaccio was the first to speak of a new way of pictorially representing man.

The new aesthetic can be called "naturalism." Its earliest expression related to the paintings of Giotto (d. 1337), which contemporaries characterized as "modern art" (*ars moderna*). In his famous *Decameron* (1353), Boccaccio has the narrator remark that Giotto

> *had so excellent a genius that there was nothing of all which Nature, mother and mover of all things, presenteth unto us by the ceaseless revolution of the*

14 Giovanni Pico della Mirandola, *Oration on the Dignity of Man*, trans. A. Robert Caponigri (Washington, DC: Regnery Publishing, 1956), 7–8.

15 Paul Oskar Kristeller, *Renaissance Thought and Its Sources*, ed. Michael Mooney (New York: Columbia University, 1979), 175.

> *heavens, but he with pencil and pen and brush depicted it and that so closely that not like, nay, but rather the thing itself it seemed, insomuch that men's visual sense is found to have been oftentimes deceived in things of his fashion, taking that for real which was but depictured. Wherefore, he having brought back to the light this art, which had for many an age lain buried under the errors of certain folk who painted more to divert the eyes of the ignorant than to please the understanding of the judicious, he may deservedly be styled one of the chief glories [of] Florence.*[16]

Here, within Petrarch's circle of early humanists, are all the marks that separate modern painting from traditional Christian iconography. "Nature" is the ultimate aesthetic standard, not a world transfigured by heaven. The work of art should be an illusion, an act of "deceiving" the viewer into thinking he is looking on an object of nature, rather than a proclamation of the gospel that illuminates the viewer about a transcendent presence beyond nature. It is the work of a "genius" with novel sensibilities, not of an ascetic who, submitting to the tradition of the Church, seeks to hand on faithfully that which he has received. Giotto was restoring a form of art that during recent centuries had lain "buried" in a sort of graveyard of high culture. It was not a thing for the ignorantly pious. And indeed, it served only the values of the "judicious," that is, those humanists who had lost confidence in the culture of the new Christendom.

The iconography of the old Christendom had been a proclamation of the gospel of Jesus Christ. It emerged within the historical shadows of the early Church and was not given doctrinal articulation until attacked by the Eastern heresy of iconoclasm during the eighth century. At the Seventh Ecumenical Council of 787 in the Greek city of Nicaea, bishops assembled to defend iconography by emphasizing that without images depicting the

---

16 Giovanni Boccaccio, *The Decameron*, trans. John Payne (New York: Walter J. Black, 1886), 303. For his part, Petrarch seems to have been ambiguous about Giotto. In his guidebook for a traveler to Jerusalem, he recommends making a stop in Naples "not to pray," as his modern editor notes, "but to admire the frescoes by Giotto." *Petrarch's Guide to the Holy Land*, trans. Theodore J. Cachey (Notre Dame, IN: University of Notre Dame, 2002), 25.

physical body of Christ, faith in the Incarnation—that God had really and not only symbolically become human—was subverted. And if icons could and even must be made of Christ, then they must also be made of His saints, in whom, to paraphrase Paul, Christ sacramentally dwells (Gal. 2:20). The Greek word *ikon* literally means "image," and it was in God's image that humanity was created. The fathers of the council claimed to be following the apostolic tradition of the Church under the guidance of the Holy Spirit.

They were convinced in this by the writings of John of Damascus, who stated in a famous iconological treatise that because of the Incarnation the material creation is sanctified within the life of the Church. A true icon, then, is not only a collection of earthly materials such as wood and paint, but a holy object in which the divine presence on earth is made real. What is more, by employing stylistic measures such as elongating the body unnaturally and using heavenly symbolism (such as the absence of natural light sources), iconographers could at one and the same time depict both the sanctified material world and the transcendent source of its sanctification.

A stylized aesthetic of what can be called "heavenly realism" became particularly noticeable in the iconography of Eastern Christendom after the confirmation of hesychasm in the fourteenth century. Iconographers did not use this term and would not have recognized a need for it, since art had yet to enter its modern ideological phase. But they were influenced by the content of Orthodox theology, especially hesychasm. Iconographers like the Russian Andrey Rublev drew upon the hesychastic doctrine of the integrated deification of man—involving both soul and body—to produce the most inspired icons in history.

In the West, the new aesthetic of naturalism pioneered by Giotto and advanced by humanist followers like Boccaccio brought an end to the possibility of heavenly realism. The fact that iconoclasm had never disrupted church life outside Byzantium resulted in an absence of theological reflection on iconography beyond its borders. In the time of Charlemagne, in fact, icons were held in suspicion but tolerated because of their evangelical function; they made effective catechetical statements about the life of Christ and His saints. Iconology as such remained impoverished. Almost all iconographical influence continued to come from the culturally more sophisticated East.

But after the Great Division, that influence stalled. As it did so, new approaches to iconography arose in the West to give expression to a new penitential piety associated with the threat of purgatorial punishment and the canonical penances that promised to preclude it. Instead of emphasizing heavenly immanence, icons in the new Christendom sought to provoke an emotional response in the viewer. Images of the Passion came to displace those of any other event in Christ's earthly ministry, depicting the Crucifixion with greater and greater levels of graphic horror. It was this approach to painting that appalled the humanists, because it was inseparable from pessimism about the human condition in a world they intended to transform.

The rise of naturalism thus brought about the end of iconography, if the latter is understood to manifest the incarnational aesthetic of the old Christendom. To use the renowned art historian Hans Belting's words about the work of art, "the new presence *of* the work succeeds the former presence of the sacred *in* the work."[17] In other words, with the rise of naturalism the artwork comes to stand alone, like the newly autonomous man of the humanists. Gone is the presence of heaven within it.

In many ways the new artwork remained Christian in content but became pagan in form. As we have seen, Petrarch and those who followed him looked to pagan antiquity for their standard of a healthy culture. Platonism displaced traditional Christianity, and as it did so ideals of physical beauty made the inherited aesthetic of spiritual realism seem crude. Humanists applied classical ideals of bodily proportion to elaborate the new aesthetic of naturalism. The example of Greek sculpture in this was particularly compelling. It provided a standard of form that could be joined to a Christian standard of content. Michelangelo's *David* is a good example. It can be interpreted as the celebration of the physical beauty of a nude boy, no different from those that proliferated in pagandom, where same-sex attraction toward youth was considered a virtue. The only thing that set Michelangelo's

17 Hans Belting, *Likeness and Presence: A History of the Image before the Era of Art*, translated by Edmund Jephcott (Chicago: University of Chicago, 1994), 459.

famous statue apart from its ancient prototypes was its Christianized title.

Because of naturalism's priorities, painters of the quattrocento began to use models extensively. Many resorted to using young women for their representations of the Madonna, as the period's standard image of the Virgin Mary holding the infant Christ came to be known. In some cases, the physical beauty of the models provoked artists to keep them as mistresses. Raphael, whom the contemporary art historian Vasari described as "a very amorous man who was fond of women," alternated between painting Madonnas and nymphs, the female models for which, it seems, he used interchangeably.[18] For instance, at the very time he was composing the famous *Sistine Madonna* (1512) on commission for Pope Julius II, he was painting the *Triumph of Galatea* for the wayward Roman banking magnate Agostino Chigi. Chigi's extravagant Villa Farnesina, newly built only half a mile from the Vatican, featured banquets at which guests were ordered to toss dirty silver plates into the Tiber because the host was too wealthy to bother cleaning them. (As it turned out, after the guests' departure servants recovered the silver by retracting nets that had been carefully positioned along the shore.)

An anecdote told by Vasari about Fillipo Lippi is even more colorful. The Florentine painter of some of the most celebrated Madonnas was "so lustful that whenever he saw women who pleased him, he would give them all his possessions just to have them, and if he could not, as a middle course, he cooled the flames of his amorous passion by talking to himself while painting their portraits." Lippi would wander the streets of Florence at night in revelry. This caused such instability in his work output that on one occasion his patron, Cosimo de Medici, actually locked him inside the second-story room of his palace until the artist completed the commission. For several days the door remained closed, until it was discovered that during the night Lippi had been lowering himself down to the street with a rope made of bedsheets, returning in the early hours to escape detection.[19]

Not all naturalistic inspiration came from models and mistresses,

---

18 Georgio Vasari, *The Lives of the Artists*, trans. Julia Conaway Bondanella and Peter Bondanella (Oxford: Oxford University, 1998), 327-28.

19 Ibid, 193.

Raphael, Sistine Madonna

however. In the case of Michelangelo, the relatively new practice of cadaver dissection enabled the artist to study the musculature beneath the skin and thereby achieve the exquisite representation of the human hand in works such as the Sistine Chapel's *Creation of Adam*. Leonardo da Vinci also availed himself of the opportunities of natural science. His drawings and notebooks include not only the famous study of bodily proportions known as *Vitruvian Man*, but a sketch of a pregnant female cadaver's bisected uterus with a fully formed fetus inside. Perhaps most disturbingly, Hans Holbein used a cadaver as a model for his stunningly morbid *Christ in the Tomb* (1522). Inspired by the recently completed *Isenheim Altarpiece*—a particularly gruesome example of the new Christendom's affective piety—Holbein's work shows the Son of God as a corpse whose fingers indicate signs of rigor mortis, whose mouth gapes in a silent scream, and whose dead eyes stare at nothing.

This new approach to painting vaulted artists to a notoriety unprecedented in the history of Christendom. The most talented were pursued by wealthy patrons prepared to endure all manner of affronts and disappointments just to engage them. Michelangelo was the most audacious in exercising the whims of artistic celebrity. During the course of fulfilling his commission to paint the Sistine Chapel ceiling, he became offended on one occasion by the pope's refusal to meet with him. Declaring he had better things to do, he petulantly left the Vatican only to be pursued by the pope's ambassadors, who, upon overtaking him, apologized on their lord's behalf and begged him to return to work. But after completing the ceiling, the genius was ordered by a scrupulous official to paint loincloths on the naked figures in the *Last Judgment*, whose anatomy the artist had rendered

Hans Holbein, Christ in the Tomb

graphically according to his naturalistic ideal. Michelangelo reluctantly complied, but in revenge he also repainted one of those being punished in hell with the official's countenance.

Perhaps most audaciously—and typical of Western art during the age of utopia—it was Michelangelo who can be credited with the first significant authorial signature. The story is that after his sculpture known as the *Pieta* had been placed in Saint Peter's Basilica, he stood in the shadows to relish the approval of those coming to view it. But the genius was affronted when one bumpkin mistakenly attributed the masterpiece to a rival artist. Simmering with rage, the sculptor returned in the evening with a hammer and chisel to engrave, across the very breast of the Queen of Heaven, "This is the work of Michelangelo the Florentine."

By the sixteenth century, then, the art of the new Christendom could not have been more different from that of the old Christendom. The West had assumed a totally new approach to beauty, one expressing the secular ideals of the humanists. The significance of these changes can be seen by contrasting certain well-known examples of painting in the East and the West.

For instance, Michelangelo's *Creation of Adam,* part of the Sistine Chapel ceiling commission, was a celebration not of man as the image of God but of man on the verge of animation to assume a promethean estate. Even God looks more like a pagan statue of Zeus than like the Word "through whom all things were made" and who became incarnate to dignify the human image. A contrast to this is to be found in Palermo on the island of Sicily, where Byzantine iconographers executed anonymous mosaics of the *Creation of Adam* during the period of Norman rule, when Orthodox and Roman Catholics intermingled—and before the Fourth Crusade burned the bridges of Christendom's reunion. Most striking is the fact that the face of Adam in the mosaic at Palermo is identical in appearance to that of his Creator, the Word Jesus Christ. Man, this stunning icon visually proclaimed, is made in the image of God.

A second contrast between the old Christendom and the new can be found in representations of the Theotokos. In the East, she continued to be rendered as *hodegetria,* that is, "she who points the way." Her head is veiled,

Christ with Adam, Monreale Cathedral, Palermo, Italy

her clothing is modest, and she literally points toward her Son as if to say, "Do not look at me, but at Him." It has been said that in Eastern Christendom all Orthodox Mariology is ultimately Christology. The Son she holds in her lap is the incarnate God, and to depict him as such requires aesthetic symbolism, not naturalism. He is represented not as a helpless infant but as a man (though in miniature) to proclaim His divine power. Arrayed in vesture, he is not only the Savior of the modestly dressed Virgin. He is the ruler of the cosmos. It is Christ who therefore becomes the real "center" of the icon, the ultimate focal point of one standing in front of it in prayer.

In the West, by contrast, Raphael's *Madonna of the Pinks* (1507) represented the Virgin Mary as nothing more than an object of charming fascination. She is simply a pretty young girl. Gone almost entirely is the halo that, according to iconographical convention, had long symbolized holiness. Also almost entirely absent is her veil, in order to display her lovely braided hair. Gone is modest attire, the better to show her smooth, powder-white bosom. More remarkably, the equally pretty baby she balances in her lap appears to be nothing more than . . . a baby.

This, along with other Madonnas of the period, is that moment in history when the incarnate God gives way to "Baby Jesus," a departure from tradition so great that it represents the transition between a paradisiacal art and a utopian one. To a member of the old Christendom, it bordered on blasphemy. In an effort to celebrate human life in a spiritually untransformed world, the artist of the new Christendom now emasculates the image of the Godman and by doing so diminishes His divinity. In this and the similar Madonnas that cascaded out of quattrocento Italy, there is in fact no indication that the little baby in its pretty mother's lap is divine, or, for that matter, that he is even Jesus. For absent also is the iconographical practice of identifying with abbreviations the name of the holy person being represented. In fact, prayer to this "Baby Jesus" is all but precluded by his aimless fascination with the flowers known as pinks. It is certainly precluded by the exposure of his uncovered genitalia.

But prayer was not Raphael's purpose. Painting had become reoriented toward the saeculum. It had ceased to be liturgical. Indeed, the only clue that the painting represented the Madonna was that it conformed in content to the standard iconography of the Theotokos inherited from and still normative in the East. A viewer with no cultural knowledge of the old Christendom could only have assumed he was looking on nothing more than a picture of a pretty young mother holding her cute little child. Through the artistic reorientation of the West, then, Jesus Christ had become an adorable baby whose passivity incites a desire to pinch him on the cheek and poke him in the belly like some fourteenth-century Pillsbury Doughboy.

A final contrast can be found in the way the angelic powers were represented. The traditional image of them was awe-inspiring. This was consistent with the scriptures, for *angelos* in Greek means "messenger," that is, mediator of communication from an awesome and transcendent God. When an angel appears to a man, his words are often "Do not be afraid," because such a messenger is fearsome. In the case of the icon of Archangel Michael in the eponymous cathedral of the Moscow Kremlin, the chief of the heavenly hosts is represented accordingly. He is armed with a sword and ready to defend the Christian people from demonic assault. A counterpart to this image is the ancient icon of the *Ladder of Divine Ascent*, executed at Saint Katherine Monastery on Mount Sinai in Egypt. It shows men climbing toward heaven while demons—represented in black silhouettes as beings with no personality—struggle to pull them off and drag them into hell. Such were the themes of angelic power and salvific struggle in the iconography of the East.

In the West, under the influence of Pico's ideal of human autonomy, angels were degraded to the status of powerless bystanders. In a world in which man was the promethean master of his own destiny, the services of the heavenly powers were no longer needed. Raphael's *Sistine Madonna* is a good example of this change. It reveals the future of utopianism, in which the angels have nothing to offer mankind. At the lowest register of the painting appear two enfeebled angel-like beings looking on with indifference. These angel-thingies are more like *putti*, or winged babies, than anything found within the tradition of the Church, biblical or otherwise. Such painting may have been Christian in content, but it was becoming thoroughly pagan in form. What is more, exactly such images of "cherubs" would come to decorate the spiritually feeble religious painting of the modern West. In fact, through mass reproduction in an age of nihilism, Raphael's conception of the putti-as-cherubs was destined for no higher purpose than bedroom posters, coffee mugs, and bumper stickers. Beyond their ability to charm, the heavenly powers in this and subsequent images became simply powerless.

It is interesting to imagine what mutual impressions would have been made in the middle of the fifteenth century had a hesychast iconographer in the East met a humanist painter from the West. Such a scenario was not implausible. The Athonite theologian Maxim the Greek, for example, had come to Moscow at about this time after living in Florence and observing the arts of the quattrocento. It is true that Byzantium had finally succumbed to Turkish conquest, her iconographers suppressed by sharia law or driven into exile. But in Russia the liturgical arts were flourishing, inspired by a resurgent national monarchy and the infusion of Athonite monasticism. There, Andrey Rublev had brought iconography to its apogee by integrating it with the principles of hesychasm. One of his most illustrious successors was

Dionisy (d. 1502), whose work is most famously preserved at the Ferapontov Monastery in the remote forests of the north. We might imagine an adventuresome Italian—Filippo Lippi (d. 1469) would do for such an experiment—ending his days in search of patrons in Moscow. Perhaps he had finally been cast out of Florence after failing to complete his commission for Cosimo de Medici. Perhaps he looked to the court of Tsar Ivan the Great as an even better opportunity for work.

However we imagine his reason for traveling to the East, Lippi would have had little to talk about in the presence of Dionisy. The latter was an ascetic, a tonsured monk whose obedience was to paint images of Christ and saints like the Theotokos in a way faithful to the tradition of the fathers. In contrast, Lippi was a rake, a reckless carouser in whose inebriated brain images of the Virgin blended indistinguishably with those of prostitutes. The Russian would have been horrified at the thought of defacing his work with a signature, whereas the Italian saw individuality as the only mark of real talent. Dionisy produced images whose only purpose was liturgical, bringing the viewer into greater communion with God. But even when painting religious images, Lippi was concerned with satisfying the vanity of his wealthy patrons as he advanced his own professional fortunes.

The imagination, of course, winces at such counterfactual contrasts. And this is a telling commentary on the history of Christendom as it entered the age of utopia. Only a century earlier, Barlaam had come to the East from Italy to teach theology in Constantinople. Though he was ultimately condemned by the hesychast councils there, his long dispute with Gregory Palamas shows that during the fourteenth century, East and West still shared a common theological language.

In the fifteenth century, however, had Dionisy and Lippi compared their works, they would have concluded they represented the values of totally different civilizations. After the Great Division, a few threads had continued to join the West to the East. Humanism now tore Christendom's paradisiacal vestment in two.

The Path of Indignation

SOME SCHOLARS HAVE SPECULATED THAT the humanists' fascination with the culture of pagandom concealed a hidden interest in paganism itself. Ficino's search for a *prisca theologia* certainly suggested this. His disciple Pico, though claiming the superiority of Christianity, was fascinated by hellenistic beliefs as well as by Jewish and Islamic ones. We have likewise met the disgruntled Greek philosopher Plethon, whose vision of a repaganized Byzantium was as delusional as it was desperate. The Turkish onslaught he fearfully awaited did not immediately threaten the West, but there the perception of cultural decline created circumstances for a similar experimentation in beliefs.

According to Jocelyn Godwin, neopaganism offered humanists an escape from the dissatisfactions of Roman Catholic Christianity—though one limited largely to fantasy.

> *In their waking life [the humanists] accepted the absurdities acknowledged as the essence and credenda of Christianity, all the while nurturing a longing for the world of antiquity and a secret affinity for the divinities of that world. No one confessed, no one described this urge, for it was never dragged beneath the searchlight of consciousness or the scrutiny of the Inquisition. It would have been suicidal, were it even possible, for anyone in Christian Europe to articulate it. But that was all the more reason for it to manifest in the favorite language of the unconscious, and of dreams: that of images.*[20]

The use of pagan motifs by artists like Michelangelo can thus be seen as an effort to redress a longstanding anthropological pessimism.

Significantly, such a cultural malaise did not substantially afflict the old Christendom. Godwin goes on to note that

> *there are those who insist that Rome had already surrendered her spiritual sovereignty, and that her embrace of a pagan aesthetic was just another stage*

20 Jocelyn Godwin, *The Pagan Dream of the Renaissance* (Grand Rapids, MI: Phanes Press, 2002), 2.

> *of decadence, from which the Eastern churches have ever held aloof. The ghastliness of the Zeus [Sistine] Chapel ceiling in the eyes of an Eastern Orthodox believer can barely be imagined by those who have been brought up to revere Michelangelo's labours.*[21]

We will discuss the revival of pagan imagery in a later chapter—and its reception by a Russian Church that sadly proved more ambivalent than Godwin's idealized characterization suggests. Spiritual culture under Ivan the Great and Peter the Great, it turned out, proved very different. But as we bring this chapter to a close, it is worth pausing to consider another dimension to the humanists' fascination with pagandom.

For whether they fantasized about paganism or not, the humanists looked to the culture it created as a balm with which to heal the ailing cosmology and anthropology of the new Christendom. Petrarch had indignantly lamented that for centuries the West had been sitting in "darkness." In a way that reversed traditional Christian cosmology, humanists like him now began to look to pagandom for "enlightenment." As we have seen, this photic symbolism originated with the gospel; its appropriation by the humanists was audacious in the extreme. As we shall see in Part II, it would eventually come to characterize the cultural revolution of the eighteenth century and even provide it with a name. For now, the reorientation of the West was more measured. Humanists were content to leave Christendom Christian, provided it submitted to a corrective baptism in the font of pagandom.

The most attractive single source for cultural recatechesis was Platonism. As we have seen, this philosophy was the preferred therapy for those suffering Petrarchan despondency. It offered hope in the form of idealism. And it was idealistic in a way that Christianity was not. Platonism looked to an intellectual pattern of perfection rather than an incarnate one. It demanded no crucifixion of the self, and, as we noted in the case of Valla, regarded traditional Christian asceticism as an impediment to human autonomy. Indeed it was. Platonism seemed to liberate the individual will without sacrifice, directing it toward unlimited potential in this world. For

21 Ibid, 8.

a culture in despair, it offered a blueprint for secular transformation.

Of all the works translated by Ficino, the *Republic* was by far the most radical. To the modern moralist it is by no means unambiguous. For instance, like the *City of God,* it accommodates slavery. But unlike Augustine and all other expressions of traditional Christianity, it also advocates infanticide. And by placing government in the hands of philosophers, it appealed to the humanists in a way that the gospel, with its lowly servant-apostles, never could. Overall, the *Republic* contains an uncompromisingly idealistic view of man's social and political potential. Unlike traditional Christianity, idealism provides a vehicle for indignation, a passion that abounded among the humanists.

These included the Englishman Thomas More (d. 1535). He was a lover of the Italian quattrocento and a friend of its northern advocate Erasmus. During his youth, in an "act of self-definition," he composed a laudatory biography of Pico della Mirandola.[22] As with Petrarch, Platonist idealism mixed in More's mind with a somber Augustinianism. Not only did he lecture approvingly on the spiritual dualism of the *City of God,* he indulged in morbid reflections on the "worthlessness of this world" through exposure to Thomas à Kempis's rueful *Imitation of Christ.*[23] In the estimation of one contemporary, More was a "man for all seasons." The multifarious complexity of his personality is revealed by the fact that as a humanist scholar he sought and obtained the highest political office under the king of England. As lord chancellor to Henry VIII, he became a merciless prosecutor of heretics, participating in their interrogation and assuring that they were "worthily burned" for their recalcitrance.[24] Yet he himself ended his days as a martyr of religious conscience resisting the Henrician Reformation, offering his head as a grim ornament for London's Tower Bridge.

In his youth More had written a literary defense of the *Republic,* seeing in it a model of what the West might someday come to be. But Platonism was not enough for him. Like his friend Erasmus, he was devoutly Christian

22 Peter Ackroyd, *The Life of Thomas More* (New York: Anchor Books, 1998), 107.

23 Ibid, 101.

24 Ibid, 305.

Hans Holbein the Younger, Portrait of Thomas More

and yearned to see the kingdom of heaven more fully manifested in this world than it was. The problem as he likely saw it was not just that Christendom continued as always to fall short of Christianity. What was most immediately of concern was the fact that the reformational culture of the new Christendom was blind to the ways in which traditional Christianity continued to offer the experience of God's presence in the world. This had been the cause of Petrarch's agony, and it was the motive behind the entire range of humanistic endeavor that followed him.

Thomas More brought the movement known as the Renaissance to a kind of completion by channeling the discontent of two centuries into a comprehensive rebuke of the new Christendom. Entitled *Utopia*, this work was an act of sheer indignation. The very word used for it was a neologism based on the Greek for "nowhere." There is not a place within the West, the author implied, in which a civilization with a supporting culture that directs its members toward the heavenly transformation of the world might be found. To locate such a "good place"—*eutopia* in Greek, a variant title that More himself explicitly alludes to in the preface—one must leave the West behind and travel, as sixteenth-century voyagers like Amerigo Vespucci were now doing, to the even farther western islands of the Atlantic.

A good society was surely not to be found in the contemporary West. Part one of the work lays out a comprehensive critique of social customs among the English which arguably applies even more to the Italy of the Medicis. *Utopia* directs its readers to a secular transformation of the world inspired by a dechristianized sense of virtue. The Utopians, for instance, do not practice any religion in particular, though they show the highest respect for Christianity when exposed to it.

More's contemporary society had fallen so far from even this standard of virtue that he is obliged to infuse the work with an unending stream of irony. The principal characters in the dialogue are an example. A narrator named Morus (from the word for "fool" in Greek—a self-deprecating allusion to the author's own name) and a traveler named Hythloday ("peddler of nonsense") discuss the vanity of their current generation.

In this sense the book links itself not only to the sarcastic social commentary of Erasmus but to the current of discontent that would erupt in the Protestant Reformation only a year after its publication. However, it is not religious doctrine and practice that fire More's indignation so much as the social and political shortcomings his interlocutors discuss. And in the second part of the work More, explicitly following the example of Plato, provides a reflection on the perfect civilization. It is not without ambiguity, for alongside economic equality and religious toleration the Utopians practice authoritarian government and euthanasia. But More, a Christian humanist who idealized the former set of practices and abhorred the latter, was not creating a blueprint for utopianism. That would come later.

After more than a century of despondency, Western Christendom invented through the genius of Thomas More a comprehensive vision of utopia. In doing so it found a means of escaping the cultural dead end in which it found itself a half millennium after the Papal Reformation. Like papal reformers and the millenarians who followed them, humanism longed for the transformation of the world. But it did so through hope in a secular future, not a heavenly present. This is what made the birth of humanism a turning point in the rise and fall of what the West once was.

CHAPTER THREE

Surrendering the Saeculum

Quattrocento humanists inherited the papal Reformation's secular model of Christian society and, lacking meaningful contact with the old Christendom (where that model had never taken root), they unwittingly accommodated it. Most of them, after all, depended on commissions and patronage from lay rulers and magnates—in other words, from exactly that part of society considered secular by the new Christendom's dualistic cosmology. Most humanists were themselves members of the laity or, to advance their careers, had undergone a purely nominal ordination. The scope of their interests was therefore limited to what was declared a spiritually untransformed world.

Yet some humanists experienced profound discomfort with the West's bifurcated model of society. Erasmus was a good example. He had taken monastic vows early in life but later obtained a dispensation to forsake them after concluding they were of no use. Though respectful of upright clergy, he regularly lambasted those who thought withdrawal from a secular life assured salvation. In his *Handbook of the Christian Soldier*, for instance, he earned notoriety for declaring that "being a monk does not make one pious." This statement would have been obvious by the standards of traditional Christianity, but in the new Christendom it was controversial. Erasmus dedicated most of his scholarly career to advancing the conviction that ordinary Christians can attain holiness as surely as the clergy.

Erasmus was a devout Roman Catholic Christian reacting against the spiritual bifurcation of society, and he was part of a generation in northern Europe that did likewise. Unlike many of their Italian predecessors, these Christians were eager to evangelize the saeculum rather than merely escape to it. However, in doing so, they mostly embraced a contemptuous cosmology. Even Erasmus, in the spirit of Innocent III, wrote a treatise entitled *On Contempt of the World*. Because of reformational Christianity's persistent pessimism about the world and man's place within it, their project ultimately failed. Instead of evangelizing the saeculum, they surrendered it.

Subverting Tradition

TO THIS TRANSITIONAL GENERATION BELONGED a Roman Catholic theologian named Martin Luther (d. 1546). Like Erasmus, he was eager to evangelize the saeculum, seeing in contemporary Christianity little more than superstition and clerical abuse. Like Erasmus, he had no hope in the papacy to lead in the enterprise of reform. An abortive pilgrimage to the Lateran Palace in Rome revealed to him how far the pleasure-minded Renaissance popes were from their somber predecessors during the Papal Reformation. Then, as a priest hearing confessions in the German university town of Wittenberg in 1517, Luther learned that the pope was selling indulgences to the laity in order to build the magnificently marbled, but in his view utterly vain, new St. Peter's Basilica.

This building would become one of the most famous symbols of Western Christendom. But it is a profoundly modern symbol and one overshadowed by irony. Though it was built as an expression of papal supremacy, its construction helped precipitate the greatest crisis Roman Catholicism has ever faced. Dedicated to the first of the apostles, it became a monument to the pagan rebaptism of the West.

The new basilica replaced St. John Lateran, the cathedral in the eastern part of Rome that, along with the adjacent Lateran Palace, had served as papal headquarters during the first millennium. It was from the Lateran

St. Peter's Square, Rome

that the Papal Reformation of the eleventh century had been launched. It was there that papal supremacy had been formulated as both a doctrine and an instrument of reformational Christianity. Having fallen into ruin during the long Avignon period, however, the Lateran Palace was demoted by quattrocento popes eager to reassert their office. They now chose the Vatican in the western part of the city. By crossing the Tiber, the papacy symbolically distanced itself even further from the East and the first millennium.

The Vatican was the site of an ancient basilica dedicated to St. Peter. In it were kept the relics of the first apostle, and above them, before the Great Schism, Pope Leo III had erected a "shield of faith" on which the Nicene Creed was inscribed without the filioque. This church was now destroyed, along with a courtyard atrium through which the faithful had once passed to enter the paradisiacal experience of the Mass. For more than a millennium, this atrium had in fact been called "the Paradise." At its center was a fountain over which sculptures of peacocks and dolphins symbolized a transfigured cosmos.

The reconstruction project, however, replaced the atrium with St. Peter's Square. The Paradise gave way to a platform for papal supremacy. Here popes could address the crowds of pilgrims who traveled to the capital of the new Christendom not only from western Europe but, as a result of

St. Peter's Cathedral, Rome

overseas expansion, from across the world. Brilliantly symbolic, the square was encircled by colonnades intended to represent the outstretched arms of the Roman Catholic Church, whose head, the pope—successor to St. Peter and vicar of Christ—welcomed the faithful.

The exterior design of the new St. Peter's Basilica was rich in Roman Catholic content but in many ways followed pagan forms. The colonnades lining the square, for instance, were topped with one hundred forty statues of saints that, with the shapely columns below them, made the structure resemble an ancient Greek temple. This was even more the effect of the basilica's façade, which featured a line of Corinthian columns centered under the triangular pediment without which few pagan temples—the Parthenon included—had been erected.

And as a final humanistic flourish, the facade of St. Peter's Basilica was marked prominently with the name of the man who saw it to completion, rather like the audacious signature of Michelangelo marking the *Pieta* (which was located within it). Along the entablature that ran horizontally above the columns was carved the statement: "In honor of the Prince of the Apostles, Paul V Borghese, a Roman, Supreme Pontiff, in the year 1612, the seventh of his pontificate." Significantly, from this inscription it is precisely the section reading "Paul V Borghese, a Roman" that appears at the center point above the entrance doors and, symbolizing his status as the Vicar of Christ, directly below the statue of the Son of God on the roofline. Thus it is the name of the building's great papal patron that stands out most prominently for those pausing at the entrance.

Most of the basilica's architectural details, as the dating of Pope Paul's inscription indicates, were incorporated after Luther's time. Nevertheless, even in the first decades of the sixteenth century there was much to aggravate the reformer. The sale of indulgences to finance construction was his main grievance. This brought attention to one of the greatest afflictions in contemporary Western culture. Like Petrarch, Luther suffered extreme bouts of guilt and despair. They led him to examine with a truly existential intensity the pessimistic penitential piety of the new Christendom.

So great was Luther's anxiety that he suffered something like a nervous breakdown during the celebration of his first Mass. So bitterly did he lament the spiritual dead end to which he had come that fellow priests recoiled when he appeared in the confessional. "Love God?" he once exclaimed after reflecting on his sense of sin. "I hated him!"

However, unlike Petrarch, he could find no consolation in humanism. Any effort to enjoy the saeculum on its own terms seemed delusional to his monastic mind. Showing affinities with a contemporary movement of the laity known as the Modern Devotion (*devotio moderna*), which had also influenced Erasmus, he was convinced that the world could never be good. And it certainly could not be redeemed with promethean fantasies about human autonomy.

So without intending to fragment an already divided Christendom, in 1517 the Roman Catholic monk, priest, and theologian launched the Protestant Reformation. Luther's famous nailing of his *Ninety-Five Theses* against the sale of indulgences to the church door at Wittenberg was intended to challenge the penitential pessimism of Rome's doctrine of purgatory and to offer a vision of authentic penance for the laity. This and the fierce polemics he subsequently launched focused especially on the doctrinal basis for indulgences, purgatory. But much of the Roman Catholic tradition soon came into his reformational line of fire. Among the practices he attacked

Martin Luther, by Lucas Cranach

were obligatory clerical celibacy, the exclusive use of Latin for the liturgy, and, of course, papal supremacy. All of these perceived errors were, like the authority of the Vicar of Christ (whom he ultimately denounced as the Antichrist), either the product of the Great Division or reinforced by it.

Luther protested the tradition, now five centuries in the making, of objectifying the saeculum by separating it from the sacred—that is, from the ascetic existence of the clergy. Much had changed in Western Europe since the eleventh century to reinforce this protest. Towns had grown in size and wealth, and the laity living in them demanded a larger share in the spiritual life of Christendom. After all, men and women had been encouraged to desire this by the papal reforms themselves, which had also targeted the saeculum for evangelization. The Franciscans, for instance, were particularly effective in cultivating urban piety. So were recent reformers such as the Brethren of the Common Life, whose semi-monastic lay congregations were concentrated in northern Germany and the Low Countries. Of great significance also was the growing tension between the papacy and the lay rulers north of the Alps. Many a king and prince resented the loss of state revenue to a voracious Vatican bent on rebuilding Rome. Rulers like Frederick the Wise of Saxony, who offered sanctuary to Luther, thereby saving him from the inquisition, were pious and dedicated advocates of a different kind of Christendom than the one that had emerged from the Papal Reformation.

So in the aftermath of the *Ninety-Five Theses,* as Martin Luther began to issue a stream of pamphlets and sermons against clericalism, the laity of Germany was ready to listen. His was an inherently anticlerical message of reform, and for this reason it was mostly communicated in the vernacular rather than in Latin. He saw the formal though often ignored ban on clerical marriage, enforced rigorously only since the eleventh century, as a betrayal of God's plan for the social order. He considered the institution of monasticism as the most egregious example of such clericalism. To make his point, he forsook his monastic vows and even married a former nun. He also insisted that the laity should once again receive the Eucharist in both forms and not, as had been the Western practice for centuries, in the form of bread alone. To this he added a call for the restoration of the early Church's practice of frequent communion, something that had long been absent from liturgical life in both the West and the East. To encourage lay engagement, he even set hymns such as "A Mighty Fortress Is Our God" to secular melodies popular in beer halls.

It is significant that the core issues by which Protestantism thus initially defined itself were, with the exception of infrequent communion, mostly nonissues in the old Christendom. Holding to the faith of the first millennium, the Orthodox had simply never adopted the practices Luther and his followers found so execrable. For the Orthodox no less than the Protestants, then, Roman Catholic abuses at the time of the Protestant Reformation were indeed the erroneous traditions "of men" (Col. 2:8). But for the Orthodox these practices were not part of tradition as such. In the East there had always been a holy tradition without which there could be no Christianity.

During the first century, Paul himself had admonished Christians to "hold to the traditions which you were taught by us, either by word of mouth or by letter" (2 Thess. 2:15). Despite this injunction from Scripture itself, Luther introduced a doctrine known as "Scripture alone" (*sola scriptura*), by which all authority is limited to the text of the Bible. This was an effort to counter the overwhelming influence of accrued Roman Catholic tradition as it had come to manifest itself by the sixteenth century. But the principle was illogical and fatally flawed. For it is a fact that Christianity spread through the oral teaching of the apostles for a generation before any of the books that would become the New Testament were written (most scholars conjecture its first book was composed only in the sixth decade). What is more, the New Testament was canonized three centuries after Pentecost by bishops following the established tradition. Only then was its content fixed with twenty-seven (and not twenty-six or twenty-eight) books. The New Testament, as anyone with knowledge of Scripture knows, contains no apostolic table of contents. It was only tradition, in short, that saved it from becoming a grab bag of spurious writings such as the so-called Gospel of Thomas (the beloved text of gnostic heretics from the first century to the twenty-first).

Nevertheless, in the Protestant polemic against Roman Catholicism the term "tradition" became increasingly derogatory. Over time, this aversion would slowly subvert the doctrinal integrity of traditional Christianity and the culture that was founded upon it.

Luther was relentless in assailing the traditions of the Roman Catholic Church. He was in character no less implacable than Pope Leo IX, who five centuries earlier had launched the reforms that now most distinguished Roman Catholicism from Orthodoxy. But if the Papal Reformation had broken resistance to change with the hammer of papal supremacy, the Protestant Reformation now attacked tradition with the sword of scripturalism. This was not, to be sure, the "sword of Scripture." That had long been used to defend tradition. By contrast, scripturalism—the claim that answers to all questions of church authority are ultimately to be found in the Bible alone—would prove even more potent in the hands of those continuing in the lineage of reformational Christianity that stretched back to the eleventh century. Scripturalism would also prove more destructive of the civilization and culture that had long been supported by tradition.

Pope Innocent's Revenge

WHAT IS REMARKABLE IS THAT despite their attack on Roman Catholic tradition, Luther and his followers adhered so closely to one of its most notable cultural outcomes, stavrocentrism. In fact, the Protestant fathers strongly reinforced what Pope Innocent III had called "contempt for the world" and went even further than he in lamenting "the misery of the human condition."

The stavrocentric culture in which Luther himself was raised had convinced him that man is fundamentally depraved. The lax morality and superstition he observed around him as a young theologian confirmed this. Like the architects of the Papal Reformation, he was strongly influenced by Augustine. It had in fact been the Augustinian monastic rule that guided his life until he decided to forsake it and marry.

In addition to a dualistic cosmology, Augustine had developed a doctrine of predestination. This was used in part to counter Pelagianism, one of the heresies against which the North African bishop fought. Pelagianism claimed that man was largely in control of his salvation. Predestination, on the other hand, asserted unambiguously that God alone determines the salvation of men. And though Augustine acknowledged the principle of free will, he introduced a radical qualification of it in what is known as "prevenient grace." In this view, original sin so disables man that he cannot will to do good without an initial impartation of grace from God. Perceiving in Pelagianism a heretical doctrine of human moral autonomy of the sort that would later be embraced by the humanists, Augustine regarded any claim about the natural goodness of humanity as a kind of idolatry. Luther, seeing in Roman Catholic practices of good works a reversion to Pelagianism, seized on the Augustinian anthropology. In fact, he went on to issue an even more pessimistic statement of it.

Luther's grim view of man overshadowed many of his writings, but none as ominously as the *Bondage of the Will* (1525). This work, significantly, was written to counter a book by Erasmus in which the humanist, encouraged by figures such as Pico and More, voiced an optimistic assessment of the human condition. Luther, with his trademark disdain for adversaries, assailed the comparatively gentle Erasmus, dismissing the latter's defense of free will as "vile trash" and expressing "indignation" that it defended human dignity with the use of literary eloquence the way that "rubbish, or dung, should be carried in vessels of gold and silver."

Polemics aside, the *Bondage of the Will* expressed the same stavrocentric piety that had so agonized humanists since the time of Petrarch. And in this the work holds an affinity with earlier lamentations about the human condition. In it the great anthropological pessimist Innocent III, whose assertion of papal supremacy had been condemned by Luther, seems to have exacted a sort of vicarious and posthumous revenge.

The reasons for this are not difficult to see. Like his humanist opponents, Luther had almost no knowledge of Eastern Christendom's optimistic anthropology. And even if he had, given his Augustinian mind he probably would have regarded the Orthodox doctrine of deification as Pelagian. Indeed, in one work he rejected what he called a "theology of glory" by which man, because of the Incarnation, is capable of attaining dignity in this life through divine participation. Against this view—so characteristic of the old

Christendom—he advanced a "theology of the cross" that leaves man with nothing but the hope of suffering with the crucified Christ until death brings final relief. Like the thirteenth-century Vicar of Christ he excoriated, Luther was held fast by stavrocentrism.

This explains why, in the *Bondage of the Will*, he unleashed a torrent of predestinarian pessimism about the human condition. Admitting to the scandal of a God who creates people only to punish them, he sternly asserted a contempt for the world as strong as that of his papal nemesis. "Doubtless it gives the greatest possible offense to common sense or natural reason," he acknowledges,

> *that God, Who is proclaimed as being full of mercy and goodness, and so on, should of His own mere will abandon, harden, and damn men, as though He delighted in the sins and great eternal torments of such poor wretches. It seems an iniquitous, cruel, intolerable thought to think of God; and it is this that has been a stumbling block to so many great men down the ages. And who would not stumble at it? I have stumbled at it myself more than once, down to the deepest pit of despair, so that I wished that I had never been made a man.*[25]

Luther was emotionally stunned and spiritually motionless before the face of a God who in his contempt for creation abandoned man to an unredeemable state.

John Calvin (d. 1564) was another Protestant father whose influence equaled Luther's and probably exceeded it. He too embraced a grim view of the human condition. Even more inclined to sever ties to a traditional Christianity he associated with Rome, he carried stavrocentrism several steps further in development. On the one hand, he built on the "theology of the cross" to elaborate an anthropological doctrine called "total depravity." In this view, all human beings, because of original sin, are completely bereft of innate goodness. Calvin also amplified Luther's doctrine of predestination. He was so eager to assert God's omnipotence and radical transcendence

25 Quoted in David Baggett and Jerry L. Walls, *Good God: The Theistic Foundations of Morality* (Oxford: Oxford University, 2011), 74–75.

John Calvin

in the face of Rome's alleged neo-Pelagianism that in addition to claiming the elect are chosen for heaven even before their conception, he declared that the reprobate are created by God for no other reason than to populate hell. More Augustinian than Augustine and more rigorously Lutheran than Luther, Calvin's doctrine of "double predestination" produced arguably the most pessimistic vision of man in the history of Christendom—prior, that is, to the atheistic age of nihilism.

Though the edifice was quite different, Calvin's view of salvation was also built on foundations dating to the early decades of the Papal Reformation. Of particular importance here was the soteriology of Anselm of Canterbury (d. 1109). The "father of scholasticism," as he was sometimes known, had famously reformed first-millennium doctrines of salvation. He focused almost exclusively on the Crucifixion of Christ at the expense of both the Incarnation and the Resurrection. Instead of an act of victory over death directed against the devil, he saw the death of Christ as an act of propitiation rendered to the Father. Christ's death appeased an offended God and restored to Him His honor. Anselm's famous principle of "satisfaction" not only invoked certain biblical statements about salvation but drew on the West's contemporary culture of feudalism. Himself trained as a lawyer within the scholastic system, Calvin elaborated on Anselm's doctrine to emphasize its legalistic elements. He found this effective in advancing his larger project of eliminating the vestiges of Pelagianism.

In the East, where the heresy of human autonomy had never become the issue it was for Augustine, Greek fathers had long assigned to man a necessary though subordinate role in salvation. Man "cooperates" with God in a relationship of divine participation. This was especially emphasized in the doctrinal tradition of deification, by which man participates directly in the life of God. Such a relationship does not overwhelm man with divine grace, though it remains asymmetrical in the sense that God and not man is its center. After all, God was not made in man's image (as pagandom had believed), but man in God's.

Calvin, on the other hand, rejected the thought of human cooperation with God. Of the two, one was totally depraved while the other was totally sovereign. He therefore went even further than Anselm by declaring that salvation consists almost exclusively in Christ's substitution of Himself for the human race on the cross. Calvin's was an image of miserable humanity shrinking back in fear as its incarnate Champion stepped forward to receive the full brunt of His Father's wrath. Without the cross, the divine Judge was compelled almost against His will to punish mankind. Calvin's doctrine of "penal substitution" was not totally absent from earlier reflections on the Crucifixion, but it so emphasized divine wrath and punishment that it represented a radically pessimistic innovation in the Western view of man. Pope Innocent might have approved.

Nor was Calvinist cosmology any more optimistic. Cursed in his depravity, predestined for heaven or hell without his cooperation, man had nothing in this life to look forward to but unremitting misery. It was inevitable, therefore, that hatred of the world and man's experience of it should seem virtuous.

> *With whatever kind of tribulation we may be afflicted, we should always keep this end in view—to habituate ourselves to a contempt of the present life, that we may thereby be excited to meditation on that which is to come. . . . We therefore truly derive advantage from the discipline of the cross, only when we learn that this life, considered in itself, is unquiet, turbulent, miserable in numberless instances, and in no respect altogether happy; . . . and in consequence of this at once conclude, that nothing can be sought or expected on earth but conflict, and that when we think of a crown we must raise our eyes towards heaven. For it must be admitted, that the mind is never seriously excited to desire and meditate on the future life, without having previously imbibed a contempt of the present.*[26]

Heaven, once the living experience of a transformed world, was now something distant from and even incompatible with the world. Protestant predestinarianism was like purgatory, the doctrine on which so much of the

26 John Calvin, *Institutes of the Christian Religion*, trans. John Allen (Philadelphia: Presbyterian Board of Publication, 1813), 856.

new Christendom's pessimistic culture had been built five centuries earlier. It too banished paradise to a postmortem afterlife.

In a book entitled *Everywhere Present*, Stephen Freeman has described the cosmology that sprang from reformational Christianity as a "two-storey universe." This is a vision of the world in which there is a God, but He has little to do with everyday experience. "It is as though the universe," the author writes,

> *were a two-storey house: We live here on earth, the first floor, where things are simply things and everything operates according to normal, natural laws, while God lives in heaven, upstairs, and is largely removed from the storey in which we live. To effect anything here, God must interrupt the laws of nature and perform a miracle.*[27]

This view of things would take time to work out and would not assume its final form until secularism had shaped it following the rise of deism in the eighteenth century (something we will explore below). But already in the sixteenth century, the anti-sacramental reflex of the Protestant counter-reformation was working ominously to remove paradise from Western culture.

With such convictions, it is no surprise that Calvin viewed the paradisiacal culture of Christendom as a wicked net of illusory entanglements. The veneration of saints' relics incensed him perhaps the most. The depiction of the Incarnation through images he viewed as almost equally idolatrous. Here he consciously brought to mind not the iconography of Byzantium so much as the modern painting of quattrocento Italy. When it came to liturgy, only prayers and practices that were explicitly sanctioned in the Scriptures were admitted. And while the use of incense and images was in fact prescribed in the Old Testament, their association with the dreadful sacrileges of popery, as the most extreme Calvinists viewed them, meant they had to go.

To establish the proper architectural setting for this new approach to Christian worship, churches were thoroughly cleansed of tradition. In

27 Stephen Freeman, *Everywhere Present: Christianity in a One-Storey Universe* (Chesterton, IN: Ancient Faith Publishing, 2010), 7.

Switzerland mobs led by Ulrich Zwingli threw statues to the ground, and in Holland a riot called the "icon storm" (*Bildersturm*) smashed stained-glass windows to pieces. The ideal Calvinist assembly hall became characterized by no more than the proverbial four walls and a pulpit. Here congregants sat on newly introduced pews to provide bodily comfort as their minds labored to comprehend the pastor's two-hour exposition of the Scriptures. Thus ended the practice of more than a millennium, when members of Christendom had stood at attention in the real presence of Christ, crossing themselves and bowing in honor of heavenly immanence.

Protestantism subverted the experience of paradise. From the start, its fathers rejected the Roman Catholic doctrine of transubstantiation, which used scholastic categories of logic to confirm the traditional Christian conviction that at the Eucharist the bread and wine truly become the body and blood of Christ. The question of Christ's presence on earth in the Mass was of such urgency that it provoked acrimonious debates among the Protestants themselves. The most notable of these occurred in 1529 at the Marburg Colloquy, where Luther battled against the minimalistic doctrine of Zwingli. Neither could agree with the other, setting a precedent for the incessant quarrels that would divide Protestants for centuries to come.

Calvin, of course, could not remain aloof from this dispute. In his *Institutes of the Christian Religion* he insisted that while Christ might be present in the Eucharist in a strictly spiritual sense, His presence had absolutely no material reality. The most systematic of all Protestant fathers, Calvin thus integrated an innovative eucharistic doctrine seamlessly into a broader cosmology in which the world was no longer capable of heavenly immanence. As his disciple John Knox asserted, Christ is "in heaven and not here."

So rather than lift the curse of anthropological pessimism imposed on the new Christendom by Pope Innocent III, the Protestant fathers actually reimposed it. The doctrines of predestination, penal substitution, and total depravity inspired a litany of new maledictions against the human condition. In fact, probably the most accomplished historian of Western religious despair, Jean Delumeau, concluded that "it was . . . in the sixteenth century, and specifically in Protestant theology, that the accusation of man and the world reached its climax in Western civilization. Never before had they been so totally condemned, and never had this condemnation reached such a large audience."[28] The irony of this was great. Luther, following the example of Erasmus, had set out in 1517 to evangelize the saeculum. However, the Protestant Reformation failed to reverse or even arrest Western Christendom's tendency to immiserate man's experience of the world. In fact, it actually increased the burden of the Innocentian inheritance.

Nor, it should be added, was that inheritance limited to theology. Innocent had been the first pope to launch a crusade against the Orthodox. Though he was initially opposed to a war against Eastern Christendom, once crusaders were in possession of Constantinople the self-proclaimed Vicar of Christ made the most of the situation by withdrawing an earlier threat of excommunication against them and then placing a Roman Catholic on the patriarchal throne. With this act, the reunion of East and West was proclaimed. In fact, it was nothing more than a short-lived imposition of papal supremacy. And it brought an end to all hopes of healing the Great Division. The Orthodox assumed an intransigent hostility to future papal gestures of good will. And for its part the West, severed permanently from the old Christendom, was now destined for the pattern of piety that would lead it into the cultural dead end lamented by Petrarch. After the Fourth Crusade of 1204, the new Christendom drifted ever further from the old, and its heavenly orientation became ever more tenuous.

Another long-term outcome of the Papal Reformation had been Pope Innocent's decision to use the military to persecute and destroy heresy. Flushed with ecclesiastical triumph in the East, he launched a war in the West against a sect of Christians who rejected the sacraments and asserted that the created world was fundamentally evil. This Albigensian Crusade (1209–1229) effectively suppressed heresy in southern France, but it established an ominous precedent for the use of violence against fellow Christians. The papal inquisition and its later Spanish variant emerged from this war and would regularize the use of torture and execution in the West.

---

28 Jean Delumeau, *Sin and Fear: The Emergence of a Western Guilt Culture, 13th–18th Centuries*, trans. Eric Nicholson (New York: St. Martin's, 1990), 27.

To the Orthodox of the old Christendom, the organized religious violence of crusades and inquisitions was as strange and disturbing as the West's long record of penitential pessimism. The East therefore had virtually no share in them.[29]

But in the West, where Protestants and Roman Catholics were becoming hardened against one another in the wake of the *Ninety-Five Theses,* armed conflict was almost inevitable.

A Neo-Reformation

AS THE CONFESSIONAL BATTLE LINES were forming, the Roman Catholic Church began a series of reforms that is usually called the Counter-Reformation. While this term serves to identify an anti-Protestant motivation, it obscures the fact that the papacy had been an advocate of reform for centuries. Recent historians, enjoying greater distance from the polarizing confessionalism that long influenced accounts of the period, have begun to take note of this. According to one, the period demonstrated "an enduring tradition of reformism in the Catholic Church."[30]

---

29 Exceptions to any rule are always to be found. It can be conceded, for instance, that several Byzantine emperors—most notably Heraklios—used religious ideals to motivate soldiers fighting against non-Christian armies. Emperor Michael III is also known for launching a war of persecution against the Paulician heretics of Armenia. In both cases these wars were acts of a state pursuing primarily geopolitical rather than ecclesiastical goals. They were not crusades in the conventional understanding of the term, as no patriarch or other clerical authority ordered or even formally endorsed them. Indeed, until the fall of Constantinople Orthodox canons against military bloodshed were kept intact, unlike the situation in the feudal West. A concession must also be made in the case of Russia, which until the rise of the Muscovite state almost completely lacked a history of Christian persecution. The exception is the case of Archbishop Gennady of Novgorod, who ordered the arrest and execution of a handful of heretics in the early sixteenth century. It is reported in the chronicles that he was inspired in doing this by the example of the contemporaneous inquisition in the West. The act was strongly opposed by a party led by Maxim the Greek, the leading theologian in Russia at the time.

30 Michael Mullett, *The Catholic Reformation* (London: Routledge, 1999), ix.

Indeed, Protestantism itself might just as well be called a counter-reformation, for, applying the transformational imperative on an institutional level, it was merely following the pattern established by the Roman Catholic Church during the Papal Reformation. What is more, most of the issues driving Luther and other Protestants were reactions against reforms introduced by Pope Leo IX and other Roman Catholics since the eleventh century. Papal supremacy, a celibate priesthood, a non-vernacular liturgy, the doctrine of purgatory, and, of course, the practice of indulgences were all examples of such reforms.

The Roman Catholic reaction to Protestantism was therefore more of a neo-reformation than a counter-reformation. Its centerpiece was the Council of Trent, which deliberated for nearly two decades, from 1545 to 1563. It confirmed many of the basic convictions under attack by the Protestants. Many of these, however, were themselves the product of reforms introduced since the Great Division. In this sense, Trent was indeed the continuation of a "tradition of reformism" that linked it to earlier events such as the Fourth Lateran Council of 1215.

But since tradition and reformism are in fact incompatible, Trent's defense of the Papal Reformation meant that it was really subverting tradition, at least in its first-millennium forms. Papal supremacy was of course one of Trent's central assertions. So was eucharistic doctrine. Traditional Christianity had always claimed that the Eucharist is the body and blood of Christ in both a spiritual and a material sense. However, the rationalization of how this occurs, known as transubstantiation, had only been established in the eleventh century. It had never been adopted by the Orthodox, whose sacramental theology by contrast remained fundamentally mystical (the Greek and Russian words for "sacrament" translate literally as "mystery"). What is more, by embracing the logic of Aristotle, scholastic theologians had introduced a formalized explanation of the Eucharist that provided Protestants with a handy sophism against which to define their "not-Catholic" alternatives.

Papal supremacy and transubstantiation were thus an inheritance of the Great Division and not of Pentecost. They were the product of reforms and not the bedrock of tradition. But as newly introduced traditions of the Roman Catholic Church, they represented the main lines of division drawn by the Council of Trent against both Orthodox and now Protestant adversaries.

As the latest of the Roman Church's reform councils, Trent also introduced certain changes. One was the decision to counter the successes of Protestant preaching and scriptural exegesis with a renewed emphasis on learning, especially among the parish clergy. Another was a rebuke of the new Italian liturgical painting and its celebration of a spiritually untransformed human nature. The kind of frescoes favored by Michelangelo, which seethed with naked muscular saints, were to give way to greater modesty. Nevertheless, this reform was a veiled recognition that iconography had largely come to an end in the West. For while during the Baroque period that followed, liturgical painting showed less undeified flesh, it remained largely sensual and would not be challenged by traditional iconography until the Western rediscovery of Orthodoxy in the twentieth century.

Restrictions on painting, however limited, might have been extended to liturgical music. Since the time of the Avignon papacy, church music had become increasingly ornate by means of the introduction of polyphony—that is, the use of several simultaneous melodies to create harmony. Since the fourteenth century, many had complained about the difficulty worshippers had not only in singing but in understanding the words of the Mass. Trent's insistence on Latin, of course, did nothing to help this, for only the clergy understood that language. What is more, a story is told of how the Italian composer Giovanni Palestrina (d. 1594) crashed one of the council's sessions and, with his gorgeous *Pope Marcellus Mass* in hand, convinced the bishops that polyphony did not necessarily make singing unintelligible. His argument was questionable, but their endorsement of it opened the door to future masterpieces of choral music such as Gregorio Allegri's celebrated *Miserere,* considered so exquisite by the pope who commissioned it that the manuscript was ordered never to leave the Sistine Chapel. Such polyphony, decorating an exclusively Latin liturgy, dignified its execution but obscured its meaning.

Another important outcome of Rome's neo-reformation was the formation of the Society of Jesus, whose members came to be known as Jesuits. Its founder was Ignatius Loyola (d. 1556), a Spanish knight who once during a convalescence was compelled by an absence of secular literature to read the *Imitation of Christ.* This caused in him a spiritual conversion, an experience he built into the monastic order he founded. In this way Roman Catholic piety became a match for the personal sense of heavenly transformation that so appealed to contemporary Lutherans and Calvinists. Ignatius's *Spiritual Exercises* cultivated the individual's will to seek God.

Through intensive discernment, Jesuits cultivated an experience of divine presence so strong that they were prepared to go anywhere in the world to evangelize and teach. With the horizons of Christendom thrown open by global exploration, they were soon on the ground in far-flung corners of pagandom such as Mexico and India. Their achievements were astonishing. Within decades, for instance, the population of Nagasaki in Japan was mostly converted. But many Japanese Christians would suffer martyrdom alongside European missionaries during the seventeenth century, when the pagan government unleashed what was perhaps the deadliest persecution since the time of Diocletian.

In China the mission of the Jesuits was more peacefully received, largely because its leader, Matteo Ricci (d. 1610), established close ties with the imperial court. He did his best to honor native customs and assimilated them into the faith whenever possible. This was not the way of the older orders of Franciscans and Dominicans, who demanded that natives in Latin America, for instance, rebuild their cultures from the bottom up after what was often a forced conversion. It was, however, the way of early Christian evangelization. Cultural assimilation occurred under Paul in Athens, where the apostle related Christ to the city's statue to an "unknown god." It also occurred under the fourth-century Ulfilas when converting the Goths, and under the ninth-century Cyril and Methodios working among the Slavs.

Sadly, a resistance to doctrinal integrity appeared among Chinese converts in the form of ancestor worship. During the eighteenth century, Ricci's heroic work was eventually undone when rival monastic orders obtained

Matteo Ricci

a papal ban on the practice, leaving the Chinese emperor baffled by such disagreements within a single church. Outraged by first Dominican and then Franciscan denunciations of nascent Chinese Christendom, the emperor ordered all missionaries expelled from his realm and made an end of the Christian mission there.

Back in Europe, the Jesuits distinguished themselves as educators, founding a phenomenal number of colleges within the first century of their existence. They immediately displaced the scholastics and became the leading force in theological reflection. Even at the Council of Trent, their arguments prevented the bishops from settling on a strict Augustinianism when formulating the doctrine of justification. As we have seen, both Luther and Calvin had pushed the Augustinian inheritance to its limit, insisting on divine predestination. The council's soteriological loophole, if it can be so called, allowed a Spanish Jesuit named Molina to neutralize the predestinarian argument by claiming that divine sovereignty was in fact better understood as divine foreknowledge.

The Jesuits became an overnight phenomenon in culture as much as in theology. It was their movement that most advanced the revolution in art and architecture known as the Baroque. The Italian quattrocento had given new life to classical tastes for symmetry and decorum, demonstrated by the façade of Saint Peter's Basilica. But now something more explosive was desired. Perhaps the impetus came from the doctrinal debates of the time or from the violence of the religious wars. One historian has explained the new aesthetic as "a highly emotional escape from the miseries of the world."[1] Another determinant was the role art could play in the evangelization of the saeculum. The Jesuits, as we have seen, were foremost among Roman Catholics in their pursuit of this goal. It is not a coincidence that the Baroque was closely associated with them. For two centuries, it would mark Christendom not only in Europe but in Asia and Latin America as well.

The earliest example of Baroque architecture is the Church of the Gesù in Rome, which was founded in 1568 as the global headquarters of the Society of Jesus. Despite its use of columns and pediments, the façade is radically different from that of Saint Peter's Basilica. Instead of classical harmony and reasoned geometry, it explodes in a call to spiritual transformation. Beneath a dramatically oversized upper pediment, straight and curved lines battle one another. But it is the latter that gain supremacy, indicated by the façade's scrolled framing and the entrapment of a lower triangular pediment within a curved one. Inside the church, the laity were directed toward the high altar by the elimination of aisles and the obstructive columns that supported them. With preaching and frequent communion as the new ideals of Jesuit worship, the design emphasis was on the pulpit and the altar.

Baroque design was intended to amaze, and the interior of another Jesuit church in Rome did this spectacularly. The Church of Saint Ignatius, built to complement Loyola's first college, featured a vast ceiling depicting "the apotheosis of Saint Ignatius." To cause amazement among the laity staring up at it, the painter intentionally applied a device known to art historians as *trompe l'oeil* ("deception of the eye"). Its purpose is to deceive viewers into feeling as if they are staring up into heaven itself. This, however, was a very naturalistic rendering of heaven. It featured breathtaking lighting, billowing clouds, and the winged babies that had become standard images of angels among humanists. The illusion the painting created was of a riot of half-naked bodies hovering above the viewer in ecstatic recognition of Ignatius's entry into heaven.

The same earthly manipulation of piety is to be found in the shrines designed for laity visiting Rome. The master sculptor Gianlorenzo Bernini

1 Quoted in Mullett, *Catholic Reformation*, 197.

Church of the Gesù, Rome

(d. 1680) used flamboyantly baroque elements in his *Ecstasy of Saint Theresa*, a shrine depicting an event in the life of the famous sixteenth-century Spanish mystic. The work is paradisiacal in that it reveals the divine participation of sanctified humanity in the present age. However, its rendering of heavenly immanence is overwhelmingly naturalistic and even sensual. The shrine is surrounded by richly marbled walls of such varying colors and textures as to distract from the spiritual significance of the scene. Behind Theresa, a spray of gilded metallic shafts theatrically descends from on high. And the countenance of the mystic herself is extravagantly emotional. Head thrown

Bernini, Ecstasy of Saint Teresa

back, eyes closed tightly, mouth gaping sensuously—she might be descending into a luxuriantly scented bath, or worse, as much as into the depths of divine communion.

The Jesuits were not content to write books and patronize baroque art. Everything they did was directed toward the defense of the papacy in lands where it was under attack. They played an important role, for instance, in reversing the flow of Protestantism into eastern European lands like Hungary and Poland. And from the latter kingdom they also advocated the conversion of Orthodox Russia to Roman Catholicism.

The Jesuits found ready, even fanatical support for this project in King Sigismund of Poland, who in 1605 launched an invasion that in some ways represents the last crusade. While it succeeded in briefly placing his son Wladyslaw on the throne in Moscow, the outrage provoked a populist war of liberation that resulted in the expulsion of the Poles and the founding of a new dynasty in Russia under Michael Romanov (r. 1613–1645). The politically opportunistic and religiously cynical invasion of the Orthodox land by Roman Catholic Poland was the low point of what the Russians later called their national Time of Troubles. It created a bitterness toward Poland and the Roman Catholic Church as strong as the resentment felt by the Greeks after the Fourth Crusade. This too would last for centuries, making the Great Schism ever more intractable.

Religious warfare failed to expand Roman Catholic Christendom to the East. But it was even more fruitless in the West. There it brought levels of destruction and death never seen before in the history of Europe.[2] The greatest catastrophe was the Thirty Years War. And when this war was finally ended by the Peace of Westphalia in 1648, it had done virtually nothing to alter the new geo-religious landscape. The new Christendom had mostly settled into the fixed confessional divisions that would mark it for centuries to come. But for some of its most sensitive and earnest intellectuals, a retreat from a religious culture was the inevitable reaction to the killing of more than fifteen million people in the name of the God of love.

---

2 For an account of the religious wars and their cultural effects, see *Age of Division*, 326–33.

The consequences of the wars of Western religion, in which the old Christendom had played no role, were catastrophically debilitating for a civilization with a supporting culture that directed its members toward the heavenly transformation of the world. As Brad Gregory notes,

> *not only did no one win in early modern Europe, but Catholics, Lutherans, Reformed Protestants, and Western Christianity in general all lost. Collectively, their conflicts amounted to an unintended disaster that has fundamentally shaped the subsequent course of Western history in ways they could not have foreseen and which nearly all of them would have deplored.*

An Orthodox Christian historian would readily agree with such a statement. And to it Gregory adds:

> *Not only did they create a poisoned legacy that has endured into the early twenty-first century. Early modern Christians themselves also unwittingly provided a firm launching pad for ideological and institutional secularization.*[3]

The wars of Western religion had the effect of permanently discrediting the very idea of the heavenly transformation of the world. The path forward, it now appeared, was secularization.

---

3 Brad Gregory, *The Unintended Reformation: How a Religious Revolution Secularized Society* (Cambridge, MA: Harvard University, 2012), 160.

CHAPTER FOUR

The Secularization of the State

SINCE THE TIME OF EMPEROR Constantine, government had been seen as a manifestation of the kingdom of heaven on earth. The Christian state was never considered—and by definition could not be—paradise itself, but it was expected to contribute to the experience of heavenly immanence. All of this was derived from the early Church's unitary cosmology. Eusebius gave expression to it, and as we saw in chapter one, the same vision was held for a time even by the cosmologically dualistic Augustine. Emperors, kings, and princes were expected to use their power to defend the vulnerable, legislate morality, protect the clergy, build churches, and support missions.

In the East, an ideal of ecclesiopolitical symphony arose in which rulers were granted broad latitude in ecclesiastical affairs with the expectation that their policies would align with those of bishops. In fact, such symphony often degenerated into a condition of caesaropapism, whereby strident emperors imposed detrimental and at times even heretical policies on the faithful. In the West, symphony remained the ideal until the Papal Reformation, when the papacy suddenly asserted political supremacy over "secular" rulers. The goal was to compel the state to honor Christian principles. This frequently had spiritually transforming effects ranging from the imposition of marital fidelity at court to the suppression of blood feuds among the nobility. In other cases, however, papal supremacy degenerated into an overbearing and self-serving clericalism.

The support that Luther and his followers received from northern European princes during the early stages of the Protestant Reformation was a sign that rulers of the new Christendom had finally, after five centuries, reached the end of their patience with papal supremacy and the political interference it entailed. Personal piety aside, King Frederick the Wise of Saxony (r. 1486–1525) protected Luther from the inquisition in order to stanch the flow of taxes to Rome. King Henry VIII of England (r. 1509–1547) went the furthest in reacting against papal supremacy. He inverted the principle to make the monarch the "supreme head" of the Church of England.

While some kingdoms were turning to Protestantism in the north, Niccolò Machiavelli (d. 1527) was advocating complete secularization of government in Italy. His treatise *The Prince* was initially reviled for its amoral political values. It offered praise, for instance, for deceit and assassination. Its humanist author did not think government should be concerned with advancing heavenly values. Breathing deeply the air of the saeculum, he was interested—like the Cesar Borgia he explicitly praised—only in power for its own sake.

What was beginning to emerge from the font of pagandom was a Christendom in which the state no longer oriented itself toward paradise. Like philosophy, art, and society, it was entering upon the path of secularization.

The Sun King

EUROPE'S MOST POWERFUL AND INFLUENTIAL state during the seventeenth century is an example of this process. The kingdom of France had endured a long and exhausting series of civil wars in the wake of the Protestant Reformation. These reached a peak in what may have been the earliest conscious application of Machiavellianism in politics: the cold-blooded massacre of Protestant Huguenots by Queen Catherine de Medici and other Roman Catholics in the Saint Bartholomew's Day Massacre of 1572. The French civil wars killed a staggering three million people—a carnage so great as to match that of the Hundred Years War. They came to an end only

Louis XIV of France

when the Huguenot King Henry IV (r. 1598–1610) agreed to accept Roman Catholicism for the sake of the crown. Yet in order to restore peace he also found it necessary to issue the Edict of Nantes (1598) granting Huguenots toleration. For this he was eventually assassinated, leaving France in the hands of the boy king Louis XIII (r. 1610–1643).

In 1624, the latter appointed as his chief minister a prince of the Roman Catholic Church, Cardinal Richelieu (d. 1642). Since the days of the Papal Reformation the college of cardinals had become Rome's main governing body, but despite early canonical bans on the practice, many also entered governmental service. Richelieu, in fact, had been raised to be a warrior. However, when his elder brother, who had been prepared for the episcopate, decided to become a monk, the aristocratic parents changed the family plan and sent Richelieu to Rome for ordination. That a cardinal was placed in charge of the administration of the French state was remarkable enough. But when, during the Thirty Years War, he formed an alliance with the Protestants against the Roman Catholic Habsburg Empire, effectively contributing to the eradication of Roman Catholic Christendom, a new phase in the history of European diplomacy had clearly arrived.

Cardinal Richelieu was set on one compelling objective, and it was not the restoration of France's formerly paradisiacal culture. It was the creation of an absolutist system of monarchy. He named his policy *raison d'etat*, or "state logic." Like Catherine de Medici's approach, it was decidedly Machiavellian. All historical obstacles to royal power were targeted for emasculation or elimination. Spiritual and other higher ideals almost became irrelevant.

The ancient nobility was one of Richelieu's first targets. He sent armies throughout the realm to knock down their ancestral castles—symbols of feudal resistance to the crown. Religion was merely a means toward the same end. In 1627 the cardinal led the siege of the Huguenot city of La Rochelle, and, wearing his episcopal robes, was the first to enter the starving city after it capitulated.

Recovering Roman Catholic populations from the Protestants may have been the papacy's objective, but it was not Richelieu's. During the Thirty

Years War he ordered the French army into battle against fellow Roman Catholics. The reason for this was simple: The Habsburg Empire that commanded them was a rival to French national power. And if in times of peace he upheld a strict preference for Roman Catholicism at home, he did this simply because it was the religion most aligned with the interests of the French monarchy. In short, he regarded Christianity as an instrument for acquiring power. It is not too much to say that Cardinal Richelieu initiated a secularization of statecraft that would lead, during the following century, to the French Revolution.

It was this model of government that Louis XIV (r. 1643–1715) inherited when he came to power. The new king was by no means indifferent to religious questions. He attended Mass regularly and, like the Puritans across the English Channel, created a vast police force to enforce public morality. This rule of law was no less implacable than its Calvinist counterparts or their God. When, for example, a common gambler was convicted of repeated blasphemy while at play, the king had him hanged. But Louis was somehow aloof from anything more than a merely formalized piety. His leading bishops and his mistress-turned-wife Madame de Maintenon (d. 1719) both commented on this. He seems to have taken very seriously his title as Most Christian King. He listened attentively when Bishop Bossuet (d. 1704) asserted that "princes are gods" who "participate" in the heavenly rule of Christ.[4] Louis had been raised in a political atmosphere permanently altered by Cardinal Richelieu, and he made absolutist monarchy his only unambiguous commitment.

He therefore styled himself the "sun king," going so far as to have a medallion cast to commemorate the fact. He would not only be the center of the French state, whose nobility would now bask in the glorious light he emitted. He would be the light of all Christendom. And indeed he sponsored a great flowering of secular culture. Richelieu had been an active patron of the arts, establishing the French Academy in 1735. Louis went further. He founded a new royal palace outside Paris and recruited Europe's greatest talents to

4 Quoted in Henri Daniel-Rops, *The Church in the Seventeenth Century*, trans. J. J. Buckingham (London: J. M. Dent and Sons, 1963), 188.

build it; and once built, to decorate it; and once decorated, to entertain the royal court within it.

The town of Versailles from which the palace derived its name was itself transformed in the process. According to the rationalism of the time, it was subjected to detailed city planning. It exuded a feeling of civic good order with its road grids and parks all laid out in geometrical patterns. The vast gardens surrounding the palace also submitted to a mathematical design with precise manicuring. Notably, these gardens featured fountains which, by their power to reverse the natural flow of water, served as the ultimate symbol of man's emerging control over the cosmos.

Inside the palace—one of the largest buildings on earth—baroque design awed visitors and demonstrated that Louis's glory was nearly equal to God's. The famous Hall of Mirrors achieved the most spectacular results. Its ceiling used the same deceptive device (*trompe l'oeil*) as the Jesuit churches in Rome. All of Christendom's dignitaries traveled to this chamber as if to the center of the cosmos. Aristocrats came to confirm their social status. Bishops came to receive their diocesan assignments. And foreign ambassadors from as far

Hall of Mirrors, Versailles

away as Siam came to pay honor to the most powerful man on earth. As they stared up into the richly painted vaults of the Hall of Mirrors, they would have been dizzied by the experience of seeing images of Louis enthroned in the heavens, surrounded not by an angelic host but by one consisting of his loyal servitors.

With his secular priorities, Louis enacted religious policies that both Roman Catholics and Protestants would find dubious. One of these was his suppression of Jansenism. During the seventeenth century an austere form of Roman Catholicism arose in France that challenged the Jesuits. The latter, in matching the Protestant call to evangelize the saeculum, had adopted penitential practices at variance with those common in the West since the Great Division. Resembling in some ways a return to the more therapeutic penance of the first millennium, the Jesuits applied a method called *casuistry* (from the Latin word for "case") that looked at reasons behind individual acts of sin. Instead of merely confronting penitents with the awful consequences of their actions, Jesuit confessors led them into a reflection on the unique and in some ways psychological complexities behind their sins. Casuistry was closely related to the devotional vision of Ignatius Loyola himself, who had emphasized the importance of introspection and the perfection of one's will. For the Jesuits, this approach promised to ease the beleaguered consciences of a laity long agonizing (as Petrarch had) over a relentlessly pessimistic piety. It also offered a shield to the laity against the dismal anthropology of the Calvinists.

It is not surprising, then, that the practice of casuistry was attacked by exactly that element of the new Christendom most attached to the Innocentian heritage. Augustinianism again intervened against a tendency toward anthropological optimism. A theologian named Cornelius Jansen (d. 1638) confronted the Jesuits with a book he entitled, appropriately, *Augustinus*. Issued in three volumes that amounted to more than thirteen hundred double-columned pages, the treatise was a manifesto of prevenient grace so massive that it would have impressed even the saint after whom it was named. Throughout, Jansen warned that Pelagianism was again on the rise in Western theology, and that the Jesuits were responsible. Their use of casuistry suggested that the inner world of the penitent was as important as God's sovereignty.

By linking his attack to Pelagianism, Jansen presented himself as a defender of the true faith. Needless to say, he knew virtually nothing about Augustine's Orthodox contemporaries in the East who celebrated the dignity of humanity and the value of a therapeutic approach to penance. What Jansen was really doing was fighting for the restoration of a one-sided vision of man that was itself a distortion of the broader patristic mind. Augustinianism's dominance among the Franks after the time of Charlemagne had served to isolate Western culture from the richer and comparatively optimistic pool of thought in the East. But by the seventeenth century, amid the furious controversies between Roman Catholics and Protestants, that patristic alternative seemed distant, strange, and suspicious. Though not himself a Calvinist, Jansen was unquestionably held in thrall by his fellow Frenchman's relentless assertions of the depravity of man and the sovereignty of God.

When a small but highly effective intellectual following appeared soon after Jansen's death, it soon earned the name Jansenism. It was most famously advanced by the French philosopher Blaise Pascal (d. 1662). His morose but brilliant work, *Thoughts* (*Pensées*), published posthumously, documents a lifetime of "despair at the human condition" (as one sympathetic historian characterizes it).[5] It was in this volume, which many modern commentators consider a classic of Western spirituality, that he uttered a curious aphorism as fit for the fourteenth century as it was for his own:

> *Man's greatness comes from knowing he is wretched: a tree does not know it is wretched. Thus it is wretched to know one is wretched, but there is greatness in knowing one is wretched.*[6]

5 James M. Byrne, *Religion and the Enlightenment: From Descartes to Kant* (Louisville, KY: Westminster John Knox Press), 92.

6 Blaise Pascal, *Pensées*, trans. A. J. Krailsheimer (London: Penguin Books, 1995), 29.

The world for Pascal could only be the enemy of the Church. In a reflection on what he imagined the cosmology of the first Christians to be, he claimed that an "essential distinction was then known between the world and the church." Because of this distinction, or division, Christians did not sanctify, let alone transform the world around them. In his grim estimation, "they were considered as two opposites, as two irreconcilable enemies."[7] With such convictions, he was naturally drawn to the Jansenist cause. At the request of its leadership, he penned a satirical attack on the Jesuits entitled *Provincial Letters*. It took the floor out from beneath them. In it casuist confessors are depicted as justifying rape and murder in light of the special circumstances claimed by penitents.

Even more influential than Pascal's literary advocacy was the Jansenist takeover of a convent outside Paris named Port Royal. There the sour predispositions about the human condition of monastics and court insiders were cultivated and sustained by some of France's most gifted theologians. Such views did not align well with those of the king, however, whose court was anything but austere. Growing weary of their influence, Louis ordered the dispersal of the convent. And though one of his many mistresses had actually died there while giving birth to his own daughter, in 1711 he had the entire structure razed to the ground.

A secondary motive lay behind this action. For a long time Louis had been at odds with the papacy over an issue that cut to the heart of Roman Catholicism. His ambition to build an absolutist monarchy required, in his view, complete autonomy from the pope. After all, since the time of Charlemagne the French Church had periodically demanded a free hand in domestic administration. This became much more controversial after the rise of papal supremacy. The most dramatic episode occurred during the reign of Philip the Fair, when the king demanded obedience from the French clergy in the face of Pope Boniface's threats of excommunication. In the ongoing struggle, the French party became known as Gallicans (from the old name

7 Blaise Pascal, "Comparison between Christians of Early Times and Those of Today," trans. O. W. Wight, in *Thoughts, Letters, and Minor Works* (New York: P. F. Collier and Son, 1910), 378–81.

for France) and the Roman party Ultramontanists (from "across the mountains," that is, beyond the Alps).

Louis XIV now revived the conflict as part of his program to assert absolutist control. In 1681, he summoned a national council of bishops in Paris. The following year the council issued four articles in support of the Gallican cause. The first declared that a sharp division existed between "spiritual" and "temporal" power, and that the pope's authority was limited exclusively to the former. This, of course, was the other side of the dualistic cosmology that had been advocated by papal reformers since the eleventh century. Now it was being used to eradicate Rome's political supremacy in France. By restricting the papacy to exclusively "spiritual" matters, the council brought an inglorious end to the very premise of the Papal Reformation. The saeculum, long targeted by clerical reformers for evangelization, had now swallowed up the sacramentum.

The Paris Council did not leave matters there. Its bishops also revived conciliarity, long the measure of authority in the Orthodox Church and tragically defeated by the papacy in the fifteenth century. The pope's authority, they declared, was subject to and not supreme over councils of bishops. Nor was his authority universal. Another article claimed that the universal faith of Rome must be conditioned by local and national variations. Finally, the papacy's authority cannot be absolute (were the bishops here making a contrast to the authority of the Sun King?). The papacy, in short, cannot be infallible.

As a result of these Gallican Articles, the Roman Catholic Church of France ceased to be limited to what the Papal Reformation had earlier made it: Roman in polity, catholic in scope, and ecclesiastical in authority. It had become something more than that. It was becoming an instrument of secular authority. Needless to say, such heady challenges to the papacy severely strained relations with Rome, and the suppression of Jansenism provided Louis with an opportunity to try to heal them. So did his decision to reverse the policy of tolerating the Huguenots by revoking the Edict of Nantes in 1685.

But as France entered the eighteenth century, there was no going back to the Christian statecraft that had shaped Western Christendom since the time of Constantine. In fact, though the Sun King's absolutist heirs would continue to support Roman Catholicism for a century more, their actions from the recesses of Versailles, when compared to those of their canonized thirteenth-century namesake Louis IX, were little more than those of the man who upon entering a brothel continues out of mere habit to cross himself.

The Waning of Puritanism

IN ENGLAND, THE SECULARIZATION OF the state had been looming since the day Henry VIII became the head of the national church. A century passed, however, before the logic of reformational Christianity finally took hold. From the time of Henry's son, Edward VI, Calvinists used their control of Parliament to "purify" the Anglican Church of Roman Catholic tradition. But in the seventeenth century a Romophilic monarchy began to resist them. When King Charles I (r. 1625–1649) appointed the liturgically conservative William Laud as Archbishop of Canterbury, these Puritans launched a revolution that came to be known as the English Civil War (1642–1651). They eventually fabricated charges of treason against Laud and beheaded him. Then came the military defeat and execution of Charles himself.

After this, a righteous commonwealth was declared under Puritan rule. Public morality was reformed, with Sunday church attendance mandated by law and the celebration of the Incarnation at Christmas—a remnant of "popery"—strictly banned. Under Oliver Cromwell (d. 1658)—who had experienced a Calvinist-style spiritual conversion—Britain became a Christian police state in which Scotch Presbyterians and Irish Roman Catholics were not only persecuted but massacred by the thousands in merciless battles and sieges.

Calvinism changed the political character of the new Christendom. But it was a change that had much in common with efforts to transform the saeculum ongoing since the time of the Papal Reformation. In his study of reformational indignation during the English Civil War, Michael Walzer noted that

Oliver Cromwell, by Samuel Cooper

the power of an ideology . . . lies in its capacity to activate its adherents and to change the world. Its content is necessarily a description of contemporary experience as unacceptable and unnecessary and a rejection of any merely personal transcendence or salvation. Its practical effect is to generate organization and cooperative activity.

"Calvinist ideology," he concludes, "can be briefly summarized in these terms. The permanent, inescapable estrangement of man from God is the starting point of Calvin's politics."[8] As we shall see, it was also the starting point of modern revolutionary ideology.

As this anthropological estrangement was beginning to occur, other Calvinists were making their exodus from a corrupted Europe to a promised land called America. In fact, the founding of New England represented in some ways the end of Christendom's paradisiacal vision of statecraft. True to its origins, the experience of the kingdom of heaven in Plymouth—the first colony founded in 1620 by a group of Anglican separatists calling themselves "pilgrims"—was decidedly pessimistic, and in the most puritanical sense of the word. Settlers established a dour social order in which dancing and all other forms of merrymaking were scorned as demonic. A decade later, another group of Calvinists came from England and founded the Massachusetts Bay Colony near Boston. During the long sail, their leader, John Winthrop, preached aboard the ship *Arabella* about the importance of the Puritan mission to settle America. New England would be a "city on a hill," he declared, and all of Europe was watching to see what she would do to reform a corrupt, old-world Christendom.

At the start, New England was a New Jerusalem, an eschatological community of God's elect. This defined her identity more than anything else. But it was an identity grounded in public morality and reformational doctrine rather than in heavenly immanence. The community was profoundly spiritual in character. The colony of Virginia to the south, for instance, might be driven by a desire for wealth and adventure, but not the Puritans. The building of settlements, the cultivation of food, the conquest of natives—all these were considered necessary but secondary to their righteous purpose.

Hence the readiness to undergo unbelievable deprivations and sorrows.

8 Michael Walzer, *The Revolution of the Saints: A Study in the Origins of Radical Politics* (New York: Atheneum, 1970), 27.

Among the hundred and two who alighted from the *Mayflower* at Plymouth in the fall of 1620, nearly half died before spring arrived. But the colonists did not see themselves as miserable refugees. "The Bay Company," wrote Perry Miller, "was not a battered remnant of suffering Separatists thrown up on a rocky shore; it was an organized task force of Christians, executing a flank attack on the corruptions of Christendom. These Puritans did not flee to America; they went in order to work out that complete reformation which was not yet accomplished in England and Europe, but which would quickly be accomplished if only the saints back there had a working model to guide them."[9] It was with this transformational purpose in mind—this "errand in the wilderness," as one preacher put it later in the century—that Britain's northernmost and most famous American colony was established.

Nevertheless, as the self-proclaimed headquarters of cosmic reformation, this city on a hill eventually ceased to emit light. By the end of the seventeenth century, her zealous divines had very little to offer an increasingly secularized England. For after the death of Cromwell, a crypto-Catholic monarchy was restored, and the homeland ceased to be a Calvinist stronghold. In 1688, a moderate Protestant political establishment enacted the Glorious Revolution, which, through the creation of a constitution the following year, brought a permanent end to confessional militancy. Varieties of Christianity were now tolerated (with the notable exception of Roman Catholicism), and a civil peace that had been wanting since the time of Henry VIII was likewise restored. It turned out that despite the promises of John Winthrop, the eyes of Christendom were no longer upon New England.

This caused an existential crisis for the Puritans there, made worse by the fact that Calvinism was in trouble throughout the rest of Europe. The reason was a decline in sympathy for its goals. The earliest Protestants had depended on a heightened popular devotion, and those who affiliated with the Reformed Church of the Calvinists proved to be the most devout. But such sympathy was in decline. And as this happened, a motivationally depleted Calvinist Christendom became the breeding ground of secularism.

---

9 Perry Miller, *Errand into the Wilderness* (Cambridge, MA: Harvard University, 1956), 11.

Holland is a good example. During the decades following Calvin's death, the land of Erasmus had become a refuge for separatists and a stage for iconoclasts. But almost as suddenly, during the seventeenth century the Dutch Republic reclined into a cozy preoccupation with worldly things. Reaping riches from an overseas colonial empire, its people spent them on building the world's largest navy, and, in moments of theological liberality, amassing the exquisite paintings of Rembrandt. In the meantime, its government relaxed restrictions on the publication of religiously subversive literature, providing a shield for skeptics and early deists like Pierre Bayle.

Other former bastions of Calvinism such as Switzerland (where Calvin created the Geneva consistory), Scotland (home of the Presbyterianism of John Knox), and, as we have seen, New England would likewise become centers of secularism during the eighteenth century. And reformational Christianity only deteriorated further after that. In fact, it is the great irony of Calvinist Christendom that it became the cradle of a post-Christian culture which by the end of the twentieth century would pioneer the legalization of prostitution, drug use, same-sex marriage, euthanasia, abortion, and perhaps in the near future, infanticide.

Back in New England, the Puritans had their own unique challenges. They embraced an innovative ecclesiology by which an episcopal hierarchy (which they considered papist) was exchanged for self-administered congregations. This eventually became known as Congregationalism and left the Puritans more vulnerable to popular indifference than emerging mainline Protestants like the Lutherans and Anglicans. For this reason, they could not easily tolerate or even survive the waning of their members' zeal. Ominously, after midcentury "the curve of religious intensity was beginning to droop."[10]

One index of decline was the settlers' indifference to religious uniformity. New England had started off as one of the most religiously repressive regions of Christendom. The pilgrims may have been victims of persecution in the Old World, but they did not hesitate to become agents of it in the new. As Miller put it, "the government of Massachusetts . . . was a dictatorship, and never pretended to be anything else; it was a dictatorship, not of a single

10 Ibid, 54.

tyrant, or of an economic class, or of a political faction, but of the holy and regenerate."[11]

Yet as more and more settlers disembarked at Boston Harbor, confessional homogeneity proved unsustainable. Even in the 1630s, for instance, theological disputes resulted in the expulsion from Massachusetts first of Roger Williams and then of Ann Hutchinson. Both relocated to Providence, where they contributed to the establishment of a new colony, Rhode Island, in which religious liberty was proclaimed by law for the first time since Emperor Constantine's Edict of Milan.

In 1659, the first of four Quakers was hanged in Boston Common after refusing to remain silent about his heterodox beliefs. These executions and the more notorious Salem witch trials of 1693 shocked many New Englanders into holding a more moderate opinion about the influence of Calvinism within government. When social cohesion demanded the persecution of heresy and moral deviance, it seemed to many, the political order was subverted.

Indeed, the Puritan zeal of second- and third-generation settlers was clearly waning by the end of the century. The key to parish membership had long been the vocal and public expression of one's personal transformation through a conversion experience. With its doctrine of predestinarian election, Calvinism emphasized righteousness over repentance and submission to a transcendent judge instead of sacramental participation in His immanent presence on earth. Eucharistic communion and access to baptism for one's children depended on one's having had a demonstrable conversion experience.

However, with growing indifference threatening to dissolve the New England commonwealth, Puritan divines resolved at a Boston synod in 1662 to adopt a measure called the Halfway Covenant. By its terms, so-called "unregenerate" members of congregations who failed to give compelling evidence of their conversion were nonetheless suffered to have their children baptized, provided lesser evidence of zeal was presented. Most congregations ultimately adopted this compromise solution, though zealots like Harvard

11 Ibid, 143.

College President Increase Mather (d. 1723) initially launched a campaign against it.

As the elect gave way before the unregenerate, then, New England experienced a kind of identity crisis. Gone now was the hope of leading the Old World back to the religion of the apostles. Gone also was the hope of establishing a perfect Christian commonwealth, a society of good moral order if not of heavenly immanence. Fallen man had proven too obstinate and the world too enticing for even that limited measure of paradise. The way forward appeared to pass through the saeculum.

For the Puritans of both Englands—the old and the new—the seventeenth century had begun with a bang but was ending in a whimper—or, to put it in their own terms, it had begun with a conversion but was ending in a compromise. Many a clergyman tried to stir up the old zeal. In the colonies, the transition was marked by the rise of a uniquely American form of political literature known as the jeremiad. Examples were issued by preachers on days of special public significance such as elections and fasts. Named for and inspired by Jeremiah's prophecies about the impending judgment of Jerusalem, these public statements combined sacred historiography with scouring homiletics, telling the story of a golden age and urging a renewed reformation to avert destruction. "Reformation hath been the design of New England," declared one not very eloquent preacher in 1674,

> *and therefore Reformation it is the profession of New England. This work of reform, it hath been (especially by this generation) (not only) much neglected, but even (almost) utterly deserted, by a general defection and declension, which we are fallen into.*[12]

For the son of Increase Mather, the format of the jeremiad was not enough. Cotton Mather (d. 1728) wrote a two-volume history of New England entitled *Magnalia Christi Americana* that worked fire-and-brimstone homiletics into what Paul Johnson has called "the first great work of literature

12 Quoted in Andrew R. Murphy, *Prodigal Nation: Moral Decline and Divine Punishment from New England to 9/11* (Oxford: Oxford University, 2009), 32.

produced in America."[13] It was also in some ways the first great recognition that New England had become a post-Puritanical civilization. It was becoming secularized.

Puritanical Christendom is established by Mather as a civilization based on a culture of reformational Christianity. Two generations of men have historically struggled against one another, he claims in the introduction: reformers and anti-reformers. And it is the latter, he laments, who have by the opening of the eighteenth century gained the upper hand through a preoccupation with earthly prosperity. They seek "to stop the progress of the desired Reformation" and "to persecute those that most heartily wished well unto it."[14] Unfaithful descendants of New England's Puritanical founders have become preoccupied with "secular concernments." Quoting a Latin adage, Mather concludes that "religion brought forth prosperity, and the daughter destroyed the mother."[15]

In the New World, as in the old, the saeculum had snuffed out the reformational lamp of Puritanism.

The Westernization of the East

AMONG THE MANY POLITICAL DIGNITARIES who made the pilgrimage to Versailles in the eighteenth century to honor France's secular magnificence was one who arrived less than two years after the death of the Sun King. Peter the Great (r. 1682–1725) was the emperor of Russia and came to the French capital to negotiate an alliance against the Ottoman Turks, the conquerors of Constantinople. He was the first Orthodox ruler to visit the West since Byzantine Emperor John VIII attended the Council of Florence under comparable circumstances.

Like the tragic figure of John, Peter was dismayed by the destructive

13 Paul Johnson, *A History of the American People* (New York: HarperCollins, 1997), 85.

14 Cotton Mather, *Magnalia Christi Americana, or, The Ecclesiastical History of New England*, ed. and abr. Raymond J. Cunningham (New York: Frederick Ungar, 1970), 2.

15 Ibid, 26–27.

Peter the Great of Russia

energy of the Turkish war machine. Like John, he was awed by the military and political strength of Western Christendom. And like John, he was prepared to impose on his people Western patterns of life in order to tap into that strength. But whereas John had failed to bring the West to the East, Peter, through force of will, would impose the new Christendom on Russia with great effect. And in doing so he altered both forever.

The process of westernization had already begun before Peter came to power. As we have seen, in the aftermath of the Protestant Reformation the papacy was eager to expand Roman Catholicism to the east. Though the Jesuit-inspired invasion of Russia had failed, important inroads were achieved with the Union of Brest in 1596. Endorsed by both Pope Clement VIII and Polish King Sigismund III, this act incorporated several formerly Orthodox dioceses of Ruthenia into the Roman Catholic Church. Known thereafter as Uniates (and sometimes as Byzantine or Ukrainian Catholics), the signatories won in exchange for their submission to Rome the right, previously denied them, of conducting church life in the manner of the old Christendom. Their services continued according to the Byzantine rite, their priests remained married, and the original form of the Nicene Creed was confessed without the controversial *filioque*. In other words, submission to Rome did not bring about a thoroughgoing westernization in anything but jurisdictional alignment.

Something more substantial was suggested in the activities of Patriarch Cyril I of Constantinople (d. 1638). He had been an active opponent of the Union, traveling to the region and spending years advocating against it. After becoming patriarch, he found that Jesuit missionaries were as active in the Ottoman capital as they had been in eastern Europe. Almost powerless to resist them, he therefore decided to make the enemy of his enemy his friend. He established contacts with the Protestants in England and Geneva, even sending his most gifted clergy to study in Calvinist institutes there.

Then, in 1629, he issued a notorious *Confession* that strongly endorsed Calvinist principles, including the doctrines of faith-alone and predestination. While the authenticity of the work has been challenged, it seems to have expressed some of the beliefs the beleaguered patriarch was forming as he sought ways of fending off Roman Catholicism in the East. He seemed to think the only way to resist Jesuit proselytism was to adopt Protestant ways of thinking. The Ottomans were all too happy to see him so struggle, as division among their Orthodox subjects only promised swifter conversion to Islam. But in the end, the sultan simply ordered Cyril's execution. And in 1672, an Orthodox Synod of Jerusalem under Patriarch Dositheos unequivocally condemned his *Confession*.

Only among the Slavs did westernization make any permanent headway. This occurred in part because the Orthodox Church in eastern Europe fell into a state of confusion during the seventeenth century. On the one hand, the Orthodox living under Western rule were continuously on the defensive against the pressures of neo-reformational Roman Catholicism. Kiev was an example. The site of the Russians' conversion to Christianity under Grand Prince Vladimir in 988, the city was overrun by the Mongols in the thirteenth century and later annexed by the Polish state. By the beginning of the seventeenth century, Kiev had become little more than a shrinking outpost on the borderland of Eastern Christendom.

Administered from a distant Constantinople, the Orthodox Church there was poor and ignorant. By comparison, the Uniates offered wealth and the promise of integration within the Polish political establishment. Many among the Orthodox nobility thus followed the example of their bishops by converting to Roman Catholicism in either its Latin or Uniate form. What is more, the Jesuits were building numerous schools for their clergy, making it almost impossible for the native Orthodox to compete. The common people were left with little more than lay brotherhoods to maintain their sense of community.

Into this situation stepped Peter Mogila (d. 1646), the most heroic defender of Orthodoxy during the period but one with a tragic flaw. Though a faithful member of the Orthodox Church, he was convinced of the intellectual and organizational superiority of the Roman Catholic Church. The only way to defend the Orthodox Church, he believed, was to embrace the theological culture that now surrounded her in the eastern borderlands of Western Christendom. This meant building an Orthodox Kievan Academy on lines similar to those of Western seminaries. It also meant adopting a scholastic form of theology.

Until this time, Orthodoxy had relied mostly on the church fathers and not on grammar or logic to express itself. Mogila changed this. He rewrote the service books using a Thomistic explanation of the sacraments. An example was the rite of confession. The Byzantine formula for absolution brought unambiguous attention to Christ as the agent of forgiveness. By contrast, under the influence of the Papal Reformation the Roman rite had come to place emphasis on the priest, who stood *in persona Christi* ("in the person of Christ") and whose ministry was an extension of that of the pope, the "Vicar of Christ."

Because of such reforms, Orthodoxy among the Russians now became increasingly clericalistic and formalistic. Mogila was the first of a line of Russian theologians to Latinize the spiritual culture of Eastern Christendom, initiating what Georges Florovsky (borrowing a term from Oswald Spengler) called the *pseudomorphosis* of Orthodox theology. Due to this "false-formation," the Russian Church was cut off from the patristic tradition and an incompatible alternative—scholasticism—began to distort her understanding of the faith.

As this was happening, westernization was beginning to alter Eastern Christendom within the Muscovite state as well. After the collapse of Byzantium, many Russians had become isolated from international Orthodoxy and especially from the role of hesychasm within it. The need for national unity and a strong absolutist monarchy to defend against the Mongols was one reason for this. In this sense, Christianity in Russia resembled that in Gallican France, and it was drawn toward a comparatively secularistic logic. What is more, some believed that the fall of Constantinople to the Turks in 1453 had been a divine judgment against the Greeks' apostasy at the Council of Florence.

Therefore, when the reformist Patriarch Nikon of Moscow (r. 1652–1666) suddenly ordered changes to the liturgy based on foreign Greek standards, the result was widespread indignation and even revolt. Talented leaders of the clergy like Avvakum Petrov entered into open resistance to the reforms, and soon a group of schismatics known as the Old Believers called for the abolition of all things foreign. Against their often xenophobic outbursts an equally reactionary party of reformers advocated the importation of foreign models of church life. Nikon himself appears to have entertained plans to raise the patriarchate above the state in imitation of the papacy. But as a Hellenophile, he also had little sympathy for the culture of the West. Other reformers were more open-minded toward that culture.

Among them was an iconographer named Simon Ushakov, who modeled his painting on the naturalism of the Italian humanists. Images became fleshly, seeking to provoke an emotional response in the viewer. They also began to depict theological abstractions rather than the deifying effects of the Incarnation. Ushakov's subjects, for instance, included the scholastically conceived "seven deadly sins," the image for which he merely copied from an edition of Loyola's *Spiritual Exercises*. Such works, according to art historian Leonid Ouspensky, "eliminated the eschatological orientation of the icon."[1] As Russia began to turn to the West, then, the most profound expression of her culture lost sight of paradise.

But neither scholastic theology nor naturalistic painting could have prepared Russia for the radical cultural reorientation forced on her by Peter the Great. Growing up in the German Quarter of Moscow, as a youth the future emperor developed a fascination with the West. Everything around him came to seem paltry and backward in light of the stories he heard about foreign lands. The fanaticism of many Old Believers, some of whom collectively self-immolated rather than submit to Nikon's reforms, reinforced a strongly antireligious temperament in Peter. His passions were directed instead toward the potential of absolutist statecraft.

He became especially engrossed in rebuilding Russia's military. As the Muscovite state had always been landlocked, Peter decided that a warm-water port and a strong navy were needed. He looked for inspiration to Holland, whose East India Company had given rise to the largest and most sophisticated navy in the world. In 1697, Peter took the unprecedented step of leaving his homeland to study shipbuilding in Amsterdam. After months working at the dockyards dressed as a common carpenter, he continued his Grand Embassy by studying government and the military in England and

1 Leonid Ouspensky, *Theology of the Icon*, vol. 2, trans. Anthony Gythiel (Crestwood, NY: St. Vladimir's Seminary, 1992), 368.

Austria. Later trips abroad introduced him to society in Germany and, as we have seen, France. He so embraced the civilization he found during his travels that upon returning to his homeland, which he considered inferior, he launched a frenetic program of reforms to make Russia Western.

Towering at over six and a half feet tall with an ambition as volcanic as his temper, Peter's will to westernize the East was unstoppable. He was always on the move, pursuing an unbounded desire to improve his "backward" homeland. He thoroughly redesigned the institutions of power, introducing a bureaucratic form of administration and opening government service to anyone with talent or ambition. But power remained his personal monopoly. Louis XIV had had an expression, *L'etat, c'est moi*—that is, "I am the state." Far more absolute than the Sun King's monarchy, Peter's government was a full-blown autocracy. Anyone who dared step in the way of his reforms was immediately eliminated. After an incident known as the Streltsy Revolt during the very year of his accession, he ordered the brutal torture and execution of more than a thousand suspects. Late in his reign, even his son and heir Alexey was arrested, tortured, and executed on Peter's orders for resisting westernization.

By emulating the political culture of kingdoms like France, Peter greatly enhanced Russia's international reputation. But life at his court was a strange mixture of royal ceremony and peasant boorishness. Upon meeting the seven-year-old King Louis XV, for instance, the Russian tsar had seized him in his massive hands and impetuously hurled him into the air. Near his new capital of Saint Petersburg, Peter tried to reproduce the majesty of Versailles by building a palace complex called Peterhof. However, amid elegant buildings and manicured gardens, its fountains included one resembling a bowl of fruit—so designed that when a dignified guest curiously reached for a piece, a jet of water would blast him (or her) in the face.

Peter detested sycophants, demanding that everyone treat him as merely the first among equals. He eschewed elegance and preferred modest living and common entertainment. His preferred residence was little more than a townhouse called the Summer Palace, modeled on the residences of Dutch merchants. An aversion for social forms made him bristle around dignitaries, especially the church hierarchy. Whereas Louis XIV treated Roman Catholic bishops with reverence, Peter considered grandiloquent titles like Eminence, Beatitude, and All-Holiness absurd. On a whim one night he organized a band of carousers called the "Most-Drunken Synod" (mimicking the Church's Most Holy Synod) and marched through the streets of Moscow singing bawdy songs in mock vestments of the patriarch.

Peter certainly had an appetite for drink. He could outperform any of his courtiers and often broke them by ordering that they draw copiously from a specially designed marble beer goblet. Always suspicious, he also used his all-night sprees to gain intelligence about potential subversion within the court. A less sinister theme of these parties, but perhaps no less unsettling, was the reformer's practice of shaving the beards of his noblemen, known as boyars, against their will. In emulation of Western manners, Peter actually tried to abolish the Russian practice of growing a beard altogether. Failing at this, he resorted to the imposition of an onerous beard tax. Peter was an enthusiast for modern medicine and dentistry, and more than one party guest was horrified to see the tsar produce a pair of pliers during the night and insist on prying an infected tooth from a merrymaker's mouth.

Though Peter displayed little piety, he was deeply concerned about the role of the Orthodox Church in the Russian state. Like Louis XIV, he realized that political strength depended on good religious order. And like his French mentor, he therefore used religion as an instrument of rule. In 1700, the patriarch of Moscow died. Church custom required the tsar to nominate a replacement. Peter declined to do so. Instead, he created a body called the Holy Synod consisting of hand-chosen hierarchs whom he could trust to run church affairs for the benefit of the autocracy.

He was advised in this and other church reforms by Feofan Prokopovich (d. 1736), who in some respects represented a latter-day Peter Mogila. Born in Kiev, educated by the Jesuits in Poland, he converted to Uniatism and traveled to Rome to pursue the study of scholasticism. However, he developed an aversion to the papacy and eventually returned to Russia and the Orthodox faith, or at least a westernized form of it. Distinguishing himself in scholarship and oratory, he was eventually called to the capital to assist the tsar in imposing secularizing reforms on Russian Christendom.

It is also possible to compare Prokopovich to Bossuet, the eminent bishop of seventeenth-century France. If the latter was an advocate of Louis's absolutism, Prokopovich was (as one historian has called him) the "chief ideologist of the Petrine state."[2] And as Bossuet supported Louis in the Gallican campaign to nationalize the Roman Catholic Church at the expense of the papacy, so Prokopovich attacked what he called "patriarchalism"—the demand by the highest clergy for independence from the state. Like Bossuet, he asserted his sovereign's "divine right" to rule and concluded that no legitimate voice of criticism could be raised against him, whether secular or religious.

For this reason, Peter's church reforms did far more than confirm the abolition of the patriarchate. They transferred religious authority to the secular state. For instance, the head of the Holy Synod was to be a layman directly responsible to the sovereign and known as the chief procurator. Peter called him the "tsar's eye." His role was not just to report potential resistance among the bishops but to manipulate them to such a degree that they would never again represent a guiding influence over Russian civilization. That was now the state's responsibility. Even the local parish priest was placed under the government's thumb. Against all canons, a royal edict demanded the seal of confession be broken and authorities notified whenever a penitent admitted a tendency toward sedition. It appears very few priests obeyed. But the precedent was portentous. Under Peter and through Prokopovich the Orthodox Church was earning a reputation as "the handmaiden of the state." The cultural effects of this would be disastrous, as we will see in Part III.

Peter's driving ambition was to raise the Russian military to a level equal to that of France, and by the end of his reign he certainly approached its fulfillment. Louis XIV had distinguished his long reign with almost incessant wars of expansion. Peter did the same. After reaching a stalemate in the south against the Ottoman Empire, he turned his attention to the Baltic.

2 James Craycraft, *The Church Reform of Peter the Great* (Stanford: Stanford University, 1971), 59.

There, Sweden had created an empire after leading the Protestant states in the Thirty Years War. In 1700, Peter launched the Great Northern War against his new enemy, winning a decisive victory at the Battle of Poltava nine years later. The war dragged on until 1721, but when it was finally ended Sweden had forever ceased to be a great power. Russia was now the mistress of the Baltic. Russia had once been an isolated principality on the eastern borderlands of Europe, but the empire created by Peter would henceforth remain a constant player in the diplomatic affairs of the West. From the Napoleonic wars to World War II, no great European conflict would be resolved without her participation.

Russia had become an integral part of Western Christendom. To be sure, she still harbored vestiges of the old Christendom. The Old Believers could certainly claim that distinction, as could a large population of monastics who had so far resisted state interference in their affairs. And it is certainly true that the great majority of the population would remain untouched by westernization for a century to come. Only at court and among the nobility did utopia become a compelling alternative to the paradisiacal culture. And so it is at the court of Peter the Great that our narrative about the desecration of the world will conclude.

In 1717, Russia's capital was relocated to the newly built city of Saint Petersburg. Neither Louis XIV's Versailles nor even Constantine's New Rome had been built on land as barren as the frozen marshes surrounding the Neva River where Peter chose to erect his new capital. But Peter demanded access to the ocean, and the Gulf of Finland provided it. The city was formally dedicated to the Apostle Peter (such was Christendom, even as late as the eighteenth century), but everyone knew it was really named after the tsar. It was certainly stamped with his personality. Thousands of peasants died in fulfillment of his orders to build the city. Scores of noblemen abandoned ancestral homes in Moscow in fulfillment of his orders to populate it. And, indeed, what emerged along the shores of the Neva was a skyline worthy of the most illustrious European capital. Its palaces and cathedrals were built in the Baroque style, avoiding any suggestion that they marked the presence of the old Christendom.

Peter-Paul Cathedral, St. Petersburg

The city's first church was a good example. The Peter-Paul Cathedral was built within a fortress protecting the city from naval attack. Its military setting was appropriate, as the bastion would eventually be used to hold the empire's political prisoners. From within the fortress's walls, the cathedral shot upward with a tall, slender spire. At complete odds with the architecture of Eastern Christendom, whose central dome symbolized the kingdom of heaven on earth, this Western device suggested that paradise was to be found only in the distant heavens, leaving the earth to utopia.

What such architecture lacked in heavenly immanence it made up for with earthly exuberance. Beyond the curvaceous baroque façade lay an even more spectacular interior. The space was filled with dazzling colors and rich ornamentation. But neither these nor the winged babies flitting about the ceiling were the most striking departure from Orthodox liturgical design. The iconostasis (icon stand) that joins the nave to the altar was a monument of earthly extravagance, a wall of sculpture saturated with gold leaf. This was the real focal point, not the naturalistic paintings swallowed up by gilded garishness. Icons had always functioned as "windows into heaven," as proclamations of the incarnational transformation of the cosmos. Here they were mere decorations, however, frivolous accoutrements to enhance a spiritually untransfigured and therefore desecrated world.

The windows to paradise were thus being shuttered as Eastern Christendom entered the eighteenth century. Significantly, Peter had nicknamed his new capital a "window on the West." And it was toward the lands of the setting sun that Russia now looked for the renewal of her civilization and culture.[3] The reorientation that had begun in Europe during the quattrocento was to become Russia's inheritance as well. Resolutely oriented toward paradise since the Great Division, she now rushed toward utopia in a fit of insecurity and confusion. In respect to that past, she was falling into a state of profound disorientation.

---

3 The Russian word for "west," *zapad*, literally means "sunset."

PART II

Disorientation

CHAPTER FIVE

Replacing Reformational Christianity

AS THE EAST BEGAN TO westernize, the West continued to secularize. We saw in Part I how secular humanism gradually displaced traditional Christianity as the cultural inspiration of Western Christendom, and how in the case of Russia, Eastern Christendom eventually followed suit. Now, as the eighteenth century opened, displacement gave way to replacement. And in this sense, Christendom began unambiguously to exchange paradise for utopia.

The two centuries inaugurated by the Peace of Westphalia on the continent (1648), the Stuart Restoration in Britain (1660), and the Halfway Covenant in New England (1662) witnessed the fundamental reorientation of Christendom. During the first millennium, culture had been oriented toward the kingdom of heaven as revealed by the gospel and preached by the Apostles. The most expressive form of this culture, sacramental worship, was literally directed toward the *oriens*, or "east." Since the fourteenth century, secular humanism had taken its place in Western culture but had not replaced Christianity even among the elite. From Petrarch to Peter the Great, the beliefs and values of Christianity and humanism had largely coexisted.

But the wars of Western religion changed this. So great was the disgrace of Christianity in its post-schism, reformational form that the elite ceased to hold to it. Some developed an emotional variant called pietistic Christianity, while others, by the early nineteenth century, abandoned doctrinal integrity altogether and embraced something that can be called utopian Christianity. But more influential were those who abandoned Christianity altogether. Following the example of seventeenth-century scientists and philosophers who were themselves intellectual refugees from the religious wars, eighteenth-century deists and nineteenth-century idealists would exchange Christianity for various forms of secular humanism. And by doing this, they introduced a counterfeit system of beliefs and values that, while capable of fulfilling the transformational imperative on exclusively secular terms, would deny to it a convincing and enduring transcendent anchor.

The two centuries joining the wars of Western religion with the rise of revolutionary ideology therefore represent in the history of Christendom a period not only of reorientation but of disorientation.

Fathers of Modernity

THE WEST'S CULTURAL REBAPTISM IN the fifteenth century had not only loosened traditional Christianity's hold on the arts. It also upended science, which, long based on Aristotle, had been enshrined within the scholasticism of the universities. Ficino provided a new way of seeing the natural world. His Neoplatonic concept of *homo faber* gave man the capacity for both understanding the world and changing it. In the heady atmosphere of the quattrocento, this inspired a wide interest in the occult. Pico was the most systematic adherent of a "white" magic, but there were many others. These strange intellectuals saw magic not as a deviation from Christianity but as a supplement to it. The intuition that an elusive *prisca theologia* had been preserved by pagandom long before the time of Christ or even Moses reinforced the promethean drive toward human autonomy.

Among those attracted to esoteric explanations of the universe and the possibilities of man's capacity to manipulate it was Giordano Bruno (d. 1600). Influenced by Neoplatonism, his phenomenally creative mind ranged between speculations about the existence of extraterrestrial life (he was one of the first to suggest the stars are suns with their own solar systems) and challenges to the doctrines of traditional Christianity. It was for the latter that he was condemned and executed by the inquisition. But before his end, he was one of the first to accept Copernicus's recently revealed but much scorned theory of heliocentrism.

Francis Bacon (d. 1626) acquired a much better reputation. He was also controversial, though this was due to his involvement in bribery at the English court (where he served for a time as lord chancellor) rather than his theological ambiguity. He is known as the founder of the scientific method. His main contribution to the study of nature was to emphasize the importance of empirical observation rather than theology or revelation. Earlier humanists such as Leonardo da Vinci had conducted experiments on natural phenomena, but it was Bacon's advocacy of this new method that most established it as the basis for modern science. But Bacon, like Bruno and Pico before him, was also fascinated by magic and believed that a secret body of ancient wisdom was available to modern men in their effort to understand and improve the world around them. As he put it in his most influential book, *The New Organon*, from the study of magic "there cannot but follow an improvement in man's estate, and an enlargement of his power over nature."[4] Promethean humanism was becoming empowered.

This was especially apparent in Bacon's utopian treatise *The New Atlantis*, left unpublished at the time of his death. Bacon knew of More's famous account of an imaginary society of justice and happiness. Like More, he located utopia in the western hemisphere—in this case on an island called Bensalem in the Pacific Ocean. But unlike his countryman, he used it as an image of a future world in which science would provide for the needs of man. "The end of our foundation," declares one of its citizens, "is the knowledge of causes, the secret motions of things; and the enlarging of the bounds of human [dominion], to the effecting of all things possible."[5]

4 Quoted in John Henry, *Knowledge Is Power: How Magic, the Government and an Apocalyptic Vision Inspired Francis Bacon to Create Modern Science* (Cambridge: Icon Books, 2002), 49.

5 Francis Bacon, *Works*, vol. 5 (Boston: Brown and Taggard, 1862), 398.

Sir Francis Bacon

And while his vision is shaped in part by Christianity, especially the Old Testament's account of the Garden of Eden and the temple of Solomon, in elaborating it he also draws, as his fascination with the *prisca theologia* would suggest, on pagandom. For him the city of Atlantis described in Plato's dialogues was not a myth but a model, an ideal society that could be reborn in a Christendom very far from the golden age.

Indeed, the spirit of much of Bacon's writing is apocalyptic. He spent time in France during the wars of Western religion there and later in life became an advocate for religious toleration. In the face of its apparent religious violence, he seems to have felt a detachment from Western Christendom's past. The golden age is thus projected into the future. We have seen how in the wake of the Papal Reformation a stream of millenarian expectation began to appear, most notably among the Franciscan followers of Joachim of Fiore. As Western Christendom's paradisiacal culture became eclipsed in the indignant effort to reform society, a need arose for an alternative experience of divine presence. Predictably, this millenarian tendency reemerged during the Protestant Reformation, violently driving the Anabaptist seizure of Muenster in 1535. It also colored Puritan hopes of religious renewal in England in the time of Bacon.

Within this millenarian context, the *New Atlantis* marks an important shift toward secularization at a time of religious confusion. Bacon was an Anglican and like other Protestants was sincerely interested in restoring Christianity's apostolic order. But he believed perhaps even more sincerely that true restoration required recovery of man's God-given rule over nature. This recovery was not a return to the past. It was a march into the future.

He called his utopian project the "great renovation" (*instauratio magna*), a phrase he used often and which even furnished the title of one of his books. The technical term *instauration*, drawn from the Latin word used for the restoration of Solomon's temple under King Josiah, meant more than mere renovation. It connoted a fresh start, a new beginning, the dawn of a new age.

It represented, in fact, the sixteenth-century equivalent of revolution. Using the term, Bacon could not help bringing to mind the pagan image of Prometheus, whom he considered the embodiment of "human nature."[6] Uplifted and empowered by his newfound autonomy, modern man would collectively use science to solve the problems that five centuries of religious reformation had failed to solve. Instead of feeling contempt for the

---

6 Quoted in Charles Whitney, *Francis Bacon and Modernity* (New Haven: Yale University, 1986), 185.

world and misery for the human condition, he would rejoice in his powers over nature. "Natural philosophy," Bacon declared, "proposes to itself; as its noblest work of all nothing less than the restitution and renovation of things corruptible."[7]

The island of Bensalem is a model for the renovation of Christendom. At a transitional moment in the rise and fall of what the West once was, it represents both a restoration of paradise and a revolution toward utopia. In Bacon's account of it, scientific learning replaces deification, scientists replace the clergy, and science itself replaces miracles. The author relates how one of the island's leaders, in boasting of the many scientific advances of his people, described a liquid that actually has the power to prolong life. The Bensalemites call their invention the "water of paradise."[8]

Francis Bacon had great confidence in the collective and cumulative achievements of science. During his lifetime, however, a rival but equally momentous form of knowledge was emerging among Western Christendom's philosophers. It applied the Promethean principle of human autonomy in an even more radical way. If Bacon had claimed nature could be understood only through human experimentation and not by divine revelation, the new philosophy claimed the very basis for knowledge was found not in man's relationship with God but in man's isolated meditation on his own reasoning.

René Descartes (d. 1650) was the most important of these rationalists and is known to historians as the "father of modern philosophy." His famous conclusion "I think, therefore I am" (*cogito ergo sum*) was one of the boldest assertions of human autonomy ever. He made it after agonizing over the dubious claims of his philosophical and religious predecessors. The effects of the wars of Western religion were the context for this crisis of epistemological faith. A Roman Catholic born in a Protestant region of France, Descartes volunteered to fight in the Thirty Years War first on the side of the Dutch Protestants, and then later in support of the German Catholic

7 Quoted in J. C. Davis, *Utopia and the Ideal Society: A Study of English Utopian Writing, 1516–1700* (Cambridge: Cambridge University, 1981), 124.

8 Bacon, *Works*, vol. 5, 400.

League. Surrounded by the death and destruction brought on by militant confessionalism, he eventually lost confidence in the truth claims of the new Christendom.

As with Bacon, then, the religious upheaval of the sixteenth and seventeenth centuries was the context for the philosophical reorientation of the West. As Brad Gregory notes in his study of the Protestant Reformation's "unintended consequences," the violent and interminable debates among Christians during this period took the floor out from underneath traditional methods of philosophical reflection. If Luther, Zwingli, and Calvin—not to mention Roman Catholic apologists—could not agree on the true nature of the Eucharist, for instance, how could any rational thinker arrive at unambiguous certitude about philosophical truth? The Protestant principle of scripture-alone had proven completely incapable of establishing a unity of belief for reformational Christianity. The Roman Catholic example of doctrinal development, yet to be formulated but already evident to contemporaries, was likewise unconvincing in its appeal to what appeared to be shifting historical traditions. In his famous *Meditations*, Descartes insisted that "everything had to be torn down to the ground and I had to begin anew from the first foundations, if I ever wanted to establish anything firm and enduring in the sciences."[9]

The first-person singular pronoun in this statement is telling. With Descartes, the ego—the "I"—becomes the conceptual center of knowledge about not only man and the cosmos, but even God. "When I make myself the object of reflection," he asserts, "I not only find that I am an incomplete and dependent being . . . but, at the same time, I am assured likewise that he upon whom I am dependent possesses in himself all the goods after which I aspire . . . and that he is thus God."[10]

Descartes applied skepticism with a productive aim; he was not a nihilist. He was in fact a believer in a time of mass belief, and it would have been unthinkable that rationalism could have led him to abandon Christianity.

9 Quoted in Gregory, *Unintended Reformation*, 115.

10 Rene Descartes, *Meditations on the First Philosophy*, in *Discourse on Method and Meditations*, trans. John Veitch (Buffalo, NY: Prometheus Books, 1989), 97.

But like Bacon, he reacted to cosmological contempt and anthropological pessimism—to say nothing of religious conflict—by turning toward the saeculum. For him, this was the realm of natural reason. It was the very realm that the scholastics since the Great Division had occupied with one foot, even as they occupied faith with the other. Indeed, Anselm, the father of scholasticism, had himself proven the existence of God on purely philosophical grounds.

In the old Christendom, by contrast, the secular philosophy of pagandom had never been elevated to such a status. Gregory Palamas, like so many Greek fathers before him, had affirmed the limited use of philosophy to achieve theological clarity. But theology itself was not a rationalistic enterprise. It was a means of communion with God. And as such, it was regulated by asceticism and the sacramental life of the Church.

From his seventeenth-century vantage point, however, Descartes knew very little of this. Sacraments and asceticism played no role in his quest for knowledge. Indignation, however, did. He perceived a grave inadequacy in the religiously based philosophy he inherited from the scholastics. Only the secular foundation of a purely natural reason, he concluded, could withstand the skepticism caused by the never-ending reformational disputes. And as for Bacon, it was this element of the saeculum that offered to the West's corrupted culture a hope for renewal, or, as the father of modern science liked to say, an instauration.

The secularization of knowledge would take centuries to play out, but even in the short term the new rationalism began to transform the culture of the new Christendom. It could be found even within theological reflections—though not, perhaps, with very convincing results.

Descartes's fellow countryman Blaise Pascal (d. 1662), for instance, used philosophical rationalism against rationalists themselves. The fervent Jansenist was known to experience visions. Yet he was also a scientist who conducted public experiments, such as one demonstrating the existence of vacuums (which Descartes actually attended). He could thus speak the language of rationalist philosophy. His most famous contribution to modern faith, in fact, was a "wager" in which he calculated, using the science of probability, the comparative advantage in being a Christian. Pascal's wager was similar in argument to the famous "proof" of God's existence rendered by Anselm in the eleventh century, as it too was based solely on natural reason and had virtually nothing to say about the gospel. The wager could support just about any belief in a higher power—even Islam—but this did not seem problematic in a society that was still predominantly Christian.

The famous wager was designed to lead a growing chorus of agnostics to the faith. It consists of deciding whether a skeptic should waste his life in obedience to a God who turns out at the end of it not to exist, or spend it in sinful pleasures only to find that God does exist. The wager was an argument particularly well suited for an age in which divine participation and heavenly immanence had ceased to orient Western culture. But a more anemic form of the Christian faith is hard to imagine.

Another contemporary who applied rationalism to Christianity was Gottfried Leibniz (d. 1716). Like Pascal, he felt obliged to defend the faith from skeptics reacting against the religious wars. One of their objections was the existence of evil. How could there be a God as Christians have always confessed Him, full of love and care for the cosmos, when events like the Rape of Magdeburg can happen? Leibniz reasoned it through and came up with an answer. In a work entitled *Theodicy* (a neologism meaning, absurdly, the "justification of God"), he explained that since God is almighty and therefore has the power to create a variety of worlds, the one he did create—ours—is necessarily "the best of all possible worlds." Seen in the light of natural reason, the philosopher cheerfully concluded, the problem of evil is really nothing more than an illusion.

Another important rationalist was John Locke (d. 1704). Like Descartes, he withdrew in disgust from the spectacle of seventeenth-century religious conflict. Like Descartes, he sought a rational foundation on which to base all truth claims, a secular epistemology. This foundation must exist prior to and independent of Christianity—even if he, like Descartes, considered himself a Christian. However, unlike Descartes, he did not locate the foundation of knowledge within himself but in the world around him. Rejecting the premise that innate ideas can unite the human mind to an external reality,

Sir Isaac Newton

he claimed that the external reality determines the ideas held by the human mind. This doctrine, known as empiricism, he presented in a famous work entitled *An Essay Concerning Human Understanding*. The essay claimed that only through sensory impressions does man understand reality. The human mind is in principle a *tabula rasa*, or "blank slate," upon which truths about the cosmos are written.

This view of reality, radically at odds with Descartes's but no less rationalistic, was particularly suited to support the work of Locke's contemporary and fellow countryman Isaac Newton (d. 1727). No father of modernity was as influential as he in establishing a secular vision of the cosmos. As a scientist, Newton was preceded by illustrious astronomers like Galileo, whose endorsement of the heliocentric universe first elaborated by Copernicus met with inquisitorial condemnation in 1633. Newton was not as vulnerable, both because he lived in England and because the focus of his studies was physics. Using a new form of mathematics called calculus (which was largely his invention), he set about the systematic explanation of many of the world's mechanical functions. Though he was himself religious, his famous work *Principia* described how the world functioned in a way free of heavenly immanence. He accepted the Christian teaching that a transcendent God had created it and even on occasion intervened in its affairs. Nevertheless, his interest in the world was purely empirical. The only inquiry worth making was the discovery and calculation of its natural laws. The two most important of these were gravity and optics, and he famously formulated each.

In a single stroke, the *Principia* offered modern Christendom a vision of the cosmos that was almost exclusively autonomous in its operations. That Newton, like many other scientists and philosophers before him, believed in occult wisdom and the practice of alchemy does not alter the fact that knowledge for him was purely rational. The mystery of the Incarnation—the heart of traditional Christian cosmology—had no place in his empiricist understanding. It is no coincidence that he came to reject the divinity of Christ.

The Pietist Reaction

AS WE CAN SEE, SEVENTEENTH-CENTURY philosophers and scientists were highly privileged members of society. The fathers of modernity were an elite. Never before had the distance between the piety of the educated and that of the great mass of the population been so great. We will consider the cultural effects of this, the latest consequence of the Papal Reformation's bifurcation of the West, when we discuss the rise of deism below. Here, it is important to consider how common members of Christendom and the pastors who led them recovered from the horrors of religious warfare.

Some, of course, had been saved those horrors. Eastern Christendom had not participated in the wars of Western religion and as a result did not experience as directly the antireligious reaction of its elite. This is not to say reformational Christianity was unknown there. We have already observed its insinuation into the theology of Peter Mogila and the administrative reforms of Feofan Prokopovich. Such westernization was still of limited influence, though. The great majority of Orthodox in Russia would not begin to taste directly of Western piety until well into the eighteenth century, when naturalistic iconography and baroque hymnography began to communicate it.

In fact, there were still strong examples of resistance to the reformational legacy. In Greece, for instance, Makarios of Corinth (d. 1805) joined forces with Nikodemos of Athos (d. 1809) to produce a massive compilation of hesychastic texts on prayer of the heart. Entitled the *Philokalia,* it was translated into Slavonic by Paisius Velichkovsky (d. 1794) and thereafter entered the spiritual bloodstream of Russia. The *Philokalia,* read subsequently not only by monks but by pious laymen as well, provided a bulwark of Eastern piety against the influx of scholasticism. However, even its coeditor Nikodemos saw value in the reformational piety of the West. He translated a work entitled *Spiritual Combat* by the Roman Catholic Lorenzo Scupoli (published in English as *Unseen Warfare*), and he used a highly legalistic method of interpreting moral canons. That the piety of the old Christendom could have intermingled so closely with that of the new Christendom in the person of Nikodemos has remained a puzzle for historians to this day.

In the West, very little understanding of or interest in Orthodoxy survived the wars of religion. There, pastors and theologians of the eighteenth century were preoccupied with moving beyond the effects of conflict. A good place to look for new approaches to piety is across the confessional killing fields of Germany. The target of nearly every Roman Catholic and Protestant army, the lands of the Holy Roman Empire became a cauldron of hatred and cruelty. In some areas, half the population was killed. This matched, more or less, the effects of the fourteenth-century Black Death.

The terrible fact that doctrinally driven men had killed as many or more Christians as disease-bearing rats caused many to reflect soberly on their faith. Philosophers like Christian Wolff (d. 1754) and Hermann Reimarus (d. 1768) abandoned traditional Christianity altogether. Most, however, sought a new form of it.

One of these was Philipp Spener (d. 1705). Though his Lutheran identity never faltered, he was a critic of the way in which the institutional church had served the interests of confessional states during the wars of religion. He believed a new reformation was needed, which he called pietism. For Spener, the key was a revitalized Lutheranism that would emphasize piety over ecclesial or doctrinal matters. It would take the place of reformational Christianity just as reformational Christianity had taken the place of traditional Christianity. At the core of the change was what he called a postbaptismal "new birth" (*Wiedergeburt*), an inner experience that spiritually transformed the believer. As he put it, the true believer must be "born again, again."

By itself this was not an innovation. It was a vision of spiritual transformation inspired by the Apostle Peter's statement that Christians become "partakers of the divine nature" (2 Pet. 1:4)—the same passage in Scripture to which Eastern church fathers frequently alluded when elaborating the doctrine of deification.[11] But if Spener's desire to revive Christian piety led him toward an Orthodox understanding of salvation, his roots in Lutheranism prevented him from moving very far. Luther's doctrine of imputed righteousness, according to which the elect play no role in their salvation but instead are made righteous by faith-alone, meant that a belief in man's deifying participation in the life of God would never flourish within pietism. The experience of conversion became the most important element in the faith.

Spener's ecclesiology carried him even further away from traditional Christianity than did his concept of piety. To combat the decadence (as he saw it) of reformational Christianity, he created a system of "little churches within the church" (*ecclesiae in ecclesia*) that diffused confessional identity. Accordingly, liturgy and the sacraments played much less of a role in these

---

11 K. James Stein, "Philipp Jakob Spener," in *The Pietist Theologians*, ed. Carter Lindberg (Oxford: Blackwell, 2005), 84–99.

churches than did Bible reading and spiritual conversation. Pietism became profoundly individualistic.

And for this reason it served the ongoing reformation of Christendom. It is not a coincidence that hymnography flourished within pietist circles, for the new birth was stimulated by a fusion of affective poetry and stirring melodies. Luther himself had set an example with his "A Mighty Fortress Is Our God," the tune for which he picked up in a local tavern. Spener's own godson Nicholas Zinzendorf (d. 1760), the patron and cofounder of the Church of the Moravian Brethren, composed hymns that were even more emotional and introspective.

Pietism's most famous musical advocate was Johann Sebastian Bach (d. 1750). Raised within the Lutheran Church and the longtime composer for Saint Thomas Church in Leipzig, he was the first in a sequence of four great composers—all of them German—who, between the quattrocento and twentieth century, profoundly changed the course of music history. Bach's style is known as Baroque and shares the same penchant for ornamentation and attention-grabbing detail that characterized the new architecture of Rome. Also of significance is the fact that the great Protestant composer—like the Jesuits—used the liturgical arts to evangelize the saeculum. Here pietism offered a more powerful model than earlier hymns from the Lutheran mainstream. Bach's texts served to convert an individual's heart more than establishing him within a confessional church. Jaroslav Pelikan noted that in Bach's compositions a major role was played by the pietist method of personal conversion, "in which the contemplation of the sufferings of Christ by the individual Christian heart was intended to reawaken the awareness of sin as the debt for which so horrendous a price had been exacted."[12] In this sense, Bach took his place within the same stavrocentric culture that had given rise to the *Dies irae* but had dismayed humanists like Petrarch for so many centuries. But if anthropological pessimism colored his liturgical works, warm melodies and dazzling ornamentation set them far apart from the culture that preceded them.

---

12 Jaroslav Pelikan, *Bach among the Theologians* (Philadelphia: Fortress Press, 1986), 62.

Johann Sebastian Bach

There are far too many examples of Bach's debt to pietism to summarize here. One example offered by Pelikan is the aria from the *Saint John Passion*, "Ponder well" ("*Erwaege wie*"), in which the colors of Jesus' bloodstained back are likened to a rainbow in the sky after the deluge of man's sins has showered down upon it. Another example is the cantata *It Is Enough* (*Ich habe genug*), which ends with the aria:

> *With gladness I look forward to my death*
> *(Ah, if only it had already come!).*
> *Then shall I escape all despair,*
> *That still enslaves me now on earth.*

More famous though less unique to pietism is the exquisite aria "Have mercy, my God" ("*Erbarme dich mein Gott*") from the *Saint Matthew Passion*. Accompanied by a solo violin, its simple but melodically piercing lament is surely one of the most beautiful hymns ever composed. But by linking the solo singer's alto voice to the violin, it moved much further than earlier liturgical music in the direction of highly sophisticated and technically challenging methods of performance.

Lutheranism was not the only Protestant faith in which the pietist impulse toward individualism and detachment from traditional ecclesiology was felt. In the Church of England, a similar dissatisfaction with institutional Christianity accompanied the resolution of the Puritan movement. One particularly discontented believer was John Wesley (d. 1791). With his brother Charles, he established at Oxford University a group known by critics as the "holy club," the intention of which was to intensify piety as a "little church within the church." After an abortive mission to the colony of Georgia, Wesley had a conversion experience in 1738 while praying with a group of Moravian Brethren in London.

This led him to assert three claims about what he considered true Christianity. First, as Spener had emphasized, true believers must experience a "new birth" after being baptized as infants. Second, the nature of their conversion experience was so pivotal that the cultivation of it became a key element in salvation. They could not simply adhere to the doctrines and fulfill the obligations of the institutional church to which they belonged. It was necessary to follow a practical "method" of life which would lead, even now in this world, to an experience of heavenly transformation.

Here Wesley found inspiration in the writings of Makarios of Egypt, whose early practice of monasticism was directed toward the experience of deification. This set Wesley apart from earlier Protestant fathers, who inherited a forensic understanding of salvation from their Roman Catholic predecessors. Calvin, the most extreme among them, expressed an Augustinian aversion to free will and the cooperation of the elect with God. Wesley self-consciously rejected this pessimistic view of man, falling back on a doctrine called Arminianism that affirmed the believer's cooperation with God. This therapeutic understanding of salvation was, as several scholars have noted, much closer to that of the Orthodox Church.[1]

1 Randy L. Maddox, "John Wesley and Eastern Orthodoxy: Influences, Convergences, and Differences," *Ashbury Theological Journal* 45:2 (1990): 29–53.

Wesley's ecclesiology, however, was not. Like Spener, his effort to correct the perceived shortcomings of reformational Christianity led him to a third claim that salvation is predominantly an individualistic event. To be sure, worship and the sacraments remained important elements in Methodism (as the new denomination he founded later named itself), and emotionally charged hymns—especially those composed by his brother Charles—became classics of Protestant Christendom. But his practice of ordaining clergy while only a priest, without episcopal authority, defied traditional Christianity.

The fruits of Wesley's innovations were stunning. Tens of thousands flocked to hear him preach in open fields. In no time at all he was surrounded by other evangelists. Among them was George Whitefield (d. 1770), who had been an early member of the Wesleys' Oxford circle and had even followed John to America. Back in England, however, he broke from his mentor. John's embracing of Arminianism, with its stigma of the ancient Pelagian heresy against which Augustine had so tenaciously fought, was too much for him. Whitefield asserted Calvinism in its most vigorous forms and now attacked Wesley for backpedaling predestinarianism.

So, as soon as the West indicated an interest in the long-forgotten East, an instinctual pessimism again intervened. And as it did so, another schism was spawned. Whitefield's theological disagreements with the Wesleys gave rise to a Calvinist variant of Methodism and the creation of a rival church. Within a century no fewer than nine Methodist denominations existed in England. In America, the number rose to more than two dozen.

The British colonies were fertile soil for pietism. A second missionary journey there by Whitefield in 1740 marks the beginning of the most important event in the history of American Christendom after the landing of the Mayflower. At the time it was dubbed the Great Awakening, a term still favored by historians. Yet what it was that awoke is difficult to measure. In some ways, it was another stage in the long decline of traditional Christianity in the West.

As we have seen, by the end of the seventeenth century Puritanism had become a spent force in New England. Calvinism, however, remained alive and well. It was the theology of choice among preachers who saw the "errand in the wilderness" wandering into oblivion like beleaguered settlers in the forests of the Connecticut Valley. King Philip's War (1675–1678), which represented the first conflict with Indians that colonists fought without British support, had wiped out a large number of New England's towns and militias. The Puritan Samuel Torrey, who has been called America's first evangelical, composed a sermon the year of the peace treaty entitled, significantly, *The Necessity of the Pouring Out of the Spirit from on High upon a Sinning and Apostatizing People.*

Reformation, to be sure, was still in the New England air. But instead of being the city on a hill that promised enlightenment to the rest of Christendom, Americans had become a people who were themselves sitting in darkness and the shadow of death. Standing foremost in the minds of preachers was the ambiguous situation caused by the Halfway Covenant. Too many congregants were simply indifferent to sainthood as defined by the Calvinist divines. A program of "covenant renewal" was introduced to revive the flagging reformation, but for several decades the most zealous preachers had little to show for it.

Then in 1734, something remarkable occurred. In the Massachusetts town of Northampton, located on the right bank of the Connecticut River, a wave of spiritual conversions began. The local preacher was Jonathan Edwards (d. 1758), and by the time he published his account of the events, dozens of other towns and hundreds of saints had experienced the new birth of pietism. When asked to explain how this had happened, he admitted he did not know. He admitted that some of the enthusiasm may have been spurious. He also acknowledged that in a few cases the initial spell of holiness had given way to demonic despair. And in at least one case—that of his own uncle—conversion was followed by suicide. But on balance, he claimed, a great revival had unquestionably occurred.

Edwards's *A Faithful Narrative of the Surprising Work of God in the Conversion of Many Hundred Souls in Northampton* was published in London in 1737 and became an instant sensation. John Wesley, fresh from his abortive visit to America and the conversion experience that followed, devoured a copy.

Jonathan Edwards

Whitefield did the same. Edwards's publishers in England had prefaced the work with a breathless statement that nothing "since the first ages of Christianity" demonstrated so surely the readiness of God to spread His kingdom "through all the nations of the earth."[2] In a flash of divine grace, America

2 Thomas S. Kidd, *The Great Awakening: The Roots of Evangelical Christianity in Colonial America* (New Haven: Yale University, 2007), 22.

went from being a nation of apostates to the restored, and reformational, city on a hill.

And so American Christendom "awoke." The revival reached a peak in 1740. That was the year that Whitefield himself returned to the colonies to conduct a preaching tour of the entire Atlantic coast. Screaming and gesticulating in his signature form of oratory, the short, corpulent, cross-eyed second father of Methodism stirred the hearts of his audiences to the breaking point. As crowds wailed and wept, thousands submitted to the new birth.

Other "new lights" of the reformation joined in. Gilbert Tennent preached an audacious sermon in Pennsylvania that was widely disseminated, partly through the press of a young Benjamin Franklin. Entitled "The Danger of an Unconverted Ministry," the sermon suggested that the vast majority of America's clergy was unregenerate, that is, reprobate. Whitefield had already provoked dismay in the clerical establishment by advocating itinerant preaching without regard for local episcopal permission. Tennent now urged congregants to shun ministers who failed to stir their thirst for conversion. Such "dead dogs that can't bark" were worthless, even if they had been canonically ordained.[3] Everything seemed to depend on the emotions.

In 1741, the most famous sermon of the Great Awakening was delivered by Edwards in the Connecticut town of Enfield. Entitled "Sinners in the Hands of an Angry God," it threw every reserve of the master preacher's oratorical skill into the effort to terrify listeners and open their hearts to conversion. In Perry Miller's insightful words, the sermon "slowly, with implacable slowness, coils a monstrous accusation against mankind, until the bow of God's wrath is bent and the arrow justifiably aimed at the entrails of the race."[4] Then Edwards lets the arrow fly.

The "vengeance of God," he declares in the opening sentence, hangs over the human race—and especially over those who, like the Israelites of old, have been made God's elect people through no good works of their own. Edwards presents a perfectly Calvinistic God whose "sovereign pleasure" and "arbitrary will" loom over the audience assembled. For sinners

3 Ibid, 60.
4 Perry Miller, *Jonathan Edwards* (Toronto: William Sloane, 1949), 145.

are now the objects of that very same anger and wrath of God that is expressed in the torments of hell: and the reason why they don't go down to hell at each moment, is not because God, in whose power they are, is not then very angry with them. . . . Yea God is a great deal more angry with great numbers that are now on earth, yea doubtless, with many that are now in this congregation, that it may be are at ease and quiet, than he is with many of those that are now in the flames of hell.

And speaking of flames, Edwards proceeds with graphic imagery to describe the depths of hell. He seems to apply the new philosophy of Locke in doing so, for in his description he does not speak of innate ideas of punishment but of empirical sensations that his listeners would recognize from the experience of a common kitchen hearth. "The wrath of God burns against them . . . the pit is prepared, the fire is made ready, the furnace is now hot, ready to receive them, the flames do now rage and glow."

Having stoked the fears of his audience to a peak of intensity, Edwards then springs on them his most famous empirical image.

The God that holds you over the pit of Hell, much as one holds a spider, or some loathsome insect, over the fire, abhors you, and is dreadfully provoked; his wrath towards you burns like fire; he looks upon you as worthy of nothing else, but to be cast into the fire; he is of purer eyes than to bear to have you in his sight; you are ten thousand times so abominable in his eyes as the most hateful venomous serpent is in ours.

Back in Locke's native land, John Wesley would have been appalled by Edwards's sermon. For in addition to learning from Makarios of Egypt, pietism's greatest critic of Calvin also delighted in the writings of the Eastern father Isaac of Syria. The principal import of these writings was that God is merciful and that His disciples, like Him, weep when they behold even the most loathsome of creatures—venomous reptiles and even the demons themselves—in a state of suffering.

Not so the Calvinist Edwards. As he reaches the conclusion of his most famous sermon, he assures his listeners that, when they are in hell,

> *God will have no other use to put you to but only to suffer misery; you shall be continued in being to no other end; for you will be a vessel of wrath fitted to destruction; and there will be no other use of this vessel but only to be filled full of wrath: God will be so far from pitying you when you cry to him, that 'tis said he will only laugh and mock.*[5]

Deism

IF PIETISM WAS REPLACING REFORMATIONAL Christianity among Christendom's remaining believers, a new religion called deism repudiated Christianity altogether. It drew on modern philosophy and science to offer an alternative faith in a time of confessional collapse.

In many ways deism brought to completion the restless efforts of the quattrocento humanists. Ficino, as we saw in chapter two, was not content with Christianity in its Roman Catholic form. He had learned too much from Petrarch's penitential agonies. A new faith was needed, he felt, something that would liberate man from the fetters of Augustinianism. The incongruous result was what Peter Gay called "pagan Christianity."[6] Christianity was on the surface preserved, but its content became increasingly the philosophies of Plato and Cicero. The Platonic Academy of Florence provided the earliest form of deism. By appropriating Neoplatonism, Ficino and other humanists like Pico recreated the human race in an entirely new image. Man was still a creature of God, but one who gains his dignity through the autonomous management of his passions and the cosmos around him.

Such an anthropology had been dimly foreseen by Ficino's paganophile Greek teachers, who in very different but equally confusing cultural circumstances, owing to the immanent fall of Constantinople, had seized on

5 *Sinners in the Hands of an Angry God and Other Puritan Sermons*, ed. David Dutkanicz (Mineola, NY: Dover, 2005), 171–84.

6 Peter Gay, *The Enlightenment: The Rise of Modern Paganism* (New York: Alfred A. Knopf, 1967), 256.

anything other than traditional Christianity. It was only Gregory Palamas and hesychasts like Mark of Ephesus who had resisted the lure of Neoplatonism. For them, man's dignification depended on sacramental communion with the New Adam, the incarnate Christ, not on the appropriation of the myth of Prometheus. The difference was between paradise and utopia.

But the promethean vision of humanism required more than a dissatisfaction with traditional Christianity. It could only assume religious proportions when the prevailing faith of Christendom was discredited by its reformational quarrels and the wars of Western religion. The seventeenth century provided a crucible for the new faith that had eluded the quattrocento humanists. By the end of that century, many intellectuals had finished with the claims of reformational Christianity in its Roman Catholic and Protestant forms. And as we have seen, two new developments in philosophy and science had appeared during the century to offer a truly humanistic faith.

Deism was based in part on the rationalism of Descartes. The father of modern philosophy had looked within his reasoning powers to find a basis on which to build faith in a deity. He could not, as we have seen, wholeheartedly embrace the Roman Catholic Church to which he belonged—neither her sacramental life nor her doctrinal tradition. These had been called into question by the challenge of Protestantism. Natural reason seemed the only resource on which a believer could depend.

Newton was the second inspiration for deism. Applying the scientific method of Bacon, he had demonstrated that natural laws govern the world. A deity had of course put these in place through an act of creation, but he saw communion with this deity as a matter of secondary importance. In fact, Newton's mechanical model of the universe inclined some to view the deity as a kind of watchmaker who, in the moment of creation, had fitted the cosmos with a mainspring—the laws of nature—and then left it to run forever under its own autonomy.

Deism depended on the apparent triumph of rationalism. Reason itself had of course long served to articulate the truths of Christianity. But in the wake of the Great Division, the distinction between faith and reason had grown in emphasis. Anselm of Canterbury famously formulated this with his slogan of "faith seeking understanding." The scholastics that followed him made faith and reason even more distinct from one another. In reaction, Luther adopted a position that would come to be known as *fideism* (from *fide*, the Latin for "faith"). It asserted that natural reason is totally incapable of serving faith and is often an idolatrous rival to it. Calvin largely endorsed this view, eager as he was at all times to expose the fundamentally depraved condition of the human mind.

The growing rivalry between faith and reason was partially resolved by a group of Huguenot theologians living in Dutch exile at the end of the seventeenth century. Breaking from the more extreme position of Calvin, they argued that Protestantism would only be victorious when reason replaced what they considered the superstitions of the Roman Catholics. Without reason, they warned, the doctrinal conflicts behind the wars of Western religion could never be healed.

Their confidence was gravely shaken, however, when a fellow Frenchman named Pierre Bayle (d. 1706) declared a complete and final division of faith and reason. Bayle was indeed a product of the age of division. Born to a Huguenot family in France, he was denied the solid education his intelligence deserved by anti-Protestant legislation. But as a youth he converted to Roman Catholicism and thereby obtained a scholarship to study at a Jesuit university. Upon completion, he promptly reverted to Protestantism and fled to Geneva (apostasy was still a criminal offense in France). Ultimately, he settled in Europe's haven of nonconformists, Holland. Though he was safe himself, his brother was imprisoned back in France and later died from the ordeal.

In the meantime, Bayle published a famous work of freethinking entitled *Historical and Critical Dictionary*. It was soon denounced by those Huguenots who had worked so hard to employ reason as a weapon against Roman Catholic superstition. Bayle's Christian faith, however, had by now been broken by the division of Western Christendom and personal misfortune. The *Dictionary* was a record of this. In three copious volumes it demonstrated innumerable ways in which traditional Christian theology was rationally inconsistent. It presented fideism—faith based on individual and often nonrational assumptions—as being the only philosophically consistent basis for belief. In contrast to Anselm's slogan, then, faith no longer sought understanding and had no need of it. The divorce earlier threatened by Luther and Descartes was now final.

Less radical views of the relationship between faith and reason were advanced in England, and it was there that deism would make its first appearance. Empiricism had opened up a new way of looking on revelation from a purely rational point of view. Locke led the way in this, having rubbed shoulders with the likes of Bayle in Holland as an exile there himself. During the Glorious Revolution he was able to return to England and helped formulate the political principles of its newly founded constitutional monarchy with his famous *Two Treatises of Government.* Locke was strongly in favor of the granting of religious toleration, something Bayle had also advocated after the revocation of the Edict of Nantes.

Locke wrote a *Letter Concerning Toleration* to support the innovative principle. Until this time, the claims of Christianity to an objective truth meant that states regarded religious uniformity—irrespective of the individual consciences of their subjects—as a necessary foundation for the social order. Bayle and Locke were some of the first to reject such legal obligations. More importantly, Locke's *The Reasonableness of Christianity* established a new basis for the Christian faith. Gone was the Church as the mystical body of Christ. Gone was the apostolic tradition that she bore throughout the course of history. Gone was the Holy Spirit who lived within her as the source and confirmation of the faith. Christianity, Locke claimed, consisted simply of the doctrines that natural reason confirmed within any truly autonomous mind. Divine revelation and even God Himself were totally secondary in importance.

Locke's optimistic religious epistemology—his belief that the autonomy of natural reason was the real basis of religion—inspired a series of works in the years that followed. As we have seen, Bayle's *Dictionary* had introduced to the West a new way of thinking about religion. One of its articles employed the word *deism* to describe a religious philosophy in which specific revelation is rejected but belief in a higher power is not. Only a year after Locke's

Voltaire

treatise on Christian rationalism, John Toland (d. 1722) published *Christianity Not Mysterious* to elaborate this new doctrine. It argued that nothing that is worthy of assent in the Christian religion requires more than reason to affirm. This did two things. First, it gave license to the growing body of Cartesian skeptics who found this or that element of traditional Christianity intellectually untenable. Second, it justified the confessional agnosticism that had come to afflict a religiously war-torn civilization. For instance, one could jettison all doctrines about the presence of Christ in the Eucharist—which none of the reformational faiths could agree on in any case—and still call himself a Christian.

Another important British deist was Matthew Tindal (d. 1733). In *Christianity as Old as the Creation,* he presented a religion that, like the *prisca theologia* of quattrocento humanists, preexisted the Bible. In fact, he claimed traditional Christianity was in many ways an accumulation of superstitions that, when stripped away, revealed an original core of pristine moral reasoning. According to Tindal, true religion is purely natural and divine revelation is irrelevant.

The eighteenth-century deists who built on Locke's empiricism were not all British. The most famous, in fact, was the Frenchman who went by the name Voltaire (d. 1778). He was born in 1694, and like many a millennial born three centuries later, his values were determined by the spectacle of a consuming conflict that took place a half-century before his birth. Instead of the horrors of Nazism, however, he looked back on the horrors of militant confessionalism. From an early age Voltaire fostered an avid interest in the history that produced the Thirty Years War. It taught him to hate Christianity. His early literary works were critical of the Roman Catholic Church and the French monarchy that supported her. His caustic attacks on both earned him a year in the Bastille—the notorious political prison in central Paris. Voltaire was later exiled to London, where he moved in philosophical circles and breathed the air of the aristocracy. He soon became an Anglophile. The two great achievements of the English, in his opinion, were religious toleration and Newtonian physics. He imported both to France on his return.

In his study of this period, the historian Ernst Cassirer stated that "the concept of original sin is the common opponent against which all the different trends of the philosophy of the Enlightenment join forces."[7] This was certainly true of Voltaire's most famous work, the short novel *Candide.* If one reads it closely, one can see it as a retelling of the Christian account of

7 Ernst Cassirer, *The Philosophy of the Enlightenment*, trans. Fritz C. A. Koelln and James P. Pettegrove (Princeton: Princeton University, 1951), 141.

paradise and the history of the world after the Fall. Yet the novel does not contain a single affirmation of heavenly immanence. Original sin is traced to man's refusal to think autonomously and his resulting tendency toward superstition.

Candide's narrative opens, significantly, in a garden of delight. There its eponymous protagonist enjoys a moment of intimacy with his paramour (a scenario the perpetually unmarried Voltaire had himself lived out on numerous occasions). But his bliss soon ends when a vengeful father discovers the lovers and casts them out of the garden. From there, the story proceeds from one unnecessary misfortune to another, documenting the misery of the human condition about which Pope Innocent and other representatives of reformational Christianity had had so much to say. But instead of blaming man's depravity, the author sees Christianity as the source of sorrow. The reader accompanies Candide through a Christendom at war with itself over ridiculous doctrinal disagreements. In one memorable scene the Spanish Inquisition is featured. Voltaire describes the infamous *auto-da-fe*, whose macabre outcome is cheerfully linked to the celebration of the Mass and the singing of a beautiful setting of the *Miserere*.

In contrast to the horrors of Christendom, the novel also presents a peaceful utopia called El Dorado. Like the happy "nowheres" of More and Bacon, Voltaire locates his utopia not in Europe but in the Americas. There men live in harmony with one another. Religious conflict is unthinkable. They have little interest in wealth and even less in the sacramental worship of God. "We do not pray to Him," explains one inhabitant. "We have nothing to ask of Him; He has given us all we need, and we return Him thanks without ceasing."[8] Voltaire's utopians are self-sufficient with no need of divine participation. They are much nearer the goal of human fulfillment than the members of Christendom. "Alas," declares the hero after returning to his homeland, "how much better it would have been for me to have remained in the paradise of El Dorado than to come back to this cursed Europe!"[9]

Unlike the biblical narrative it parallels, the novel does not culminate

---

8 Voltaire, *Candide* (New York: Dover, 1991), 44.

9 Ibid, 66.

Jean-Jacques Rousseau

with a restoration of paradise. Salvation for Candide is the realization that there is no deity that cares about man's condition on earth and that the only rational response is to make the world a happier place within which to live. The hero asks a dervish he encounters for wisdom into the reason man suffers—something Leibniz's *Theodicy*, in Voltaire's judgment, had gotten completely wrong. Indeed, that book had been conceived in reaction to the enormous and apparently random suffering caused by the deadly Lisbon earthquake of 1755. Rather than optimism about providential love—which for Leibniz ensured the best of all possible worlds—the pagan sage speaks to Candide of divine indifference. "When his highness sends a ship to Egypt," he asks, "does he trouble his head whether the mice on board are at their ease or not?"[10] In other words, the deity who created the world and placed man at its center has absolutely no interest in any of it.

This deistic conviction brings a closure to the novel's repudiation of Christian cosmology. It represents, for its apostate Roman Catholic author, an eighteenth-century resolution of Petrarch's fourteenth-century agony over divine absence. Candide, now finally "enlightened" by deism, famously announces in the final sentence, "Let us cultivate our garden." That is, let man, severed forever from divine communion, become the sole master of his destiny.

In terms of artistry and rhetorical power, the only rival to Voltaire in advancing eighteenth-century deism was his fellow Frenchman and intellectual sparring partner Jean-Jacques Rousseau (d. 1778). These two intellectual titans spent almost as much time battling one another as they did combating Christian culture. For instance, when Rousseau published a critique of the aristocratic culture to which Voltaire was so attached, praising instead the primitive conditions of American natives, the latter wrote a sarcastic reply:

> *I have received your new book against the human race and thank you for it. Never was such cleverness used in the design of making us all stupid. One longs upon reading your book to walk on all fours. But as I have lost that habit for more than sixty years, I feel unhappily the impossibility of renewing it.*[11]

There was a work that received Voltaire's praise, however—or at least a section of a work. The book was entitled *Emile,* and it was Rousseau's vision of a new method of education that would cancel forever the influence of

10 Ibid, 86.

11 Quoted in Frank Pierrepont Graves, *Great Educators of Three Centuries* (New York: Macmillan, 1912), 85.

Christianity in the West. The section Voltaire enjoyed was its famous digression called "The Profession of Faith of the Savoyard Vicar."

This discourse is one of the most winsome cases for deism ever written. It opens with the teacher disarmingly assuring his charge that "I do not want to argue with you or even attempt to convince you."[12] As coercion and threats can never be the basis for moral formation, neither can manipulation. An eighteenth-century reader would immediately have contrasted such wisdom with the militant evangelism of reformational Christianity. As for teaching itself, even that is an act of love rather than pedagogy. "Always remember," the vicar states, "that I am not teaching my sentiment; I am revealing it."[13]

The vicar's most important revelation is "natural religion." He contrasts it not only with the dogmas of Christianity but with its morality and worship. "The greatest ideas of the divinity come to us from reason alone."[14] Here he joins other humanists in advancing in an almost slogan-like way the principle that faith—and certainly faith-alone—is the source of all darkness. Reason-alone, on the other hand, enables a mind to admire the world as a mechanism created by a great though remote divine mechanic. "I am like a man," the vicar exclaims, "who saw a watch opened for the first time and, although he did not know the machine's use and had not seen the dial, was not prevented from admiring the work."[15] All that man needs to guide him in virtue and fulfillment is natural reason and a conscience uncomplicated by dogma or revelation.

Deism rose to prominence during the course of the eighteenth century and represented the religious battle line for the humanists' assault on Christianity. But it was never more than a temporary position from which to advance to higher ground. In the following century, it would evolve into atheism. Nevertheless, under fire from deism's partisans, some of the final territories of Christendom's paradisiacal culture had now been captured and placed under the flag of utopia.

---

12 Jean-Jacques Rousseau, *Emile: Or, on Education*, trans. Allan Bloom (New York: Basic Books, 1979), 266.

13 Ibid, 277.

14 Ibid, 295.

15 Ibid, 275.

CHAPTER SIX

Benightenment

IN OUR TIMES IT IS always assumed and often argued that secularism is what carried the West away from a religious culture, serving as the agent rather than the outcome of historical change. A secularization thesis claims that nonreligious values will progressively supplant Christianity (and all other religions), and that this process began in the eighteenth century with a movement most historians call the Enlightenment.

Often unnoticed is the fact that this term, coined by advocates of secularization and uncritically perpetuated by popular culture, was itself appropriated from Christianity. It was the Church that originally used the language of illumination, declaring that Jesus Christ is the "light of the world." The world, which long "sat in the shadow of darkness," has because of the Incarnation "seen a great light." Because the Church is the body of Christ and His mystical presence on earth, she becomes also the "light of the world." By proclaiming the gospel, she brings about the transformation of the world and is the only true measure of its enlightenment.

The eighteenth-century intellectuals who were pleased to call themselves *philosophes* ("philosophers") seized on such symbolism even as they repudiated the gospel. They considered Christianity a cause of blindness, not illumination. For them, Petrarch's condemnation of Christian culture as *tenebrae*, "darkness," replaced the Incarnation as a new starting point in the history of the West. Filled with indignation, they set out to abolish the influence of Christianity with the confidence that doing so would open the way to the secular counterfeit of paradise, utopia.

Anti-Evangelism

IN A FAMOUS STUDY NEARLY a century ago, the historian Carl Becker turned common assumptions about this project on their head. *The Heavenly City of the Eighteenth-Century Philosophers,* published in 1932, revealed that in a movement that expressly sought the radical secularization of the West, there were many religious and even quasi-Christian themes. Alluding to Augustine's model of a distant and future paradise in the *City of God,* Becker proposed that the advocates of secularization were really "nearer the middle ages, less emancipated from the preconceptions of medieval Christian thought, than they quite realized or we have commonly supposed."[16] Such men, he claimed, "demolished the Heavenly City of St. Augustine only to rebuild it with more up-to-date materials."[17]

While Becker's assessment is counterintuitive and today accepted only conditionally, it brilliantly captures the manifest zeal men like Voltaire had for reforming the beliefs and values of Christendom. They approached their project not as the mere rationalists they are often presented as being but as men invested in the cultural transformation of the West. And in this they showed themselves heirs to the transformational imperative in its reformational mode. The desire to reform their civilization and its supporting culture was as much an influence on their activities as the science and philosophy they employed to justify it. Intellectual heirs of Isaac Newton and John Locke, they were at the same time moral heirs of Gregory VII and John Calvin. Perhaps more so. For like the leaders of reformational Christianity, whether Roman Catholic or Protestant, these eighteenth-century secularists

---

16 Carl L. Becker, *The Heavenly City of the Eighteenth-Century Philosophers* (New Haven: Yale University, 1932), 29.

17 Ibid, 31.

"were not primarily interested in stabilizing society, but in changing it."[18]

Yet it is of course incontestable that the eighteenth century produced an unprecedented attack on Christianity—greater than any since the days of pagandom. And it is equally incontestable that this attack issued from the estrangement of otherwise principled and morally idealistic members of Christendom who were seeking the transformation of the world. Scandalized by the wars of Western religion and the acrimony of reformational Christianity, they could not fulfill the transformational imperative through heavenly means. In their indignation, they turned their moral zeal toward a saeculum surrendered by reformational Christianity.

The eighteenth-century attack on Christianity was a culture war in which intellectual commanders known as *philosophes* ("philosophers") marshalled support from cadres of disaffected literati. Voltaire, in some ways the commander-in-chief, was continuously writing letters to his followers urging them to take more vigorous action against the religious establishment. "Strike, and hide your hand," he wrote to one literary collaborator. "I hope that every year each of our fraternity will aim some arrows at the monster, without its learning from whose hand they came."[19] By "monster," he meant Christianity.

This militant brotherhood fought on a variety of fronts. The most memorable was undoubtedly the *Encyclopedia*. Edited by Denis Diderot (d. 1784) and Jean D'Alembert (d. 1783), the work was a massive undertaking, like nothing that had gone before it. It drew heavily on the new science and philosophy to make its arguments against Christianity. Between 1751 and 1772, it generated more than seventy thousand articles on virtually all subjects of knowledge.

In some ways the *Encyclopedia* was an *anti-evangelion*, a body of writings designed to refute the gospel (*evangelion* in Greek) and replace it with an alternative standard of "good news." This was no easy thing to do in a period when censorship protected the public from what was considered blasphemy

18 Ibid, 97.

19 Quoted in Will and Ariel Durant, *The Story of Civilization, Volume IX: The Age of Voltaire* (New York: Simon and Schuster, 2011), 126.

The frontispiece of the Encyclopedia *depicts Truth on high between Reason and Imagination. Below this group are speculative philosophers, and below them artists.*

and indecency. In fact, publication was shut down more than once, and the authors were compelled to cloak their views within the appearance of respect for the faith. An article on "Christianity," for instance, was because of its prominence carefully written by Diderot to avoid any controversy. Other articles on more obscure topics, however, were designed to sow doubts about the faith. One simply entitled "Priests" subtly subverted the reputation of the Roman Catholic clergy by using the pagan priesthood for its content. Articles on topics like "God" would draw the reader into noncontroversial details only to direct him to related articles such as "Demonstration" which, as Will and Ariel Durant put it, "laid down principles of evidence lethal to miracles and myths."[20] The censorship could scarcely keep up with the subterfuges, and thousands of readers closed the *Encyclopedia* a good deal more skeptical about Christianity than when they had opened it.

Other fronts were more public. In 1761 a young convert from Protestantism to Roman Catholicism was found hanged in his parents' home in Toulouse. The father, a Huguenot named Jean Calas, was arrested on suspicion of killing his son in a religiously induced rage against France's majority faith. A Roman Catholic mob demanded retribution. The fact that Calas's maid, herself a Roman Catholic, declared his innocence mattered little. He was ultimately found guilty and condemned by the local officials. His sentence included ceremonial torture in the public square, during which each of his limbs was pulled out of its socket and then shattered with iron bars. Somehow, Calas survived the ordeal long enough to be finished off by the executioner by strangling.

Voltaire, on hearing of the episode, "let loose the loudest and most sustained cry of his whole career."[21] For him, one of two equally appalling examples of religious violence had been committed. Either the verdict was justified and Jean Calas's Calvinism had led him to commit filicide; or it was a travesty and the Roman Catholic tribunal had put an innocent man to death in order to satisfy popular fanaticism. Voltaire threw himself into an

---

20 Ibid, 109.

21 Alfred Owen Aldridge, *Voltaire and the Century of Light* (Princeton: Princeton University, 1975), 297.

investigation of the matter and, concluding the latter scenario had occurred, obtained a highly publicized exoneration of Calas.

Publications like the *Encyclopedia* and public actions like the Calas investigation earned the philosophes a reputation as advocates of skepticism and enemies of superstition. And so they were. But theirs was really an attack on one particular form of religion—that cultivated in the West since the Great Schism. To read their innumerable accusations against Christianity is to be confronted with the record of uniquely Roman Catholic and Protestant doctrines and abuses. The Orthodoxy of the first millennium, while not exempt from attack, was a much smaller issue for them. A few examples of their anti-evangelical campaigns will illustrate this.

Voltaire was fond of using a slogan he invented when signing his name to letters. It was "Crush Infamy!" (*Ecrasez l'infame!*). By all accounts, the infamy in question was Christianity in the historical forms with which he as a Frenchman was familiar. When he spoke of it, he often had in mind the religious violence that was a unique feature of the new Christendom but not of the old. For instance, in *Candide*, nearly every instance of cruelty represents a facet of reformational Christianity since the Great Division.

Crusades, unknown until introduced by Pope Urban II at the end of the eleventh century, are frequently in the background of Voltaire's narrative. Heretics, first systematically persecuted by Innocent III in the Albigensian Crusade, are a focal point of undeserved suffering. The Spanish Inquisition, featured in the unforgettable scene involving baroque liturgical chant, was the direct outcome of that crusade. Jews, persecuted widely in the West since the time of the crusades, are burned to appease the capricious deity who, according to the Roman Catholic clergy, caused the Lisbon earthquake. Battles are fought between Roman Catholics and Protestants. And members of Protestant sects such as the character James the Anabaptist are themselves unjustly targeted for abuse. Throughout all of this, it is unbridled clericalism—another outcome of the Papal Reformation—that receives the author's most biting satire.

Voltaire's war on the infamy of reformational Christianity only intensified after the publication of *Candide*. During his final years he lived in the town of Ferney on the French side of the Rhone River opposite Geneva. His chateau there became a pilgrimage site for secularists and one of Europe's principal centers of antireligious propaganda. From this "factory" of pamphlets and sermons (as one historian describes it) he brought attention to those features of Christianity that were particularly associated with reformational disputes.[22] For instance, in his sarcastic and intentionally blasphemous way, he ridiculed the main parties of the sixteenth-century eucharistic dispute whose positions we reviewed in chapter three: "The Catholics profess that they eat God and not bread, the Lutherans eat both God and bread, the Calvinists eat bread but not God."[23]

Other members of the anti-evangelical brotherhood also emphasized the specifically Western features of what they considered a corrupt Christianity. Violence was the favored vice. Diderot, who approvingly nicknamed Voltaire his "dear Antichrist," concocted a playful myth about the origins of religion. It featured a misanthrope who so hates humanity that he withdraws from it to live in a cave. But unable to shake his hatred for the race to which he belongs, he decides one day to curse it by releasing a poison called religion. Emerging from his hermitage, he baits his neighbors with the formerly unknown name of "God." And from the moment this "abominable name" is uttered, Diderot sneers, the human race began "to argue, to hate each other, and to cut one another's throats."[24] Yet violence sometimes appeared the only means by which utopia could be achieved. In another passage the editor of the *Encyclopedia* notoriously declared that human happiness would remain elusive until such time as "the last king is strangled with the entrails of the last priest."

The philosophes did not limit their attacks to only Western expressions of the faith, of course. As their enemy fled in disarray, they pursued him into his most ancient strongholds. The Bible and early miracle accounts offered favorable battlefields for their rationalism. Voltaire never tired of mocking

---

22 Paul Hazard, *European Thought in the Eighteenth Century*, trans. J. Lewis May (New York: Meridian Books, 1963), 412.

23 Durant, *Age of Voltaire*, 127.

24 Peter Gay, *The Enlightenment: Age of Voltaire*, 372.

the scriptures and using the record of violence in the Old Testament to delegitimate the gospel of love. One of his more notable parodies is of the genealogy of Jesus, where he uses the Old Testament to trace not who "begat" whom but who "assassinated" whom.

Like Scripture, the place of miracles in traditional Christianity was selected for special ridicule. It was contrasted to the cosmology of modern science. The concept of the watchmaker deity inspired by Newton suggested that every event in the natural world had a natural and not a supernatural cause. To think otherwise was "unenlightened." Paul-Henri Holbach (d. 1789) wrote a treatise entitled *System of Nature*, which declared the world entirely free of heavenly immanence. "Men have completely failed to see," the atheist complained, "that this nature, lacking both good and evil intentions, merely acts in accordance with necessary and immutable laws when it creates and destroys living things."[25] Miracles therefore had no place in Western Christendom's new cosmology. As the atheist David Hume (d. 1776) wryly put it in his *Enquiry Concerning Human Understanding*, "We may conclude that the Christian religion not only was at first attended with miracles, but even at this day cannot be believed by any reasonable person without one."[26]

A New Vision of History

DESPITE THESE AND MANY OTHER attacks on Christianity in general, the philosophes were always drawn to its Western forms in particular. First and foremost, they hoped to dismantle Augustinianism. They were not, of course, the first to do so. As we have seen, the humanist project had originally been propelled by a reaction to the pessimistic view of man that Augustine's doctrine of grace and original sin entailed. Cut off from the East after the Great Division, Western Christendom had experienced an atrophying of its formerly paradisiacal culture as Augustinianism came more and more to preponderate.

---

25 Norman Hampson, *The Enlightenment: An Evaluation of Its Assumptions, Attitudes and Values* (London: Penguin Books, 1968), 94.

26 Ibid, 120.

Petrarch had been only the first to perceive the problem and in his reaction turned to the spiritually untransformed saeculum. His Neoplatonic followers did likewise. Their newly defined humanist values—elaborated within the paganly born-again culture of the new Christendom—soon determined their religious values. Thus, as Ernst Cassirer noted long ago, "the Renaissance strove for a religion of affirmation of the world and of the intellect, a religion which conceded to both their specific value, and which found the real proof and seal of divinity not in the degradation and destruction of the world and the human intellect but in their exaltation."

And while the humanists sought in Neoplatonism an alternative to the incarnational anthropology of church tradition, they did not directly attack the faith. Humanism in its initial form, according to Cassirer, "does not approach Christian dogma in an inimical or skeptical manner; it attempts rather to understand and to interpret the dogma itself in such a way that it becomes the expression of a new religious attitude." That attitude produced the syncretism of Ficino and the promethean optimism of Pico. The reconciliation of man with God therefore "was no longer looked for exclusively in an act of divine grace; it was supposed to take place amid the activity of the human spirit and its process of self-development."[27] In other words, the autonomous values of humanistic religion during the quattrocento began to challenge Augustine's extreme teachings about grace and the human condition.

But this all came to an end with the Protestant Reformation. Luther and Calvin both saw in the religion of the humanists the specter of Pelagianism and therefore placed their movements firmly back under the dependable but anthropologically deflating dominion of Augustinianism. Whatever forms it took during the sixteenth and seventeenth centuries, reformational Christianity held in common a view of man's depravity and the world's accursedness. And it was this—the pessimistic soul of the new Christendom—that the philosophes finally renounced during the eighteenth century. The overthrow of Augustinianism united them in a single objective. Their struggle

27 Cassirer, *Philosophy of the Enlightenment*, trans. Fritz C. A. Koelln and James P. Pettegrove (Princeton: Princeton University: 1951), 137–38.

was to break, in Cassirer's words, "the power of medieval dogma." In this conflict, "Augustinianism is now attacked not in its consequences and direct influences but at its very heart. The concept of original sin is the common opponent against which all the different trends of the philosophy of the Enlightenment join forces."[28]

And in this the philosophes succeeded. They may have failed to inaugurate a perfect society. But by the end of the eighteenth century, amid the bloodshed of revolution, they, like the papal reformers of the eleventh century, had changed the character of the West forever.

Hence their imposition of a new model of historical identity. For those who joined in the building of utopia, the world was no longer defined by the Incarnation. It could not be so defined, in part because according to the deists (to say nothing of their atheistic allies), God cannot and would not become human. Doing so would rend the Newtonian fabric of nature and strip man of his autonomy. The Augustinian model of human history—shared in this case with Eusebius and virtually all other Christians until the time of Joachim of Fiore—had used the Incarnation as the pivotal point in history. Once God became man, paradise had entered the world and through the sacramental life of the Church would continue to sustain it until the Second Coming. This latter dogma was likewise cast aside by the philosophes. Instead of a world transformed by heavenly immanence and divine participation, faithfully awaiting the consummation of its history, they rushed to build a different world in which the saeculum and not the kingdom of heaven is the source of fulfillment.

Rejecting the paradisiacal vision of history, then, secular humanists advocated a utopian alternative. This is the origin of the familiar tripartite model of history still predominant in the West today. Like an iron rack, it fixes all human experience to one of three periods: the "ancient," the "medieval," and the "modern." It is not an objective model (despite uncritical use by academics) and is designed to dignify only the last period within it. To this end, the tripartite model subverts the value of the "middle ages," which are reduced to nothing more than a bridge—however long and complex—between a

28 Ibid, 141.

tragically distant pagandom and secular modernity. Here the philosophes took their cue from Petrarch, who regularly disparaged the millennium that preceded his generation. As we have noted, he called it a period of "darkness." Elaborated by his humanist successors, the time between Constantine and the quattrocento came to be dubbed the "dark ages."

But darkness is relative, as Jesus stated when He revealed that men can actually be benighted by a false enlightenment—and in such cases, He remarks, "how great is the darkness!" (Matt. 6:23). The secularists who advanced their anti-evangelical vision of "enlightenment" often did so with a sense that Christianity was responsible for the abundant evil in Christendom. As we have noted, their point of departure was the religious violence, injustice, and superstition that had seemed to overwhelm the West since the eleventh century.

And it is unquestionably the case that their activities helped bring an end to much that was ugly about their civilization. Voltaire's challenge to the harrowing injustice of the Calas affair is only one example. Another was Charles Montesquieu's *The Spirit of the Laws* (1748), which demonstrated how a separation of powers improved government and protected it from tyranny. Yet another was Cesare Beccaria's *On Crimes and Punishments* (1764), which helped liberate the justice system from cruelty and the principle of retribution. Nevertheless, by attacking Christian culture at its roots, the philosophes also opened the door to a great darkness, one the gospel had long dispelled. Their actions benighted their culture even as they delusively thought they were enlightening it.

An effort to use the Church's imagery of darkness against her is found in the work of the Englishman Edward Gibbon (d. 1794). His *History of the Decline and Fall of the Roman Empire* is a masterpiece of historiography. It is also a masterpiece of secularist rhetoric. It uses its subject as a case study of how Christianity ruined the greatest state in the history of pagandom.

Like his fellow philosophes, Gibbon was raised within a culture of confessional conflict, even if outright war was a thing of the past. His religious development paralleled that of the skeptic Bayle. Raised an Anglican, he converted to Roman Catholicism under the influence of its polemics, but then

Edward Gibbon

reverted to his native faith after being threatened with disinheritance by his father. The memory of such instability became an embarrassment to the proud rationalism he cultivated as a man of letters. The deism of the philosophes proved more convincing than a gospel disputed by its own advocates.

Eventually he abandoned Christianity altogether. Then, sitting atop the ruins of Rome one day and brooding on the loss of pagandom, he conceived one of the most famous narratives in the history of historical writing.

The six-volume *Decline and Fall* gave Gibbon the opportunity to lay out the new tripartite model of Western history and direct it toward the formation of a post-Christian Christendom. It opens with Rome enjoying her greatest prosperity, about a century before Constantine's conversion. Then, after that event, everything goes downhill as the West enters "the darkness and confusion of the middle ages."[29] Documenting with obvious delight the most scandalous events in the history of Byzantium, Gibbon concludes that the ruination of Roman civilization was due to a toxic mixture of caesaropapism, clericalism, and popular superstition. A once vigorous pagan civilization was swallowed up by Christendom. As a result, in the East it was finally conquered by the Turks, whereas in the West it degenerated into the disgraceful activities of the papacy.

As he reaches the end of his narrative, Gibbon turns to the heroic effort to restore the ancient glory of Rome during the Rienzo revolution. But otherwise, he tells the story of a civilization with a supporting culture that failed to transform the world in a productive way. The rhetorical force and elegance of his style assured that no one who closed the sixth and final volume of the history could ever argue otherwise.

There was indeed something contrived in Gibbon's famous effort to rewrite the history of Christendom. Becker was one of the first to take note of this. On the one hand, the work effectively "sought out the enemy in his stronghold and made the direct frontal attack on the Christian centuries."[30] On the other hand, its secularistic bias prevented it from capturing the true experience of its human subjects. This flaw produced monotony.

> *In the pages of the* Decline and Fall, *we seem to be taking a long journey, but all the time we remain in one place: we sit with Gibbon in the ruins of*

---

29 Edward Gibbon, *The Decline and Fall of the Roman Empire*, vol. 1 (New York: Peter Fenelon Collier and Son, 1900), 4.

30 Becker, *The Heavenly City*, 116.

> *the Capitol. It is from the ruins of the Capitol that we perceive, as from a great distance, a thousand years filled with dim shapes of men moving blindly, performing strangely, in an unreal shadowy world. We do not enter the Middle Ages, or relive a span of human experience: still we sit in the ruins of the Capitol, becoming cramped and half numb listening, all this long stationary time, to our unwearied guide as he narrates for us, in a melancholy and falling cadence, the disaster that mankind has suffered, the defeat inflicted by the forces of evil on the human spirit. The* Decline and Fall *is a history, yes; but something more than a history, a memorial oration: Gibbon is commemorating the death of ancient civilization; he has described, for the "instruction of future ages," the "triumph of barbarism and religion."*[31]

Gibbon's masterpiece, in short, was a narrative of the West that could be used by the anti-evangelists to justify the repudiation of Christianity's role in shaping it.

As a whole the philosophes believed the future would be freed of such "darkness." Their model of history served a strictly secular modernity. Augustine had framed history between the First and Second Comings of Christ. They reframed it between the rebirth of pagandom and the coming of utopia.

The one important difference was that for traditional Christianity, paradise was already present in the world. This had begun to change in the West after the Great Division, when the culture of purgatory began to shift the experience of paradise to an incomprehensibly distant "afterlife." But now, secular humanism projected utopia to an even more evasive state of "not yet." If in the eleventh century the new Christendom had begun to replace a culture of divine presence with one of divine absence, now, in its incipient modern phase, it promised to restore a kind of presence—one defined exclusively by man—only at some indeterminate point in the future.

And this was probably its genius. Never satisfying its members, always demanding of them further transformation, and directing all attention to

31 Ibid, 117–18.

the saeculum, post-Christian Christendom generated a longing that could be satisfied only by revolution.

But a great obstacle blocked the road ahead.

Benighted Absolutism

TREATISES AND HISTORIES WERE NOT going to change the world. Power was needed, and the philosophes were encouraged by seeing that by the end of the eighteenth century the courts of Europe were beginning to respond to the anti-evangelical program. Nevertheless, the absolutist regimes that ruled continental Europe would prove ambiguous partners in utopian transformation.

One of the most promising regimes was in Germany. Frederick the Great (r. 1740–1786) had been raised in an unusual religious atmosphere. His father, King Frederick William I of Prussia, was a Calvinist whose fear of eternal punishment had been softened through contacts with Lutheran pietists. This did not shield the son from a court tutor who did everything he could in secret to impart the doctrine of predestination (and was eventually fired for doing so). The result was a future ruler who came of age disgusted by the doctrinal disagreements and anthropological pessimism of his surrounding culture. Frederick's reaction was to rebel against his father in just about every way, including by rejecting Christianity. After escaping the gloom of Berlin for the refined and sensuous court of Saxony at the age of sixteen, he resolved to rule his lands in a very different way from what either reformational or pietistic Christianity prescribed.

Frederick's love was for the arts. During his youth he assembled a huge library and began writing poetry. He learned how to play the flute and even composed pieces for the instrument. After ascending the throne, he built for himself a palace in the town of Potsdam near Berlin and named it Sans-Souci (French for "without cares"). Designed in the new Rococo style (which exceeded even the Baroque in its ornamentation) and standing on a promontory above a terraced hillside, the modest but delightful building resembled in many ways the palace of Peterhof. This was appropriate, for like Peter the

Frederick the Great of Prussia

Great, Frederick the Great intended his court to be a point of contact with the new culture emanating from more progressive lands to the west.

Frederick was oriented above all toward the writings of the French philosophes. He became a voracious reader and wholly assimilated their values. "The more thoroughly he penetrated this body of thought," wrote one biographer,

> *the more strongly he came to accept the belief that lay behind every aspect of the Enlightenment: with the help of reason it should be possible not only to reach a sounder understanding of the world but also to make it a better, freer, and happier place. Few men of his century held this hope with such enthusiasm. . . . Theological dogma and positive Christianity he dismissed forever. At the beginning of a new epoch in the world's spiritual development, he felt himself called on to assume a royal charge which would enable him more than any of his contemporaries to turn the ideals of the new age into reality. . . . The remnants of the Middle Ages and of centuries of stifling illusion were to be cleared away.*[32]

The philosophes' royal disciple adopted their language, claiming on one unguarded occasion to speak German only with his horse. With time, he adopted the practice of signing his letters "the Philosophe of Sans-Souci." This met with no objection from the likes of d'Alembert, whose *Encyclopedia* was published more freely in Prussia than in France. Rousseau also had much to praise in the monarch despite holding radically republican views. When a warrant was issued in France for his arrest following the publication of *Emile*, he was offered protection in the lands of Frederick. But the most famous act of recognition came from Voltaire. At Frederick's invitation, he moved to Potsdam and lived at the king's side, consulting with him on matters relating to philosophy, the arts, and government. Frederick's ongoing support for religious toleration, scientific studies, and the arts was influenced by his famous long-term house guest. It is appropriate that it was Voltaire, the king of the philosophes, who dubbed Frederick a "philosophe on the throne."

To the south, Prussia's greatest rival looked on with a mixture of admiration and fear. The Holy Roman Empire had also seen the accession of a new ruler in the year Frederick came to power. But there the circumstances were far more ambiguous. Because of her sex, Maria Theresa (r. 1740–1780), by Habsburg custom, had not been eligible to succeed her father, Emperor

---

32 Gerhard Ritter, *Frederick the Great*, trans. Peter Paret (Berkeley: University of California, 1968), 51–52.

Charles VI, when he died. An Austrian legal resolution called the Pragmatic Sanction was introduced to allow her to do so, but many of the empire's territory-hungry neighbors conveniently declined to honor it. One of these was Prussia, and within months of Maria Theresa's accession Frederick had ordered his formidable armies into the Habsburg territory of Silesia. When the War of the Austrian Succession came to an end, the new empress had lost Silesia but gained legitimacy within a reduced Holy Roman Empire. This she ruled forcefully, reforming state administration and the military according to the example set by Prussia. Frederick's vision of secular monarchy, however, repelled her.

Her son and successor, Joseph II (r. 1765–1790), was a different matter. He proved to be a model philosopher-emperor. Raised by superstitious and disciplinarian tutors, educated by pedantic Jesuits, the heir to the throne assuaged his contempt for Christianity by turning to the works of the philosophes. He was forced to wait in the political wings for fifteen long years as a powerless co-emperor. The throne was still warm from Maria Theresa's presence when upon her death Joseph began to reverse her religious policies.

Prior to that date, he had already done much to cultivate a secular culture in Vienna the way Frederick the Great had in Potsdam. Among Joseph's priorities was the expansion of the city's musical infrastructure. Concert halls and opera houses began to grow in size and influence. This was the beginning of that marvelous century when the city brought forth a stream of great composers, including Joseph Haydn, Wolfgang Amadeus Mozart, Ludwig van Beethoven, Franz Schubert, and Johannes Brahms.

Mozart—the second (along with Bach, Beethoven, and Wagner) of the quartet of Germans that most changed modern music—arrived in the city as the art form was transitioning from a means of worship to an end in itself. Bach had already started down this road, balancing his text-based cantatas and masses with purely instrumental concertos and orchestral suites. His use of the complex form of fugue (in which a theme enters multiple times, forming simultaneous melodic lines) would have been welcomed as an example of the rationalism in which philosophes delighted. Some of his last works became extraordinarily cerebral, such as the labyrinthine *Musical Offering*—a

Wolfgang Amadeus Mozart

piece composed in response to a challenge presented to him at the court of Frederick the Great.

Vienna's classical school of composition was heir to the Baroque tendency toward secularization and brought it to completion. It was in the Austrian capital, for instance, that the sonata form was perfected. Employing an almost geometrical model, the sonata presents three sequential melodies in a perfectly symmetrical way: a first melody is introduced and developed; then a second; and finally, the first is reintroduced and exhausted with new variations.

Mozart (d. 1791) was the finest product of Viennese musical classicism. In the entirety of his output—cut short by death at the age of thirty-five—liturgical compositions are both greatly outnumbered and overshadowed by purely secular ones. His most famous exception—the *Requiem*—only proves the rule. Even more than Bach's famous Mass, it discourages prayer by assigning to the choir such complex and demanding vocal gymnastics as to force its "audience" into awed silence. Especially noteworthy in this respect is the use of ornate melisma—the drawing out of a syllable over multiple notes, designed to serve a composition's melody rather than the text's meaning. This was not new. Ancient Byzantine chant used the device, as did an emerging form of polyphony in Russia known as *znamenny* chant. But melisma assumed unprecedented complexity in the new Christendom during the eighteenth century. In that part of Mozart's *Requiem* known as the "Kyrie eleison" ("Lord Have Mercy"), it becomes quite impossible for a member of the audience to sing (or in most cases understand) the second word. The journey away from Gregorian liturgical chant that Palestrina's polyphony charted during the sixteenth century had reached its destination.

But on the secular side of Mozart's scale of output rest some of Christendom's most brilliant works of music. They include the *Turkish Piano Sonata* (showing off the new form with dazzling improvisations). Also employing sonata form but rendered by a chamber orchestra is the now culturally ubiquitous *A Little Night Music* (*Eine kleine Nachtmusik*). Then there are the serious compositions. The gravity of the opening melody of the Twentieth Piano Concerto and the exquisite charm of the second movement of the Twenty-First Piano Concerto are unprecedented. His symphonies were even more profound. They were modeled after the new compositional form perfected by fellow Viennese Joseph Haydn (d. 1809). The latter had composed more than a hundred symphonies, many with curious thematic devices. One, the *Clock Symphony*, used the orchestra in the second movement to imitate the ticking of a timepiece, and by doing so suggested the growing influence of secular timekeeping and mechanical invention in the West. Needless to say, Mozart soon outdid his master. His symphonies imbued non-textual music with a transformational power formerly possessed only by the Mass.

His three final symphonies are recognized for carrying the form to a new level of expression. Though the Thirty-Ninth Symphony opens with a slow overture in homage to Haydn, it soon expands into something unforeseeable by anyone who might have looked on music as mere entertainment. For its part, the Fortieth Symphony is almost harrowing in its intensity. It opens with a cry of anxiety as fluid and unsettling as the thirteenth-century "*Dies irae*" in which so much of Western Christendom's pessimism had found a voice. The Forty-First Symphony—Mozart's last—was soon nicknamed for the ruler of the pagan gods because of its sheer strength. Its peremptory opening can indeed be likened to Jupiter hurling thunderbolts down on man from heaven. Famously, however, it shifted the most important movement to the final position. As its turbulent themes find a dizzying resolution, the work ends with a rolling coda full of energy and drama. Who needs liturgy? a bewigged Viennese nobleman might have reflected when the conductor's baton was finally lowered. The fullness of human experience can now be experienced in a concert hall.

And not just there. The opera house was also being filled with an unprecedented depth of human experience by Mozart. His comedy *The Marriage of Figaro* and tragedy *Don Giovanni* would leave audiences speechless for centuries to come. But *The Magic Flute* went further. It was the product of the composer's experiences with Freemasonry, a close-knit and ritualistically elaborate movement to marshal the powers of the saeculum toward progress. Freemasons were typically contemptuous of the Roman Catholic Church and sought to replace its influence with a purely secular form of reformation. *The Magic Flute* displays some of Mozart's most technically brilliant choral pieces, such as the aria "Hell's Vengeance" by a character named the Queen of the Night—most probably an allusion to the pious Maria Theresa. The opera exudes optimism for the future. The final act, for instance, ends with a chorus's transformational declaration:

CHAPTER SIX

When mercy and justice spread glory on the path, then the kingdom of heaven will come to earth, and mortals will resemble gods.

Joseph's court was not only an inspiration for the secularization of the arts. It was also a center for the suppression of traditional Christianity. The philosopher-emperor proved himself more responsive to the period's anti-evangelism than any other major European monarch, and more radical in applying it. Liberalization of censorship and religious toleration for the many Protestants, Orthodox, and Jews of his realms almost went without saying.

It was for restrictions he imposed on the historically predominant Roman Catholic Church that Joseph earned notoriety. Not only did he create an autonomous episcopate along the lines of that of Gallican France, he forbade the issuance of papal bulls without imperial authorization. He did not stop there. Like Frederick, he was swayed by utopian contempt for asceticism and prayer. Accordingly, he abolished a third of Austria's monasteries, seizing their vast landholdings in the name of a secular state. Orders like the Benedictines, Franciscans, and Dominicans were henceforth dissolved. Joseph applied the same logic to the liturgical calendar. Valuing industry over worship, he abolished a large number of saints' days. He even intervened in the Roman Catholic Church's sacraments. He declared marriage a purely civil institution and, for the sake of frugality, actually forbade funerals that used anything but simple pine coffins.

When a dumbfounded pope appeared at the Viennese court in 1782 to negotiate a compromise, the imperious Joseph all but ignored his presence. The distant heir to Emperor Henry IV—the eleventh-century nemesis of Gregory VII, who famously stood in the snows of Canossa begging for absolution—Joseph brought a decisive end to eight centuries of papal supremacy in the Holy Roman Empire. Perhaps he considered it a kind of revenge.

Art and secularization were also prominently linked at the court of Catherine the Great of Russia (r. 1762–1796). She had come to power unexpectedly. The Lutheran daughter of a German prince, she had been married to Tsar Peter III while he was still only the heir. She soon learned to detest her husband, who by virtue of both his youth and his temperament proved himself grotesquely immature. He continued to play with toy soldiers well into their marriage and gave more attention to military drills than to domestic relations. It took him no fewer than twelve years to consummate the marriage.

In the meantime, the intelligent and ambitious young princess alternated her time between lovers and the works of the French philosophes. Under these influences she became a deist and began to plan for how she might rule Russia alone as a progressive monarch. When Peter finally acceded to the throne, she swiftly arranged a palace coup that resulted in his arrest and summary execution. Catherine thus became the empress of Russia in her own right.

Her reign was in many ways the fulfillment of Peter the Great's, and as a result posterity bestowed on her the same epithet. Catherine the Great shared her predecessor's contempt for the old Christendom and the Orthodox Church's influence on Russian culture. Erecting a famous statue of Peter known as the Bronze Horseman on the banks of the Neva, she advanced his policy of integrating Russia ever more closely with the West. Her main achievements in this were cultural. She continued the building program of Saint Petersburg, ordering the erection of palaces, churches, and schools. All were designed in the late Baroque or Rococo style to link the city with Rome and Paris.

Her most famous architectural achievement was the expansion of the Winter Palace, situated on the Neva upstream from Peter's statue. She playfully called the annex her "hermitage." But instead of prayer, the opulent structure was designed to support a growing collection of secular paintings like no other in the world. Needless to say, the Hermitage did not display icons or any other form of native Russian art. Only Western European works produced since the quattrocento were catalogued in its vast expanses. Like Peter's efforts to turn Russia into a mighty European military force, Catherine's promotion of the arts aimed to make her adopted homeland more like the culture she had left behind in Germany.

In this she followed in the footsteps of the Philosophe of Sans-Souci. As

Michelangelo, The Creation of Adam. *Sistine Chapel, Rome*

Andrea Pozzo, ceiling of the Church of St. Ignatius, Rome

Iconostasis, Peter-Paul Cathedral, St. Petersburg, Russia

Nicolas Poussin, Bacchanalia

François Boucher, The Toilet of Venus

Caspar David Friedrich, Wanderer above the Sea of Fog

Caspar David Friedrich, Woman before the Rising Sun

Ilya Repin, The Volga Boatmen

The Apotheosis of Washington, *Capitol Building, Washington, DC*

Vasily Perov, Paschal Procession

Church of the Savior on the Spilled Blood, St. Petersburg, Russia

Vasily Perov, Monastic Refectory

Statue of Lenin, Finland Station, St. Petersburg, Russia

a wise philosopher-tsaritsa herself, she too corresponded with Voltaire and d'Alembert. She consumed the great treatises on government by Montesquieu and Beccaria. And though Petersburg was thrice as far from Paris as Potsdam, she matched Frederick's protection of Rousseau by inviting the celebrated Diderot to her capital when his *Encyclopedia* began to face censorship problems.

Catherine kept herself well apprised of the policies of other absolute monarchs in Europe. Like Joseph II, she held monasticism in high contempt. In 1764, she actually anticipated and exceeded Josephinism by seizing the Orthodox Church's monastic lands and dissolving nearly two-thirds of all monasteries. By this time, the hierarchy had been completely demoralized by the absence of an autonomous patriarchate. What is more, the long-term effect of dissolving independent sketes like those of the sixteenth-century non-possessors (in which hesychasm had flourished) was that wealthy monasteries of scale were easily targeted for state appropriation. As in the case of Peter's abolition of the patriarchate, a compliant and spiritually weakened hierarchy thus failed to resist its deistic sovereign. Only one bishop of note objected: Metropolitan Arseny of Rostov (d. 1772). He denounced Catherine's land seizure and condemned the hierarchs of the Holy Synod as guard dogs who passively watched the theft of the Church "without barking."[1] Arseny paid dearly for his independence. He was arrested on Catherine's orders, dragged before the Synod for trial, and summarily thrown into prison, where he was subsequently starved to death.

Needless to say, when Catherine issued an ambitious but abortive instruction to convene a special commission representing all elements of Russian society to consider how progressive reforms might be introduced, the clergy were not invited.

However, by imitating and even placing herself out in front of the policies of Western monarchs, she would soon realize that progress was a sword that cut both ways.

---

1 Quoted in Isabel de Madariaga, *Russia under Catherine the Great* (New Haven: Yale University, 1981), 116.

A Surge of Indignation

ON THE OPPOSITE END OF Europe, the court that had set the tone for eighteenth-century absolutism was descending into a morass from which it would never emerge.

On the one hand, Versailles remained the emblem of so-called enlightened statecraft. The Sun King's successor, Louis XV (r. 1715–1774), welcomed innovations in financial policy and commerce. During the first part of his long reign he depended on the practical mind of Cardinal Fleury, the chief minister, whose primary goal was keeping France out of costly wars.

Unfortunately, the martial record of Louis XIV made that difficult, especially after Fleury's death and Louis's assumption of absolutist prerogative. In North America, France now possessed most of the territories west of the British colonies, and around the throne were many advocates for driving France's age-old enemy into the Atlantic. Desire for Canadian furs and careless diplomacy therefore led to a war against the British colonies, known to English speakers as the French and Indian War. Before this was concluded to British advantage, however, a much greater conflict erupted in Europe. This Seven Years War (1756–1763) was a devasting setback for France. She was forced to cede all her American territories. Furthermore, she emerged from the catastrophe with debts as great as those accrued by the spendthrift Sun King.

As the finances and diplomatic reputation of France were sinking, so was the moral character of her court. Louis XV had grown tired of the plain-looking and otherwise unexciting Queen Marie within a decade of their marriage. He began to seek alternative sources of feminine inspiration. Thus began one of the most notorious sagas in the history of royal adultery.

That history was a long one, but it took on a new character during Louis's reign. In the past, traditional Christian values of spousal fidelity had not as a rule been challenged openly, even when a monarch's lust matched his power. At times the popes and patriarchs had even distinguished themselves in demanding, upon pain of excommunication, that rulers desist from adulterous relationships.

Secularization had begun to change this. Repudiating Christianity, many of the philosophes rationalized a new approach to sexuality. Diderot, for instance, penned an imaginary encounter between European explorers and Tahitian pagans, claiming that man, in a civilization "happier" than Christendom, was naturally unconcerned with monogamy. More privately he complained that "evangelical perfection" was "nothing but the deadly art of stifling nature."[2] Hume the atheist asserted that marital fidelity is merely a social "utility" without which "such a virtue would never have been thought of."[3] Many of the philosophes were bold enough to live out their "enlightened" approach to sexuality. Voltaire, d'Alembert, and Rousseau never married and kept mistresses throughout their lives. Others, like Diderot, married but also kept mistresses. And if children were born to their mistresses, as happened five times in the case of Rousseau, they were promptly abandoned to an orphanage.

Then there was the Marquis de Sade (d. 1814). The orphaned victim of a religious upbringing in which flagellation was practiced, he developed a sexual fascination with pain and cruelty. Rousseau had confided similar fantasies in his autobiographical *Confessions,* as well as sexual experiences involving groups of people of both sexes. De Sade took such behavior to an entirely new and morally unrestrained level. As a philosophe himself, he wrote plays and novels graphically describing sexual behavior totally at odds with the values not only of Christendom but of the mainstream of classical pagandom. The only exception in the latter case would be the court circles of profligate Roman emperors like Tiberius or the bacchanalias of ancient Greece, in which worshippers of Dionysus assembled in secret to practice orgies, and, in some cases, the abduction, rape, and ritual murder of young girls. The orgy became de Sade's preferred form of sexual relationship, and this, along with regular blasphemies and an advocacy for abortion, resulted on multiple occasions in his arrest. The proto-postmodernist's most nihilistic novel was in fact written while he was confined to a cell in the Bastille.

A few miles away from that notorious prison, the palace of Versailles

---

2 Peter Gay, *The Enlightenment: The Science of Freedom* (New York: Alfred A. Knopf), 194.

3 Ibid, 200.

was also becoming a laboratory of moral experimentation. Louis XV never descended as low as de Sade, to be sure. In fact, he was still regarded by much of the populace as a pious descendant of Saint Louis. At his coronation he imparted the same charismatic "healing touch" to those in attendance that his ancestors had imparted. But his adherence to traditional Christian morality was selective. Some of what the serial sexual criminal de Sade enacted on individual occasions, the divinely chosen King Louis accomplished over the course of a long reign.

It started with a girl named Louise Julie de Mailly-Nesle. Aware of the king's dissatisfaction with his wife, Cardinal Fleury (of all people) proposed that he satisfy himself with the girl as a mistress instead. To repeat: taking a mistress was nothing new in the history of Christendom. But the secular values that now ruled its rulers had changed things. They served to free Louis from the vows of his marriage and endowed his lust with a sort of benighted legitimacy. Before long, he was looking for additional mistresses.

Louise Julie's aristocratic family itself provided some of them. After making the first daughter his "official mistress" (there was actually such a title), he proceeded to seduce and keep as temporary mistresses no fewer than three of her sisters. To obtain one who was already engaged, like King David of old he first ordered the fiancé into battle with hopes of his death. When the young man returned to Paris unscathed, Louis arranged to have him seduced and then released evidence of the affair to the girl. After this she reluctantly surrendered to him. And so it went through the sequence of sisters. One actually died while giving birth to Louis's son. When the king had exhausted the resources of the Mailly-Nesle family, he turned to other beauties from cultured and therefore secularized backgrounds. Mistresses came and went with almost dizzying frequency. Louis even resorted to sending scouts into Paris to locate girls and bring them back to the palace for a night or two.

By far the most notorious of Louis's innumerable mistresses was Madame de Pompadour (d. 1764). She all but ruled the French court from the moment she became the official mistress until the day she died. She is most famous for her patronage of the arts. She not only lavished the crown's resources on interior design and paintings but used them effectively to advance her own position at court.

In doing so she also advanced the aesthetic of rococo in Western painting. Closely related to the secular values of Saint Petersburg's architecture, such painting was extremely naturalistic. Its seeds had already been sown, as we have seen, during the quattrocento. The Venetian painter Titian (d. 1576) had gone much further than fellow humanists in drawing on the culture of pagandom for his inspiration. Whereas Raphael had painted Madonnas that were pagan in form but Christian in content, Titian produced female images that were pagan in both form and content. His *Venus of Urbino* is the most famous and radical example. During the seventeenth century the innovative choice of subject was taken up by the Frenchman Poussin, who gained fame for images of both Venus and the pagan rite of the bacchanalia.

But it was not until the eighteenth century that the transition from the Virgin Mary to Venus was complete. Until then, traditional Christianity continued to hold the upper hand in depictions of feminine beauty. The still-popular Madonnas oriented female humanity toward the greatest saint in history, whose experience of paradise was so tangible that no earthly need for a man touched her. The content of female beauty in Western painting continued to be spiritual rather than physical, despite a tendency in form toward the sensual. We have already noted, for instance, the case of Bernini's sculpture of Teresa of Avila. But in the eighteenth century, a pronounced emphasis on the purely physical beauty of female humanity began to take hold within cultured circles under the influence of the secular values of the philosophes. Venus, the goddess of sexual desire, displaced the Virgin Mary and became the ultimate standard of feminine perfection.

Madame de Pompadour, at the heart of the anti-evangelical culture, quite literally embodied this new principle. She was physically beautiful, and she promoted a cult of eroticism at the French court. To do so, she used leading painters such as Francois Boucher (d. 1770). This master of rococo was already known in Paris for applying naturalism more boldly than any previous painter. He used color and lighting to celebrate the physical beauty of the body. His Venuses were unlike most of those of the past in that they were neither monumental nor mythological. They were set rather within the intimate space of the bedchamber, exactly where any male advocate of the new morality would have liked to imagine them.

Like Raphael, Boucher employed young female models to achieve his naturalistic goals. One was a desperately poor Irish girl named Marie-Louise O'Murphy. The daughter of a prostitute, she offered herself to Boucher, and the result was a work entitled *Young Girl Reclining*. It shows a completely naked girl of thirteen lying provocatively on a bed. Word of the titillating innovation quickly reached Versailles, where Madame de Pompadour was eager to supply subordinate mistresses for the king. Doing so demonstrated her own leadership of the court and assured that she would maintain Louis's favor. In this case, too, she need not fear losing the status of official mistress since Marie-Louise was from a lowborn family.

As the king enjoyed another palace hookup, Madame de Pompadour returned to Boucher with requests for additional works. One of the most famous was *Venus Consoling Love*. It was originally hung at Versailles, and rumors swirled that the enticing woman at its center was none other than the official mistress herself.

Outside Versailles, however, taste was not so refined. In the slums of Paris, a body of Frenchmen known as the *sans-culottes* ("those without breeches")—named for the absence in their dress of the elegant silk trousers worn by the aristocracy—were embracing a different sort of secular culture. At the center of it was what is known to historians as the *libelle*, the salacious pamphleteering that inflamed social resentments and exaggerated (if such was possible) the moral corruption of the court. The libelle was not pious in any sense, and it drew on the same currents of anti-evangelism in making its case against the monarchy. It was a kind of secularized puritanism. Nor was it scrupulous about facts. Its goal was to satisfy the interests of an increasingly literate but unsophisticated urban proletariat. To do so, it presented the court as a den of outrageous sensuality and greed.

A pamphlet ironically entitled *The Fasts of Louis XV*, for instance, described how the king's agents regularly scoured Paris for girls to add to the royal "harem." At two a week, it calculated, the total number of court mistresses had risen in a single decade to approximately one thousand. Apart from the moral outrage of it all, such a practice had nearly bankrupted the regime, since after satisfying the sovereign each courtesan was entitled to an extravagant severance payment. The salacious work also brought attention to Madame de Pompadour's successor, Madame du Barry (d. 1793). She was a young woman more than thirty years Louis's junior who had risen, to emulate the style of the libelles, from the brothels of Paris to the lap of the king. "Louis XV remained always the same," the anonymous author declared,

> *that is always up to his neck in filth and voluptuousness. Despite the desperation of his starving peoples and the public calamities, his mistress grew so wild in her prodigality and pillaging, that in a few more years she would have brought the kingdom down, had not the death of the despot put an end to her extravagance.*[4]

Such was the reputation of the monarchy among the common people.

But if moral issues were beginning to detach the population from the crown, economic ones would soon grow even more destabilizing. By the end of the eighteenth century, government finances were entering a state of crisis. Before the Sun King died, he had confessed in a moment of atypical diffidence that he had been "too liberal" in waging war. His heirs inherited the sins of the father. Louis XV, despite Cardinal Fleury's efforts, also jumped hastily into conflicts like the Seven Years War. And Louis XVI (r. 1774–1792), soon after his accession, lashed out against Britain once again by joining in the costly War of American Independence.

By 1788 the treasury was exhausted, and no more loans could be obtained without a major concession to the nobility. In desperation, Louis called together the Estates General, constituting, as Catherine the Great's abortive special commission had, representatives of major social groups. It was organized into three estates: the clergy, the nobility, and everyone else (such as peasants, workers, and the nascent bourgeoisie). Louis XVI hoped that the

---

4 Quoted in Robert Darnton, *The Literary Underground of the Old Regime* (Cambridge, MA: Harvard University, 1982), 145–146.

assembly would support him in an effort to solve the financial crisis.

However, the progressive ideals disseminated by the philosophes had become too much a part of the political culture by now for this ploy to work. In the newly formed United States of America, for instance, a truly rational system of government had been created. Montesquieu's mechanism of checks and balances was being built into an historically unprecedented written constitution. The Declaration of Independence had not only severed a newly liberated nation from institutions of the Old World; it inspired the Old World to follow suit.

France provided an atmosphere in which such utopianism could aspire to power. First, it possessed a network of reform-minded institutions known as Masonic lodges. These had been formed by the social and economic elite during the past century to counter the influence of the clergy in society. They were committed to improving society by applying rationalistic philosophy and science. They also provided their own sense of identity and even cultivated secret quasi-religious rituals to rival those of the Roman Catholic Church. Even more important than Freemasonry was an expanding network of literary salons. These offered a platform for discussing the most progressive ideas of the past century. Many salons were run by noblewomen like Madame Necker (d. 1794), the wife of Louis's finance minister, who used social connections to invite celebrated philosophes to speak about their vision of utopia.

Masonic lodges and literary salons, as well as the libelles, contributed to the formation of what can be called a "civil society," a body of public opinion that is both educated and critical about the civilization in which it operates. The anti-evangelical philosophes provided the content of this emerging public opinion. For while Christianity, with its enlightened vision of the kingdom of heaven, had much to criticize about the order of things in the world, participants in civil society obeyed an unwritten rule by which affirmations of the gospel were considered retrograde, barbaric, or simply in poor taste. As in the classrooms of twenty-first–century Western universities, discussion about change for the better was only encouraged when it moved in a secular direction.

Yet the looming upheaval was not completely free of the past or of the influence of reformational Christianity within it. In fact, the emerging civil society grew out of a lineage dating to the Papal Reformation. That movement had also looked on the contemporary condition of the West as an intolerable shortcoming. It too was driven to make it better. Likewise, it was led by an elite—in this case clerical—that defined itself against the governments of the time. The Papal Reformation had adhered to a cosmology—Augustinian in provenance—that set the clerical elite against a saeculum that it alone had the wisdom to improve. And as did the philosophes and their followers, the papal reformers had intended radically to transform the world.

The eighteenth-century heirs of the Papal Reformation would likewise do so in a state not of humility and repentance, but of indignation. It was this passion that Voltaire had so well captured in his slogan "Crush Infamy!" It perfectly characterized the utopian transformation that was to come.

Revolution

LOUIS XVI HAD CALLED FOR THE convocation of the Estates General, and as the year 1789 opened it began to assemble. Most of the clergy of the first estate and nobility of the second estate were prepared to work with him, provided doing so did not require them to pay new taxes. Those within the third estate, however, began to demand more than financial reform from the profligate and bankrupt monarchy. Many of its Masonic and salon-attending representatives were eager to apply the critical views about government that now circulated freely within civil society.

It was at this moment that the vision of Jean-Jacques Rousseau became decisive. Only he seemed to offer an effective rebuttal to Augustinianism and the legacy of anthropological pessimism that stretched back to the Great Division. He had done so in a work entitled *The Social Contract*. In it he dismissed Voltaire's and Leibniz's struggles with theodicy. Such a project, he argued, was fundamentally flawed. For in his view the real source of evil is not to be found in the nature of man and his relationship to God but rather in the social organization of man. "Man is born free," he famously declares in the book's opening, "yet everywhere he is in chains." Contrary to what Augustine claimed, man is born good. But as he enters human society after birth he becomes corrupted by avarice, lust, and pride. A fervent deist, Rousseau here leaves deity out of the picture. All evil arises in man's relationship to other men, but this is not intrinsic to human beings as such. There is therefore no need of theodicy.

The polis or state is the source of evil. Rousseau's genius is to solve the philosophes' dilemma without surrendering the humanistic affirmations of man and the world in which he lives. For he declares in *The Social Contract* that the restoration of innocence is possible. But it cannot be attained in society as it has come to be, nor can it be achieved through a flight from society (for the individual always needs his fellow men). The solution to the problem of evil is to be found in the transformation of society.

The state in which men will achieve utopia is one in which a "general will" replaces the individual will imposed from without by corrupted social institutions. Only this general will can offer man escape from an evil that is neither natural nor supernatural. To institute this freedom from evil requires tremendous idealism and self-sacrifice. It requires, inevitably, a revolution.

And if, Rousseau added, there are those who selfishly resist the act of transformation—as there will necessarily be—such enemies of utopia will have to be "forced to be free."

When the Estates General finally convened in May of 1789, a crisis confronted the absolutist monarchy. The third estate fell under the influence of intellectuals and lawyers who demanded the formation of a national assembly to serve the interests of the majority of the population and not only those of clergy or nobility. When Louis scoffed, leaders of the third estate fomented an insurrection among the sans-culottes in Paris. On July 14 the Bastille—symbol of absolutist repression—was seized and its garrison brutally massacred. Its commander was beheaded by the mob. Raised upon a pike, his lifeless face gazed down upon the liberated crowds marching through the streets below. The act was only the beginning of a process of bloodletting that would come to be known as the Reign of Terror.[5]

5 For the first three years of the revolution, indiscriminate violence was much

The Bastille

In the meantime, the self-proclaimed National Assembly created a constitutional monarchy modeled on that of Britain. One of its first acts was to confiscate all property belonging to the Roman Catholic Church. Next, all monastic orders were dissolved. Early in 1790, a law called the Civil Constitution of the Clergy demanded that Roman Catholic priests and bishops swear an oath of obedience to the revolutionary government. Separating them from the authority of the papacy, the legislation was in a real sense the logical fulfillment of Gallicanism and the centuries-old anticlerical aversion to Rome's highly centralized administration. Nevertheless, the great majority of the clergy remained faithful to their tradition and refused to take the oath.

The resistance provoked by these anticlerical actions led to an intensification of the revolution. To make things worse, in 1791 Louis attempted to flee France in disguise, only to be recognized at the frontier and forced to return to Paris. In 1792 Austria and Prussia invaded France to defend the principle of absolutism, but a hurried campaign of national conscription served to keep the enemy at bay. The invasion, combined with the untrustworthiness

---

more contained than during the period 1792–1794. It is the latter period that is usually associated with political terror, but the distinction is unnecessary and ignores the use of unexpected and unlawful political violence from the fall of the Bastille forward.

of the king, caused great insecurity among the revolutionaries. Radicals used this as a pretext to massacre hundreds of people languishing in the capital's prisons. The reasoning, if there was any, was that among the thieves and counterfeiters in jail were a number of counter-revolutionaries who would welcome the invaders. The first to go were Roman Catholic priests, who were chased down and hacked to pieces in the courtyards of the disbanded monasteries that had been made to serve as prisons. Then, early in the following year, King Louis XVI and Queen Marie Antoinette were publicly executed to put an end to any hopes for a restoration of absolutism. The method used was the newly invented guillotine, designed in the spirit of Beccaria to make executions less traumatic for the condemned. The guillotine also made public executions more efficient. It soon became the symbol of a galloping terror.

With France rid of her royalty, power transferred to the hands of the most radical party of revolutionaries, the Jacobins. Their leader was Maximilien Robespierre (d. 1794), a deist who believed strongly in Rousseau's doctrine of the general will. He was a fervent utopian. In one of many eloquent speeches before the legislature he set out "to mark clearly the aim of the Revolution." Fervidly, he proclaimed that

> *we wish in a word to fulfil the course of nature, to accomplish the destiny of mankind, to make good the promises of philosophy, to absolve Providence from the long reign of tyranny and crime. May France . . . become the model to the nations, the terror of oppressors, the ornament of the universe; and in sealing our work with our blood may we ourselves see at least the dawn of universal felicity gleam before us! That is our ambition. That is our aim.*[6]

Robespierre was joined in his vision by fellow radicals like Jean-Paul Marat (d. 1793) and Georges Danton (d. 1794). Together, they intended to eradicate the nobility, the clergy, and any other element opposed to a republican utopia. Robespierre oversaw the terror as head of a Committee for Public

6 Quoted in R. R. Palmer, *Twelve Who Ruled: The Year of the Terror in the French Revolution* (Princeton: Princeton University, 1989), 275–76.

Safety, which issued thousands of death sentences between 1793 and 1794. Nevertheless, leadership of it was not particularly safe. Marat was assassinated while taking a medicinal bath. Danton, who unlike Robespierre was subject to bouts of conscience, was eventually taken to the guillotine for apparent disloyalty.

In the meantime, the revolution was opening opportunities for secularization never dreamed of by the most radical of the philosophes. In 1793 the government decreed that France would no longer abide by the Christian calendar. Instead of using the Incarnation as the beginning of the calendar, linear time would thenceforth be marked from the birth of utopia, that is, the year in which monarchy was abolished. This was a step beyond the tripartite modern model employed by Gibbon. Like the incarnational calendar's organization of time before and after the coming of paradise, the revolutionary one organized the world before and after the coming of utopia.

The names of months were likewise changed and holidays like the weekly Lord's Day abolished. Streets and other public places were in many cases renamed. Paris's famous promontory Montmartre became Mount Marat. More ambitiously, a group of enthusiasts invented an atheistic cult of reason and reassigned a desecrated Notre Dame Cathedral as its center. Inside the nave of this newly designated Temple of Reason, a mountain supported by wooden scaffolding was erected. On the "feast of reason" an actress dressed in an ancient Roman toga decorated with the revolutionary tricolor ritualistically ascended its heights to the delight of onlookers. Upon reaching the summit, she entered a makeshift Greek "temple of philosophy," before which stood torchlit busts of a secular trinity consisting of Voltaire, Rousseau, and the American revolutionary Benjamin Franklin.

Curiously, the cult of reason was strongly opposed by Robespierre. He saw it as too provocative in a recently Christian political culture, and in any case as a deist he believed with Voltaire and Rousseau that respect was due to the divine though impersonal source behind reason. Therefore, he replaced the cult of reason with a cult of the Supreme Being. In 1794, he ordered a leading artist named Jacques-Louis David (d. 1825) to organize an elaborate outdoor "Festival of the Supreme Being."

David himself had earned the respect of revolutionaries for his anti-evangelical paintings. One entitled *Death of Socrates* drew upon the imagery of Christ's Passion, but for secularist effect. It depicted the great pagan philosopher at the moment of his suicide bravely pointing upward toward the "truth," as twelve disciples including Plato prepare to go out into the world to teach his philosophy. David was also an advocate for the pseudo-deification of Marat. He contributed to the revolutionary terrorist's posthumous cult of personality by painting another image knocked off from those of Christendom—in this case Michelangelo's *Pieta.* The *Death of Marat* shows the martyr for utopia lying dead in his bathtub with a look of deep serenity, suggesting that the cause for which he gave his life would—like an anti-gospel—live on to "enlighten" the world after him.

The dechristianization campaign was not content to limit itself to festivals and paintings. Christians faithful to the gospel—and in France this meant primarily Roman Catholics—were regularly persecuted and put to death by the regime. We have already noted the targeting of priests during the 1792 September Massacres. As the terror accelerated the following year, the Committee of Public Safety sent out "representatives on mission" to towns and provinces where counter-utopian resistance was strongest.

In 1793 a rebellion erupted in the Vendée region in the west. Paris responded ruthlessly. It dispatched an army to wipe out all resistance, much of which was closely affiliated with the Roman Catholic Church. Tens of thousands were executed summarily with sabers, muskets, and the guillotine. In one episode, the committee's representative lined victims up in front of open trenches and wiped them out with grapeshot. Women and children were not spared. In fact, pregnant women were especially hated as the mothers of a recalcitrant population that refused to assimilate to an anti-Christian republic.

To the north, in the town of Nantes on the Loire River, the terror was particularly hideous. There, a zealous representative on mission named Jean-Baptiste Carrier (d. 1794) grew impatient with the sluggish work of the guillotine. To speed things along, he ordered the refitting of river barges to include a large plug in the hull. He then filled the barges with people—men, women, children, and especially priests. This latter category of society was in fact placed first in line, and some barges appear to have had only clergy on them. Carrier then ordered the barges pushed out into the river's current and the hull plugs pulled out. With all hatches closed and locked, there was no way for the people on board to escape. Thousands were executed by drowning in this way. Eyewitnesses of the horror—many of them republican soldiers—could not forget the screams of the families below decks as the barges slowly listed and then sank into the deep. Carrier was pleased with the results, and, alluding to the practice of drowning unwanted kittens, nicknamed the Loire the "revolution's bathtub." In all, the creation of utopia in the Vendée claimed the lives of nearly four hundred thousand Roman Catholics. That figure constituted about half the region's population.

The deaths of those opposed to the creation of a post-Christian Christendom were tragic. But as Christians, many were witnesses to a conviction that paradise is not of this world. Among the hundreds of prisoners languishing in the prisons of Paris in 1792 was a man named Nicholas le Clercq. He was a lay member of the Roman Catholic religious order of the Christian Brothers. His work had been to educate poor children whose parents could not afford school tuition. By definition, the revolutionaries regarded him as a dangerous enemy. And so they arrested him. On the day they did so, just before they arrived, Nicholas wrote a letter to his pious sister. It begins with a sense of foreboding. "If God permits," he writes, "I shall come and join you and mingle my tears with yours." But then the tone suddenly changes, and foreboding gives way to courage and even hope. "But no!" he adds immediately,

> *What do I say? Why should we weep when the Gospel tells us to rejoice when we have something to endure for the Name of Christ? Let us then suffer joyfully and with thanksgiving the crosses and afflictions which He may send to us.*[7]

Two weeks later, the revolutionary mob stormed into the prison in which Nicholas and other victims of utopia were being held and put them all to

7 Quoted in Warren H. Carroll, *The Revolution against Christendom* (Front Royal, VA: Christendom Press, 2005), 159.

death as part of the September Massacres.

In the end, the French Revolution served up justice of a sort, even for its victims. Readers may have taken notice of the fact that a great many of the dates of death for personages discussed in recent pages belong to 1793 or 1794, years when the Reign of Terror was at its peak. These personages include opponents of the revolution, but they also include its advocates. Revolutionaries, after all, tend to kill their own. And so it may be appropriate to conclude this account of the French Revolution and the first half of this book by considering the final days of Maximilien Robespierre.

As a radical among revolutionaries and the dominant personality on the Committee of Public Safety, Robespierre had overseen and in some cases ordered the executions of some of the revolution's chief enemies. He supported the September Massacres. He was also there when Louis XVI and Marie Antoinette were dragged through the streets and placed under the blade of the guillotine. He was there when his coconspirator in terror Danton met a similar end. Through it all, Robespierre always seemed to have the upper hand. When he entered the legislature, its rowdy atmosphere would fall to a hush—less out of respect than out of fear.

Then, on a hot July day in 1794, dated by the revolutionary calendar as 9 Thermidor, he gave a speech in the chamber that had a very different outcome. He had delivered an eloquent tirade about the revolution and its enemies—a standard theme for him—but after he returned to his seat, an uproar suddenly broke out among the delegates. The deputies, it seemed, had finally had enough. "Down with the tyrant!" they yelled. It seemed inconceivable that they would dare reproach the revolution's chief dealer of death, yet they did. He returned to his feet to confront the irreverent assembly. But its members howled all the louder, "Down with the tyrant!"

For the consummate terrorist, it was now clear what was happening and how it would end. Robespierre managed to make his way back to his apartment that evening, but at about two in the morning the police arrived. Then, in an effort to cheat them, he took out a pistol and shot himself. The ball, however, only took off part of his jaw.

The next day, the man who had sent so many innocent victims to their deaths was sent to his. As the hissing blade of the guillotine came rushing down upon his neck, one of the most benighted phases in the new Christendom's effort to build utopia without Christianity finally came to an end.

The Execution of Robespierre

CHAPTER SEVEN

New Hopes and Expectations

THE FRENCH REVOLUTION STIRRED HOPES and expectations for a better world. The wave of optimism released by the philosophes could not be stopped even by an event as appalling as the Reign of Terror. Republicanism might transmogrify into Napoleonic imperialism, and this might precipitate the reactionary intervention of Europe's most conservative powers, but less than a generation after the fall of Robespierre utopia was again an inspiration. New revolutionary ideologies arose to serve it, and in the newly formed United States of America a stable democracy seemed to many to secure it. New forms of Christianity even appeared that promised the coming of a perfect world.

Reacting to the Revolution

THE FRENCH REVOLUTION HAD BEEN a catastrophe for Christendom. It not only brought into being the tempest of political terror. It provoked in reaction the mobilization of armies against France, and this in turn led to yet more violence. And when the "revolutionary decade" that began with the fall of the Bastille was finally brought to an end, a new period of upheaval was already underway. This would in fact last another decade and a half.

By the end of 1799, the revolution had spent itself. With the Reign of

Terror ended, France's government was now in the hands of a small body of moderates. They sought a figurehead for the regime that would help them reestablish order and prevent a return to violent chaos. They thought they had their man in the famous general Napoleon Bonaparte (d. 1821).

Since the invasion of Austria and Prussia in 1792, he had defended France's borders and led her armies to victory beyond them. He had earned enormous popularity in doing so. What is more, in 1795 he effectively defended the government against a Roman Catholic royalist insurgency in Paris. He was merciless in doing so, firing grapeshot into the crowds. Once appointed to the largely honorary position of first consul in 1799, however, the formerly unpolitical soldier showed a taste for power and overthrew the government on November 9 (18 Brumaire by the revolutionary calendar). Napoleon now created a dictatorship that in the form of the French Empire—proclaimed in 1804—made a mockery of republicanism.

In his domestic policy, Napoleon proved an agent of secularism. Though he did not share Robespierre's inclination toward terror, he did share the Jacobin's deistic convictions. He would not tolerate the reestablishment of the Roman Catholic Church with the authority she had held before 1789. However, in light of the counter-revolutionary rebellions of the Vendée and Paris, he decided to restore peace with Rome. In a Concordat of 1801, Roman Catholicism was recognized as merely the religion of "the majority" of Frenchmen. In return, bishops were required to swear an oath of loyalty to the emperor on being appointed by him. In fact, Napoleon demanded that French Christianity be subordinate to the government. And the Concordat, even more than the Gallican Articles of Louis XIV, achieved this.

What is more, in 1804 Pope Pius VII traveled to Paris and formally recognized Napoleon as emperor. He even brought with him a replica of Charlemagne's crown. But if he intended to repeat the act of Leo III centuries earlier in making himself the source of the ruler's authority, he was bitterly disappointed. Standing in a restored Notre Dame Cathedral (the makeshift mountain of "enlightenment" inside had since been dismantled), Napoleon seized the crown from the pope and himself placed it on his head. There was to be no question of papal supremacy. In fact, Napoleon's opinion of the pope remained condescending and even abusive throughout his reign. In 1809, to "reclaim" the lands Charlemagne had long ago donated to the papacy, he sent his army into Italy to seize the Papal States and placed Pius under arrest. The pope was later transferred to France, where for years he languished morally (though not physically) as Napoleon's prisoner at the palace in Fontainebleau.

A secular vision of modernity also guided Napoleon as he smashed his way through the armies of Christendom. He never repudiated the revolutionary ideals of "liberty, equality, and fraternity," and in this sense he was less of a reactionary than a republican. As a result of the many battles his military genius secured for the French, he carried revolution and its secular logic another step forward.

His great adversary became Russia, who refused to comply with a French boycott of British goods called the "continental system." Frustrated by the defiance of Tsar Alexander I (r. 1801–1825), Napoleon invaded Russia in 1812 in one of the boldest invasions ever. More than half a million French and allied soldiers crossed the border and in little time made enormous headway toward Moscow. Napoleon was hoping so to frighten Alexander that the latter would sue for peace.

But as the weeks passed and diplomatic overtures went unanswered, Napoleon realized a great battle would be needed to shake his adversary. On September 7 the two armies met on a field near Borodino, a village about eighty miles from Moscow. Tens of thousands of men—perhaps a total of seventy thousand—fell in a single afternoon. Yet the battle was not decisive, as the Russians withdrew in good order. The French were forced to continue marching into enemy territory. Napoleon entered Moscow on the Feast of the Elevation of the Cross—September 14—to find the citizens had set their city on fire to keep it from his grasp. To demoralize his enemy, the deist converted the Kremlin cathedrals into horse stalls. But the absence of food and supplies forced him to retreat westward within a month.

Alexander continued to refuse negotiations. He had met the French invasion with a defiant manifesto declaring that a "Holy Russia" would not negotiate with the anti-Christian successor to the Jacobins until every enemy soldier had been expelled from the country. Unlike his grandmother Catherine, Alexander was a Christian influenced as much by Western pietism as by Orthodoxy. He saw it as a spiritual calling to defeat the one whom many in Europe considered the Antichrist.

Napoleon's Retreat from Moscow, by Adolf Northen

But in the end it was Napoleon who defeated himself. Vainly convinced of his invincibility, he had fatally underestimated Russia's capacity for war, as well as the severity of the Russian winter. He had launched his campaign with more than half a million men in June. By December, only about twenty thousand limped across the Neman River on the Prussian frontier in their flight toward France. A famous map by statistician Charles Minard would later display graphically the scale of French losses.

Though Napoleon fought on after returning to Paris, he was now doomed. In 1813 the Battle of Leipzig (also known as the Battle of the Nations due to the many combatants allied against France) resulted in a staggering hundred thousand casualties—more than in any battle theretofore in the history of Christendom. It was a major defeat for the French and Napoleon was forced to abdicate the following year. He was exiled to the tiny Mediterranean island of Elba, where legend has it British guards taunted him for lacking enough "elba-room" for his ambitions. Amazingly, the unrelenting warlord escaped confinement and rallied a new army in 1815. At the Battle of Waterloo, however, he was decisively defeated by an international coalition including Russia, Britain, Austria, Prussia, Sweden, and Spain.

The whole of European Christendom had been forced to endure an upheaval caused by the forging of utopia. In this something unprecedented had occurred. There had always been wars, but there had never been wars that so consumed the complete energies of a civilization. In the past, conflict was accepted as a given but was limited by the political and economic investments of the crown or aristocracy that waged it. Common people followed their commanders into battle but without the sense of transforming the world in doing so. Even the consuming wars of Western religion had been waged to achieve finite confessional ends.

The wars unleashed by the French Revolution were different. They were no longer ordinary in the sense of being finite. They were extraordinary in the sense of being world-changing. They were the direct outcome, as historian David Bell notes, of a lethal combination of "the intellectual transformations of the Enlightenment" and the "political fermentation" of the French Revolution.[8]

The initial reaction to this cataclysm was a concerted effort to step back from what was considered the abyss of republicanism. The victorious leaders of Europe wanted to reestablish the political *status quo ante*. The Congress of Vienna that convened in 1815 thus restored monarchy to France as if the revolution had never happened. It also created a diplomatic balance of power to prevent her from ever causing such upheavals again. The agreement was not particularly creative, especially because its architect, Austria's foreign minister, Klemens von Metternich (d. 1859), was really committed only to maintaining the integrity of absolutism. Neither France nor Britain, where constitutional monarchy continued unimpeded, was likely to cooperate very long with a reactionary foreign policy. Russia, Austria, and Prussia, on the other hand, did.

In fact, at the incentive of Tsar Alexander, these three easternmost great powers forged a curious agreement called the Holy Alliance. The Russian ruler had grown to be something of a mystic during the war against Napoleon. Inheriting Petersburg's eighteenth-century court, he had not been raised to think of himself as a devout Christian ruler. In fact, he had not even read through the New Testament until shortly before war broke out.

8 David A. Bell, *The First Total War: Napoleon's Europe and the Birth of Warfare as We Know It* (Boston: Houghton Mifflin, 2007), 9.

When he did so, it was under the influence of an imported German pietism. What is more, Anglican ecclesiology was adapted to Russian needs according to one statute declaring the tsar the "supreme head" of the Orthodox Church. There was little respect for tradition in all of this, and the product was what Georges Florovsky called a "mongrel form of Christianity."[1] But such was the situation for those sovereigns who, through ideological reaction to the revolution, grasped at what faith they could find in a court culture now bereft of traditional Christianity. This is all there was to inspire the Holy Alliance.

Under such circumstances, the agreement was never acted on to any real effect in the decades that followed. At most it produced a spirit of politicized ecumenism in that the signatories were respectively Orthodox, Roman Catholic, and Protestant. Each declared a readiness to assist the others in reestablishing and preserving a Christian basis for government. But what exactly that meant was never defined. As Metternich cynically observed, "What is in fact nothing can only produce nothing."[2]

A more sophisticated Christian reaction to the revolution issued from the pen of Joseph de Maistre (d. 1821). As Sardinia's ambassador to Russia during the wars, he had ample opportunity to observe the doctrinal confusion of Alexander's court, and as a Roman Catholic of ancient noble lineage, he was in a position to offer a correction to it. Like Alexander he was a child of the eighteenth century, and he had even taken a youthful interest in Rousseau. But dispossession of his family estate in Savoy during the Terror quickly led to the repudiation of republican sympathies. He became one of the period's leading reactionaries, a virulent but brilliant critic of the philosophes.

Maistre was similar in some ways to his counterpart Edmund Burke (d. 1797), whose *Reflections on the Revolution in France*, published in England in 1790, provided an uncanny prediction of the terror that was then still to come. In Burke's judgment, terror was inevitable when abstractions took the

1 Georges Florovsky, *Ways of Russian Theology*, part 1 (Belmont, MA: Nordland Publishing, 1979), 168.

2 Quoted in Arthur J. May, *The Age of Metternich* (New York: Holt, Rinehart, and Winston, 1963), 19.

place of customs. Both men believed good government does not issue from reasoned treatises and bills of rights. Justice and social well-being depend on tradition, which will be different for every state insofar as every people has a unique historical experience behind it. Only by following the accumulated wisdom of the past can a government protect its populace from the ambitions and passions of idealists and revolutionaries. The dreams of Rousseau, they claimed, are fantasies at best and demonic delusions at worst.

Maistre, however, was more extreme than Burke in laying down a doctrine of conservatism. The Anglo-Irishman had not been opposed to revolution as such and sympathized with both the Glorious Revolution and the American Revolution. "A nation without the means of reform," Burke once said, "is without the means of its survival." Maistre was not so optimistic. In fact, in his war on the philosophes he sought to ally himself with their primordial enemy, Augustine. He claimed that since all men are incapable of willing good, it is necessary to restrain them with a paternalistic and unyielding state. In the words of Isaiah Berlin, Maistre was convinced that

> *men are by nature evil, self-destructive animals, full of conflicting drives, who do not know what they want, want what they do not want, do not want what they want, and it is only when they are kept under constant control and rigorous discipline by some authoritarian elite—a church, a state, or some other body from whose decisions there is no appeal—that they can hope to survive and be saved.*[3]

Maistre not only embraced an anthropology reminiscent of that of Innocent III, he actually called for a return to papal supremacy over the governments of Europe, beginning with France. Such a position ran against everything that had happened from the Sun King to Bonaparte. Yet its quixotic character aligned with the ultramontanism emerging among Roman Catholic intellectuals eager to restore a form of Christian statecraft that, now long-lost, had once defined what the West was.

---

3 Isaiah Berlin, "The Counter-Enlightenment," in *Against the Current*, ed. Henry Hardy (New York: Penguin, 1979), 21.

CHAPTER SEVEN

Refining Republicanism

THE WALL OF CONSERVATISM—EVEN ITS most religious layers—did not prevent a resurgence of republicanism in the decades following the Congress of Vienna. Try as they might, Metternich and other political reactionaries across Europe could not capture and re-imprison the revolutionary ideas that had been released by the Pandora's box of 1789.

The French Revolution had made much of an ideological trinity introduced first by the republican Robespierre: *liberty, equality, fraternity.* They were often heard on the lips and seen on the banners of French soldiers as they marched their way through Europe. The words were somewhat indistinctly formulated in the heady years of the terror, and they began to seem outright hypocritical under Napoleon. But when they reappeared after 1815, they began to assume a more refined meaning. In fact, they came to signify the primary ideals of one or another revolutionary ideology.

Liberty can be seen as the primordial slogan of liberalism. This ideology set the interests of the individual—especially of men with property and education—in the forefront of utopia. It sought to advance the freedoms of the citizen against the power of the state. It was closely aligned with the *laissez faire* (French for "allow to act," or, idiomatically, "hands off") economic theory of Adam Smith (d. 1790). Liberalism became the ideology of the great majority of middle-class republicans in places where commerce and industry were expanding. This included not only Metternich's Austria but even more so Germany and France. England was the leader in industrialization. There liberalism as an ideology found the perfect home within the constitutional monarchy, where parliamentary representation expanded at the expense of a monarch who increasingly "reigned but did not rule."

On the continent, liberalism was more disruptive. It was in fact by definition revolutionary, for there absolutist monarchs continued both to reign and to rule. In 1825 a conspiracy of liberal Russian officers who had tasted of Western manners while occupying Paris tried to overthrow Nicholas I (r. 1825–1855). Known as the Decembrist Uprising, the effort failed miserably. Austria and Germany likewise suppressed any signs of liberal conspiracies. Only in restoration France was the ideology effective, especially after

The Decembrist Uprising

the Bourbon dynasty was overthrown in the July Revolution of 1830 and a constitutional monarchy under King Louis Philippe created. Under the new regime, liberals like Francois Guizot (d. 1874) used legislation to expand popular education at the expense of the Roman Catholic Church. Liberals, like the eighteenth-century philosophes that inspired them, usually saw Christianity as an enemy of progress and enlightenment. In Roman Catholic lands they were relentlessly anticlerical.

The second republican ideal of the French Revolution had been *equality*. It was seen to serve the interests of laborers and became the basis of the ideology of socialism. The ideal still had a long way to go. Only in the second half of the century would socialists begin to make themselves felt in political life through the demographic results of the industrial revolution. However, even before factories came to mark the cityscapes of Europe, socialist philosophers advocated radical changes to benefit all laborers, especially those engaged in agriculture. Here again a notable hostility to Christianity was evident.

One of the earliest socialists was Charles Fourier (d. 1830). He contrasted himself to John the Baptist by calling himself the "postcursor" of Christ whose prophecy was that of reason rather than faith. Like other secular humanists before him, and with an involuntary stab at Augustine, Fourier "believed in the essential goodness of man and considered salvation, fully obtainable on earth, to lie in the complete release and full play of all passions."[4] His main concept for a socialist utopia was something called a phalanstery. This was an enormous building in which workers would live, work, and recreate. There they would also procreate. They would carry on amorous relations without marriage, since as Diderot and others had shown, "Edenic" societies like that of Tahiti had supposedly achieved happiness without that social "institution." Fourier even looked forward to the restoration of pagandom's practice of infanticide as a means of sustaining the freedom of the working class to live by its passions.

Another leading socialist philosopher was Henri Saint-Simon (d. 1825). An admirer of Francis Bacon, he foresaw a utopia of scientific advances and technological improvements. The clergy of "medieval" society, as he conceived it, would be superseded in modern times by technocrats and industrialists. His was less an attack on Christianity than an effort to usurp its moral principles in support of the secular ideology. His final treatise was entitled *The New Christianity*, and in it he argued that the essence of the faith was reducible to caring for one's neighbor and the poor. The rest was superstition. Like Fourier's life, Saint-Simon's was one of frustration. His work was scarcely read by anyone, and at one point he even shot himself in despair. Astonishingly, he managed to fire six rounds into his head without doing any more damage than blinding one eye. He died years later in obscurity.

The French Revolution's final republican ideal was *fraternity*. Still inchoate in 1789, by the middle of the nineteenth century it became a slogan for those seeking the formation of sovereign nation-states. As a revolutionary ideology, nationalism was new in history. National feeling had always existed, of course, but only through the secularization of the state during the seventeenth and eighteenth centuries in places like Louis XIV's France could

4 Nicholas Riasanovksy, *The Teaching of Charles Fourier* (Berkeley: University of California, 1969), 100.

it become a vehicle for republican aspirations. Like socialism, its time was yet to come. But by the end of the nineteenth century, nationalism would alter politics and bring an end to the carefully designed diplomatic "concert of Europe" arranged in 1815.

Nationalism was also like socialism in its appeal to a Christianity denuded of the kingdom of heaven. For instance, Giuseppe Mazzini (d. 1872) spoke regularly of the Roman Catholic faith to his fellow Italians. However, he scuttled all but the vaguest of its statements about brotherly unity. In *Faith and the Future*—a work, like Saint-Simon's *New Christianity*, projected into an unfulfilled future—he replaced doctrinal tradition about the Incarnation with the ideology of national sovereignty. In the old order of divine-right monarchy, he argued, the divine remained exclusively transcendent. But through republicanism the deity became truly immanent in the life of the nation.[5]

The three republican ideologies of liberalism, socialism, and nationalism simmered under the tight lid of reactionary conservatism during the decades following the Congress of Vienna. Then, in 1848, they blew the lid completely off. The explosion began in France. In February, King Louis Philippe, constitutional monarch though he was, fled as a republic was again declared. The excitement of this event was felt throughout continental Europe. Revolutionaries in Italy, Germany, and even Metternich's Austria took to the streets and the landed estates to demand new governments.

Of the great powers of continental Europe, only one remained unperturbed. Russia lacked the political, social, and intellectual infrastructure that made radicalism so volatile in the West. In fact, in the spirit of the Holy Alliance, Tsar Nicholas I even resolved to help put down the revolutions through military intervention. To this end, an aristocratic ball was suddenly interrupted one evening when the tsar walked in and declared, "Gentlemen, saddle your horses! France has again declared herself a republic."

The Russian army never needed to march on Paris, however. Within a short span of time, the revolutionary outbursts died out on their own or

5 Salo Wittmayer Baron, *Modern Nationalism and Religion* (New York: Harper and Brothers, 1947), 52.

were put down with force by governments. Throughout Germany, republicans were divided between mutually exclusive ideals of constitutional monarchy and national unification. When an assembly of revolutionaries known as the Frankfurt Assembly finally sent a delegation to the king of Prussia with a condescending invitation to rule a united Germany as a constitutional monarch, the absolutist Frederick William IV scoffed, "I would never accept my crown from the gutter." Shorn of popular support, the Assembly was arrested the following year.

In Austria, things were more ominous for the government. In an empire containing numerous nationalities subordinate to the Germans, nationalism promised to bring the monarchy to its knees. But when a Hungarian uprising began to march on the capital, it was taken by surprise as the Russian army attacked from the rear. Though Metternich was forced to flee Vienna, the Habsburg monarchy was consequently saved.

Only in France did the revolutions of 1848 fundamentally alter the political landscape. There socialists succeeded in introducing a welfare system of state-run workshops, and universal male suffrage was introduced to elect the president of a Second Republic. A plebiscite was held in 1849, and the winner turned out to be the nephew of Napoleon Bonaparte. It was not a good sign. Louis Napoleon had little interest in the republican ideals of the revolutionaries. Perhaps it was genetic. For as the bad memory of political upheaval faded, France's first president began to dream about filling his famous uncle's dictatorial shoes.

There was one modern state in which republicanism was neither revolutionary nor inherently antireligious. This was the United States of America. Her system of government was based from the start on the principle of popular sovereignty. The origins of this are to be found, in the first place, in the congregationalist polity of churches during colonial times. The absence of a strong hierarchy in the Puritan tradition, coupled with the anti-ecclesial spirit of the Great Awakening, made American Protestantism a vehicle for representative government. What is more, the pietistic value placed on religious individualism cultivated an attitude toward authority that inclined it toward constitutional protections.

Another way in which the Awakening cultivated the formation of a republic was the optimism it exuded. Even Edwards, whose grim *Sinners in the Hands of an Angry God* filled congregants with terror, emphasized in other contexts the great opportunities opening up for American Protestants who took religious transformation seriously. Alan Heimert noted that by embracing a postmillennial view of history—in which Christ's fearful judgment is expected to come only after a long reign of peace and prosperity—Edwards and other evangelicals stimulated hopes that a broadly equitable society could be created. The result was "an optimistic view of history."[6] This Christian conviction dovetailed, paradoxically, with that of the anti-evangelical philosophes, whose struggle against Augustinianism had similar goals. Both, it turned out, were utopian. Thus when British tyranny became seen as intolerable under King George III, American Protestants linked arms with American deists in 1776 to declare their independence.

That the "founding fathers" were often deists who held traditional Christianity in contempt proved of little significance. Unlike in France, where revolution resulted almost inevitably in antireligious terror, no such religious turbulence troubled the American Revolution. Perhaps the most notorious case of apostasy was that of Thomas Jefferson (d. 1826). A thoroughgoing Francophile who did what he could to defend French excesses, Jefferson was known to have opposed the influence of the Christian clergy at every turn. For him history "furnishes no example of a priest-ridden people maintaining a free civil government."[7] But this was still a long way from Diderot's notorious slogan that human freedom would not be achieved until the last monarch had been strangled with the entrails of the last priest.

At the end of his life, Jefferson composed a deistic account of the life of Jesus—whom he respected, as Voltaire had, only as a moral genius. The work was dubbed the "Jefferson Bible," and it was a reworking of the Gospels. Jefferson confided in a friend that the project was an effort "to separate the

---

6 Alan Heimert, *Religion and the American Mind: From the Great Awakening to the Revolution* (Cambridge, MA: Harvard University, 1966), 62.

7 Quoted in Sandra Rebok, *Humboldt and Jefferson: A Transatlantic Friendship of the Enlightenment* (Charlottesville: University of Virginia, 2014), 56.

Thomas Jefferson

diamonds from the dunghill." That is, the canonical Gospels were a deposit of superstitious excrement that nevertheless contained a number of admirable moral principles. Faithful to the tenets of deism, however, Jefferson refused to peddle any of their miracles. So in his account, Jesus of Nazareth is not the Son of God, nor is He born of a virgin, but takes His place in a long line of Jewish rabbis to preach a morality of love and humility. When the religious and political authorities—the predecessors to the Roman Catholic Church and her allied monarchs—decide to put Him to death, He dies nobly like Socrates. And that is the end of Thomas Jefferson's anti-Gospel. There is, of course, no Resurrection in it.

But such deism was not imposed on a predominantly Christian society through radical, culture-altering legislation as it had been in France. Significantly, the Jefferson Bible was in fact never published. Nor were the views of other apostate founding fathers such as Benjamin Franklin, Ethan Allen, or, perhaps, George Washington.

An exception was Thomas Paine. He was an advocate of independence and used his talent for rhetoric in *Common Sense*, one of the most stirring documents of the American Revolution. Later, during the French Revolution, he returned to Europe to participate in the excitement. He defended republicanism against Edmund Burke's *Reflections* by writing a treatise entitled *Rights of Man*. But his most antireligious work was *Age of Reason*, written in part while languishing in a Parisian prison during the Reign of Terror. In it he tore into Christianity as even Voltaire had failed to do. For this militant deist, the historical faith of Christendom is nothing but "a fable, which, for absurdity and extravagance is not exceeded by anything that is to be found in the mythology of the ancients."[8]

Nevertheless, when the founders met at the Constitutional Convention in 1787 (where Jefferson was absent and Paine played no direct role), the resulting form of government was thoroughly republican without being anti-Christian. Indeed, freedom of religion was enshrined within the First Amendment of its Bill of Rights. That the same amendment prevents the government from establishing a state religion was not seen as a strike against Christianity. The absence of an official religion was considered an advantage to Christian statecraft of the time, contrasting with overbearing examples from the Old World like Roman Catholic France, or, more distantly, Orthodox Byzantium. It was the close relationship between throne and altar that had, after all, provoked anticlerical hostility to religion during America's sister revolution across the Atlantic.

The anti-Christian utopia of France had failed, while the religiously constituted American republic was thriving. This is the paradox that attracted the interest of Alexis de Tocqueville (d. 1859). In 1831, the French aristocrat traveled to the United States to study how Christendom's most boldly designed republic operated. What he found was a modern polity strengthened rather than weakened by Christianity. "Never before have I been so conscious," he wrote to an acquaintance back in Europe, "of the influence of religion on the social and political state of a people since my arrival in America."[9] In a book entitled *Democracy in America*, he laid out the many factors that contributed, for good and ill, to the remarkable success of the new republic.

He was particularly impressed by the way in which the sectarian Calvinists of New England had laid a foundation for American democracy. "Puritanism," he wrote, "was not only a religious doctrine, but also at several

---

8 Quoted in David L. Holmes, *The Faiths of the Founding Fathers* (Oxford: Oxford University, 2006), 42.

9 Arthur Kaledin, *Tocqueville and His America: A Darker Horizon* (New Haven: Yale University, 2011), 300.

points it was mingled with the most absolute democratic and republican theories."[10] Religion did more than cultivate political values, however. It created social obligations that anchored democracy's otherwise individualistic tendencies. This addressed one of the greatest concerns among philosophers in the nineteenth century: How could the freedoms of a liberal democracy be so trained as to maintain a commitment to the common good? For de Tocqueville, individual liberty was by nature dangerous to the community. It could easily degenerate into competitiveness or indifference. In an economic mode, it could also dissolve the moral bonds of society. But when liberty was disciplined by Christianity, whose gospel valued both social obligations and personal restraint, republicanism seemed to flourish.

De Tocqueville was not always optimistic about the American republic, however. Noting the almost unlimited economic opportunities of a country whose western frontier was forever being extended, he found everywhere a relentless spirit of enterprise that tended toward materialistic preoccupations. He also feared the polity would become satisfied with a government of shallow demagogues rather than refined statesmen. Here he contrasted sharply the example of President Andrew Jackson (r. 1829–1837) with founding fathers like George Washington. Religion was perhaps the greatest cause for circumspection. The notebooks de Tocqueville kept during his travels contain decidedly pessimistic observations about the quality of popular piety. As a Roman Catholic with Jansenist tendencies, he looked aghast at untamed evangelicalism.

In one account he has a fictional observer comment on a Methodist camp gathering in which a sermon is given on God's wrath equal in intensity to the most harrowing declarations of Jonathan Edwards. The preacher

> *spoke of the perversity of man and of the inexhaustible abundance of divine vengeance. . . . He explored one by one the dread mysteries of the next life. He drew a picture of the Creator busy piling up generations in the pits of*

10 Alexis de Tocqueville, *Democracy in America*, trans. James T. Schleifer (Indianapolis: Liberty Fund, 2012), 54.

A Methodist Revival in the USA (1839), by J. Maze Burbank

> *hell while just as indefatigably inventing torments as inventing sinners. I was transfixed by anxiety, the congregation even more than I: terror was expressed in a thousand ways on their faces, on which repentance showed itself as despair and frenzy. Women lifted their children in their arms and uttered mournful cries, others beat their forehead on the ground, men writhed on the benches or rolled in the dust while loudly confessing their sins. As the preacher's movements became faster and his descriptions more vivid, the congregation's passions seemed to grow, and it was often difficult not to believe that one was in one of the infernal places the preacher was describing.*

What is interesting in this account is the continued spell—under the most modern of all Western governments—of an unbalanced Augustinianism. The spectacle of pessimism and despair was overwhelming. "Penetrated by horror and full of disgust," the fictional observer declares, "I fled." But then de Tocqueville has him utter a cry for the God of the first millennium. "Creator and Guardian of all things," he asks, "would you recognize yourself in the horrible portrait that your creatures here made of you? Is it necessary to debase men through fear in order to raise them to you?"[11] The same question had been put by Petrarch and the humanists of the quattrocento.

And so the pietistic Christianity that de Tocqueville observed in the new republic was ambiguous. It drew all men to respect democracy. But it also made all men slaves of an impassioned piety that tended to serve individual concerns. This individuation of belief, he claimed, created a religion of the public sphere or of civil society. Because believers had little or no experience of a transcendent God present in this world through ecclesiality and a sacramental liturgy, they reverted to a faith in an immanent body politic that took the place of such a God.

In this way democracy became a substitute for heavenly immanence. It became a kind of religion. And once it did so, public opinion threatened to become a tyranny comparable to the religious regimes of the Puritans or Louis XIV. The "tyranny of the majority" emerged from de Tocqueville's book as the great threat to American public life.

But there was another side to American Christianity that was even more prone to democratic excesses.

Utopian Christianity

THE UNITED STATES CONSTITUTION'S DISESTABLISHMENT clause reflected the eighteenth-century aversion for state religions. But it also spoke volumes about the unique circumstances of Christianity in America. The ecclesiological minimalism inherited from the Great Awakening made the law almost necessary for civil peace. What is more, a new awakening was about to begin, so radical in its ideology that the first would seem almost conservative by comparison.

That awakening was in some ways a reaction to a doctrinal form of Christianity called unitarianism. Its earliest advocate was William Channing (d. 1842). He appropriated the humanism of the deists but tried to maintain a minimum of continuity with New England's congregationalist past. He rejected Calvinism outright as a religion of fear in which man had no hope

11 Quoted in Kaledin, *Tocqueville and His America*, 303.

of personal transformation or joy. In his view, Christianity was legitimately concerned only with improving the human condition in this world. In a published address entitled "Unitarian Christianity," he argued that mysteries like the Trinity and the divinity of Jesus were to be abandoned in favor of doctrines that natural reason alone could comprehend. Unitarianism represented the rebirth of Christianity in a modern, utopian form. That its break from tradition was motivated by uniquely Western patterns of Christianity—anthropological pessimism in particular—is demonstrated by the fact that it simultaneously asserted a belief in divine participation.

In an essay entitled "Likeness to God," Channing revived the ancient conviction—still emphasized in the East after the Great Division—that human nature is fulfilled through communion with God. However, after so many centuries of separation from first-millennium Christianity and fighting against Puritan deviations from it, he presented a very secular account of "man's participation in the divine nature." He expresses an almost morbid concern with renouncing the pessimistic legacy that Calvinism had bequeathed. "Say not," he admonishes, "that man's business is to think of his sin, and not of his dignity." He attributes the fearsome transcendence of Calvin's sovereign God to the effects of human culture, particularly the example of kings and tyrants. "True religion," he counters,

> *is not the adoration of a God with whom we have no common properties; of a distinct, foreign, separate being; but of an all-communicating Parent. . . . That religion has been so dispensed as to depress the human mind, I need not tell you; and it is a truth, which ought to be known, that the greatness of Deity, when separated in our thoughts from his parental character, especially tends to crush human energy and hope. To a frail dependent creature, an omnipotent Creator easily becomes a terror, and his worship easily degenerates into servility, flattery, self-contempt, and selfish calculation.*

Here the father of American unitarianism summarizes the long-term effects of reformational Christianity. To recover the lost culture of the first millennium, however, he turned not to traditional Christianity but to secular humanism. He transferred divinity to human nature. Expropriating the anthropological principle of man as the image and likeness of God without any consideration of its incarnational basis, he baldly proclaimed "the divinity of human nature." His conclusion is that "the idea of God, sublime and awful as it is, is the idea of our own spiritual nature, purified and enlarged to infinity. In ourselves are the elements of the Divinity."[12]

All of this provided a background to what historians rather unimaginatively call the Second Great Awakening. It broke upon the new republic before the ink had dried on the Bill of Rights. Its character was much what the first had been: a fervid reaction to popular preaching emphasizing emotional rather than sacramental or ecclesial experience. It began with the same kind of outdoor preaching in large informal gatherings. Its leaders were mostly itinerant, and the assembled audiences were often unchurched settlers along America's vast western frontier.

Kentucky's Cane Ridge Revival of 1801 was an early example. During the course of a week, thousands came to hear preachers from denominations including Methodists, Presbyterians, and Baptists. Communion was offered, but without any sense of community beyond the warm feelings of diverse believers. Ecstatic outbursts were common, with people shouting, dancing, and even speaking in tongues. Some even crawled around on all fours to demonstrate the divine presence.

The entire western frontier of New York was another evangelical hotspot. It came to be dubbed the "burned-over district" because of the intensity of its revivals. Its most famous preacher was Charles Finney (d. 1875). He rejected completely the rationalistic faith of New England's unitarians. Instead, he emphasized the believer's personal relationship with a living and immanent Jesus. Departing from the long-term Protestant preoccupation with reforming Christianity, he turned to reforming the individual. Due to the wide range of confessions in America, he all but dismissed the importance of doctrinal integrity. All that mattered was a heartfelt conversion. From this, he argued, it was possible to achieve human perfection in this life. The purpose

12 William Ellery Channing, "Likeness to God," in *Transcendentalism: A Reader*, ed. Joel Meyerson (Oxford: Oxford University, 2000), 3–20.

of a preacher is simply to provoke the desire for conversion. Taking his cue from George Whitefield, Finney developed an arresting manner of address in which individual listeners were challenged by name to renounce their sins and accept Jesus as their savior on the spot. He used several devices to enhance the dramaturgy of conversion. One was the placement of converts within the audience who testified to the new birth. Another was the "anxious seat," a bench placed in front of his stage to which he called those desiring conversion. This was the origin of the modern altar call. Hundreds came.

The confusion of confessions at these revivals dismayed Joseph Smith (d. 1844), a recent settler in western New York. Caught up with his parents in the wildfire of emotions, he had a conversion experience in which all Christian confessions were revealed to be false. He then encountered a spiritual being who told him he would be the founder of the only true religion on earth. Like many Protestants since the time of Luther, Smith saw his work as an act of restoration. Disdain for tradition had been the defining feature of Puritanism, and even after the Calvinistic legacy waned, American Protestants loved to hate the Roman Catholic Church. Even so, Smith's calling was an extreme case: He would restore an original religion that since the time of the Apostles had totally ceased to exist on earth. The New Testament, he was told, was incomplete and traditional Christianity spurious. A "great apostasy" had overshadowed the history of Christendom from the age of the Apostles to the birth of the American republic. "We believe," Smith later declared apocalyptically,

> *in the literal gathering of Israel, and in the restoration of the Ten Tribes; that Zion will be built upon this continent; that Christ will reign personally upon the earth; and that the earth will be renewed, and receive its paradisiacal glory.*[13]

The spirit that communicated these convictions was named Moroni, and under his guidance Smith discovered long-buried golden tablets that

13 Quoted in J.F.C. Harrison, *The Second Coming: Popular Millenarianism, 1780–1850* (Oxford: Routledge, 2012), 180.

rendered, in an obscure language, the full revelation of what he was told was the true religion. Furnished with a pair of crystal eyeglasses to interpret them, Smith then recorded what he called the Book of Mormon. In 1830 he founded the Church of Latter-Day Saints, known commonly as Mormons.

As the spirit's "latter-day" revelation to Smith indicates, more than simple religious zeal was beginning to awaken within the camp meetings organized by Finney and other evangelicals. An expectation of deliverance from a deadened Christendom was stirring. Doctrinal tradition and liturgical practice no longer revealed a spiritually transformed world to the revivalists shouting and weeping in the tent chapels of the American frontier. This is not because "paradisiacal glory" could never be attained on earth. It is true, as we saw in chapter three, that their Calvinist heritage resisted such an experience. But the promise of worldly transformation had not died out, as the humanists that had gone before them toward utopia had made so clear. It had merely been secularized. And now, as citizens of the new republic, American Christians also set out to build their own version of utopia.

The catalyst for this was the rise of millenarianism. Calculated expectation of an eschatological thousand-year period associated with the Second Coming of Christ had largely been absent in the history of Christendom until this time. Traditional Christianity proclaims that Christ will come again in glory to judge the living and the dead. In connection with this, a mysterious period of "a thousand years" in which the saints will reign with Christ is related in Revelation (20:1–7). This obscure statement did not greatly shape traditional Christian cosmology. After all, from the beginning Christians claimed that the kingdom of heaven is already present in the world through the sacramental and liturgical life of the one holy, catholic, and apostolic Church. Only after the eleventh century did millennialism emerge, when the longing for paradise in this age began to be stifled.

The health of a paradisical culture can in fact be measured in part by the absence of messianic expectations; the experience of heavenly immanence and divine participation in this age preclude an anxious need for an end to the world. Such anxiety began to appear in the culture of Western Christendom only with the onset of reformational values after the Great Division. As we have noted, it took form first in the Joachimites and later in the Anabaptists. Both cultivated a violent reformational disdain for the Christianity of their time—the first looking for relief to the papacy and the second to the eradication of the same. American Protestantism, with its Puritan heritage, possessed a similar tendency toward anthropological pessimism and cosmological contempt. Once religious revivalism began, therefore, the floodgates of millenarianism were opened.

Predictions about the Second Coming were quick to come. The most influential was that of William Miller (d. 1849), a one-time deist who returned to his childhood Baptist faith after a conversion experience. After a thorough reading of the Old Testament, he came to hold the "premillennialist" view that Christ will return to earth before the millennium. By the time his scriptural research enabled him to make a prediction, a large and expectant following had materialized. With millions of tracts distributed, a veritable church known as the Millerites emerged. Such was the spirit of the times. With initial reluctance, its leader settled on 1844 as the year of the Second Coming. At first he indicated the event would occur on March 21, the spring equinox (an important date in determining the date of Pascha each year in traditional Christianity). When that date came and went, he and the Millerite leadership returned to the Scriptures and came up with a new date in April. That too passed without cosmic incident. The Bible was again consulted, and again a new date was determined. Again nothing happened. By October, it was evident that Miller, even with his Bible, was incapable of calculating the end of the world.

The resulting "great disappointment" left the Millerites in confusion. Some found their way into other millennialist movements like the Adventists, who themselves soon divided into rival churches. The largest, known as Seventh-day Adventists, used scripturalism to replace the traditional weekly celebration of heavenly immanence on the first day of the week—eschatologically dubbed by early Christians the "eighth day"—and reverted to the preincarnational preference for the sabbath. Other Millerites gravitated toward the United Society of Believers in Christ's Second Appearing, known as the Shakers. Founded in the eighteenth century, this ever-dying body of sectarians (a rule of celibacy prevented sustained membership) held a central doctrine that must have provided relief to the prediction-weary Millerites: Ann Lee, its founder, had claimed there was no need to calculate the Second Coming, for it had already occurred—and what is more, she herself was Christ in female form.

The perils of calculating the Parousia assured that among America's revivalists it was the "postmillennialists" who would keep the upper hand. They believed the Second Coming of Jesus would occur only after the millennium. During this time, the spiritual conversion of the human race would occur. This had been Jonathan Edwards's tentative view of the matter. Postmillennialist divines were not obligated to produce a date but rather a state of mind. Their project was to prepare for the Second Coming by creating a better world, even if it had yet to taste of paradise. In this way they became agents of utopia.

The first half of the nineteenth century witnessed so many utopian experiments that it would be impossible to summarize them. "It was a time," as one historian puts it, "when the imminence of paradise seemed reasonable to reasonable people."[14] Not all experiments were undertaken for Christian ends. Some began with Christianity but ended as almost exclusively secular affairs.

The case of Harmony in Indiana is an example. The town began as a Christian utopia. It was founded in 1814 by a group called the Harmonites who followed the teaching of a German immigrant named George Rapp (d. 1847). This pietist visionary, under the influence of Spener, saw in the wars of the French Revolution the impending apocalypse and in the person of Napoleon the Antichrist. He called his followers away to the wilderness of the American frontier, there to await the end of the world. In the meantime, Harmonites converted forests into fields and built all sorts of productive enterprises such as a dye works, a woollen mill, and a distillery. They held all things in common like the original disciples, and like the Shakers they practiced celibacy.

---

14 Chris Jennings, *Paradise Now: The Story of American Utopianism* (New York: Random House, 2016), 3.

Within a decade, however, they had tired of their enterprise and sold the town to another utopian visionary, the Welsh industrialist Robert Owen (d. 1858). He renamed the town New Harmony and invested even more in its infrastructure. But he was thoroughly secular in outlook, and the eschatological spirit soon faded. With time he too abandoned the town. There is something of an irony, though, in the fact that old man Rapp's kooky mysticism finally caught up with Owen, who at the end of his life embraced esoteric beliefs and spent his final years conversing through seances with eminent deists like Thomas Jefferson.

Another Christian utopia turned secular was established in Oneida, New York. Its founder was the visionary John Noyes (d. 1886). Like Joseph Smith, he was a product of the burned-over district. One night during a four-day revival organized by Finney he had broken into a nervous sweat and stayed up until dawn reading the Scriptures. Having experienced a conversion, he later declared, "My heart was fixed on the millennium, and I resolved to live or die for it."[15] Noyes entered seminary but found the Calvinistic doctrine of human depravity stultifying. He turned instead to perfectionism, the doctrine springing out of the revivals that placed man's salvation in his own hands. As taught by luminaries like Finney, perfectionism was a reversion to the Pelagian autonomy against which Augustine so rigorously fought. Noyes drank deeply from the intoxicating brew. He even visited Finney on one occasion to discuss the possibility of becoming morally perfect. The master stopped short of such a possibility; the student Noyes leapt into the abyss.

Oneida was Noyes' way of proving Augustine—and all of Western Christendom with him—had been terribly wrong. It was premised on the premillennialist belief, picked up in the flurry of debates during the time, that Christ had already returned to earth, and had done so as far back as AD 70. As the Romans sacked the Jewish temple, all the apostles were raised into heaven and Christian perfection on earth ceased. Now was the time to hasten a second and final resurrection to bring the creation to its fulfillment. Modern man was called to pursue and achieve moral perfection, not through communion with God, but through communion with fellow men.

15 Ibid, 303.

Mansion House and community members, Oneida, New York

Oneida's mode of life was centered, as Fourier's phalanstery had been, on a single building. As might be expected, all property in the Mansion House was to be held in common. Furthermore, children born in the commune were to be raised by the community, not by their parents (whose access to them was strictly regulated). And when it came to procreation, Noyes introduced the practice for which Oneida is most often remembered. He called it "complex marriage." The sacramental union of husband and wife was abolished and replaced by "free love" (another of Noyes' utopian terms). Because residents were perfect, Noyes taught, they were not bound by the morality of the past. Noyes himself had long claimed to have achieved a state of sinlessness, and so it was incumbent on him to set the example. Accordingly, all girls upon reaching the age of fourteen were initiated into complex marriage by him.

And since the community was attaining sinlessness, Noyes took care to maximize the fruit of their complex unions. Oneida became the first place on earth to practice eugenics. A man and a woman were scientifically selected by a committee headed by Noyes and then sent into one of Mansion House's reproduction chambers to produce an offspring superior to any that would have resulted without such methods. "We believe," Noyes optimistically announced in the first annual report, "that the time will come ... when scientific combination will be applied to human generation as freely and successfully as it is to that of other animals."[16]

Reformational Christianity was becoming a thing of the past, and even its pietistic alternative, cultivated in the tents of America's great awakenings, was fading in influence. Defined by secular hopes and expectations rather than by paradise, utopian Christianity was in some cases surpassing deism as a force of progress.

16 Ibid, 361.

CHAPTER EIGHT

A Counterfeit Communion

DEISM HAD THROWN THE SPIRITUAL culture of Christendom into confusion. By severing the world from heaven, it set man on a path very much like the descent from a mountaintop. The trek started amid brilliant landscapes inspiring hopes and expectations. But as it proceeded, broad vistas began to give way to claustrophobic forests. The bracing atmosphere of the summit changed to the musty scent of arboreal decay. Modern man found himself a long way from the heights of spiritual transcendence.

Only a few paths lay open to him. He could of course return to the summit and gaze from there on paradise. But in his increasingly benighted state this was unlikely, at least for now, when the nihilistic outcome of secular humanism had yet to be fully exposed in total war and totalitarianism. Along the path that continued downward, a fork offered two further options. One was to accept the loss of transcendence and enjoy the increasingly rugged deistic landscape on its own terms. The other option was to mystify that landscape, to imbue it with a transcendent presence it did not, in its deistically immanent state, innately possess.

One of the first to take this second path was himself a deist. Jean-Jacques Rousseau had never been at home among the philosophes. His dispute with Voltaire after the Lisbon earthquake—when he defended his deity by blaming mankind for the disaster—revealed a strangely mystical side to his cosmology. Likewise his anthropology. Though he was prone to bouts of intense alienation from society, he longed for communion with other men and felt intense pain at his estrangement from them.

It was thus by a metaphorical descent from the heights of paradise such as I have described that Rousseau brought his long and brilliant career as a writer to an end. His final work was entitled *Reveries of a Solitary Walker.* In it more than once the deist expresses his subjective perception that the world and man within it are bound together by a transcendent benevolence. Having reached the fork in Christendom's descent from paradise, then, he shunned the path of sterile immanence. For him, that which led toward a mysterious if elusive transcendence was the only way toward utopia. But the falsity of that transcendence would lead to a counterfeit experience of divine communion.

Correcting the Deists

ROUSSEAU HAD BEEN REMARKABLE FOR locating transcendence in the faculty of human subjectivity. For him the individual was the center of the world.

This emphasis on subjectivity was seized upon by the German philosopher Immanuel Kant (d. 1804). Born to a strict pietistic household in Koenigsberg, Kant never left the East Prussian town and spent his lifetime teaching at its university. In fact, he came to be known to its citizens for a walking routine so precise that some set their clocks by it. A story tells how one day at five o'clock he did not appear for his habitual circuit around the public park. As it turned out, that day he had landed on a copy of Rousseau's *Emile* and was thrown so far off balance by it that he lost all track of time.

Kant had been struggling to find an answer to the empiricist claims of David Hume—that all knowledge comes from outside the individual and that the mind is therefore the product of nothing more than sensory impressions. Rousseau's claim that knowledge begins within the mind of the individual enabled Kant to turn empiricism on its head. The result was what has been called a "Copernican revolution" in philosophy. It brought the claim that man can experience transcendence through an experience called "sublimity." Suddenly, the world was no longer consigned to sterile immanence.

Immanuel Kant

A series of innovative claims could now be made, and all of them boded ill for deism. For one, Kant brought unprecedented attention to the knowing faculties of the individual subject. He placed intuition at the center of that process, displacing not only observation (as had been the case for Locke) but rational reflection (as had been the case for Descartes). This is not to say that he was a critic of the rationalism we explored in chapter five. In many ways, his thought was its culmination. He even published a famous essay entitled "What Is Enlightenment" in which he spoke the language of the philosophes, dismissing the history of Christendom as a period of intellectual immaturity. Nevertheless, as the product of a pietistic upbringing, he hoped to salvage from what he considered the ruins of traditional Christianity a strong basis for personal morality.

With the principle of subjective moral reasoning in place, Kant was able to lay out a series of "categorical imperatives" that all men must follow. The most important of these was treating every human being not as a means toward an end but as an end in himself. Kant linked the absolute validity of these imperatives to the natural cosmos. In a beautiful, anthropologically affirmative statement (which was later inscribed on his tombstone), he declares:

> *Two things fill the mind with ever new and increasing admiration and awe, the oftener and more steadily we reflect on them: the starry heavens above and the moral law within. . . . The former view of a countless multitude of worlds annihilates as it were my importance as an animal creature. . . . The second, on the contrary, infinitely elevates my worth as an intelligence by my personality, in which the moral law reveals to me a life independent of animality . . . a destination not restricted to conditions and limits of this life, but reaching into the infinite.*[17]

With intense subjectivity, Western Christendom seemed to recover the majestic dignity of the human being. Prometheus was not only powerful—his moral worth was infinite.

Finally, and most radically, Kant broke from virtually all previous philosophers in asserting that reality is in the end the product of the human mind. The subjective character of human understanding forced him to concede that the object of knowledge—what he called the "thing-in-itself"—could never be known as it truly exists, but only as the mind constructs it. This principle was especially true for God. The concession was in some ways reminiscent of traditional Christian epistemology, which claimed that God Himself cannot be known in His essence. In the Roman Catholic Church, scholasticism had established an epistemological barrier between heaven and earth by asserting that only an intermediary "created grace" enables man to know an otherwise totally transcendent God. Even more sharply does Kant's position differ from Orthodox doctrine. As we saw in the case of hesychasm, Orthodoxy claims that while the divine essence is unknowable,

---

17 Immanuel Kant, *Critique of Practical Reason*, trans. Thomas Kingsmill Abbott (Mineola, NY: Dover, 2004), 170.

divine energies enable man to participate directly and without intermediation in the life of Christ, who is the Truth.

It was this anthropological question—this fading echo of paradise—that propelled Western philosophy into one of its most creative and influential periods. Metaphysical idealists, as they came to be known, sprang to lecture podiums throughout Germany in answer to the question of man's capacity to know the divine. The groundwork had in some ways already been laid, insofar as German intellectual life during the eighteenth century represented something of a "counter-Enlightenment." The preeminence of French literary figures over professionally trained philosophy professors was resented east of the Rhine, as were the armies of Napoleon when they came.

Already, a movement known as *Sturm und Drang* ("Storm and Stress") had opposed rationalism with subjective feeling. The best example of this was Johann Wolfgang von Goethe's *Sorrows of Young Werther,* which sympathetically told the story of a young man's unrequited love. The philosopher Johann Hamann—like Kant, from Koenigsberg—treated reason as the enemy of religion. He claimed to look on logical argumentation with the same suspicion with which "a reasonable girl looks on a love-letter."[18]

Kant's principle of subjective reason was taken up with particular enthusiasm by Johann Gottlieb Fichte (d. 1814). He went so far as to claim that the individual subject, or ego, was the actual source of all existing things. This enhanced tremendously the importance of the individual and placed him, as it were, at the center of the universe. Another German idealist, Friedrich Schelling (d. 1854), applied this understanding of the individual to creativity, especially in his account of the production of art. He called it "nature-philosophy" (*Naturphilosophie*) and claimed the individual is the nexus between the immaterial realm of heaven (or "the ideal") and the material realm of earth (or "the real"). It was an impetuous effort to make of the artist a prophet, and it drifted very close to pantheism.

Nature-philosophy was also a secularization of Christian doctrines like the Incarnation. Schelling and the other idealists were strongly influenced

18 Quoted in Robert Alan Sparling, *Johann Georg Hamann and the Enlightenment Project* (Toronto: University of Toronto, 2011), 18.

by theology. Many, in fact, started their careers in seminary. But even so, they could not bring themselves to speak the language of traditional Christianity, let alone work within it. Their preference was to speak not about God but about what they called the "Absolute." Perhaps this was due to the fact that they had undergone intellectual formation in the prevailing atmosphere of deism. Perhaps it was a sign of how much had changed in Christendom since 1054, or even since 1517. Nevertheless, as Frederick Copleston long ago noted, "it is clear that a central theological theme, namely the relation between God and the world, looms large in the speculations of the German idealists."[19]

That theme is especially evident in the work of Georg Wilhelm Friedrich Hegel (d. 1831). He it was who, more than others, earned for the philosophical movement provoked by Kant the label "idealism." The term had been used in the past to characterize the thought of Plato and to distinguish it from the "materialism" of other ancients.

Hegel was indeed an heir to Platonism. Drawing on the legacy of quattrocento philosophers like Ficino, he asserted that there exists a transcendent reality beyond the visible world that determines its form. He called this reality the "World Spirit" (*Weltgeist*). But unlike Plato, he conceived of it as being so intimately involved in the visible world as to be inseparable from it. This aligned him with Neoplatonism, which had been applied by Pico when rescuing the West from its pessimistic anthropology. Like his Italian predecessors, Hegel wanted to establish the dignity of man in the face of values that seemed to subvert it. For him, deism may have rescued humanity from the clutches of Augustinian depravity, but it did so at the expense of the transformational imperative. Without a transcendent source of transformation, the idealist believed, modern man would be condemned to a static existence in society and nature. He would be kept to the downward path of sterile immanence. The French Revolution, with its unrelenting pressures of republican conformity, had demonstrated this.

Drawing on the concept of the knowing subject, Hegel now reversed it.

---

19 Frederick Copleston, *A History of Philosophy*, vol. 7 (New York: Doubleday, 1965), 12.

If Kant had indicated that man imposes himself on God without ever fully comprehending the divine, Hegel claimed the World Spirit—his idealist substitute for God—comes to realize itself through the experiences of man. This was a doctrine with potential far more revolutionary than anything Rousseau and the other philosophes had devised. For it endowed the entire history of the world, not just individuals, with a transcendent purpose. Put differently, the purpose of the transcendent World Spirit was to change the course of history. This is not to say Hegel was a revolutionary. He himself was a political conservative living in an absolutist monarchy during a period of political reaction. Indeed, his thought served to justify the Prussian monarchy. However, since man and the history he makes are understood as the self-realization of the World Spirit, the door was opened to political change in either a conservative or a revolutionary direction.

Hegel thus revived Christendom's transformational imperative. To do so, he famously appropriated from Fichte a model of change called the *dialectic*. According to this model, a tripartite process of linear development occurs when a primitive "thesis" is opposed by a more advanced "antithesis" to produce a yet higher "synthesis." Accordingly, Hegel claimed that throughout history the World Spirit had been operating dialectically to produce yet fuller expressions of its self-realization. And this process, of course, would only continue into the future.

The deists had advanced secular humanism far beyond the dreams of the quattrocento, but man's promethean autonomy placed him in a world—so different from that of Neoplatonism—with no transcendent connection to the heavens. German idealism restored this connection. And it did more. By conjuring what Hegel called the World Spirit, it placed the deity in the service of Prometheus. Modern man was freer than ever to build utopia.

The sensation was intoxicating. Charged with the new philosophy, an increasingly post-Christian Christendom entered the most turbulent yet brilliant period of its history. The generation that drew from the wells of German idealism was given a uniquely ecstatic vision of the world and man's place within it. The spell was at once earthly and heavenly. Everything in the world was bathed in a new light. But the source of its radiance was not of the world. Nature seemed to have become supernatural.

This is how the cultural movement known as romanticism was characterized by the acclaimed historian M. H. Abrams. In a book entitled *Natural Supernaturalism,* he revealed the ways in which, in the decades following the French Revolution, literature and philosophy sought to bridge the chasm between heaven and earth. Artists and thinkers remained preoccupied (as their eighteenth-century predecessors had been) with the saeculum. But they were obsessed with filling it with a sublimity that only transcendence could provide. They infused nature with supernature. Under such circumstances, they could not avoid the cultural legacy of the Incarnation. The result was "the secularization of inherited theological ideas and ways of thinking."[20]

Yet humanism in a romantic form was, for all its longing and urgency, a profoundly deceptive movement. The transcendence it offered was a human invention that could never unite the creature with his Creator. Indeed, in some of its most devoted disciples, it led to a state of alienation so complete as to precipitate self-destruction. We will consider this dark side of romanticism below. But even in its most creative forms, the movement generated disappointment and ennui.

Genius and Its Inconstancy

ONE EXAMPLE OF THIS IS the role romanticism assigned to individual genius. Human creativity has perhaps never been so extolled as it was during the early nineteenth century. The period gave rise to a veritable cult of the artist. But the role of creativity was not limited to the arts. Every individual's faculty of imagination became a bottomless source of inspiration. It turned life into a journey, often circuitous in form, that led from the earliest stirrings of desire during childhood to their fulfillment in old age.[21]

This model of individualism was attractive to the growing middle class,

---

20 M. H. Abrams, *Natural Supernaturalism: Tradition and Revolution in Romantic Literature* (New York: W. W. Norton, 1971), 12.

21 Abrams makes much of the "circuitous journey" contained within romantic narratives.

which possessed a leisure and refinement formerly reserved for the nobility. Now that leisure could be used to enhance an otherwise mundane domestic and urban environment. Here a sensitivity to the passions was essential, cultivated by novels read in the shadows of the drawing room and by operas watched amid the glitter of the opera house. Artists stirred the public's emotions, and as they did the world became a field of adventure.

Romantic genius became more formative than liturgical prayer. Its conception of creativity certainly differed greatly from that of traditional Christianity. In Christendom, creation had long been the preserve of the Creator. Man, baptized into the sacramental body of Christ, was initiated into a lifetime of participation in divine creativity. He became a co-creator. But such a sacramental understanding of human creativity depended on humility. Only this virtue could assure that the imagination avoided demonic influence and thereby transgression. Humility's opposite, indignation, would disorient creativity by separating it from the will of the Creator. This is what befell Eve on hearing the serpent speak of a divine conspiracy to leave her in ignorance. It was also the motive passion of that first true artistic genius in history, the architect of Babel, who was indignant that man could not ascend to heaven autonomously.

Indignation fueled much of the genius of romanticism. A good example of this is the case of Ludwig van Beethoven (d. 1827). There was, to be sure, more than a little cause for him to feel dissatisfied with the order of things—or so his hagiographers were to tell us. To begin with, his father was a tyrant. He would descend into drunken rages on a regular basis, howling at his son and beating him for not mastering his lessons on the piano. Ludwig's mother died at an early age. Then, still in his twenties, the budding musician discovered that he was slowly losing his hearing. In an outburst recorded in what is known as the "Heiligenstadt Testament," self-pity and despair took over. The occasion was a realization that he would almost surely never escape deafness. But he rages at the world around him. The testament is composed as a final word to his brothers. But, as one biographer notes, it also appears to have been addressed "to his friends, to the world at large, or to God."[22] It is

22 Barry Cooper, *Beethoven* (Oxford: Oxford University, 2008), 128.

Ludwig van Beethoven

an accusation against a society that does not appreciate or understand him, in part because of his deafness-induced aversion for it. The musician even speaks of the possibility of suicide.

Beethoven eventually recovered from his despair. But contempt for the world around him never ceased. A series of friendships and even family relationships was ruined by his misanthropy. He even destroyed the reputation of his sister-in-law after the death of his brother, using the courts to wrench her underage son from her so that he would be made the legal guardian. The boy later tried to kill himself in despair. As for Beethoven, he never married or (as far as we know) had children. His caustic indifference to others prevented anything more enduring than a series of passing affairs with aristocratic beauties, some of whom were themselves married.

With an ambition of spectacular proportions and no empathy to restrain it, Beethoven took his place as one of the four greatest composers in the history of utopia. He turned the symphony into a monument. His first two works in this form had been conceived within the mold cast by Mozart and Haydn. But the third shattered that mold. It was dedicated initially to the man who was at the time shattering the mold of monarchy, Napoleon Bonaparte. However, on learning that the "servant of revolution" had declared himself an emperor, the composer went into a rage and ultimately renamed the work simply "Heroic." The extant title page with its violently scratched-out dedication still records his indignation.

This *Eroica Symphony* (1804) introduced a new kind of music to a post-Christian Christendom. It was designed to do what liturgy had formerly done: transform the world. An increasingly secularized Viennese society was used to looking on music as mere entertainment, as an ornamental conclusion to an otherwise lighthearted evening of eating, drinking, and dancing. The self-serious Beethoven intended to alter this. His symphony was not to be an afterthought. It was to be the goal of a day lived in expectation of personal fulfillment. Like a church, the concert hall was to be a place of reverence in which transformation occurred. Thus, instead of creating a slow, luxurious overture in the style of Haydn, he opens the work with a twofold slap in the face. A pair of sudden, arresting notes swings outward from the orchestra, as it were, to tell the frivolous audience to stop talking and pay attention: something transcendent has come upon them! And if there be any within that audience who hoped to get to bed early (groggy, perhaps, from too much champagne), they were subjected to the longest symphony ever produced—twice the length of anything by Mozart.

The composer had no doubts the investment of time was worth it. For music had now been recreated to change one's life. The second movement was a sign of this, for it broke from previous molds by being assigned dramatic significance greater in importance than its tempo designation. It was entitled "Funeral March" (the tempo was set at *adagio assai,* or "very slow"), and accordingly it was filled with gravity and emotion. But it was the fourth movement that stood out most. Opening with a furious statement of angst (the almost spasmodic bowing of the violins is considered one of the most demanding acts a concert violinist can perform), it ultimately finds a tenuous equilibrium. The movement makes use of a melody invented for an earlier work entitled the *Creatures of Prometheus,* a telling allusion for the secular humanist. After exploring a wide range of variations, it reaches a finale that leaves the audience—if it has been listening attentively—utterly thrilled and totally exhausted.

Having given the symphony a form that most historians call "romantic," Beethoven went on to compose works that defined the Western canon for a century. Among them is the Fifth Symphony, known for the theme of "fate." It earned its nickname from the famous eight notes with which it opens, arguably the most recognizable in classical music. They were said by a critic to sound like the knock of fate at one's door. Within no time at all the movement swings upward toward crescendo after crescendo, a musical device perfected by the composer to advance his emotionalistic program of personal transformation. The fourth movement culminates even more dramatically than the *Eroica* with a cascade of so-called false endings, on the cusp of each of which the listener would be justified in thinking the work had reached its conclusion. This was another device designed to exhaust the emotions of the listener. In a sense, there is no real ending to the world invented by the greatest of romantic composers. There is only life, surging forward at all times. Depending on how one counts, the Fifth Symphony comes to an end at least eight times.

Beethoven's most celebrated symphony would be his last. In terms of breaking existing molds, his genius now surpassed all earlier compositions with the possible exception of the *Eroica.* If the earlier symphony had doubled the length of the norm, the Ninth Symphony adds half as much content again to exceed an hour in performance. What is more, it takes the unprecedented step of adding a full choir with a quartet of soloists. Mozart had, with the exception of operas, largely left textual music behind. Beethoven seems to have decided this was conceding too much to liturgy, which, by his humanistic standards, was an inferior means of experiencing transcendence. He too had tried his hand at a *Missa solemnis,* but even more than Mozart failed to produce anything liturgically convincing. The Ninth Symphony, on the other hand, was a blockbuster of secular creativity.

Its genius is concentrated in the final movement, which constitutes nearly half the work. The opening sections recapitulate the melodies of the movements that have gone before, rather like an old man reviewing memories of a life fully lived but awaiting a final illumination. That light then breaks forth in the melody that still makes the work famous—more famous than any other of the composer's incomparably creative works. The melody is played first by the cellos, then by the violas, and finally by the violins—in other words, rising through the tonal mediation of the strings like a kind of melodic daybreak.

Then the singing begins. Beethoven decided to use a poem by the romantic Friedrich Schiller entitled *Ode to Joy.* It is perfectly utopian in its vision of a human brotherhood established through the autonomous agency of man. Though it speaks generically of a deity, the Incarnation is irrelevant. The world will be transformed through an abundance of emotional good will. A crescendo of drums, "Turkish percussion" (popular in a Vienna no longer threatened by the declining Islamic empire to the south), and singing confirms this, the most musically utopian of compositions.

For a civilization used to fasting on the desiccated rationalism of the philosophes, Beethoven was nourishment indeed. Yet his was only one of many offerings at the banquet table of romanticism. In its new mode of secularism, Christendom inspired many an artist to offer similar fare. Each considered himself a prophet to the spiritually washed-out culture of the eighteenth century.

One of the most famous was in fact a "she." Mary Shelley (d. 1851) composed *Frankenstein* in 1818 to depict what she considered a "modern Prometheus." The short novel was a narrative of liberation from man's ancient dependence on a deity. It tells of a young doctor's efforts to create life by his own power in the form of reanimating the dead. The protagonist is the victim of a mother's early death and resolves, with great indignation, to teach himself how to bring the dead back to life. He is an autodidact—the ideal of romantic creativity. And after much labor and sacrifice—including the rejection of his know-nothing university professors—he succeeds. But in doing so, he unleashes a monster on the world that only he can stop. Shelley composed her work under circumstances not greatly different from those of Beethoven. But instead of musical crescendos, she charged her prose with agonizing outcries. The genius of her protagonist is demarked by such a multitude of emotive monologues as to make the false endings of the Fifth Symphony seem tepid.

As *Frankenstein* revealed, creative genius could be volatile. This is especially visible in the case of the poet Percy Bysshe Shelley (d. 1822). He happened to be the lover and eventual husband of Doctor Frankenstein's creator. He also shared her fascination with promethean humanity, entitling one of his dramas *Prometheus Unbound.* That work was inspired by John Milton's *Paradise Lost,* which, though composed by a devout Puritan, had somewhat unintentionally presented a vengeful Satan as its hero. An indignant Prometheus seemed to Shelley a more compelling figure by virtue of being uncomplicated by Christian theology.

Shelley was, in fact, an atheist who waged an unceasing literary campaign against the religion of Christendom. One of his early works was a pamphlet entitled *The Necessity of Atheism.* Despite this, he was morbidly and in some ways superstitiously attracted to the occult. He looked on creative writing as a sort of communion with a transcendent intelligence not unlike the Absolute of the German idealists. Contact with it was unreliable, however. In fact, the high-strung poet experienced agony and even madness in its absence.

A great contrast is presented by the liturgical poets of the old Christendom, who could by their faith endure the absence of creativity. Saint John of Damascus, for instance, composed his famous hymns about the Resurrection of Christ only after enduring a long period of silence imposed not by himself, or even by God, but by a misguided abbot. Unlike Beethoven in the face of impending deafness, John in the face of literary inactivity did not

The Funeral of Shelley, by Louis Edouard Fourier

plunge into confusion and suicidality. Communion with the incarnate God sustained him whether he was experiencing creativity or not.

Shelley's "Hymn to Intellectual Beauty," by contrast, is one of the darkest expressions of artistic production in the history of the new Christendom. It opens with a statement about the inconstancy and faithlessness of his transcendent inspiration:

The awful shadow of some unseen Power
Floats though unseen amongst us,—visiting
This various world with inconstant wing

Yet this mysterious power cannot be forgotten or ignored. Its inconstancy causes despair, perhaps akin to that experienced by Beethoven when confronted by his approaching deafness. Several lines reflect on the instability of the poet's relationship with the power.

Spirit of Beauty, that dost consecrate
With thine own hues all thou dost shine upon
Of human thought or form,—where art thou gone?

Why dost thou pass away and leave our state,
This dim vast vale of tears, vacant and desolate?

Shelley finds encouragement in the memory of past cases of communion with it.

While yet a boy I sought for ghosts, and sped
Through many a listening chamber, cave and ruin,
And starlight wood, with fearful steps pursuing
Hopes of high talk with the departed dead.

Yet despite his own faithfulness to the power, it never bestowed on him creative stability.

I called upon poisonous names with which our youth is fed;
I was not heard—I saw them not—

And yet,

Sudden, thy shadow fell on me;
I shrieked, and clasped my hands in extacy!

The mysterious presence of the power flashed into existence suddenly, providing everything for which the poet had been waiting. As a result,

I vowed that I would dedicate my powers
To thee and thine—have I not kept my vow?

But creativity remained elusive.

Shelley thus expressed anxiety about the inconstancy of his genius. Having rejected Christianity, he had nothing but the vague language of the occult on which to draw to express his experience of transcendence.

With beating heart and streaming eyes, even now
I call the phantoms of a thousand hours.

And with this miserable confession, his greatest poem on creativity comes to an end. In parting, the atheist pathetically asks the fleeting spirit of genius to bless him as "one who worships thee."[23]

Nature and Its Impersonality

AS SHELLEY'S PLEA FOR INSPIRATION shows, romantics subjected themselves to powers they could not control, which they found especially in nature. Schelling's nature-philosophy claimed that the human subject is but a conduit or self-consciousness of nature. For the German idealist, nature is not the sum total of its parts but a living unity. It is an organism. Rationalism distorts it by dividing its many parts and placing them under the microscope of analysis. Nature, for Schelling, is similar to Hegel's World Spirit. It seeks self-consciousness. And the way it does this is through man.

For romantic humanists, the concept of a world acting as a subject rather than object of knowledge served to elevate the value of nature. This was striking in light of the industrial revolution then underway in much of Europe, and it is certainly not a coincidence that the idea gained traction as the earliest railroads began slicing their way through pristine landscapes, leaving noxious plumes of smoke in their wake. Romanticism served as a corrective against the eighteenth-century mechanistic view of creation that had made the exploitation of nature possible.

Yet romanticism's exaltation of the cosmos was very different from what had occurred under the influence of traditional Christianity. The Incarnation had dignified the entire creation, not only man's place within it. Having entered His creation and taken a physical body to Himself, the transcendent God elevated matter in a way no human being ever could.

---

23 Percy Bysshe Shelley, "Hymn to Intellectual Beauty," in *Shelley's Poetry and Prose*, ed. Donald H. Reiman and Sharon B. Powers (New York: W. W. Norton, 1977), 93–95.

One example of the early Church's sanctification of matter was the annual outdoor blessing of springs, rivers, and lakes on the Feast of Theophany (Epiphany). The depiction of Christ and His saints in icons further enhanced the glorification of the cosmos. But perhaps the greatest expression of Christianity's affirmative cosmology was the design of liturgical architecture. In the West, consecrated basilicas oriented space toward heaven, symbolized by the altar table. In the East, a central dome above the nave came to symbolize the transfiguration of the world through sacramental worship. From animal statuary carved on Gothic cathedrals in France to fresh-cut greenery placed in parish churches at Pentecost in Russia, nature was transformed through the worship of a transcendent God.

By contrast, romantics transformed the world by linking it to the subjective feelings of humanity. An example is found in the poetry of William Wordsworth (d. 1850). Few writers have so famously celebrated the beauty of nature as he. Traveling to rustic regions such as northwest England's Lake District, he would hike for miles in search of the perfect vista. Much of his writing was based on notes recorded in a journal he kept in his pocket. In "I Wandered Lonely as a Cloud," he communicates to his reader an extremely subjective experience of natural wonder.

I wandered lonely as a cloud
That floats on high o'er vales and hills,
When all at once I saw a crowd,
A host, of golden daffodils.
Beside the lake, beneath the trees,
Fluttering and dancing in the breeze.

This delightful scene does not stand objectively before the poet's eyes, however. Nature possesses a value in direct relationship to the reflective subject that observes it. At first, Wordsworth proves unworthy of the scene.

I gazed—and gazed—but little thought
What wealth the show to me had brought.

But then the scene immediately changes, and we are back with the poet in his domestic environment. It is here, within a stifling civilization, that nature's beauty is truly appreciated. Memory of it serves to restore the soul.

For oft, when on my couch I lie
In vacant or in pensive mood,
They flash upon that inward eye
Which is the bliss of solitude;
And then my heart with pleasure fills,
And dances with the daffodils.[24]

Wordsworth was a sophisticated thinker, and most of his poems are more complex than this. Some took the theme of nature-worship to the point of pantheism. His "Intimations of Immortality," for instance, speaks of a "celestial light" that bathes all of nature. This light is a sort of divine presence not unlike Shelley's "unseen power." In fact, without any reference to the sacraments, the poem is remarkable for its evocation of heavenly immanence. Instead of liturgical worship, the poet finds communion with the absolute in birds and lambs, trees and flowers, valleys and hills, sunshine and moonshine.

Yet in typical romantic fashion, the poet's soul experiences agony. As transformative as nature is, communion with it is unstable.

It is not now as it hath been of yore;—
Turn whereso'er I may,
By night or day,
The things which I have seen I now can see no more.

Again, Shelley's experience of the inconstancy of genius comes to mind. According to Wordsworth,

---

24 William Wordsworth, "I Wandered Lonely as a Cloud," *Complete Poetical Works* (London: Macmillan and Company, 1896), 205.

The Rainbow comes and goes,
And lovely is the Rose,
The Moon doth with delight
Look round her when the heavens are bare,
Waters of a starry night
Are beautiful and fair;
The sunshine is a glorious birth;
But yet I know, where'er I go,
That there hath past away a glory from the earth.

The fall from a state of communion with nature is due not to any deficiency of nature itself but to man's inability to see into its mysteries, to become fully self-conscious of it, and even to submit to it. This represents man's fall, though not from God but rather from nature. It occurs when the soul is born into the world from a preexistence beyond it.

Our birth is but a sleep and a forgetting . . .[25]

The child's delight in existence is a sign of the memory of preexistence, but it soon fades. And as the grown man becomes ensnared by the traps of society, he loses the ability to know his former bliss.

Fatalistically, the poet concedes that only death offers the soul a return to the fullness of communion. Wordsworth's account of this "circuitous journey" (to quote Abrams) provided comfort to a generation disillusioned by deism and the mechanical denigration of the cosmos. Rousseau, looking on from the sterile eighteenth century, would certainly have appreciated it.

Finally, life was once again filled with an experience of transcendent purpose. The mysterious presence of a power beyond the human personality but intimately interacting with it was recovered. Romanticism's mystification of nature was an obvious effort to glimpse once again the lovely mountain peak of paradise.

---

25 William Wordsworth, "Intimations of Immortality from Recollections of Early Childhood," *Complete Poetical Works*, 357–61.

Echoes from that peak reverberated throughout the first decades of the nineteenth century. The ears of innumerable artists became attuned to it. Beethoven, for instance, composed some of his most memorable compositions as meditations on the mysterious powers of nature. While the gentle opening movement of his Fourteenth Piano Sonata (the *Moonlight Sonata*) was only after its completion likened to the nocturnal dance of moonlight on the surface of a lake, the Sixth Symphony (nicknamed *Pastoral*) was conceived from the start as a reflection on pastoral landscapes.

Ever breaking the mold, the composer assigned the work five movements rather than the conventional four. Each captures one or another impression of man's experience of the natural world. The fourth movement, called "The Storm," is unforgettable. It begins with a nervous bowing of cellos that resembles the crackling of atmospheric electricity. Violins communicate the restless shifting of clouds overhead. And then, suddenly, lightning bolts strike. Drums explode and horns scream. Torrents of rain come down through the descending notes of the strings. The wind howls via the woodwinds, and for a moment a piccolo even captures a screaming gust passing violently through the trees overhead. Then, as suddenly as the storm appeared, it dissipates. The orchestra falls silent, and low drum rolls of distant thunder indicate it has moved on to other landscapes. The subjective listener is left soaked in sweat if not rainwater and thrilled by his encounter with the transcendent grandeur of nature.

The German painter Caspar David Friedrich (d. 1840) was another to hear the dying echoes of Christendom's paradisiacal culture. He too held a radically subjectivistic view of creativity. "An artist should not paint what he sees before him," he was fond of saying, "but what he sees within him." This is striking for one who painted landscapes and almost nothing else. By depicting the majesty of nature, he believed he was revealing the absolute that abides in every man. An early expression of this is his Tetschen altarpiece. Unlike all depictions of the cross for use on an altar table made in the past, this one shows a Crucifixion set in the mountains. Fir trees and turbulent purple clouds are as important in it as the body of Christ, which almost merges indistinguishably with the cross on which it hangs. Set as the backdrop for the Roman Catholic Mass, the work represents nature as a sacrament.

Friedrich's paintings contributed visibly to the utopian disorientation of the West. In the old Christendom, orientation had been liturgical. People were directed by traditional Christianity toward the kingdom of heaven, which is not of this world. Friedrich's paintings served the humanistic project of reorienting Christendom toward a spiritually untransformed world. The way in which they do this is brilliant. His stunning landscapes frequently employ a single human figure as an orienting device. This figure is never shown facing the painting's viewers but rather turned with his back to them, as a priest might be at the head of a liturgical assembly. The effect is to direct viewers toward the landscape in front of the figure. There, a transcendent nature offers transformation.

Woman before the Rising Sun is perhaps the most pantheistic example, as the singular figure holds her hands out in the ancient orans position of supplication as the sun breaks over the eastern horizon in front of her. Other landscapes are even more refined and therefore more liturgical. *Two Men Contemplating the Moon* is thoroughly Wordsworthian in its nature-worship. The romantic poet's "I Wandered Lonely as a Cloud" is brought to mind by Friedrich's *Woman at the Window*, in which a lone woman transcends a claustrophobic domesticity by gazing toward a horizon of trees and open sky.

Perhaps the most memorable of Friedrich's liturgical landscapes is *Wanderer above the Sea of Fog*. It depicts a singular figure standing atop a mountain peak not unlike those to which Doctor Frankenstein had been drawn during his most creative spells. Below him, piercing the mists here and there, are mountain peaks. The man stands above the earth, godlike in his autonomy. The work might even be compared to the portrait of individual self-confidence and strength that is *Blue Boy* by Thomas Gainsborough. But though Friedrich's man too is handsomely dressed, there is something about his contact with nature that is unsettling. His hair is disheveled by a wind that also carries the fog in disparate directions. There is a sense of instability, even impending chaos. In Friedrich's romantic masterpiece, man stands grandly on the summit of the earth; yet even there he appears vulnerable.

Nature compensated for the loss of a paradisiacal culture in the new world as in the old. In New England, Puritanism had by this time finally run its disquieted course. Its indictment of human nature could no longer be squared with the achievements of the eighteenth century. For those who found the recurring awakenings of evangelicalism unseemly, a new form of Christianity was offered by unitarianism. As we saw in the previous chapter, advocates like William Channing claimed human nature possesses a kind of autonomous divinity. However, even this utopian form of Christianity was too traditional for some intellectuals.

One of these was Ralph Waldo Emerson (d. 1882). He himself had been a unitarian minister for a time before resigning to pursue intellectual inquiry more freely. He was deeply influenced by German idealism and the claim that transcendent reality is not known through Scripture or tradition but through subjective reasoning.

In 1838, Emerson was invited to speak at the commencement ceremonies of Harvard Divinity School, which had by now abandoned its Calvinist heritage in favor of unitarianism. Emerson scandalized even these modernists, however, by asserting that Jesus is not divine. Interestingly, his way of introducing the assertion was to contextualize it indignantly within the history of Western religious violence. He has an imaginary opponent declare, "I will kill you, if you say that [Christ] was a man." Such times are past, the radical announces to Harvard's graduates. "Historical Christianity has fallen into the error that corrupts all attempts to communicate religion."[1]

Emerson's break from unitarianism created a new religious movement known as transcendentalism. As much a philosophy as a religion, it took humanism a step further toward actual atheism. In an important work entitled *Nature*, Emerson stated that "the imagination may be defined to be, the use which Reason makes of the material world." Like Hegel's World Spirit, a transcendent power named Reason realizes itself through human faculties such as the imagination and intuition. Emerson shared Wordsworth's sense

1 Ralph Waldo Emerson, "An Address Delivered before the Senior Class in Divinity College," in *Nature, Addresses, and Lectures* (Boston: Houghton Mifflin, 1898), 117–48.

that childlike naivety was necessary to develop these faculties. Traditional doctrine and worship, on the other hand, only impaired them. "The lover of nature is he whose inward and outward senses are still truly adjusted to each other; who has retained the spirit of infancy even into the era of manhood. His intercourse with heaven and earth, becomes part of his daily food." Recommending the unspoiled woods as the realm of "perpetual youth," Emerson goes on to conclude that through submission to nature,

> *I become a transparent eye-ball. I am nothing. I see all. The currents of the Universal Being circulate through me; I am part or particle of God.*[2]

This kind of language resembles the mysticism of an earlier period in the history of Christendom. But unlike the Christian self-effacement of a Jacob Boehme (whom he studied), Emerson had no place in his views for dogma. The heretical Emanuel Swedenborg was more to his taste. But even that fellow traveler into the wilds of nature-worship carried with him the unwanted luggage of historical Christianity.

In the end, Emerson's heart went to Hindu classics like the *Bhagavad Gita*. He was one of the first Western thinkers to draw on such works. From them he developed a belief in a deity he called the "Over-Soul" that permeates all of nature and joins all individuals together within it. Communion with this transcendent force is not possible because it is not a person. Man finds his salvation by living in harmony with nature alone. In an essay elaborating the Over-Soul, Emerson alluded to Calvinism's harsh doctrine of predestination and offered his Hindu-inspired naturalism as an alternative to it. The impression made is that the resilient legacy of anthropological pessimism, which the freethinker would have found all around him growing up in New England, played an important role in his radical turn to utopia.

Emerson's pantheistic anti-evangelion was indeed particularly well suited to the utopian project underway in the American republic. It excited the early members of the Transcendentalist Club that assembled around him

2 Ralph Waldo Emerson, "Nature," in *Transcendentalism: A Reader*, ed. Joel Myerson (Oxford: Oxford University, 2000), 125–60.

in Boston. Some ran off to put his vision into practice in a short-lived community named Brook Farm. Residents of the farm included Nathaniel Hawthorne, who would go on to author one of the greatest American novels, *The Scarlet Letter.* Another was Bronson Alcott, who, in addition to pioneering new methods of childhood education, raised a daughter named Louisa May Alcott, who authored another classic novel, *Little Women.*

But it was Henry David Thoreau (d. 1862) who most famously applied transcendentalism to life. He built a cabin on Walden Pond near Concord, Massachusetts, and lived there for two years as a kind of individualistic utopian experiment. In the book he later published bearing the name of the pond, he extolled a way of life lived in harmony with the Over-Soul. Nature is the only orientation a religious person should have, Thoreau wrote. His account repeats Emerson's dissatisfaction with the perceived absence of heavenly immanence in the natural world. "God himself culminates in the present moment," he asserts, "and will never be more divine in the lapse of all the ages."[3] Mutually exclusive forms of Christianity were as numerous in New England as Walden's species of flora, and unlike the latter, Thoreau had no interest in them. America would be a better place, he thought, if her interests were limited to this world. In a journal entry recorded a few years before setting out for Walden, the pantheist confessed simply, "I suppose that what in other men is religion is in me love of nature."[4]

Love and Its Unreliability

IF ROMANTICS WERE DEPRIVED OF stable personal communion with their transcendent God-substitute, they were comforted by the promise of extraordinary attachments to members of the opposite sex. No period in the history of Christendom has so exalted—sometimes to the point of absurdity—the experience of being in love. Under the circumstances, such

3 Henry David Thoreau, *Walden and Other Writings*, ed. Brooks Atkinson (New York: Modern Library, 1965), 87.

4 *The Quotable Thoreau*, ed. Jeffrey S. Cramer (Princeton: Princeton University, 2011), 191.

attachments could assume a quasi-religious character. And as the historian H. G. Schenk put it, they "did not remain always this side of idolatry."[5]

In its heavenly transformation of the world, Christendom had long placed the relationship between a man and a woman within a sacramental context. The liturgical rites accompanying marriage were late to develop in Byzantium, only becoming fixed after the sixth century. In the West, formalization took even longer and was not set until the eleventh century. Nevertheless, from the beginning the Church invested every union of husband and wife with a sacramental rather than a secular significance. In the New Testament, Jesus blessed the marriage at Cana with His presence, and not without a sacramental act of changing water into wine. Paul could at times speak of the physical dimension of marriage in pragmatic terms, but it was he who articulated the most glorious vision of it: the relationship of a husband to his wife, and of a wife to her husband, was both an image of and a participation in the relationship of Christ to His Church. Christian marriage, in short, was a relationship involving three persons: a husband, a wife, and God.

Because of this, marriage was above all a relationship of divine love. God's love for the world was expressed in various ways in the Scriptures, but the most recurring definition of it is as sacrifice. Rendered as *agape* in Greek and *caritas* in Latin, this sacrificial dimension of love is imaged by Hosea's selfless pursuit of the unfaithful Gomer. It is fulfilled in Christ, who is love incarnate. According to the Apostle John, "God is love" (1 John 4:16). And according to the same apostle, "God so loved the world as to give to it his only begotten Son, that whoever believe in him shall not perish but have eternal life" (John 3:16). Through the Incarnation, God imparts this love to men. It is this that deifies the human race, as Paul indicates by declaring that in contrast to all other human virtues, "love never ends" (1 Cor. 13:8).

Another type of love found in the Scriptures is what the Greeks called *philo*, a sentiment of affection and attachment that is centered on the ego and falls short of selflessness. It is not bad, merely imperfect. It belongs, in Augustinian terminology, to the saeculum. Significantly, it is this type of love that Peter

5 H. G. Schenk, *The Mind of the European Romantics* (London: Constable, 1966), 154.

confesses to Christ when the latter twice asks him on the beach, "Peter, do you love (*agape*) me?" The apostle responds with honest contrition, "You know that I love (*philo*) you." Only in the third instance does Christ condescend by changing His question to "Peter, do you love (*philo*) me?" (John 21:15–19).[6]

A third form of love recorded in the Scriptures is *eros*, or erotic desire. This is used in statements expressing the Creator's desire for communion with His beloved creation. In the Old Testament it was expressed most vividly in the Song of Songs. In the New Testament it is expressed in allegories of Christ as a Bridegroom desiring his bride the Church. Such imagery did not, of course, displace the predominantly sacrificial character of divine love but augmented it.

Traditional Christianity was consistent in proclaiming divine love as the heavenly virtue in which a man and a woman, through the sacrament of marriage, participate. And because divine love is heavenly and not secular, it is eternal. In Western Christendom, this was expressed in the rite of matrimony by the mutual pledge of spouses to love one another "until death do us part." In Eastern Christendom, it found expression in the newly joined spouses thrice circling the temple—the symbol of heaven—while wearing eschatological "crowns of glory."

In the new Christendom of the romantics, this all began to change. On the one hand, erotic love became an *ersatz* (or "substitute") religion. On the other, by severing itself from sacrificial love, it ceased to be reliable.

Both extremes were expressed by the poetry of Lord Byron (d. 1824). In "She Walks in Beauty," he records the effect of a young married woman on his tender heart. His impression is infused with nature-worship.

She walks in beauty, like the night
Of cloudless climes and starry skies;
And all that's best of dark and bright

6 After receiving the Holy Spirit and participating in the sacramental life of the Church, Peter subsequently acquired divine love and died in an act of sacrifice by being crucified as Christ had been (only upside down, since he considered himself unworthy to share in the same death as his Lord).

Meet in her aspect and her eyes:
Thus mellow'd to that tender light
Which heaven to gaudy day denies.

The short poem concludes with lines expressing the woman's transcendent purity:

A mind at peace with all below,
A heart whose love is innocent![7]

In another poem, the same poet caustically observes the end of a tender romance.

So we'll go no more a-roving
So late into the night,
Though the heart be still as loving,
And the moon be still as bright.

For the sword outwears its sheath;
And the soul wears out the breast,
And the heart must pause to breathe,
And Love itself have rest.

Though the night was made for loving,
And the day return too soon,
Yet we'll go no more a roving
By the light of the moon.[8]

A more dramatic point of reference is the tangled society kept by Percy Shelley. The tormented genius's radical conception of love can be found in

---

7 *The Poetical Works of Byron*, ed. Robert F. Gleckner (Boston: Houghton Mifflin, 1975), 216.
8 Ibid, 229–30.

his earliest large work, *Queen Mab*. The poem is a utopian manifesto in the form of a fairy tale. Put differently, it is the author's earlier essay *The Necessity of Atheism* rendered into verse. The poem was so radical that Shelley was forced to distribute copies surreptitiously to avoid prosecution.

Every page of the work breathes indignation for the crimes and superstitions of a specifically Western form of Christianity. For instance, an Anselmian foil is perceptible in its reference to a wrathful God's offended "honor." A Calvinist foil is discernible in that same God's statement "few will I elect." Overall, Christianity is presented as the story of a malevolent deity calling his followers to unending hatred and violence. This finds expression in one of many stanzas:

Yes! I have seen God's worshippers unsheathe
The sword of his revenge, when grace descended,
Confirming all unnatural impulses,
To sanctify their desolating deeds;
And frantic priests waved the ill-omened cross
O'er the unhappy earth: then shone the sun
On showers of gore from the upflashing steel
Of safe assassination, and all crime
Made stingless by the spirits of the Lord,
And blood-red rainbows canopied the land.

Such is the theological context for the poet's most utopian statement about love in the society of the future.

To be free, he declares, erotic love must reject any limitation of its autonomy, whether religious or social. "Love withers under constraint," he warns in a footnote, "its very essence is liberty." Therefore, "a husband and wife ought to continue so long united as they love each other: any law which should bind them to cohabitation for one moment after the decay of their affection, would be a most intolerable tyranny."[9] Shelley resolved to live by this principle, and in the most liberal sense.

9 Percy Bysshe Shelley, "Queen Mab," in *Shelley's Poetry and Prose*, 14–68.

It is a great irony that the quotation about marriage above comes from a work dedicated to his first wife, Harriet. With romantic charm, that dedication concludes:

Then press into thy breast this pledge of love,
And know, though time may change and years may roll,
Each flowret gathered in my heart
It consecrates to thine.[10]

Shelley had eloped with the sixteen-year-old Harriet against her father's will. After dragging her from place to place as he worked to start his career, he lost interest in her when she gave birth to an unwanted daughter. He had always reproved himself for giving in to society's expectation of marriage, and he resented Harriet's accusations that he was carrying on affairs under her nose (which he was). After three years of marriage, therefore, he abandoned her, pregnant with a second child, to elope with another sixteen-year-old. The discarded Harriet eventually drowned herself in one of London's public parks.

The new love was Mary Wollstonecraft. We met her earlier as Shelley's second wife and the author of *Frankenstein*. She actually wrote her famous novel while living with Shelley and her half-sister on Lake Geneva within sight of the picturesque Alps. Lord Byron was one of their regular houseguests, and the two men enjoyed sailing the lake and climbing the mountains as they talked about the virtues of free love.

In no time at all, Byron had seduced Mary's half-sister. But that was not the worst of it. Percy also began an affair with the girl. Then, when the offended Mary objected, he talked his wife into a having an affair with an old college friend of his who happened to be staying in their sexually liberated household. Indeed, as one biographer has commented, Shelley's "utopian scheme for a commune based on shared property and sexuality"—long ago advocated in *Queen Mab*—very nearly found its fulfillment

10 Ibid.

on a small scale amid the romantic landscapes of Switzerland.[11]

Not every romantic was so open-minded. The life of Scottish poet and novelist Walter Scott, for instance, was unmarked by utopian promiscuity. But he was rather the exception than the rule. The great majority held traditional Christianity's vision of love in contempt. Some, like George Sand (d. 1876), matched Shelley's infidelity. This Frenchwoman was famous for her depiction of personally transformative love. Her many novels featured young women whose passion for lovers carried them out of the doldrums of daily routine and onto a pinnacle of vitality. She lived out the same passions—in one case conducting an affair with the Polish composer Frédéric Chopin—and they finally led her to abandon her husband and children.

Perhaps the most notorious disciple of eros was the German composer Richard Wagner (d. 1883). He was the last of the four greatest composers in the age of utopia, though his contribution to Western music hinged on a vision of art edging toward the precipice of nihilism. One of his early operas, however, expressed with music what Byron and Shelley had been arguing in verse. *Tannhäuser* involved public performances with large-scale financing, in contrast to the small print run and clandestine distribution of *Queen Mab*. This meant that it had to conform more obviously to conventional tastes, and Wagner was careful to cloak its revolutionary exploration of free love.

The plot displays the new Christendom's tension between Venus and the Virgin Mary. An eponymous hero struggles between his love for both Venus (an actual character in the story), who inspires his most transcendent experience of love, and a virginal sweetheart named Elisabeth. We meet him first in the realm of Venus amid a choreographed bacchanalia. In the final act, both women beckon to him, one for ecstasy and the other to undergo repentance. In line with the bourgeois tastes of the time, it was necessary for Elisabeth to prevail. She dies in the final act while praying to the Virgin Mary for Tannhäuser's salvation. The hero then renounces Venus and falls over dead with the words, "Holy Elisabeth, pray for me!" But it is clear from the life Wagner lived that his true goddess was Venus.

---

11 Anne K. Mellor, *Mary Shelley: Her Life, Her Fiction, Her Monsters* (New York: Routledge, 1988), 30.

Venus and Tannhäuser, by Lawrence Koe

He was married early to a simple girl named Minna, who was in some ways a model for Elisabeth. She followed him throughout Europe as he searched for commissions, always supporting him and making sacrifices for his sake. Yet in every city they lived in—however briefly—he seems to have betrayed her. In one case, a wine merchant threatened to shoot the composer after discovering his wife's plans to run off with him. In another, a generous patron found his wife had been seduced while the maestro was living at the patron's expense in his own house. Yet another case involves a loyal advocate of Wagner's revolutionary style who came to stay with his own new wife in tow. Her name was Cosima, and she was the daughter of Franz Liszt. Soon, Wagner was producing children with her under the very nose of his friend. As for Minna, she was abandoned and later died in despair.

Wagner's subsequent marriage to his paramour (the friend had finally granted Cosima a divorce "for the sake of Wagner's genius") did not lead to anything resembling sacrificial love. Venus and not the Virgin Mary remained his guiding muse. In fact, his infidelities only multiplied. One day, the second Frau Wagner answered the door to find an embittered female singer in front of her, claiming the maestro had deflowered her during rehearsals for the upcoming opera *Parsifal*—a story, ironically, of a man who renounces sexual love. It is said that when the long-suffering second wife confronted Wagner about the situation, the composer suffered a stroke and fell over dead on his piano keyboard. Strangely, it took more than a day for the mortician to pry his body out of the clutches of the disconsolate Cosima. Such was the cult of romantic genius, however unreliable its pseudo-incarnations might be.

What is perhaps most remarkable in the case of Wagner is that, adulterer that he was, he bestowed on Western civilization a composition without which a great many heirs to romanticism cannot in their minds be properly married. His opera *Lohengrin* is in many ways a standard romance, but its third act features an invigorating prelude that culminates in the most famous wedding march ever composed. That this music actually became necessary for a modern bride to feel whole as she walks down the aisle is almost comical in light of the composer's adulterous manner of life. It is certainly a kind of revenge for the man whose preference for free love had been stifled by the bourgeois scruples of his contemporaries.

Through the celebration of genius, nature, and love, then, the romantics restored a kind of transcendence to Western culture. But just as the heavens seemed to be opening to them, the earth began to fall away beneath their feet.

The Descent into Madness

SECULAR HUMANISM WAS A COUNTERFEIT faith for Christendom. In the form of romanticism, it exchanged a paradise of divine communion for a utopia of earthly passions. And no matter how transcendently romanticism might have conceived those passions, in the end they remained passions.

The original Latin meaning of *passio* was "that which holds one fast." Passion could mean suffering, as in the case of Christ's death, or strong emotion, as in the case of desire. A passion did not establish one's control over the world but rather one's subjection to it. This is suggested in English by the related word *passive*. Seen in this etymological light, the romantic trust in the passions contained an element of delusion. By placing their hope for transformation in feelings, they surrendered much of the dignity inherited from traditional Christianity.

In the old Christendom, heavenly transformation had always been an experience involving both a transcendent God and an immanent human being. This had become possible only through the Incarnation. The sacramental life of the Church enabled man to participate in his salvation. Paul's word for this participation was *synergy*, or "cooperation." Its aim was the deification of man and the transfiguration of the world.

As we have seen, first Augustinianism and then Calvinism minimized and finally eliminated completely the human role in the process of salvation. Secular humanism had been the corrective reaction. But by the nineteenth century it could no longer obscure the fact that promethean man, to whom the humanists assigned autonomy, was becoming increasingly passive in the experience of transcendence. He was, in fact, becoming heteronomous—that is, he was increasingly "ruled by another." And the other by whom he was ruled was no longer the incarnate Godman, Jesus Christ, whose perfectly reliable love for the world was a union of agape and eros. There was now another "other" that ruled modern man through transcendent passions, but this power was by no means clearly identified by the vocabulary of modernity. Hegel's World Spirit, Shelley's Spirit of Beauty, Emerson's Over-Soul, and Wagner's Venus were all attempts. But they proved entirely ephemeral. Traditional Christianity, on the other hand, had the vocabulary to identify such exogenous forces in the spiritual life. It called them *demons.*

One of the most prescient statements about the spiritual condition of the West under the influence of the passions was made by the French romantic Hugues Lamennais (d. 1854).

> *When the faith that once united a man with God and raised him to God's level begins to fail, something terrible happens. The soul, impelled by its own gravity, falls incessantly and without end, carrying with it a certain intelligence detached from its principle, and which clutches at all that crosses its path as it falls, now with a sad restlessness, now with a joy resembling the laughter of a madman. . . . In the shadowy abyss whither he plunges he carries with him his inexorable nature, and from world to world the echoes of the universe repeat the heart-rending plaints of this creature who, having departed from the place that the Almighty organizer in His vast plan has allotted to him, and henceforward incapable of anchoring himself, drifts without rest amidst the whole of creation like a battered vessel tossed hither and thither by the waves on a deserted ocean.*[12]

12 Quoted in Schenk, *The Mind of the European Romantics*, 85–86.

For Lamennais the soul's fall from the heights of paradise led inexorably downward, toward despair and even madness.

Sometimes its fall was broken by hope in a future utopia. Shelley was an example of this. The poet regularly alarmed his wife Mary and those around him with a stated fondness for death. But it was modified by a somewhat abstract hope for progress. In "Ode to the West Wind," he repeated the call expressed in *Queen Mab* for a revolutionary transformation of society. But it was couched in the imagery of death. Once again, the poet summons an impersonal being to guide his genius:

Wild Spirit, which art moving everywhere;
Destroyer and Preserver, hear, O hear!

Surrendering his identity to this spirit, he likens it to an autumn wind that sweeps dead leaves across the landscape. He himself becomes a seed-bearing leaf. He begs that his utopian vision for the future may thus be cast abroad by the Spirit-Wind, even as it brings about his annihilation.

Make me thy lyre, ev'n as the forest is:
What if my leaves are falling like its own?
The tumult of thy mighty harmonies
Will take from both a deep autumnal tone,
Sweet though in sadness. Be thou, Spirit fierce,
My spirit! Be thou me, impetuous one!
Drive my dead thoughts over the universe
Like wither'd leaves to quicken a new birth;
And, by the incantation of this verse,
Scatter, as from an unextinguish'd hearth
Ashes and sparks, my words among mankind!
Be through my lips to unawaken'd earth
The trumpet of a prophecy! O Wind,
If Winter comes, can Spring be far behind?[13]

13 Percy Bysshe Shelley, "Ode to the West Wind," *Shelley's Poetry and Prose*, 221–23.

By the time he wrote this poem, Shelley's thoughts were increasingly unstable. He had long suffered from nightmares and hallucinations. By 1822, he was having suicidal thoughts so compelling that he actually procured poison. He also reported a dream in which he strangled Mary. His growing mania was ended only when a squall sank his poorly designed custom sailboat off the coast of Italy. Ten days later his corpse drifted ashore and was identified only with difficulty due to the ravages of fish. It was burned on the beach in the style of pagandom. Byron attended.

Another poetic reflection on death is fellow English romantic John Keats's "Ode to Melancholy," which, after relating the joy felt in communion with one's beloved, ends with these ominous verses:

She dwells in beauty—Beauty that must die
And Joy, whose hand is ever at his lips
Bidding adieu; and aching Pleasures nigh,
Turning to poison while the bee-mouth sips:
Ay, in the very temple of Delight
Veil'd Melancholy has her sovereign shrine,
Though seen of none save him whose strenuous tongue
Can burst Joy's grape against his palate fine;
His soul shall taste the sadness of her might,
And be among her cloudy trophies hung.[14]

Keats died even younger than Shelley—at twenty-five years of age, from tuberculosis. Byron too, for that matter, reached only his thirty-seventh year. It is a striking fact that so many of the romantics died tragically young through sickness, accident, or suicide.

Self-destruction was an unmistakable tendency of the romantic mentality. As early as the proto-romantic Storm and Stress movement, excessive emotion and desperate desire led fictional personalities of the German imagination to a suicidal end. The great example is Goethe's tragic hero

14 John Keats, "Ode to Melancholy," in *Selected Poetry*, ed. Paul de Man (New York: Signet, 1966), 254–55.

Werther (discussed above), who falls in love with a young married woman whom he cannot possibly have. One day while he is considering his agony, he finds himself pacing back and forth on an anthill, destroying the innocent creatures under his feet. He weeps uncontrollably. Later he finds that someone has cut down a venerable walnut tree whose shade he used to enjoy with his beloved. Again he weeps uncontrollably. Finally, when weeping no longer brings comfort, he shoots himself.

The hero of *The Beautiful Mill Girl* (*Die schöne müllerin*) by Franz Schubert (d. 1828) is another example of self-destructive madness, produced when romanticism had reached its maturity. The tale told in this song cycle is desperately sad. Again a young man falls in love with a young woman, and at first she seems to accept him. He brings pretty blue flowers to her home in the woods. But one day he hears a hunter's horn through the trees, and upon arriving at the home of his beloved, he finds the telltale hunter's gun leaning against the fence. His transcendent love betrayed by the girl, he turns instead to the only lover he can trust. He embraces death by drowning himself.

The final song of the cycle is entitled "The Brook's Lullaby." It is a heartbreaking record of the way the passion for erotic transcendence can result, in the absence of divine love, in annihilation of self. The reliable stream now entwines its arms around the boy, jealously keeping humanity at bay and whispering promises of a counterfeit communion.

Rest well, rest well!
Close your eyes!
Weary wanderer, this is your home.
Here is constancy;
you shall lie with me,
until the sea drinks up all brooks.

I shall make you a cool bed
on a soft pillow
in this blue crystal chamber.
Come, come,

all you who can lull,
rock and lull this boy for me!

When a hunting-horn echoes
from the green forest,
I shall surge and roar about you.
Do not peep in,
little blue flowers!
You will give my slumberer such bad dreams.

Away, away
from the mill-path,
wicked girl, lest your shadow should wake him!
Throw me
your fine shawl,
that I may keep his eyes covered!

Good night, good night,
until all awaken;
sleep away your joy, sleep away your sorrow!
The full moon rises,
the mist vanishes,
and the sky above, how vast it is.

Such words are as heartbreaking as they are chilling.

In some cases romantic madness was mixed with homicide. The phenomenally original *Symphonie fantastique* by Hector Berlioz (d. 1869) featured a narrative program in which the protagonist becomes infatuated with a beautiful girl he spies from a distance but can never win. In this case the scenario was not copied from Goethe or any other predecessor in romantic mania but from real life. The composer himself went completely off the rails after seeing an Irish actress play Shakespeare's Ophelia in Paris one night. He never had a chance to speak with her after the performance (though he would later meet, marry, and then divorce her). He went home like a man possessed and began to compose what in the years that followed would become his greatest work.

Berlioz's autobiographical program of unrequited love leads the hero to an obsession so strong that it causes hallucinations. As the hero moves through city and countryside, he is transfixed by the image of his beloved. The experience is communicated to the audience by an invention of the composer called the "fixed idea" (*idée fixe*). According to this device, a melody is played to represent the man's passion for the girl. In each of the work's five movements, this melody abruptly interrupts others representing normal life experiences, such as a ball and the natural landscape. When the man finally realizes he will never have the object of his desire, he resorts to opium. Then, in his delirium, he dreams he first murders the girl and then is executed for the crime. After his head is cut off at the guillotine, his soul descends into hell, where the composition concludes amid a bacchanalia-like witches' sabbath. Few romantic works are so illustrative of Lamennais's vision of plummeting madness.

Nevertheless, a rival is found in not only the work but the life of Peter Ilyich Tchaikovsky (d. 1893). Though he never indulged in fantasies of violence, his life and work were equal to and in certain respects exceeded the extravagant agonies of Berlioz. There is after all something affected about the Frenchman's unrequited love, whereas with the Russian genuine suffering was an unshakable reality throughout his life—from the nervous insecurities of childhood to the violent, thirst-induced death throes with which it unnecessarily came to an end.

Tchaikovsky can serve as encouragement to any late bloomer who discovers a passion for life after childhood is spent. He grew up in the Ural provinces with little idea that he would become Russia's most famous composer. He was certainly suited for creativity, however. He showed a precocious interest in playing the piano—so much so that his mother found it necessary to lock the keyboard after bedtime. As a little boy, he would run about the house crying in the middle of the night that he could not rid his mind of the melodies that haunted it. He suffered acute anxiety from the beginning. An unforgettable impression was made on him when his mother, having deposited him in distant Saint Petersburg to be raised at a boarding school, bade him farewell to return to the provinces. The boy pathetically raced after her and tried to climb up the side of the carriage before falling off and sobbing in the dust as he watched her disappear into the distance.

Eventually, however, Tchaikovsky found his way to one of Russia's newly established musical conservatories—the cultural fruit of westernization. There he showed a talent for melody and dance, and both became trademarks of his compositions. His anxieties did not dissipate, however. His earliest conducting was done with a morbid sensation that his head would somehow fly off into the audience in front of him, and he often waved the baton with his right hand while holding his forehead firmly and anxiously with the left.

From the beginning his music was intensely emotional. His earliest success, the *Romeo and Juliet Overture* (with its famous love theme), is an example. Late works like the ballets *Swan Lake* and *The Nutcracker* are others. He was drawn compulsively toward tragic subjects. This may have been due in part to his lifelong struggle with depression. Even amid standing ovations and critical praise, he often felt miserable and alone. His condition was greatly intensified by the fact that he was homosexual. Diary entries and letters to confidantes reveal an almost bottomless agony that he would never find happiness amid the swirling gaiety and robust masculinity of high society. In a fit of despair, he married a young female student from the conservatory in order to fit in. The relationship nearly pushed him to the point of suicide, though he went no further than half-heartedly trying to induce a life-threatening case of pneumonia by standing up to his waist in the near-frozen Moscow River one night in a drunken stupor. At about the same time, a wealthy heiress became his benefactor, providing much-needed funding and encouragement. However, she refused ever to meet with him, and when she later abruptly withdrew her support, the composer was left with fears that she too had become disgusted with him.

Tchaikovsky's music never ceased to be on edge emotionally. Sometimes the effect was explosive. The opening of the Fourth Symphony is the orchestral equivalent of a nervous breakdown. It begins with an insistent phrase sounded by horns and trombones, which is then repeated even more manically by the trumpets. Eventually gaining equanimity, the first movement proceeds along a mostly conventional but emotionally inadequate sonata form, returning in its conclusion to the crashing anxiety with which it opened.

Adelaide Giuri as Odette in Swan Lake

Tchaikovsky's agony could also be subdued, and this produced a sequence of melancholy works that no other composer has ever matched. The gentle sadness of *Melancholy Serenade* (*Serenade melancholique*) is an example. More unsettling is the Serenade for Strings. Its opening fit of grief is eloquently resisted by ascending notes, like an effort to inhale between sobs. After a few moments of this struggle, the work gains its composure. But it never achieves anything approaching serenity. And toward the end of the final movement, after a dance-like energy has gained momentum, the initial theme of grief returns unexpectedly to suppress such merriment.

Another work of melancholy, the Piano Trio, is positively unsettling in its relentlessness. It is astonishing that three instruments can create such a storm of passionate despair. Tchaikovsky was a romantic in the lineage of Beethoven, and though he indulged in sentimentality he never betrayed, as many modernist composers would later do, the principles of vigor and form. The trio's final movement is interesting, however, for it lacks the crescendo of romantic convention. To be sure, it also has a sort of false ending, but it is nothing like the device pioneered by Beethoven. It consists of a slow descent into oblivion in which it is difficult for the listener to identify the very last, sorrowful note.

And this innovation brings us to the last, greatest, and darkest of all Tchaikovsky's works. The Sixth Symphony was completed shortly before the composer's death, about which more will be said below. It was soon nicknamed the *Pathétique* for its intense pathos and emotion. Like its melancholically themed predecessors, it opens with uncertainty. But instead of mere sentimentality, the tone is now one of grave foreboding. Deep notes of a bassoon bring the work slowly alive, like a man rising from his bed in the morning sunlight but seeing nothing but the darkness of depression. After more than two minutes of grim uncertainty, the mood lifts and lighter instruments—violins and flutes—announce a melody of hope. This is developed beautifully. But lest the audience think the opening had only been a passing mood, trombones and drums disrupt the lighter melodies, and a clutching listlessness returns.

The movement never recovers hope. In fact, it takes a turn for the worse when, after a dramatic stop, the brass again erupts with the help of the drums to announce the most terrifying sequence of the work. For some five minutes, the composer's agony grows slowly toward a crescendo, marked finally by dramatically rising notes in the trombones again. When it reaches its breaking point, the orchestra collapses with another stop, and for a long moment there is only silence. This, finally, is followed by a heartrending sigh of resignation from the drums. By this point the symphony's statement has effectively been made. There still remains more than a half-hour of some of Tchaikovsky's most beautiful music to be heard, but it is only a postscript to the cry of defeat announced in the first movement.

What remains is nevertheless worth considering in light of the romantic descent into madness. The second movement uses dance-like melodies to lighten the effect of the first movement, matching in charm the touching second movement of the Fourth Symphony. The third movement is unique. It is full of zest and the will to live. It culminates in a drum roll finale equal to anything produced by Beethoven. It is pure strength. Yet it is, of course, only the penultimate movement. Tchaikovsky, following the precedent of the Piano Trio, now does something in his last great work that is revolutionary. He assigns the final, fourth movement a tempo of *adagio lamentoso* ("slowly, lamentingly"). Instead of a crescendo-laced fanfare, the last word of his greatest work would be spoken in a terrified whisper. It was not so much a funeral march—such would have been too heroic—as a lonely graveside lament. It opens with as much anguish as the *Serenade for Strings*. But now there is no resistance to the specter of despair. The man returns to his bed, as it were, to await the end. The final impression is of a body being slowly lowered into the grave.

Tchaikovsky premiered the Sixth Symphony at the Hall of the Nobility in Saint Petersburg on October 16, 1893. Nine days later he was dead.

Accounts of what happened in the interval and why it happened have long animated biographies of the composer. In recent years, some advocates of homosexuality have claimed the composer was the victim of a homophobic conspiracy that forced him to take his life. This is almost certainly not true. He does not seem to have intentionally taken his life, and there is no convincing evidence to support such a claim. However, intentionally committing suicide and acting recklessly with disregard for the value of life are two different things. Tchaikovsky did not commit suicide, but in the end he succumbed to an attack of demonic despair that crippled his instinct for self-preservation.

The composer's letters during the weeks and even days before his death make it clear he fully intended to continue living and working for years to come.[15] Yet several days after the premier of the Sixth Symphony, he found himself in the passionate grip of despair. Even if not suicidal, the mind of one suffering from depression can find itself momentarily trapped in hell.

When Tchaikovksy was dining with friends one evening on Nevsky Prospect, a waiter appeared at the table with a carafe of unboiled water. At that time, an epidemic of cholera was ravaging Russia's capital. Tchaikovsky knew very well the dangers of drinking unboiled water under such circumstances. But with indifference to death, the lifelong victim of depression who had once courted death in the frozen waters of the Moscow River poured himself a glass and recklessly swallowed its contents. Within hours his stomach began to ache. A day later he was forced to withdraw to the small apartment

15 Just four days before he died, for instance, the composer was writing a letter to a contact in Odessa negotiating an upcoming performance in the southern city. This is hardly the act of a man planning suicide. See Alexander Poznansky, *Tchaikovsky's Last Days: A Documentary Study* (Oxford: Oxford University, 1996), 80.

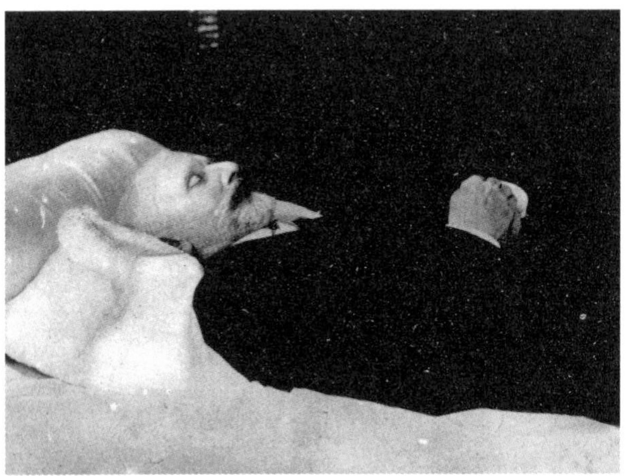

Tchaikovsky on His Deathbed, by Nikoai Gunviser

of a friend. There in a back room, on October 25, 1893, he died the horrid death of a cholera victim, unable to keep nourishment and water down and slowly perishing of dehydration.

There was nothing romantic or even melodious about Tchaikovksy's death. Yet it has an unavoidable parallel in the famous *adagio lamentoso.* As the final movement of the Sixth Symphony reaches a crescendo of agony two minutes before its end, the trombones make a prominent reappearance. But now an instrument known for its strength—for expressing man's irrepressible passion for the world—announces a conclusion to the impossible struggle of a spiritually untransformed life. The sheer authority of these instruments solemnly brings all the work's melodies to an end, at which point strings carry the man—and the audience with him—into the terminal oblivion of the saeculum.

PART III

The March of Progress

CHAPTER NINE

Godlessness and Its Contradictions

ROMANTICISM FAILED TO RESTORE THE world's link to heaven. Within a few decades, its idealist metaphysics ceased to be convincing, and in any case its celebration of the passions led adherents to the brink of despair and in some cases madness. It turned out that replacing the Incarnate God with an impersonal World Spirit or Over-Soul created more problems than it solved. The world, it seemed to many, could never again enjoy the heavenly immanence it lost under the influence of traditional Christianity.

A kind of transcendence was possible, some claimed, but only by linking the present generation to one yet to come.

The Kingdom of Posterity

IF THERE WAS ONE GOAL most served by secular humanism during the nineteenth century, it was progress. Belief in the improvement and even perfectibility of the world was not exactly new. It was the progeny of reformational Christianity, a child that somehow came forth from the convulsions of the seventeenth century even as its mother died in childbirth. And since *reformatio* itself had been the offspring of traditional Christianity's transformational imperative, progress itself could trace its lineage all the way back to the origins of Christendom.

No sense of progress preceded Pentecost. Pagandom had assigned the world a high value but no particular purpose. After the Incarnation, the world was filled with the divine presence, and this transformed it. For a millennium, the world was endowed with an utterly unique dignity. Only after the Great Division was this called into question, as the clerical hierarchy of the West subjected it to institutional reformation. As we have seen, first popes and then Protestants diminished the world's value by driving the kingdom of heaven from it. The reaction of humanists, especially after the wars of Western religion, was categorical.

But as they attempted to restore the goodness of the world through secularization, they could not ignore the transformational imperative. Even in its post-Christian condition, Christendom demanded some kind of transcendence. As early as the eighteenth century, the philosophes had been confronted by this problem. As Becker noted,

> *In order to defeat Christian philosophy the Philosophers had therefore to meet it on the level of certain common preconceptions. They could never rout the enemy by denying that human life is a significant drama—the notion was too widely, too unconsciously held, even by the Philosophers themselves, for that; but, admitting that human life is significant drama, the Philosophers could claim that the Christian version of the drama was a false and pernicious one; and their best hope of displacing the Christian version lay in recasting it, and in bringing it up to date. In short, the task of the Philosophers was to present another interpretation of the past, the present, and the future state of mankind.*[1]

In response, they sought transcendence through a communion not with God but with human posterity.

> *The new heaven had to be located somewhere within the confines of the earthly life, since it was an article of philosophical faith that the end of life is life itself, the perfected temporal life of man; and in the future, since the temporal life of*

1 Becker, *The Heavenly City*, 123.

> *man was not yet perfected. But if the celestial heaven was to be dismantled in order to be rebuilt on earth, it seemed that the salvation of mankind must be attained, not by some outside, miraculous, catastrophic agency but by man himself, by the progressive improvement made by the efforts of successive generations of men.*[2]

A century before romantics uttered pleas to a transcendent yet impersonal spirit found in genius, nature, and love, the philosophes had prayed fervently to a generation transcending their own. "O posterity," cried the atheist Diderot,

> *holy and sacred! Support of the oppressed and unhappy, thou who art just, thou who art uncorruptible, thou who wilt revenge the good man and unmask the hypocrite, consoling and certain idea, do not abandon me!*[3]

So, when the romantics failed to provide a transcendent being whose worship did not exact the destruction of personality, all that remained was man, projected into the future. This resulted in a new form of secular mystification, that directed toward posterity.

One advocate was Auguste Comte (d. 1857). He was in many ways an eighteenth-century philosophe born after his time. He was an admirer of the Jacobins and welcomed the promises of revolutionaries in 1848. He was also a disciple of Saint-Simon and actually served for a time as his secretary. Like his mentor and the other more radical philosophes, Comte was an atheist. He did take one idea from his own time, however. This was what historians call "historicism." It was closely related to the claims made by Hegel that history is unfolding in a linear direction that inevitably produces higher and more advanced states of civilization. Any given historical reality is not considered on its own terms but only in relationship to what has come before it and what comes after it. Historicism framed the identity and value of every phenomenon by its role in the march of progress.

---

2 Ibid, 129.

3 Ibid, 150.

Auguste Comte

Like his eighteenth-century predecessors, Comte was enthralled by the sciences. He believed there is no more certain form of knowledge than that gained, as Bacon long ago claimed, through empiricism. He took this conviction and placed it at the center of his explanation for the advance of history. In a six-volume work entitled *The Course of Positive Philosophy*, Comte laid out a majestic theory of historical progress. It consists of discrete stages. Strikingly, these match in number those of Joachim of Fiore. But whereas the twelfth-century mystic looked to the culmination of history in an age of the Holy Spirit, the nineteenth-century atheist looked to an age of "positive science." Comte's two earlier ages he called successively the age of "theology" and the age of "metaphysics."

The whole scheme was a fantasy of rationalism triumphant. According to it, human history commenced when man began using his intelligence to understand the world through religious categories. These could not sustain themselves forever, since reason (and here he spoke like the latter-day philosophe he was) was absolute. Thus, man came to realize as he pondered the mysteries of Christianity that certain patterns of truth lay behind dogmas, and this gave birth to metaphysics. From the time of Aquinas to that of Kant, metaphysicians had tried to explain the world through quasi-religious patterns of thought—hence the romantic recourse to World Spirits and Over-Souls. Only now, in the nineteenth century, has the futility of their project been exposed. This leaves history only one final stage, that of science. And there will be no further stages, the prophet announces, because no higher form of reason exists. History will be fulfilled when religion and its bastard offspring, metaphysics, disappear forever into the primitive mists of an unrecoverable past.

Comte's scientific millennialism came to be known simply as *positivism*, and it stamped Christendom with a profoundly secular character. More than anything the eighteenth-century philosophes had done, it created a mythos of deterministic rationalism. Progress is inevitable, it claimed, and as history advances, religion necessarily disappears from human society. It is not a coincidence that Comte invented the word *sociology* to explain how the human condition would be understood on purely empirical grounds once Christianity was excluded from science. Though the mark positivism left faded with time and lost many of its details, like an ill-considered tattoo its blurry outlines are still visible in the so-called new atheism of twenty-first–century Christendom.

An old atheist who admired positivism back when it first appeared was

John Stuart Mill (d. 1873). He was a child prodigy, as close to pure intellect as any human being has ever been. The son of an English historian and economist, he soon shared and then surpassed his father's range of interests. He started learning the Greek language at the age of three. At eight years he moved on to Latin. Of the disciplines he mastered as a youth, philosophy proved the most fruitful. But he also gained a command of algebra, political economy, logic, and biology. He was still a preteen when he conducted a study of scholasticism. All this did not mean he denied himself occasional distractions. For instance, he delighted in reading about scientific experiments of the day, and this activity proved to be one of the "greatest amusements" of his childhood.[4] Other children played cricket.

Among the influences on Mill as a young man was the work of a family friend, Jeremy Bentham. An eccentric philosopher shaped by the eighteenth-century philosophes, Bentham became notorious for bequeathing his body to science as something of a joke, but also as an example of how even in death a human being can have a utility. The corpse was duly dissected by a friend and then artificially preserved as an "auto-icon" for posterity to venerate. It can still be seen sitting in a chair at the entrance to University College in London.

Of more lasting influence was Bentham's moral philosophy, called *utilitarianism*. It was based on an atheistic conviction that human life has no higher purpose than the acquisition of pleasure and happiness. Mill embraced this hedonistic view, though he modified it to give priority to intellectual rather than sensual pursuits. Then one day as a young man he stumbled across the work of Comte and discovered a way of making human happiness the historical goal toward which all mankind strives.

At a period of crisis in the history of Christendom, Mill provided a way toward a post-Christian culture. Utilitarianism served as an atheistic system of good and evil. Grounded in purely secular values, it provided a philosophically convincing alternative to Christianity. As Mill asserts in a work entitled *Utilitarianism*, the creed of the future establishes

---

4 John Stuart Mill, *Autobiography*, ed. John M. Robson (London: Penguin, 1989), 35.

John Stuart Mill

> *that actions are right in proportion as they tend to promote happiness, wrong as they tend to produce the reverse of happiness. By happiness is intended pleasure and the absence of pain; by unhappiness, pain and the privation of pleasure.*[5]

5 John Stuart Mill, "Utilitarianism," in *Essential Works of John Stuart Mill*, ed. Max

In this simple formula a revolution in morality was occurring. Good and evil are no longer established by a transcendent God, uniting man through moral practice with paradise. Instead, man is imprisoned by a closed ethical system determined by this world. For the author, of course, there is nothing more than this world, and so no problem of transcendence exists. The scholar ate, as it were, and was satisfied. But for Christendom, with its transformational imperative, utilitarianism was a confection with little substance. Nevertheless, by being baked into the loaf of positivism it could sustain the delusion that man will eventually find his fulfillment in this world.

For it was to the future that Mill cast his most utopian promise, individual liberty. In *On Liberty,* he laid out the conditions under which modern man might find perfect happiness. Unlike Luther's treatise under the similar title *Freedom of the Christian,* Mill's defines human freedom politically rather than spiritually. Its point of reference is utopia, not paradise. As the source of human happiness, political liberty is presented from the very first paragraph as "the vital question of the future." The possibility of its attainment has only recently become possible due to "the stage of progress into which the more civilized portions of the species have now entered."[6]

In a real sense the treatise brings to fulfillment the first of the French revolutionary slogan's tripartite ideals—liberty. It advances the freedoms of the individual against authority. Mill denies the state any coercive powers whatsoever, provided the individual does not impose on the individualism of his fellow citizens.

> *The only freedom which deserves the name, is that of pursuing our own good in our own way, so long as we do not attempt to deprive others of theirs, or impede their efforts to obtain it. Each is proper guardian of his own health, whether bodily, or mental or spiritual. Mankind are greater gainers by suffering each other to live as seems good themselves, than by compelling each to live as seems good to the rest.*[7]

Lerner (New York: Bantam, 1961), 194.

6 John Stuart Mill, *On Liberty* (Mineola, NY: Dover Publications, 2002), 1.

7 Ibid, 10.

This was a manifesto. And as it was being published, liberalism was beginning to transform the West.

Progress

LIKE THE CHRISTIANITY IT REPLACED, positivism was a faith supported by observable miracles. It is an incontrovertible fact that throughout the second half of the nineteenth century the conditions of civilization improved in real and dramatic ways. We can see this by returning to the three regions of Christendom explored in chapter four.

In the formerly Puritan lands of Britain and North America, economic prosperity and political freedom were advancing with breathtaking momentum. By midcentury, England had become the first industrial economy in history. The invention of machinery like James Watt's steam engine made factory production possible and unimaginably prosperous. The reduction of tariffs—in line with Smith's laissez-faire principle—opened markets, and this in turn increased profits. Banks appeared, and as capital was concentrated in them, capitalists began to reinvest it to expand the economy even further. Once the steam engine was placed on rails or in the bellies of ships, England became the center of a flourishing global market.

English capitalism created a growing middle class that lived in burgeoning manufacturing cities like Manchester. Never before had prosperity been so open to talent—and never before had so many talented entrepreneurs sought prosperity. The accumulation of wealth came at a cost, however. The industrial labor force shared in very little of the prosperity and endured a ghastly condition of life. For its part, the new middle class attained its wealth only at the cost of traditional patterns of morality. It had little use for the cooperative values of traditional Christianity.

Instead, capitalists competed with one another for control of the free market. Cutthroat practices proved necessary for survival. The factory owner who paid his workers the least could as a result charge the least for his goods. This served to drive his competitors out of business. Nevertheless, with an ever-growing economy, more middle-class businessmen came to benefit from industrialization than be eliminated by it. By the end of the century, the English middle class had largely displaced the ancient aristocracy in economic power, though not yet in cultural taste.

Britain's sister civilization across the Atlantic had, by the end of the nineteenth century, also managed to industrialize. The American republic was not only progressive in its economic growth, however. Like Britain, she was ruled by a representative form of government that encouraged popular participation. By the end of the century, most men could vote—a precedent that Britain soon followed through electoral reforms.

Also remarkable was the expansion of liberties for groups historically excluded from power. Slavery was a bane to both countries, though in Britain it was limited to overseas colonies and not practiced domestically. The institution was effectively abolished by Parliament in 1833. The impetus for this can be traced to traditional Christianity, which since the time of Emperor Constantine had placed restrictions on slaveowners' powers over their subordinates. The gospel subverted slavery, as suggested by Paul's declaration that "there is neither slave nor free" but "all are one in Christ Jesus" (Gal. 3:28). After the eleventh century, reformational Christianity set an even higher standard, by which popes intervened to impose or encourage more merciful behavior upon the Western elite. Though the colonization of the New World mostly defied rather than fulfilled the gospel's standard of justice, popes did occasionally intervene on behalf of the native population against rapacious Christian slavers. Finally, pietistic Christianity began in the eighteenth century to emphasize the believer's affective sympathy for others and responsibility for social reform.

A convert to this form of evangelicalism was the Englishman William Wilberforce. Using his influence in Parliament, he introduced the abolitionist cause there. In 1807 it resulted in the official abolition of the slave trade. This was followed in 1833 (the year of Wilberforce's death) by a parliamentary act abolishing slavery altogether in most parts of the British Empire.

In America, slavery was opposed by many in the North on religious grounds, even as it was defended by others in the South for reasons often mixed with Christianity. Many abolitionists were secular in their values. In any case, being central to the Southern economy, slavery could not be abolished so easily as in the British Empire. A dreadful Civil War was necessary for that. And even after the war ended in 1865, and slavery with it, blacks continued to exist as second-class citizens for a very long time. But an enormous step in the direction of progress had occurred.

The liberties of women were also advanced in Anglo-American Christendom during the nineteenth century, though only after the First World War would they include the right to vote. "Suffragettes," as female advocates of voting rights were called, were inspired by the same liberalism that motivated reforms of the male electorate in Parliament and Congress. They were supported by a growing number of philosophers who considered individual rights a matter for both sexes.

John Stuart Mill's *The Subjection of Women* argued that the exclusion of women from politics was a remnant of primitive civilization and that a truly progressive society would bring an end to it. Unlike the case with abolitionism, there was less in the way of Christian influence in early expressions of liberal feminism. But the legacy of Christian anthropology played a real role all the same, Mill's prejudice against the past notwithstanding. In the same verse from the New Testament quoted above in reference to racial equality, Paul declared that in Christ there is likewise "neither male nor female." It is not a coincidence that both the abolition of slavery and the advancement of women's rights arose first in Christendom, even when carried forward by atheists like Mill. For it was traditional Christianity that, in comparison with all other world religions, uniquely dignified all human beings—especially those kept on the margins.

In France, progress was more directly associated with an assault on Christianity than in Britain or America. The Third Republic, founded in 1871, pitted secularistic republicans supported by the industrial and urban middle class against monarchists supported by the Roman Catholic clergy and peasantry. As in the case of the First Republic, leaders of the Third Republic defined progress as the eradication of traditional Christianity. With the republicans' control of the parliament, a policy known as *laïcité* was introduced to eliminate the vestiges of clerical influence in schooling. In 1882 religious topics were banned in public schools and clergy excluded from teaching in them. Under the influence of Prime Minister Emile Combs (r. 1902–1905), the republican government further reduced the influence of Roman Catholicism. Turning for support to Freemasons, liberal politicians forcibly closed all of France's Roman Catholic parochial schools. Church properties were seized and clergy driven from the country. In 1905, a law formally established the separation of church and state, to the great disadvantage of the former.

Throughout the late nineteenth century, Russia was seen as the most backward of all great powers. Yet she too showed a remarkable capacity for progress. After being humiliated by an alliance between the British and the French in the Crimean War, Tsar Alexander II (r. 1855–1881) introduced a series of bold reforms. These included the introduction of representative assemblies of noblemen in the provinces and the improvement of the court system. The most important of the Great Reforms, however, was the emancipation of the serfs. By the middle of the nineteenth century, Russian society included some fifty million agricultural laborers with virtually no rights. They were dependent on local landowners and obligated by law and custom to work for them. Their offspring inherited the same obligations. Because Russia was an autocracy without any restrictions on the powers of the tsar, Alexander was able to liberate the serfs by edict in 1861.

The contrast with the more progressive republican United States is remarkable. In the New World, the deadliest war in American history was necessary to free fewer than five million blacks from slavery. In "backward" Russia, ten times that number were liberated from serfdom peacefully with nothing more than the tsar's signature.

As in America, those freed faced unbearably difficult economic and social conditions during the decades following the emancipation. It was at the very end of the century that Russia finally began to industrialize, taking her place as the world's fifth-largest economy by the eve of the First World War (after Britain, Germany, France, and the United States). The government's resistance to liberalism contributed to a revolution in 1905 which, while generally unsuccessful, did result in a constitution called the

Fundamental Laws. According to it, a representative assembly called the Duma was created that provided a platform for progressive political forces during the decade before the First World War.

If industrialization and political reform were the vanguard of progress, they marched in company with other startling achievements. We have already noted the role of the steam engine. Other inventions contributed greatly to the sense that a new stage in human civilization had begun. These included the Bessemer process (1856), which provided inexpensive steel for large-scale manufacturing, and the Haber process (1909), which provided chemical fertilizer for large-scale agriculture. But inventions were by no means limited to economic development. Communications were improved with the transatlantic telegraph (1858) and telephone (1876). Domestic life was improved with the phonograph (1877) and incandescent light bulb (1879). Journalism was improved with the typewriter (1867) and the camera (1888). Travel was improved by the automobile (1886), and the airplane (1903) promised revolutionary improvements in the more distant future.

The march of progress through Europe and America was marked by the introduction of a new institution called the world's fair. The first of these was held in London in 1851. That year, a prosperous and proud industrialized Great Britain hosted a gathering of economists and journalists from throughout the West and even the world. This Great Exhibition featured the construction of an assembly hall made of iron and glass. It was dubbed the Crystal Palace, and nothing like it had ever been erected. It stood higher than the tallest trees of Hyde Park and contained exhibits of modern technology. Britain's industrial

The Crystal Palace, Hyde Park, London

rivals were impressed by the spectacle but not intimidated. Industrialized France, for instance, hosted a world's fair in 1889 and used the event to construct arguably the most famous monument in modern Europe, the Eiffel Tower.

Evolutionism

SCIENCE FLOURISHED ALONGSIDE ECONOMIC AND political progress. In fact, discoveries in physics and chemistry stood behind many of the technological inventions reviewed above. But biology was the discipline that was most dramatically advanced during the late nineteenth century. Credit for this goes to Charles Darwin (d. 1882), who introduced evolutionism. Though initially a theory explaining the diversity of animal life, it soon became, in the hands of the discoverer himself, a way of radically reconfiguring Western anthropology.

Darwin is famous for his empirical approach to the study of biology. He obtained passage on the *H.M.S. Beagle* and in places like the Galapagos Islands studied animal life in precise detail. Returning to England with copious notes and expanding his insights with research at the London Library, he ultimately published *On the Origin of Species* in 1859 (the same year Mill's *On Liberty* appeared). This work advanced a law of "natural selection" which all species of animal are said to obey. It claims that environmental factors determine the success of a given species, causing in some adaptations to survive and in others extinction. Individual members of a species who adapt to their natural environment pass on their superior traits through procreation, and this superiority enables the species to survive. The most important adaptive trait, Darwin claimed, is competition.

Darwin's theory directly subverted the biblical account of life's origins. This actually caused him great distress. But by this time he had reached the conviction that Christianity was an outdated explanation of the world. He had been much affected, for instance, by the positivism of Comte. Equally debilitating to his faith was the study of theodicy, a pursuit inherited from the rationalistic theology of the eighteenth century. Darwin

The Eiffel Tower, Paris

descended from a line of unitarians and was predisposed toward agnosticism. When his beloved ten-year-old daughter Annie died of an agonizing stomach disease, he lost all faith in a personal deity. For him the world became utterly void of a divine presence.

Darwin's agnosticism was the product of both a skeptical temperament, shared with the likes of Comte, and a moral aversion for theodicy. "I can indeed hardly see how anyone ought to wish Christianity to be true," he confided in an early but later expurgated version of his autobiography.

> *For if so, the plain language of the text seems to show that the men who do not believe, and this would include my Father, Brother, and almost all my best friends, will be everlastingly punished. And this is a damnable doctrine.*[8]

Like that of other unbelievers since the wars of Western religion, Darwin's predisposition toward secularism was driven by indignation.

It is quite impossible to separate the scientist from the conditions of his laboratory. We can imagine Darwin, home from his five-year voyage aboard the *Beagle*, walking through central London on his way to the London Library. Every day he might pass a particular street corner where, in the gloomy rain for which the city is famous, a young woman stands as close to the building as she can. We might call her Mrs. Gumdrop. She is poor. She is also a widow, her husband having perished when his hands were sheared off in a factory accident the previous year. A recent immigrant from the countryside, he left behind no extended family, no community of villagers to support a widow and orphans. The middle-class factory owner preoccupied with the bottom line certainly did not offer compensation. Around the woman stand a brood of young children with desperation in their faces. They realize that the rumbling, blood-tinged cough that periodically overwhelms their mother while they stand together in the cold is tubercular, and there is little hope she will recover. What will happen to them after that is a thought too terrifying to consider. For now, they do their best to smile at

8 Quoted in Gertrude Himmelfarb, *Darwin and the Darwinian Revolution* (Chicago: Ivan R. Dee, 1996), 385.

Charles Darwin

the passersby, placing their dwindling hope on the alms jar they have placed before them on the sidewalk.

Darwin pauses at the sight of this family. He takes in Mrs. Gumdrop's deep and hopeless stare. He glances over the dirty-faced children. He tips his top hat uneasily. He then drops a coin into the jar before turning to resume his march to the library.

When, several blocks further down the street, he steps into its genteel reading room, the impression of the perishing family cannot be shaken from his memory. It sits in his mind as he pores through stacks of books, pursuing the key to understanding the biological principle of nature. And with time, a conviction takes form: Nature is not what the romantics claimed it to be. It does not communicate the presence of a benevolent if impersonal spirit. It is utterly indifferent to the creatures who depend on it. It is devoid of feelings like affection. It leaves its children to compete with one another, and the weakest among them it selects for elimination.

> *Hence, as more individuals are produced than can possibly survive, there must in every case be a struggle for existence, either one individual with another of the same species, or with the individuals of distinct species, or with the physical conditions of life.*[9]

These words, recorded in the *Origin,* indicate how directly influential the industrial revolution and utilitarian morality were in shaping one of the greatest scientific theories of modern Christendom.

In 1871 Darwin published *The Descent of Man,* a treatise applying natural selection to the human race. It introduced an evolutionary anthropology whose principle of transformation was naturalistic rather than heavenly. This claimed that man is nothing more than an animal, and as such is determined by the biological forces of evolution. The argument was supported by a recent development in etymology. The term *homo sapiens* had been introduced earlier in the century, replacing the traditional Latin descriptor of the human race, *imago Dei* ("image of God"). Darwin's treatise elaborated this fateful secularistic transition. Man, Darwin claimed, had not been created from nothing by God. He had evolved through natural determinism from apes. Death, attributed to sin in both Genesis and Romans, was now

9 Charles Darwin, *On the Origin of Species* (Minneapolis: Lerner Publishing, 2018), 45.

presented as nothing more than the natural and inevitable condition of humanity from its earliest stages. What is more, Darwin's work suggested that man was not the highest form of life an exclusively natural world had to offer. Consistent with the positivists' faith in the future, it allowed for and even encouraged hope that man would continue to evolve. Someday, perhaps, humanism itself would disappear as humanity was superseded by a superhumanity.

Evolutionary anthropology provoked a vigorous reaction within Victorian civil society, sparking an early skirmish in modern Christendom's culture wars. The key event was a debate organized at Oxford University in 1860 pitting Anglican Archbishop Samuel Wilberforce against "Darwin's Bulldog," Thomas Huxley. Amid shouts of praise and censure from the crowd, the two exchanged both learned and ad hominem attacks on their opponents. Wilberforce asked sarcastically if it was Huxley's maternal or paternal lineage that descended from an ape—to which Huxley replied that it would be preferable to descend from an ape rather than from an archbishop whose fanatical attachment to religion made him reason less effectively than an ape. Like many exchanges in twentieth-century culture wars, the debate seems to have changed very few minds. Wilberforce emerged as the hero of religious complacency and Huxley as the hero of "agnosticism"—a word he actually coined.

A movement soon arose that sought to apply Darwin's theories to society. It is known as social Darwinism, and its most famous advocate was Herbert Spencer (d. 1903). A scientist in his own right, Spencer actually coined the phrase "survival of the fittest" as an alternative to "natural selection" after reading the *Origin* for the first time. But he had already established himself as a leading sociologist and philosopher. He had been influenced greatly by Comte's project of establishing a purely empirical science of society called sociology. For him the key to doing this was found in evolutionary theory.

Applying Darwinism to society, Spencer emphasized the innate competition that exists between individuals. Here he was also influenced by Mill's utilitarianism. The only measure of society's value is its happiness, and this depended on the fittest of its members having the freedom to compete successfully against those whom nature has selected for elimination. In the absence of a transcendent source for transformation, as traditional Christianity offered, all that was left was the natural law of the survival of the fittest. Spencer's conclusion was that organized relief for the poor—those in society whom nature has selected for elimination—must come to an end. He did not begrudge personal acts of charity, as he considered altruism to be a trait of the fittest. However, he strongly opposed using the state to limit artificially the dominance of superior members of the species. Had he passed the corner on which Mrs. Gumdrop and her brood stood hovering in the cold, he would no doubt have turned the other way—though on further thought, he might also have paused to drop a coin into the jar for the sake of his personal moral integrity.

Another social Darwinist was Francis Galton (d. 1911). He shared Spencer's dismay at efforts to organize care for society's poor. He went further than Spencer in denouncing even private charity. Such actions were, in fact, uncharitable in light of evolutionism. When society sustains the life of its unfit members, he argued, not only are their lives of misery elongated but the progress of the fittest is impeded. Galton was a statistician at heart (he helped invent the modern questionnaire) and he determined that British society's most powerful elements were reproducing at a rate far lower than that of the poor. Wealthy middle-class sons devoted themselves to getting ahead by forgoing families in their early years, whereas the working class married young and produced large families. Such was the example of our young Mrs. Gumdrop, whose brood was numerous. And we can be assured that had Galton passed her on his way to the London Library, the sound of her rasping cough and the sight of her shivering children would have filled him with contempt. No coin would have landed in their jar on that occasion.

The perpetuation of the poor through charity had to come to an end, Galton warned, if the greatest nation on earth were not to descend into demographic oblivion. In fact, the agnostic closely linked Christian compassion for the unfit with the practice of stifling procreation among the fit. He used what Petrarch had called the "dark ages" as a negative example. "The long period of the dark ages under which Europe has lain is due," he wrote in a work entitled

Francis Galton

Hereditary Genius, ". . . to the celibacy enjoined by religious orders on their votaries."[10] The only way to save the West was to supplement the law of natural selection by encouraging the fit to procreate and the unfit to desist.

Galton coined the term *eugenics* to describe the way in which social policy experts like himself could achieve this. Opposed to all forms of state-directed charity, he advocated state-directed programs to isolate socially

10 Quoted in Michael Blumer, *Francis Galton: Pioneer of Heredity and Biometry* (Baltimore: Johns Hopkins University, 2003), 81.

unfit people and prevent their procreation. "I think," he reflected in his autobiography, "that stern compulsion ought to be exerted to prevent the free propagation of the stock of those who are seriously afflicted by lunacy, feeble-mindedness, habitual criminality, and pauperism." As ominous as this sounds, it was overshadowed by more private statements. "Except by sterilization," he confided to a sympathizer, "I cannot yet see any way of checking the produce of the unfit who are allowed their liberty and are below the reach of moral control."[11]

Galton inspired the formation of a Eugenics Education Society in 1907. It was dedicated to lobbying Parliament to put social Darwinism into law. The old eugenicist served as its first president. In 1913 the Mental Deficiencies Act granted the state the power to institutionalize the mentally unfit. In the United States eugenicists went further. More than a dozen states introduced involuntary sterilization laws. In California, some twenty-five hundred "imbeciles" suffered this fate before the First World War.

At about this time, in 1912, the Eugenics Society back in Britain hosted the First International Congress of Eugenics. Its president, fittingly, was Charles Darwin's son Leonard. His rather indignant address indicated how far Christendom had come under the influence of positivism, utilitarianism, and social Darwinism.

> *The unfit amongst men are now no longer necessarily killed off by hunger and disease, but are cherished with care, thus being enabled to reproduce their kind, however bad that kind may be. . . . The effects likely to be produced by our charity on future generations is, to say the least, but weakness and folly.*[12]

The ancient virtue of charity—of sacrificial and divine love—had now, in a post-Christian Christendom, been transvalued into a vice.

11 Ibid, 83.

12 Quoted in Donald De Marco and Benjamin D. Wiker, *Architects of the Culture of Death* (San Francisco: Ignatius Press, 2004), 102.

CHAPTER NINE

Religions of Humanity

YET DESPITE THE EFFORTS OF agnostics, Christianity continued to hold the hearts and minds of the vast majority of those living in the West. Philosophy and the secular arts, of course, only penetrated so far into the popular culture. But even among intellectuals the repudiation of the original source of worldly transformation could still be unsettling. The nineteenth century therefore witnessed an effort to make Christianity relevant to Christendom's new secular elite.

The precedent was set by the German theologian Friedrich Schleiermacher (d. 1834). He had been raised by a Reformed pastor and sent as a youth to schools in which pietism was the prevailing religious mentality. As we noted in chapter five, pietism placed feeling over doctrine in reaction against the rationalism of the Protestant establishment. The pastor's son delighted in his experience of divine mercy and love.

However, as he learned more about his Calvinist heritage, he began to have doubts. In a letter to his father, he recorded a growing sense of dismay at stavrocentric doctrines still retained in the legacy of reformational Christianity. "I cannot believe," he wrote, "that the eternal true God called himself the son of man, or that his death was a substitutionary atonement, for he himself never expressly said this, and I cannot believe it was necessary; God made us for striving, not for perfection. He cannot want to punish us eternally because we are not perfect."[13] In this lament, the youth alludes both to traditional Christian doctrines about Jesus' divinity and to reformational ones about divine wrath and penal substitution. In his mind, the two are inseparably linked. By turning his back on the latter, he also found it necessary to reject the former.

By the end of the eighteenth century, secular humanism had exposed reformational Christendom's contempt for the world. Utopia was a counterfeit of paradise, but it provided a desperately needful mechanism for worldly transformation. The philosophes had shown an exuberance for the creation

---

13 Quoted in Helmut Thielicke, *Modern Faith and Thought*, trans. Geoffrey W. Bromiley (Grand Rapids, MI: William B. Eerdman's Publishing, 1990), 169.

even as they rejected the Creator's presence within it. Schleiermacher could not ignore or repudiate this new secular culture. Mozart's symphonies were too delightful. In fact, leaving the grim atmosphere of the pietist seminary, he fully embraced secular culture. He became friends with the idealist philosopher Friedrich Schlegel and was soon moving in the circles of early romantics. Like Ficino before him, he sought escape from Christian pessimism in the writings of Plato.

But Schleiermacher never lost faith in Christianity. In fact, he became an advocate for a totally new form of it often called liberal Protestantism. It would just as well be named utopian Christianity, for it was fundamentally shaped by secular humanism. Like Schlegel, he fell under the influence of Kant's teaching that the individual subject is the center of all knowledge. Since the Absolute cannot really be known, all the believer can do is affirm a religion of individual feeling and experience. In this respect liberal Protestantism was the successor to pietistic Christianity, though it abandoned even the minimalistic doctrine still held by the latter.

Schleiermacher published a series of sermons entitled *On Religion: Speeches to Its Cultured Despisers,* in which he advocated this new form of Christianity. It was the first time, interestingly, that religion as such had been identified as a phenomenon distinct from normal life. Until then, Christianity had been taken for granted in Christendom. Fathers had proclaimed, theologians had argued, deists had criticized—but no one had ever thought of it as a "generic something."[14] Secularization was responsible for this.

In *Speeches,* the transcendent God is secondary to man, who in an almost Hegelian way becomes the individualistic realization of a divine infinitude. Schleiermacher criticized reformational Christianity's tendency to deny divine participation, dismissing "the usual conception of God as one single being outside of the world." The "true nature of religion," he countered,

> *is neither this idea nor any other, but immediate consciousness of the Deity as He is found in ourselves and in the world. Similarly the goal and character*

14 Wilfred Cantwell Smith, *The Meaning and End of Religion* (Minneapolis: Fortress Press, 1991), 45.

> *of the religious life . . . is the immortality which we can now have in this temporal life.*[15]

In Eastern Christendom, hesychasm had always asserted the possibility of man's participation in divinity during this life while simultaneously asserting the absolute transcendence of God. The two were held together in a mysterious paradox. Doctrinal integrity about the Incarnation assured this. Since the Great Division, however, the West had begun to lose contact with doctrines supporting a paradisiacal culture. Barlaam repudiated hesychasm, and his protégé Petrarch turned instead to the saeculum. In a very real sense, Schleiermacher's rejection of divine transcendence for the sake of the human experience of living in this world was unnecessary. But considering the cultural oblivion of the second-millennium West, it was inevitable.

From Spener to Wesley the road of pietism had been paved with emotions, not dogmas. In the person of Schleiermacher, that road now reached a dead end. The utopian Christianity he offered to successors—whether "cultured" or not—was a travesty of the apostolic faith. Its fundamentally humanistic character ensured that nothing more than utopia could spring from it.

Several examples soon appeared of where Schleiermacher's subjectivism was to lead. One was a scholar named David Strauss (d. 1874). A student of Schleiermacher, he wrote a notorious *Life of Jesus* in which he denied his subject's divinity. This was not particularly new. What was innovative was his distinction between what he called a "Jesus of history," who did exist, and a "Christ of faith," who did not. Applying new methods of biblical criticism, he dismissed the New Testament's accounts of miracles as nothing more than the inventions of the apostles. More radical still was Ernest Renan (d. 1892), whose own *Life of Jesus* not only repeated the denial of divinity but presented its subject as a man motivated by anxieties about his religious identity.

Perhaps the most humanistic reconfiguration of Christianity was that undertaken by Ludwig Feuerbach (d. 1872). His *Essence of Christianity* was the work of an atheist, but one profoundly moved by the power of religion

---

15 Friedrich Schleiermacher, *On Religion: Speeches to Its Cultured Despisers*, trans. John Oman (New York: Harper and Row, 1958), 101.

to express the ideals of humanity. The work was shaped by a radical interpretation of Hegel in which human subjectivity, rather than being an expression of the Absolute, is in fact the very source of a fictive deity's apparent existence. This subjectification of reality became known as Left Hegelianism and reduced all metaphysical beliefs to mere projections of the human personality. "The personality of God," Feuerbach claimed,

> *is thus the means by which man converts the qualities of his own nature into the qualities of another being—of a being external to himself. The personality of God is nothing else than the projected personality of man.*[16]

The usurpation of Christianity by secular humanists reached its most elaborate form in the writings of Auguste Comte. There an entire system of pseudo-religiosity was invented by the father of positivism as the bond of social life in the coming age of science. Comte called it a "religion of humanity." It represented a bizarre appropriation of Roman Catholic piety and liturgy. It came into being, significantly, when the atheist had become estranged from his wife. He fell in love with a married woman named Clotilde de Vaux. Though he never consummated his infatuation, the young beauty deigned to meet with him regularly at his home on Wednesday evenings, sitting in an armchair and nursing his loneliness with her charming conversation. Then, after a year of this, she suddenly died. Comte was shattered. He now looked on the armchair as a relic of the transcendent joy he had felt in those moments when he had been in the woman's presence.

It was a presence he could not name, but the armchair became what holy places had long been for traditional Christianity. He did his best to organize the mystery with the use of reason. For the remainder of his life, he used his drawing room to enact elaborate rituals in memory of Clotilde. These included festooning the armchair with flowers and treating it like an altar. He would kneel before it thrice a day and intone formalized utterances in her memory. Soon, he extended the rites to exemplary people who had come

---

16 Ludwig Feuerbach, *The Essence of Christianity*, trans. George Eliot (New York: Harper and Row, 1957), 226.

before Clotilde. And in this way, a pseudo-religion serving positivism began to emerge. Abolishing saints' days, Comte developed for the posterity he expected a "positivist calendar" that would direct worship toward the highest examples of humanity. After undergoing a rite of "incorporation" seven years after death, great men would be enrolled in this calendar for veneration. And since religion, however humanistic, needs leaders, he planned out a positivist priesthood. It would be staffed by married men with scientific credentials. Auguste Comte himself would preside over it as a kind of pontiff.

Needless to say, nothing ever came of Comte's religion of humanity. There was something decidedly deranged in its conception. What is more, post-Christian rituals could not yet compete with those of traditional Christianity. Totalitarianism would be a much more effective organizing force, as would professional football and the Sunday newspaper. But these had to await an age of nihilism. For now, utopian rituals never moved beyond Comte's drawing room.

There the atheist knelt, worshipping nothing, living out the remainder of his life in an imagined communion with posterity. One can only wonder about his sanity during his final years, when he alternated between writing about a godless future and prostrating before an empty armchair. As one historian has marveled, "the spectacle of the Pontiff of Positivism on his knees before the armchair and bouquet of flowers—a relic of the happy Wednesday visits of Clotilde—reviving with intense concentration her radiant figure and then rekindling his emotions to exalted stages of elation, is one of the most tragic examples in all history of a genius's loss of mental health, clearly traceable to his rejection of the God of reason and revelation."[1]

Mill certainly marveled. He cut off what had been a lively correspondence with Comte after learning about the religion of humanity. For the English utilitarian, the system was an absurdity and an embarrassment. What is more, it threatened individual liberty. In his *Autobiography* he called it "the completest system of spiritual and temporal despotism, which ever yet

1 Quoted in De Marco and Wiker, *Architects*, 141.

emanated from a human brain."[2] Comte's desperate effort to mystify society, he continued, "stands as a monumental warning to thinkers on society and politics, of what happens when once men lose sight, in their speculations, of the value of Liberty and Individuality."[3]

Mill was blessed not to live to see the Bolsheviks ignore his warning when creating the cult of Lenin. Indeed, as the nineteenth century became the twentieth, liberalism and the preeminence of the individual only seemed to be gaining ground in the West, and especially in England. The father of liberal individualism would have enjoyed the serene self-confidence of his fellow-countryman Edward Elgar's *Pomp and Circumstance* March No. 1 (1901)—a work which would become, almost ad nauseam, the theme melody of future Anglo-American commencement ceremonies. Even more to his liking would have been the character of Sherlock Holmes. An always-autonomous master of logic, Arthur Conan Doyle's fictional detective was the embodiment of Mill's secular utopia.

And yet there was even in the great sleuth's personality something uncanny, something in search of transcendence. Playing his violin in a fit of melancholy, injecting cocaine to escape boredom—Holmes represented both the epitome and the limit of rationalism. He perceived things the eminently practical Doctor Watson never could. "Life is infinitely stranger than anything which the mind of man could invent," Holmes once confides to his assistant. "If we could fly out of that window hand in hand, hover over this great city, gently remove the roofs, and peep in at the queer things which are going on, the strange coincidences, the plannings, the cross-purposes, the wonderful chains of events, working through generations, and leading to the most *outré* results, it would make all fiction with its conventionalities and foreseen conclusions most stale and unprofitable."[4]

Perhaps this is why in Holmes's last appearance, a story entitled "His Last Bow," optimism and foreboding are strangely intermixed. The story,

2 Mill, *Autobiography*, 163.

3 Ibid, 164.

4 Arthur Conan Doyle, "A Case of Identity," in *The Illustrated Sherlock Holmes* (New York: Clarkson N. Potter, 1984), 31–42.

featuring militarism and written in the fateful year of 1914, puts Holmes and Watson together in the final scene. "As they turned to the car," Conan Doyle writes, "Holmes pointed back to the moonlit sea and shook a thoughtful head."

> *"There's an east wind coming, Watson."*
>
> *"I think not, Holmes. It is very warm."*
>
> *"Good old Watson! You are the one fixed point in a changing age. There's an east wind coming all the same, such a wind as never blew on England yet. It will be cold and bitter, Watson, and a good many of us may wither before its blast. But it's God's own wind none the less, and a cleaner, better, stronger land will lie in the sunshine when the storm has cleared.*
>
> *"Start her up, Watson, for it's time that we were on our way."*[5]

But before we reach the storm for which fictional England's greatest rationalist longed, it is necessary to consider another development that carried utopian Christendom to the brink of nihilism.

5 Arthur Conan Doyle, "His Last Bow," in *His Last Bow: A Reminiscence of Sherlock Holmes* (New York: A. L. Burt, 1917), 282–308.

CHAPTER TEN

A Path of Destruction

IT IS AN IRONY THAT the land in which the unrealized aspirations of the French Revolution would find fulfillment was that very land that had put an end to Napoleon's war of "enlightenment." The Russian Empire had been the first to defeat the French army. She played an important role at the Congress of Vienna and sponsored the conservative Holy Alliance against further occurrences of revolution thereafter. She had proven impervious to revolutionary subversion in 1848. Indeed, as we have seen, it was she who, under Tsar Nicholas I, suppressed the Hungarian uprising on behalf of Austria.

The fiascos of 1848 weighed heavily on Europe's revolutionaries. Clearly, romantic idealism was not effective in overthrowing tyranny and backwardness. The Frankfurt Assembly had proven this. So had the outcome of France's Second Republic. Formed in 1848, it degenerated into a new dictatorship under Louis Napoleon during the years following his election as president. After that, revolutionaries realized they needed to take stock of reality. They realized now that the masses were not as reliable as they had hoped and expected.

The time had come to withdraw from the barricades and discuss among themselves, in the security of the drawing room, the demands of the future. Liberals, already encouraged by political reforms in Britain, would celebrate victory in France's Third Republic after 1871. Nationalists, at least in Germany, would celebrate victory when a unified German Empire was finally created under Prussian leadership in the same year. Socialists, however, would remain frustrated. Their demand for social and economic equality would continue only within a political underground, ignored by all the European powers until the First World War.

But it was in Russia, the bastion of the old Christendom, where socialists would find conditions most favorable for resuming the liberating and violent march of progress.

The Rise of the Russian Intelligentsia

THERE WAS A REASON FOR this. Though westernized since the time of Peter the Great, Russia with her Orthodox Christian heritage provided an environment more combustible than that of any other modern European land in which the imperative of secular transformation might act.

Most Russians were still untouched by secular humanism. Modernity had penetrated only court circles and the socially remote lives of the nobility. In fact, during the nineteenth century (as readers of Tolstoy are aware), conversation among Russia's elite was often conducted in French. In St. Petersburg—that "window on the West"—architecture mimicked the style of European capitals, and clothing fashion was no different. The common people, however, continued to live by patterns established long before Peter's reign.

The culture secular humanism penetrated, therefore, was not that of the distant West, where first reformational, then pietistic, and finally utopian forms of Christianity facilitated modernity. It was one still shaped by traditional Christianity. And when secular humanism came into contact with it, something like an explosive reaction resulted.

The cultural gulf that divided Russian society was symbolized by two very different national figures who died within a decade of each other. One was Alexander Pushkin (d. 1837). A distant descendant of Peter's African servant Hannibal, he was born into the world of high society. He did not learn Russian until after he had mastered French, and as a child he wrote plays in both the style and language of Voltaire. At the newly established

Imperial Lyceum outside Petersburg, he soon showed a talent for Russia's emerging secular literature. He identified with the classicism of Gavrila Derzhavin (who hailed him pompously as a "second Derzhavin").[6] He was also a notorious seducer of the local girls, and, on one occasion, mistakenly accosted a lady-in-waiting to the royal family. After leaving the Lyceum, Pushkin joined a literary group advocating a westernized reform of the Russian language. It positioned itself against those maintaining cultural ties to the old Church Slavonic. The group was known as the Arzamas Society, after a town in central Russia.

Exiled to the Russian Caucasus after writing a poem praising liberalism, Pushkin conducted affairs with married women and as a consequence fought occasional duels. During this time he also declared himself an avowed atheist. Some of his unpublished poetry reflected a complete disdain for the traditional Christianity that surrounded him. He descended into writing vile blasphemies about three of its features: the Eucharist, the Resurrection, and the Virgin Mary.[7] His views changed somewhat after he returned to Petersburg following the Decembrist Uprising. Invited back into courtly circles, he modified his earlier seditious and anti-Christian social criticism, turning to the more inward high romanticism that made him revered to this day as Russia's national poet. It was at this time that installments of the epic poem *Eugene Onegin* began to appear.

Rising to the height of fame, Pushkin married a noblewoman and settled into the whirling social life of the capital. Yet the sordid ways of the secularized nobility, at which he himself was so expert, eventually caught up with him. When a French nobleman named Georges d'Anthès began openly to flirt with Pushkin's charming wife, the poet challenged him to a duel. An exchange of pistol shots on the banks of the Chyornaya River the following morning wounded both men. Pushkin's wound proved fatal. He was but thirty-seven years old.

Less than fifty miles from the town of Arzamas, after which Pushkin's westernizing literary society was named, was another town named Sarov. It

6 T. J. Binyon, *Pushkin* (New York: Vintage, 2002), 34.

7 Ibid, 134–35.

was home to a monk named Seraphim (d. 1833). He lived by values almost totally opposite to those of Pushkin, yet like the poet he would come to play an enormous role in shaping modern Russian Christendom. His life was not nearly so well documented as the poet's, as he left no writings to posterity. What is known is that his life was centered on traditional Christianity.

St. Seraphim of Sarov

At the age at which Pushkin would leave the lyceum to enter the elegant world of Petersburg, Seraphim was leaving the world to become a monk. As a poet, Pushkin would imbibe deeply the secular values of the early romantic movement. As a monk, Seraphim spent his time reading the Scriptures and supplementing them with ancient church fathers like Makarios of Egypt. Pushkin would carry on animated discussions with fellow writers about the prospects for progress in the West. Seraphim practiced prayer of the heart, which had begun once again to filter into Russia through hesychastic writings from the East. For him, progress consisted in spiritual transformation.

To experience this, he withdrew from the main monastery to live as a hermit in the forest wilderness. There in isolation he voluntarily endured loneliness, hunger, demonic thoughts, and, on one occasion, a brutal attack by thieves that left him crippled. Forest animals, on the other hand, were drawn to him and received food from his hands. A bear even sat at his feet as if in the presence of Adam in paradise.

Heavenly and not secular transformation was indeed Seraphim's goal in life. And with time he achieved measurable progress in it. The most revealing evidence was the flood of pilgrims who began to visit his hermitage for spiritual counsel in his final years. One of these was a pious nobleman named Nicholas Motovilov. The latter recorded a discussion with the elder one winter in a snow-covered forest glade. In this dialogue, Seraphim speaks of passages in the Scriptures, such as the Transfiguration, where God revealed His presence on earth through the bodily senses. The hermit declares that these revelations demonstrated that the kingdom of heaven can become fully manifested in this world, transforming it, if only momentarily, into paradise. "Some people say these texts are incomprehensible," he observes,

> *or else they deny that man can see God with the eyes of the flesh. This incomprehension is due to the fact that we have lost the simplicity of the early Christians and, with our so-called enlightenment, we plunge ourselves into such dark ignorance that what was easily understood by the ancients escapes us.*

Noting the benighted rather than truly enlightened character of secular humanism, Seraphim insists that humanity can find its proper fulfillment only through "the acquisition of the Holy Spirit." For in the Scriptures, "God, the grace of the Holy Spirit, was not seen in a dream or ecstasy, nor only in the imagination, but in reality and in very truth." This of course was what Gregory Palamas had asserted during the fourteenth century when defending hesychasm against Barlaam. Seraphim likewise affirms that the kingdom of heaven is experienced "even now" in a spiritually transformed world. And as he does so, Motovilov remarks that the elder's face miraculously began to shine like the sun in the middle of the snowy glade, revealing a participation in the transcendent divinity of the Holy Spirit.

For those who were prepared to listen, Seraphim thus revealed at a time of growing apostasy the paradisiacal vision of the old Christendom. The contrasts between him and his partial contemporary Pushkin are remarkable. If, as we have seen, the poet blasphemously mocked three particular features of Orthodox piety, the hermit humbly lived by each of them. Seraphim prepared for eucharistic communion on every Lord's Day by walking to the monastery church and confessing his sins. As for the Resurrection, visitors would often find him in his cell singing the hymns of Pascha, and his customary greeting throughout the year was "Christ is risen!"

Finally, the Virgin Mary was for Seraphim a great cause of hope—an example of feminine beauty incomparably more inspirational than the goddess-like beauties of St. Petersburg—and on one occasion he spent four hours in her presence, speaking with the heavenly host that surrounded her. Indeed, Christendom's struggle to choose between the Virgin Mary and Venus was lived out in the way each of these famous Russians died. Pushkin's life ended in an act of violence provoked by a lurid case of adultery. Seraphim was found dead one day kneeling before an icon of the Mother of God.

It is remarkable that though they were contemporaries, it is likely neither Seraphim nor Pushkin ever knew of the other's existence. Such was the state of Russian Christendom in the wake of westernization. And as the nineteenth century advanced, so did the post-Petrine cultural divide.

This was marked by the formation of a body known as the intelligentsia.[8] Like French civil society before the revolution, members of this group were educated about their civilization and highly critical of the powers that had influenced its formation. More than their eighteenth-century predecessors, they were acutely conscious of the relationship between past and present. They sought to historicize their movement and by so doing made the revolutionary spirit they fostered a truly millenarian force. Historians often observe that their solutions to problems tended toward maximalism. They were rarely interested in compromises or moderation. This can be attributed to the influence of Orthodox Christianity. In the East, the transformational imperative had not been modified by reformational Christianity as it had in the West following the Great Division. In the absence of an institutionalized context for its expression, the imperative remained as potent and disruptive as it had been during the first millennium.

An early example of this tendency was the brief work of a friend and inspiration to Pushkin, Peter Chaadaev (d. 1856). In 1836 he published the first in a series of *Philosophical Letters.* The series was profoundly shaped by German idealism, with the Neoplatonist effort to fill the world with a

---

8 Long ago the late Daniel Brower called the usefulness and even sociological coherence of this term into question, but its denotation of a radicalized civil society prior to the Russian Revolution recommends its continued use. Daniel Brower, "The Problem of the Russian Intelligentsia," *Slavic Review* 26:4 (December, 1967), 638–47.

transcendent presence. Chaadaev framed history around an Absolute spirit that progressively discloses itself within the historical life of men. During a period of self-imposed exile in the West, Chaadaev appears to have converted to Roman Catholicism. He may also have come across the reactionary writings of Maistre. In any case, he integrated the Roman Catholic Church into his idealist model, making her the Absolute and the papacy the principle of world unity.

Apart from these philosophical points, his *First Letter* is significant because it presents Russia as an ecclesiastically isolated and culturally sterile onlooker to the unfolding of world history. Reversing the Orthodox view of the Great Schism, he blames Eastern Christendom for losing contact with the West. The tragedy of 1054 for him is not that a paradisiacal culture ceased to animate Western Christendom, but that the utopian culture that took its place never breached the walls of the East. As a result, even after a century of westernization, Russians continue to lack any share in a truly universal and historical culture. Significantly, Chaadaev's *Letter* was originally written in French. It was signed from Necropolis—that is from Russia, the "City of the Dead."

Chaadaev "set Russia on fire," to quote the French traveler Marquis de Custine. In response to the provocative *Letter*, a generation of intellectuals came alive to what were called the "burning questions" of their time. Whither Russia? What is the West? Can Christendom be modernized? The answers they gave aligned them with one of two ideological parties, known subsequently as the Westernizers and the Slavophiles. Both were radically critical of the status quo, especially the institutions of autocracy and serfdom, and the character of the Orthodox Church. Tsar Nicholas I was comparatively serene about these questions. He issued an ideology called "official nationality" that rested on three principles: Orthodoxy, autocracy, and Russian nationality. As for Chaadaev's radical challenge, the tsar ordered the writer arrested and officially declared him insane. The one-time intellectual provocateur was subsequently permitted to publish only one additional work. It was entitled *The Apology of a Madman.*

We will consider the role played by the Slavophiles in the next chapter.

Here the activities of the Westernizers reveal how maximalism shaped Russia's contribution to the socialist march of progress.

Vissarion Belinsky

One of the first to distinguish himself by an affiliation with secular humanism in the West was Vissarion Belinsky (d. 1848). A self-proclaimed socialist, he looked to the improvement of Russia's peasant masses as the most important mark of progress. In the repressive political environment of autocracy, however, it was not possible to write openly about such goals. He therefore looked to art as the means of combatting social evils. Belinsky was delighted to find in the works of Nikolay Gogol an exposure of the suffering caused by serfdom. However, when the author of the socially critical *Dead Souls* later revealed conservative sensibilities and faith in Orthodox Christianity, Belinsky attacked him with a complete lack of moderation.

> *Advocate of the knout, apostle of ignorance, champion of obscurantism and reactionary mysticism, eulogist of Tatar customs—what are you doing? . . . Look at what is beneath your feet: you are standing on the brink of an abyss. That you should tie in your ideas with the Orthodox Church I can understand—it has ever been the support of the knout and the toady of despotism; but why do you bring in Christ? . . . He was the first to teach men the ideals of liberty, equality, and fraternity. . . . According to you the Russian people are the most religious people in the world; that is a lie! . . . The Russian speaks the name of God while scratching his posterior. . . . Take a closer look, and you will see that the Russian people are deeply atheistic by nature.*[9]

9 *Russian Intellectual History: An Anthology*, ed. Mark Raeff (New York: Harcourt, Brace, and World, 1966), 253–61.

These indignant words tie Russia's social injustice (symbolized by the "knout" and "Tatar customs") to the influence of traditional Christianity. This association, while little more than rhetoric, made an effective premise from which to argue that solutions to Russia's burning questions were to be found in secular humanism.

And what of the West, where that philosophy was now flourishing? A year after the publication of Belinsky's letter, it was thrown into chaos by revolution. As we have seen, 1848 saw uprisings in France, Italy, Austria, and Germany. Belinsky died before they could run their course. But other Russian Westernizers were on hand to observe and in some cases even participate in the longed-for socialist transformation of the world.

One of those who rushed into action was Alexander Herzen (d. 1870). According to his biographer, "he had been waiting for the Second Coming of the [French] Revolution during most of his life."[10] He could not stand the thought of being left out. He was already a political exile from Russia due to his earlier radicalism there. Arriving in Paris, however, he soon lost confidence in the newly formed Second Republic. Its suppression of a workers' insurrection in June revealed to the socialist that the march of progress still had far to go. With an indignation matching Belinsky's, Herzen condemned the revolution's half-measures and sentenced them to a violent death.

> *Paris! How long did that name burn as a lodestar for the nations; who did not love it, did not bow to it? But now its time is past; let it disappear from the stage. . . . What will come of this blood [of workers spilled by liberals]? Who knows, but no matter what the issue it is enough if in this paroxysm of madness, of revenge, of discord, of retribution that world perishes which oppresses the new man, preventing him from living, keeping the future from being born—and this would be magnificent, and so I say: long live chaos and destruction! Vive la mort! And let the future be born.*[11]

---

10 Martin Malia, *Alexander Herzen and the Birth of Russian Socialism* (New York: Grosset and Dunlap, 1961), 369.

11 Quoted in ibid, 373.

Mikhail Bakunin

This was all written well before Louis Napoleon betrayed the revolution by nullifying the Second Republic and creating a Second Empire. But by then the maximalist Herzen had turned his hopes toward Russia, which he was beginning to think was the only land in Christendom where a total transformation of society might be possible.

Another Russian hoping to set the world on fire was Mikhail Bakunin (d. 1876). In 1848 and 1849 he frantically traveled throughout Western Europe seeking a revolution to lead. He did not quite succeed in this, though he did finally join German workers on the barricades in Dresden. Before traveling westward, he proved even more radical than Herzen. Seemingly, he had been born a revolutionary. He reacted violently to the sensation of hearing romantic music. While still a teenager, for instance, he attended a performance of Beethoven's Ninth Symphony with its utopian "Ode to Joy" about universal brotherhood. The expression on his face during the experience, according to a companion, was of someone "ready to destroy the entire world."[12] Bakunin early discovered the writings of Feuerbach and other Left Hegelians and quickly embraced their atheism. He also seized on their dialectical model of thought and worked it into a theory of revolution.

This he presented in a work entitled *The Reaction in Germany*, which put forward one of the most extreme statements of revolutionary millenarianism yet. It notoriously advocates violence and destruction as ends in themselves, providing an early argument for anarchism. In it Bakunin expresses an almost religious longing for "a qualitative transformation, a new, vital, and life-creating revelation, a new heaven and a new earth, a young and magnificent world in which all present discords will resolve themselves into harmonious unity." This, after all, had been the spirit of the "Ode to Joy."

12 Quoted in Aileen Kelly, *Mikhail Bakunin: A Study in the Psychology and Politics of Utopianism* (New Haven: Yale University, 1987), 24.

And like Comte, Bakunin also seeks to integrate religious feelings into the creation of a secular utopia. "We must not only act politically," he insists, "but in our politics act religiously." He concludes the work by projecting his own maximalist tendencies on modern Christendom in general.

> *All peoples and all men are filled with a kind of premonition, and everyone whose vital organs are not paralyzed faces with shuddering expectation the approaching future which will speak out the redeeming word. . . . Let us therefore trust the eternal Spirit which destroys and annihilates only because it is the unfathomable and eternally creative source of all life. The passion for destruction is a creative passion, too.*[13]

The Dresden Uprising, like others in 1848 and 1849, collapsed in the face of counter-revolutionary resistance. Wanted by three different governments (those of Russia, Austria, and Saxony), Bakunin was passed from one prison to another until he found himself back in Petersburg's Peter-Paul Fortress for political criminals.

Strangely, his revolutionary career was just getting started.

Marxism

IN THE MEANTIME, THE FAILURE of the revolutions of 1848–1849 left many socialists deeply disillusioned. Karl Marx (d. 1883) was one of these. As a Left Hegelian, he had spent years preparing for the insurrection that would transform a broken saeculum into utopia. He collaborated with Friedrich Engels in composing a rousing work entitled *The Communist Manifesto* intended to give it direction. No sooner was the *Manifesto* published in early 1848 than the day of fulfillment seemed at hand. But then everything collapsed, and Marx was forced to flee to England. He did not lose his faith, though. He was certain that through the new sciences of

13 Michael Bakunin, "The Reaction in Germany," in *Russian Philosophy*, ed. James M. Edie, James P. Scanlan, and Mary-Barbara Zeldin (Chicago: Quadrangle Books, 1965), 385–406.

Karl Marx

sociology and economics, a new path forward would be found.

Marx had begun his revolutionary career as a romantic. As a young man he studied at the new University of Berlin. It was from there that Hegel had ruled modern philosophy as its most celebrated voice, and his legacy continued to overshadow the university after his death. So did those of other German idealists, such as Fichte and Schelling. Marx was enthralled by the intellectual atmosphere even as he felt contempt for the city's growing middle class. He turned to poetry for expression. His verse filled no fewer than three notebooks and was mostly dedicated to his sweetheart, Jenny, whom he would eventually marry. Other poems were more philosophical, but all were romantic in tone. According to one biographer, they were strongly characterized by "the familiar subjectivism and extreme exaltation of the personality of the creative artist isolated from the rest of society, while seeking, at the same time, for a community of like-minded individuals."[14] As we saw in chapter eight, this profile fit just about every romantic.

Marx's early verse possessed a definably Promethean quality. For instance, one poem declared:

With disdain I will throw my gauntlet
Full in the face of the world,
And see the collapse of the pigmy giant
Whose fall will not stifle my ardour.

Then I will wander godlike and victorious
Through the ruins of the world
And, giving my words an active force,
I will feel equal to the creator.

This heroic disdain for reality and defiance of its creator also stood at the center of Marx's doctoral dissertation. By now he had become closely affiliated with the Left Hegelians and embraced their atheism. Indeed, this first major piece of the philosopher's scholarship was completed in the same year as Feuerbach's *Essence of Christianity*. The latter work's claim that religion is a projection of the human personality is echoed in statements by Marx such as the following:

14 David McLellan, *Karl Marx: His Life and Thought* (London: Macmillan, 1973), 22.

> *As long as a single drop of blood pulses in her world-conquering and totally free heart, philosophy will continually shout at her opponents the cry of Epicurus: Impiety does not consist in destroying the gods of the crowd but rather in ascribing to the gods the ideas of the crowd.*[15]

What separates the young Marx from Feuerbach, however, is the primacy he assigns to collective rather than individual projection. His atheism was not to be that of a liberal but that of a socialist.

The radicalism of his doctoral thesis earned Marx a terrible reputation with the authorities, and he found himself barred from a teaching position in Prussia. However, this could only recommend him to the growing body of radical philosophers and socialists who were preparing for the coming upheaval. One of these breathlessly reported in a letter that the newly recognized but unemployable doctor of philosophy "is a phenomenon that has made an enormous impression on me, even though I am active in the same field."

> *You can prepare yourself to meet the greatest, perhaps the only real, philosopher now living. Dr Marx—that is the name of my idol—is still a very young man (about 24 years old at the most), who will give medieval religion and politics their death blow. He combines with deepest philosophical earnestness the most biting wit. Imagine Rousseau, Voltaire, Holbach, Lessing, Heine and Hegel united in one person, I say united, not thrown together—and you have Dr Marx.*[16]

The object of this adulation was soon catapulted to preeminence among Europe's revolutionaries, writing, with his "biting wit," some of the most trenchant criticisms not only of contemporary capitalism but of what he disdainfully labeled "utopian socialism" as well. Protest as he might, however, Marx's philosophy was thoroughly utopian.

---

15 Quoted in Leszek Kolakowski, *Main Currents of Marxism*, vol. 1, trans. P. S. Falla (Oxford: Oxford University, 1978), 103.

16 Quoted in *The Portable Karl Marx*, ed. and trans. Eugene Kamenka (New York: Penguin, 1983), 22.

In any case, so biting was his wit that many socialists were as alienated from him as the workers were from the factory owners. His preferred epithet for other writers was "idiot," and variations of it profusely pepper his private correspondence. In this way, he was a bearer of the romantic cult of neglected genius even as he moved further and further away from romantic subjectivism. A fellow revolutionary who met Marx in 1848 had been expecting a noble-minded defender of the poor. "This expectation," the man later wrote,

> *was disappointed in a peculiar way. Marx's utterances were indeed full of meaning, logical and clear, but I have never seen a man whose bearing was so provoking and intolerable. To no opinion which differed from his own did he accord the honor of even condescending consideration. Everyone who contradicted him he treated with abject contempt; every argument that he did not like he answered either with biting scorn at the unfathomable ignorance that had prompted it, or with opprobrious aspersion upon the motives of him who had advanced it. I remember most distinctly the cutting disdain with which he pronounced the word "bourgeois"; and as a "bourgeois"—that is, as a detestable example of the deepest mental and moral degeneracy—he denounced everyone who dared to oppose his opinion.*[17]

The polemical dehumanization of "enemies" even within the revolutionary movement—something that would reach monstrous proportions under Lenin—can be traced to Marxism's founding personality. This was unquestionably a function of the new Christendom's virtue of indignation, which, released by the Papal Reformation and harnessed by the humanists, was becoming increasingly prone to violent destruction.

Once settled in the safety of liberal England, Marx undertook the scientific validation of the claims he had been making since his doctoral dissertation. He became a regular at the London Library. There, over the course of three decades, he conducted the research for what became his magnum

17 The words are those of the famous memoirist and American immigrant Carl Schurz. Quoted in ibid, 29–30.

opus, *Capital* (*Das Kapital*). He wished to dedicate the work to Darwin, whose theory of evolution Marx wholly embraced, but was turned down—presumably because the liberal biologist was disturbed by the socialist's calls to revolution. Marx and his family lived in poverty most of the time, though he was supported by regular gifts from Engels. Both socialists identified with the historical destiny of the working class, but both were of decidedly middle-class origin. Marx was the son of a prosperous lawyer. Engels's father was actually a factory owner.

Despite his ties with the bourgeoisie, Marx produced the most effective argument for its destruction in history. His system, later known simply as Marxism, began with an appeal to science. Since the time of Francis Bacon, philosophers had often opposed empiricism to metaphysics. As we have seen, Comte brought this struggle to a conclusion by historicizing it: the father of positivism claimed that science would one day supersede metaphysics (as well as theology) as the only valid source of knowledge. Marx now combined the empirical method of positivism with the dialectic of Left Hegelianism to produce a brilliant and rousing account of the end of history in the destruction of capitalism.

Unlike Comte's, Marx's utopia would rise through social cataclysm. The opening sentence of the *Communist Manifesto* is the key to understanding its realization. "The history of all hitherto existing society," it asserts, "is the history of class struggles." Comte had placed his hope in the advance of science. Marx placed his in class conflict. "Two great hostile camps" face each other across the modern economic battlefield, he claimed: the bourgeoisie and the proletariat. Both have come into existence only in recent times through industrialization. And both are now irreconcilably opposed. The former has taken control of society with its ownership of capital. Not only factories and banks, but government and even culture serve its material interests. But at the same time it cannot do without a subordinate class. And though subordinate, the proletariat has this: that as the bourgeoisie continues to oppress the workers, it sows the seeds of its own destruction. For eventually, as capitalism advances, the proletariat will grow so large and its misery so great as to provoke in it a rebellion the likes of which the world has never before seen. This cataclysmic "proletarian revolution" will bring an end to capitalism and produce the everlasting peace that Marx called communism. Without private property, there will be no more inequality and therefore no more cause of oppression. History's final "mode of production" will wipe away every tear from the human eye.

For Marxism, then, violence is the engine of progress. Like Comte, its author envisioned an unfolding of history from lower to higher stages of development, culminating in a final state of utopian perfection. Positivism had laid out three such stages. Marx (like Augustine, strangely) claimed to discern six. These were primitive communism, before private property was introduced; slavery; feudalism; capitalism—the present stage; socialism (an intermediate stage during which the state "withers away"; and industrial communism, when the human race reaches a kind of economic full circle, sharing all economic resources in common. It was a millenarian fantasy, framed in secular form for its modern readership. But it made its case with a mountain of data and therefore passed the test of empiricism (at least for a generation, after which new research began to reveal significant fallacies). To all who had lost faith in both Christianity and its transcendent substitute, idealism, Marxism promised worldly transformation.

What is more, according to Marxism a revolutionary utopia was assured. For by claiming that economic and not intellectual forces drive progress, it eliminated the problem behind the fiasco of 1848. Progress did not depend on effective revolutionary organization. It was inevitable as long as the capitalist economy continued its insatiable drive for more markets and greater profits. Like the Second Coming of Christ, then, nothing could prevent the proletarian revolution—not even human depravity.

Marxism's similarities to Christianity have long been noted. Its linear conception of eschatological time, its attribution of human suffering to a primordial transgression (the introduction of private property), its promise of inevitable justice for the oppressed—all have an undeniably religious quality. Marx's condemnations of contemporary capitalism have been compared to the thunderings of Old Testament prophets, and his attacks on rival socialists to polemics against heretics. In fact, many historians have concluded that Marxism became as influential as it did because it provided an ersatz religion to those experiencing a loss of confidence in post-reformational Christianity.

The comfort and complacency of the Protestant clerical establishment and the generally uncomprehending and reactionary character of the Roman Catholic hierarchy greatly facilitated this. One worker in London at the end of the century described how Christianity had come to appear as a defender only of the well-to-do in his impoverished neighborhood.

> *Our attitude towards religion was—that somewhere in the skies was a God, the Father of the human race, and the Maker of the World. To certain favoured individuals He was kind, and provided good food and raiment in return for a regular attendance at church. The people in our street, especially our own family had been overlooked by God, and it was foolish to expect deliverance from our troubles by any other source than our own abilities.*[18]

Such a view of things was a tragedy, considering Christianity's historical defense of the poor in both the East and the West. The social gospel movement among Protestants and Pope Leo XIII's bull *Rerum novarum* (1891) were both examples of a sincere effort to address the suffering of the working class at this time, but both were belated and had only minimal effect. Leo's successor Pius XI would later acknowledge the loss of the working class to socialism, calling it "the greatest scandal of the nineteenth century."

In the meantime, Marxism mounted an unremitting challenge to Christianity. From his earliest writings, Marx himself had expressed hatred and contempt for the historical faith of his civilization. He called religion the "opium of the masses," likening it to a drug given by oppressors to the oppressed to induce a forgetfulness of oppression. Here he claimed to discover something never noticed before about the faith: Christian piety, he asserted, was uniquely suited to serve the class interests of the bourgeoisie because it redirected hope from this world to a future state of happiness

18 Quoted in Hugh McLeod, *Religion and the People of Western Europe, 1789–1989* (Oxford: Oxford University, 1997), 120–21.

beyond it. Furthermore, with its teaching about the cross it assigned a salvific power to suffering. This made its adherents indifferent to the effects of economic exploitation.

It hardly needs saying that both points applied to a uniquely stavrocentric conception of Christianity. During the first millennium, traditional Christianity's metamorphocentric piety had not only directed hope toward a paradise beyond the grave but experienced it "even now" in this life. Second, traditional Christianity, while seeing in the cross the only true path toward salvation, did not celebrate the suffering of this world as such. As much as participation in Christ's Crucifixion served to transform the believer spiritually, so did participation in His Resurrection through the liturgy and sacraments. From the start, Marx's trenchant attacks on Christianity only convinced those who had little practical experience of traditional Christianity—which, nine centuries after the Great Division, constituted the vast majority of people living in Western Christendom.

There is one final point to be made about the relationship of Marxism to the working class. In developing the mechanism of class conflict, Marx introduced a principle called "immiseration." Because of its exploitative character, capitalism necessarily causes greater degrees of misery among the workers who submit to it. To increase profits, capitalists must always be finding new ways to limit and even decrease the wages of their employees. Over time, this causes greater and greater hardship for the worker and his family. Ironically, Marx welcomed the process of immiseration. For without it, the working class would never become sufficiently violent to overthrow capitalism.

Which brings us back to Mrs. Gumdrop and her children. In the last chapter we left her and the orphans on the sidewalk of a London street, huddling together in the hope of stirring compassion in passersby. One day they might have seen another middle-class man turn the corner, top hat towering over a long shaggy beard, and approach their lowly post. By now the woman is sitting on the ground, unable to stand because of her tubercular fits. Her children are fewer in number, one or two having died for lack of nutrition and medical attention. But still the jar stands on the sidewalk, and still all eyes look hopefully to the well-dressed gentleman as he approaches.

Karl Marx is on his way through the drizzling fog to the London Library, where he is conducting research on *Capital.* He pauses. Like Darwin, Spencer, and Galton before him, he takes in the pathetic sight. As a fellow evolutionist, he recognizes in it the consequences of natural selection and the struggle for existence. But unlike his liberal predecessors, he is a socialist dedicated to the revolutionary abolition of the conditions responsible for such misery. And so, without even tipping his hat (a bourgeois custom after all), he marches past the widow and orphans and continues his march. For to drop a penny into their jar, or even to stop and comfort them with words of compassion, would be to counteract the principle of immiseration and suppress their desire for revolutionary destruction. Secular humanism had in its scientific mode taught him—as it had taught his spiritual fellow-travelers the liberal social Darwinists—that there is no place in a post-Christian Christendom for unconditional love.

And indeed, Marx himself never befriended a worker, never spent time among the poor sharing their sorrows. For him as for so many other revolutionaries, his interest in the suffering of the masses was abstract. The closest he ever came to having a relationship with a real worker, in fact, was in the case of his maid, Helene Demuth. Having recruited her from among the impoverished German peasantry, he used her throughout the years to keep his house, run his errands, and cook his meals. He also used her for sexual gratification. By her he sired a son, who presumably on Marx's orders was sent off immediately after birth to be raised as a foster child in a working-class family. The father of Marxism never again saw the boy, nor wanted to do so. After all, he had a revolution to lead.

The Eleventh Hour

BY THE MIDDLE OF THE nineteenth century, socialism had become the prevailing ideology within Russia's newly formed intelligentsia. Ironically, socialism gained even more ground after the Great Reforms. As we noted in the previous chapter, Alexander II—the "Tsar-Liberator"—had abolished serfdom in 1861, to the acclaim of all advocates of progress. On the surface, the reforms would have seemed certain to win the loyalty of progressive intellectuals. From exile in London Herzen sensed this, repeating Julian the Apostate's cry of defeat in the face of Christian statecraft. "Thou hast conquered, O Galilean!" he declared. But the emancipation went poorly. Freed peasants lacked sufficient land, a large proportion of which remained under the control of the nobility. Amid the uncertainties of what would come next, Russia's intellectuals resumed their frenetic discussion of the burning questions about progress.

One famous example was the fictional Yevgeny Bazarov, protagonist of the novel *Fathers and Sons* by Ivan Turgenev (d. 1883). He is an atheist interested only in science and what it can do to improve the human condition. Like the ideal positivist, he passes his time in laboratory experiments, breaking from them only to make condescending criticisms of the remnants of religious piety in the society that surrounds him. He is a utilitarian to boot, declaring at one point that "a decent chemist is twenty times more useful than any poet." Most famously, Bazarov declares himself to be a "nihilist," bringing the word into wide currency within the intelligentsia. It denoted a philosophical rejection not of all values but only of those that represented the old Christendom. "What's important," he declares, "is that two times two makes four; all the rest's nonsense."

With a belief in progress as uncompromising as the peasants' Christianity, Russia's intellectuals followed the example of Bazarov in rejecting everything in their traditional culture. Some even adopted the label of nihilists. In a novel entitled *What Is to Be Done?* Nikolay Chernyshevsky (d. 1889) depicted a group of young people who start a cooperative to promote socialism and women's liberation. They too are atheists. But they are depicted as totally dedicated revolutionaries, denying themselves all forms of pleasure in the same way traditional Christians practice asceticism. In one of the novel's scenes, the heroine, Vera Pavlovna, has a dream in which she beholds with joy an image of the Crystal Palace and interprets it as a promise of Russia's future after a transformative revolution.

Many artists turned to painting in the effort to direct Russia toward utopia. As Belinsky had shown, under autocracy art could be socially transformative. The dominant style was known as "realism" and drew its inspiration from the West. The French anarchist Gustave Courbet (d. 1877), for instance, had broken with romantic and idealistic depictions of common people and used art to promote revolution in works such as *Stone Breakers.* In Russia, a group of painters with socialist sympathies used realism to set themselves apart from the mainstream type of painting associated with the Academy of Arts. They called themselves the Itinerants (*Peredvizhniky*).

One of them was Vasily Perov (d. 1882). His paintings brought attention to the ignorance of the Orthodox clergy and what, in the artist's mind, were the shortcomings of traditional Christianity. His *Refectory,* for instance, depicts bloated monks quarrelling over food and wine as servants struggle abjectly to assist them. A visiting wealthy noblewoman is given preference while a poor widow and her children are ignored. All of this takes place in the hypocritical presence of a large crucifix. Another painting entitled *A Homily in the Village* shows the congregation of a dreary parish church. Some are quarrelling, some are romancing, and some have fallen asleep. Only naive children appear interested in what the old priest is saying about an outdated faith. Perov's *Village Procession at Pascha* is brutal in its presentation of the old Christendom. As a drunken priest staggers out the front door of a village church, a server collapses next to him, a woman rouses another peasant who has passed out, and an icon procession wanders off aimlessly into the distance. One of the icons being borne is upside down.

Perov was joined in his social criticism by the even more accomplished Itinerant Ilya Repin (d. 1930). Repin dedicated his talent to themes that were more political than religious. One painting cheerfully depicted the annual commemoration of the 1871 Paris Commune in France and another the granting of the October Manifesto during the 1905 revolution in Russia. Even more directly subversive was *They Did Not Expect Him,* showing the return home of a wornout but dignified political convict. *The Arrest of an Agitator* shows a defiant revolutionary being detained by the police. Repin's most majestic tribute to progress is *The Volga Boat Haulers,* based on the practice of moving shipping upriver in central Russia using draft workers.

Harnessed to a ship flying the imperial flag (and therefore representing the Russian state), the workers look more like animals than men. Only one figure suggests hope—a youth pulling himself upright and staring into the distance as if toward the coming revolution.

The Great Reforms not only failed to raise Russia to the economic level of the West. They failed to arrest the intelligentsia's surge toward revolutionary destruction. An example was Bakunin, whom we last observed in the Peter-Paul Fortress languishing under guard for serial acts of sedition. Amazingly, the inveterate revolutionary managed to obtain transfer to a remote town in Siberia, and once there he escaped. Traveling around the globe through Japan and the United States, he finally reached Herzen in London and from there plunged back into the revolutionary underground.

In 1869, Bakunin was living in Geneva when a young émigré revolutionary named Sergey Nechaev appeared. This junior revolutionary told tall tales of imprisonment in the Peter-Paul Fortress and of government torture. All of them were deceptions designed to obtain the famous anarchist's backing. When Nechaev claimed to be at the center of a nihilist conspiracy numbering thousands in Russia, Bakunin was beside himself with excitement. This was, after all, everything for which he had been waiting. He sent off epistles to the old guard describing the young man's "immense love" for the people and "virginally pure integrity" in planning the long-awaited and now impending apocalypse.[1] In his infatuation he even began calling Nechaev his "young barbarian."[2]

Bakunin offered guidance in drawing up a document called the *Catechism of a Revolutionary*, which was intended to be a handbook for the coming revolution. It was as if traditional Christianity's ascetic vision of sacrificial love had been demonically transmuted into a manifesto of hatred. The document breathed the spirit not of warm humility but of cold-blooded indignation. It declared the revolutionary to be doomed to die like a martyr in the struggle against injustice, while at the same time he must be utterly ruthless in destroying every person who stood in his way. People were to be treated

---

1 Kelly, *Mikhail Bakunin*, 280.

2 Ibid, 170.

simply as means toward the end of class violence. Three categories of women, for instance, were described and the value of each set as contingent on her level of support for conspirators. All acts of deception and violence were justified insofar as they advanced the liberation of the people. "Our task," the manifesto concluded, "is terrible, total, universal, and merciless destruction."

Having obtained Bakunin's backing, Nechaev soon put the *Catechism* into effect. He returned to Russia and there began to organize a circle of conspirators dedicated to the "merciless destruction" of the existing social order. To make his leadership more effective, he arranged the murder of one of the circle's members in order to create a bond of fear among the others. The affair came to the attention of Fyodor Dostoevsky, who had once been active in the intelligentsia (his first novel, *Poor Folk,* had been praised by Belinsky). After seeing the brokenness of humanity in a prison camp and returning to the Orthodox Church, Dostoevsky had become an opponent of the intelligentsia's cult of progress. Nechaev's murder of a fellow revolutionary, when it was finally reported, provided the novelist with material for his most political work, appropriately entitled *Demons* (sometimes translated as *The Possessed* or *Devils*).

As for Bakunin, he learned only later, after handing over a large sum of money to Nechaev, that he had been duped. But by then his reputation was ruined. The retributive Marx personally oversaw his expulsion from the Worker's International on the grounds of embezzlement. The father of anarchism died an outcast.

In the meantime, a revolutionary conspiracy had arisen back in Russia to take the life of the tsar. It originated in a movement known as populism (*narodnichestvo*), which sought to provoke a mass uprising through heroic acts of revolutionary violence. The conspiracy was inspired partly by the Nechaev-Bakunin *Catechism.* Before that work had been released, however, a populist who had been inspired to give himself to the cause of revolutionary progress after reading *What Is to Be Done?* approached Alexander II in a park in the capital, pulled out a pistol, and fired point blank. Miraculously, the bullet missed. On another occasion, terrorists who had obtained the schedule for the imperial train detonated a charge beneath it, causing it to derail and

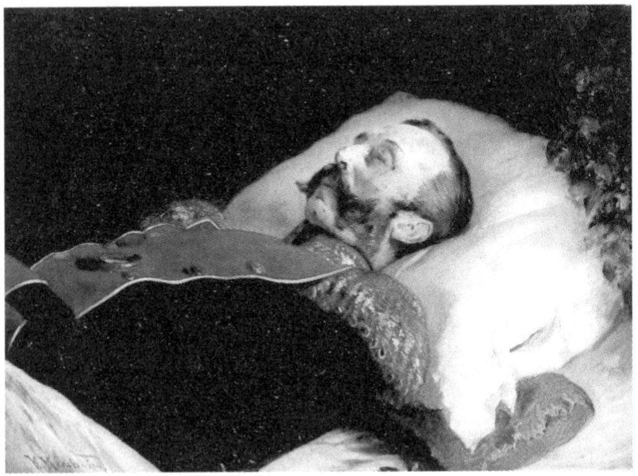
Tsar Alexander II on his deathbed

crash. Miraculously, the tsar climbed out of the wreckage. Another group of terrorists managed to get an agent into the Winter Palace to plant a bomb under the room where Alexander was scheduled to be at a certain hour of the day. Miraculously, the tsar had been detained down the hallway, and the bomb went off without hurting him. Then, in 1881, the tsar was traveling down a canal embankment in Petersburg when a revolutionary jumped out from behind a corner to hurl a bomb underneath his carriage. The vehicle was blown to pieces. Yet miraculously, out of the wreckage climbed the apparently indestructible tsar.

But as Alexander was tending to his wounded driver, another terrorist appeared and threw a bomb directly beneath his feet. As it detonated, it blew off most of his lower body. Finally, the liberator of Russia's serfs was dead.

Contrary to Nechaev's hopes, however, the tsar's death did not precipitate a revolutionary cataclysm. Just the opposite occurred. In the wake of the shocking assassination, the government canceled its liberal policies, and many of the Great Reforms were downscaled. Peasants in the countryside, who had often reacted with cold indifference to revolutionary agitation, began turning socialists in to the police. And without popular support, the populists had become a contradiction in terms.

In their place, a new element entered the revolutionary intelligentsia. It was dominated by Marxists. In 1898, just as industrialization was getting underway, the Marxist Social Democratic Party appeared. It soon split into two rival factions, the Mensheviks and the Bolsheviks. Each regarded the other as the most contemptible of heretics.

Vladimir Lenin (d. 1924) was the founder of the Bolsheviks. He was the brother of an executed populist revolutionary and was convinced that progress would come only through the application of scientific socialism. In 1902 he published a treatise under the recognizable title *What Is to Be Done?* In it he argued for a small, militantly dedicated party unconcerned with the preferences of the still tiny working class. This, he conceded, was the only way of advancing Marxism in a land in which the vast majority of workers were peasants and a true proletariat had yet to form. In the 1905 revolution, the Bolsheviks sprang into action but were soon forced into hiding after the issuance of the October Manifesto. Like Rienzo following his first insurrection in Rome, Lenin fled Russia with the intention of returning one day to finish the job.

The founder of Bolshevism matched Nechaev as a professional revolutionary prepared to build utopia at any cost. Not all members of the intelligentsia shared his ruthlessness, however.

In the aftermath of the deadly and destructive events of 1905, a group of former socialists published a collection of essays calling on the intelligentsia to repent of its violent proclivities and atheistic values. The book appeared in 1909 and was entitled *Landmarks* (*Vekhy*). In it some of the most highly credentialed former socialists attacked the westernizing legacy of contempt for the old Christendom. One of the greatest mistakes, they claimed, was to place indignation before the virtue of humility. They traced this legacy not only to Chaadaev but even further to Peter the Great himself. One of these former socialists was Peter Struve, who had been the author of the very charter of the Marxist Social Democratic Party. Another was Nicolas Berdyaev, who had spent time in prison camps for Marxist activities. Yet another was named Sergey Bulgakov (d. 1944). He had been a Marxist economist before discovering that numerous calculations and predictions made by the "scientific socialist" Marx had turned out to be fallacious. All three former revolutionaries had by now repented of their destructive activities and returned to the Orthodox Church.

Sergey Bulgakov (in dark clothing)

Bulgakov's contribution to *Landmarks* was entitled "Heroism and Asceticism: Reflections on the Religious Nature of the Russian Intelligentsia." On the eve of the most destructive revolution in history, it confronted the intelligentsia with the pseudo-religious tendencies of its values. Only in Russia, he noted, has socialism assumed such a maximalist character. Drawing on the ascetical tradition of Orthodox Christianity, it has surpassed all Western revolutionary movements and now, because of its intensity, stands ready to destroy everything to achieve its sacrificial goal. "A certain otherworldliness, an eschatological dream of the City of God, of a coming kingdom of justice (under various socialist pseudonyms), and a striving to save mankind—if not from sin then from suffering—comprise, as is well-known, the invariable and distinctive characteristics of the Russian intelligentsia."

Bulgakov contrasts traditional Christianity's doctrine of the Incarnation with secular humanism, noting that the former is focused on the Godmanhood of Jesus Christ whereas the latter, in a promethean way dating from the quattrocento, has become obsessed with what he calls "mangodhood."

> *Rejecting Christianity and its norms, our intelligentsia accepts along with atheism—or rather, instead of atheism—the dogmas of the religion of man-Godhood in one or another of the variants elaborated by the Western European Enlightenment, and then turns this religion into idolatry. The basic dogma characteristic of all these religions is the belief in man's natural perfection and in unending progress realizable through man's own powers.*

Nearly a century had passed since Russian Christendom had been confronted by the opposing visions of Pushkin and Seraphim. Now, at the eleventh hour, a prodigal son pleaded with his former accomplices to repent of the destruction with which they threatened Russia and the world. It was not too late, Bulgakov insisted, to restore a civilization with a supporting culture that instead of building utopia at any cost, directs its members toward the heavenly transformation of the world.

> *The world-view and spiritual make-up of the people is determined by Christian faith. However great the distance here between the ideal and reality, however dark and unenlightened our nation, its ideal is Christ and His teaching, and its norm is Christian asceticism. . . . Like the icon-lamps that flicker in monastic cloisters, where the people have gathered over the centuries seeking moral support and teaching, these ideals, this light of Christ, have shone on Russia. And inasmuch as they possess this light, our people—I will say this without hesitation—for all its illiteracy, is more enlightened than its own intelligentsia.*[3]

Like Seraphim of Sarov, Bulgakov saw a great darkness—a great benightenment—swiftly approaching post-Christian Christendom.

3 Sergei Bulgakov, "Heroism and Asceticism: Reflections on the Religious Nature of the Russian Intelligentsia," in *Landmarks*, ed. Boris Shragin and Albert Todd, trans. Marian Schwartz (New York: Karz Howard, 1977), 23–63.

CHAPTER ELEVEN

Judgment

THE RUMBLINGS OF THE RUSSIAN intelligentsia were scarcely heard in other parts of Western Christendom. More ominous were the demands of nationalists. Since the fiascos of 1848, they had infiltrated every corner of political life. After the unification of Germany, ethnic nationalism appeared to be the genius of secularization. Deviating completely from traditional Christianity—which, as we have seen, declared the unity of all nations and races in Christ—it divided Christendom like no other force since the Great Division.

Ironically, in its division the West found a new path toward secular transformation—one paved with nationalist politics, racial science, and militarism. Though the nations of the West were not yet ready to renounce completely the Christian ties that linked them, they now exulted in differences that defied the gospel. Tragically, such differences, artificially enlarged by secular humanism, led them to an event more destructive than any before in Western history.

A Landscape of National Monuments

BY THE BEGINNING OF THE twentieth century, the West had become a civilization marked by secular monuments, many of which were nationalistic in character. If in earlier stages of its history Christendom had expressed universal Christian ideals with public buildings like Hagia Sophia and Saint Peter's Basilica, by the end of the nineteenth century these ideals had given way to national pride and ethnicity. Not all were necessarily exclusive of other peoples. After all, progress was seen as a universal force. But the ideology of nationalism required each people to distinguish itself from others by giving priority to its own unique experiences. Progress may be universal, but it realized itself—like Hegel's World Spirit—through the historical achievements of particular nations.

This was true of the newest among them, the United States. Its capital of Washington, DC, was by the middle of the nineteenth century beginning to accumulate public buildings grand enough to match those in the old world. The Capitol is the best example. A form of it was built early in the century, but with the westward expansion of national territory and the addition of new states, it was soon too small to accommodate the growing size of Congress. For the new republic, progress and territorial expansion went hand in hand. As the building was progressively augmented, the original dome topping it became asymmetrical and needed replacement. Shortly before the Civil War, a huge cast iron dome was designed to replace this. War delayed the project, but in 1863 the building was completed with the help of Russian engineers who had recently designed the massive Saint Isaac Cathedral in Petersburg. With this addition, the Capitol became an important symbol of American nationality.

The Capitol's most interesting feature is the dome's interior. It features a giant mural known as *The Apotheosis of Washington.* The composition was designed and executed by a painter with experience in Rome. There, Michelangelo's grand dome atop Saint Peter's Basilica featured an upper oculus through which an image of a bearded God the Father hovered overhead amid a host of baby angels. *The Apotheosis of Washington* imported the baroque style of reformational Christianity but did so to create an expressly secular effect. At the center of it, America's first president takes the place of the Trinity's First Person. Now it is Washington who hovers above those assembled in the rotunda below, transforming their experience of the world with a transcendent nationality.

The heavenly transformation of liturgical space had been an important feature of the old Christendom, exemplified by Constantinople's famous Hagia Sophia. There an icon of Christ Pantocrator was painted within the dome. The Head of the Church, Jesus Christ, was depicted raising His right hand to bless worshippers below. In the *Apotheosis,* Washington Pantocrator uses his right hand not to bless but to gesture to an angelic figure next to him holding the fasces (a bundle of rods surrounding an axe), the symbol of political power. With his left hand Washington holds a sword. And below him is another angelic figure wielding a sword in one hand and a red-white-and-blue shield in the other. Not exactly the Archangel Michael doing battle against the Church's spiritual adversaries—the figure instead does battle against America's military enemies.

The great powers of the Old World also built monuments expressing a transcendent experience of nationality. France had been the earliest to do so. During the revolution, republicans had intervened in the construction of a cathedral dedicated to Saint Genevieve and redesignated the building a secular Pantheon. Inspired by the temple to all the gods of Roman pagandom, it became the resting place for the relics of famous Frenchmen such as Voltaire and Rousseau. Another important symbol was the Arc de Triomphe (1836), located at the center point of the city's famous boulevard the Champs-Élysées and commemorating the fallen soldiers of the revolutionary and Napoleonic wars. We have already discussed the Eiffel Tower (1889), which, in addition to serving as a radio antenna, marked the centennial of the Storming of the Bastille. The tower demonstrated French industrialization and technological modernity, which by the end of the nineteenth century had become national achievements.

England, France's historic enemy, also featured various monuments to her modern military and political achievements. In London these included Trafalgar Square (1844) with its column commemorating Admiral Nelson's victory against the French navy during the Napoleonic wars. England's most famous political monument was undoubtedly the Parliament Buildings, rebuilt after a fire destroyed the originals in 1834. By the middle of

Parliament Buildings, London

the nineteenth century, nationalism called the prevailing neoclassical style—favored by revolutionary France—into question.

A driving influence in the new design decision was the work of a young architectural genius named Augustus Pugin (d. 1852). He advocated the abandonment of styles associated with the previous century, such as Palladianism (a geometrically balanced and classically inspired design style then dominating British and American architecture). Interestingly, Pugin was a convert to Roman Catholicism, and this informed his contribution to the Parliament Buildings. In a sense, his work represented a loss of confidence in the liberal Protestantism of the Anglican establishment, compromised as it was by rationalism.

Such convictions paralleled those of the Oxford Movement, a group of theologians seeking a return to traditional Christianity in the middle of the century. Their most famous representative was John Henry Newman (d. 1890), who like Pugin converted to Roman Catholicism. Others, like Edward Pusey, remained within the Anglican Church but brought to it a revival of sacramental liturgy that continues to this day in the form of

Anglo-Catholicism. The movement advanced an interest in "medieval" themes in art and especially in architecture. Thus, when the Parliament Buildings were rebuilt under the direction of Charles Barry, he chose a neogothic style and turned to Pugin for guidance.

The large complex that subsequently dominated Westminster on the northern bank of the Thames River featured pointed arches, stained glass windows, and figures sculpted into the façades. It was surmounted by several towers, the most dramatic of which was that enclosing the clock known as Big Ben. The Parliament Buildings were completed in the middle of the nineteenth century, just as the Great Exhibition was being held at Hyde Park. Together with the Crystal Palace, they demonstrated that Great Britain was both the technological leader of modern Christendom and a nation with strong ties to a distant national past.

As Britain entered the twentieth century, her ideals were further elaborated by the Victoria Memorial (1911). Its symbolism included Progress personified by a sculpted youth bearing a flaming torch. Queen Victoria had ruled for most of the previous century, overseeing the consolidation of

"Progress," detail of the Victoria Memorial

Britain's overseas empire. The monument therefore recognized this achievement with winged figures symbolizing imperialism as well as various naval allusions. Victoria had been declared empress of India, and Britons would have seen in the monument an affirmation of their nation's possession of a vast array of colonies scattered across the globe. In addition to its inroads in Southern Asia, Britain had joined other Western powers to carve up virtually all of Africa by the beginning of the twentieth century.

Reflecting on this, a disciple of Galton named Karl Pearson (d. 1936) wrote a work combining imperialism with social Darwinism. Entitled *National Life from the Standpoint of Science*, it approaches "mankind as a product of nature." Man is not, as in traditional Christianity, the image of God. Such a belief is merely quaint in the aftermath of the so-called Enlightenment and the discoveries of nineteenth-century science. *Homo sapiens* is instead simply a species of animal, and the quality of its civilization—its progress index—depends directly on the unrestricted law of "natural selection." Just as Spencer and Galton had used Darwin's law to justify the elimination of the lower orders of British society, so Pearson uses it to justify the subjugation and conquest of the "lower races" of Africa. "History shows me one way," he explains, "and one way only, in which a high state of civilization has been produced, namely, the struggle of race with race, and the survival of the physically and mentally fitter race."[4] For Britain's twentieth-century heir to the social Darwinist movement, national progress was inseparable from biological racism.

Austria undertook even more substantial rebuilding than England in order to mark her unique national character. Since the dissolution of the Holy Roman Empire in 1806, she had become a territorial empire with interests no longer tied to Roman Catholic Christendom as a whole. Her core territories surrounding Vienna were German, but most of her population was non-German. After its rise later in the century, nationalism thus became her Achilles heel, as we saw in the case of the Hungarian Uprising. In addition to the Hungarians, Austria's German minority ruled peoples as

---

4 Karl Pearson, *National Life from the Standpoint of Science* (London: Adam and Charles Black, 1905), 21.

diverse as Poles, Ruthenians, Romanians, Croatians, and Italians.

But if she could not claim to be of a single ethnicity, Austria did have a claim to being a great political and cultural power. Monumental constructions in her capital city displayed this. The Hofburg Palace had long been home to the Habsburg Dynasty, but it was expanded magnificently during the nineteenth century. As a demonstration of the empire's modernity, an enormous building project was undertaken after the revolution of 1848 had passed. It centered on the demolition of Vienna's ancient walls and in their place the construction of a circular boulevard named the Ringstrasse. Along its circuit, stately buildings like the Opera House (1869) were erected. The capital of Western music also became marked by monuments to native composers like Mozart, Beethoven, and Franz Schubert. Recognition of others, such as Johann Strauss, Anton Bruckner, and Gustav Mahler, would have to await the aftermath of World War I.

"Sabers, Helmets, and Feathers"

AUSTRIA'S CLAIM TO LEADERSHIP IN German politics and art was challenged during the second half of the nineteenth century. The revolutions of 1848 had thrown the governments of all the smaller German states to the north into confusion. When the greatest among them, Prussia, arrested the ill-fated Frankfurt Assembly, it became clear to many that the ideologies of liberalism and nationalism could not, when combined, bring revolutionary progress to Germany. Liberalism would have to go.

From this realization arose one of the most remarkable and destabilizing agents of modern Christendom, Otto von Bismarck (d. 1898). In the aftermath of the revolutions, he became chancellor of Prussia under King Wilhelm I (r. 1861–1888) by advocating a nationalism shorn of the liberal ideal of democracy. Through "blood and iron"—that is, through military aggression—he promised to pacify the former revolutionaries by creating a united Germany under Prussian monarchy. The series of wars he unleashed to do so culminated with the defeat of the Second French Empire in 1871. The heir to Napoleon Bonaparte, Emperor Napoleon III, was subjected to the disgrace of being captured on the battlefield and forced to abdicate. The French, ordered by their conquerors to appear at the Palace of Versailles for terms of surrender, were forced to cede the territory of Alsace-Lorraine. This rich region straddling the Rhine River had long been contested by nationalists because of its mixed ethnicity. To add insult to injury, the French were forced to make the concession in the famous Hall of Mirrors—symbol of their now fading national glory. The blow was nearly too much for them to take. From that moment, one word was on the lips of every French nationalist: *Revanche!*

As a result of German unification, Wilhelm's title was changed from king to *Kaiser* (emperor). To create at least the impression of sovereignty, a Reichstag (or parliament) was introduced and all men were given the right to vote for its representatives. To mark this sign of national progress, a grand new Reichstag Building (1894) was erected in Berlin overlooking the Spree River.

Bismarck, however, remained the evil genius behind both the imperial throne and the parliamentary podium. To consolidate ethnic unity, he launched a program against the Roman Catholic Church called the *Kulturkampf* ("culture struggle"). It sought to reduce the power of Rome within the borders of the German Empire. The program resorted to imprisonments of clergy and the expulsion of international elements such as the Society of Jesus. It was not intentionally secularistic, as Bismarck hoped to exchange ultramontane influence for that of pietism. Nevertheless, the same humanistic forces that advocated secularism in the newly created Third Republic west of the Rhine used the culture struggle to subvert Christianity in all its forms east of it as well.

By waging a war of territorial expansion under the banner of ideological nationalism, Bismarck greatly undermined the diplomatic stability that had been in place since the Congress of Vienna. Nevertheless, he did recognize limits, and after the defeat of France he declared Germany a satisfied power and began arranging alliances designed to maintain the status quo. In creating a Second German Empire with self-conscious allusions to the defunct Holy Roman Empire, he had directly challenged the position of Austria. In fact, one of his wars of unification had been directed against Germany's most powerful southern neighbor. For these and other reasons, Bismarck's first arrangement was a Dual Alliance with Austria. That this would alarm Russia was certain. However, the chancellor brilliantly convinced the latter to sign a Reinsurance Treaty soon after. By its terms, both Germany and Russia pledged neutrality toward each other if the other were attacked. With republican France unlikely to win Russian support, and Britain pursuing a policy of "splendid isolation" behind her overseas empire, it seemed as though Bismarck had secured lasting peace.

But in 1890 a personality very different from Wilhelm I came to the throne. Wilhelm II (r. 1888–1918) was an unbalanced militarist. He regarded the alliance system as a clipping of the empire's wings and therefore began immediately to dismantle it. His first act was to dismiss the Iron Chancellor. With Bismarck out of government, Wilhelm canceled the Reinsurance Treaty with Russia. France, desperate for an ally against her tormentor, did the unthinkable and negotiated a treaty with an ideological adversary. The Franco-Russian Alliance emboldened France, reassured Russia, and threatened Germany with a two-front war. Despite the growing fears of his generals, Wilhelm forged ahead with military expansion, building a top-of-the-line steam-powered navy that ensured that if and when conflict arose, Britain would align with her historic enemy, France, along with Russia. In the meantime, Germany joined in the competition for overseas colonies, demanding, as one member of the Reichstag put it, an equal "place in the sun."

And if the British Empire had been ideologically supported by social Darwinism, Germany had her own equivalent of Karl Pearson. His name was Ernst Haeckel (d. 1919). He was one of the most prolific and influential biologists of the period. He was also one of Darwin's strongest continental supporters and traveled to England to meet the father of evolutionism. The latter privately remarked that Haeckel "was one of the few who clearly understands Natural Selection."

The German had repudiated the Protestantism in which he was nominally raised and became an activist in popularizing a strictly scientific anthropology rid of centuries of religious beliefs. His influence was tremendous. A work entitled *Natural History of Creation* (1868) went through twelve editions, and another entitled *Riddles of the World* (1899) introduced half a million readers to the principle of natural selection. A geneticist in Berlin spoke for the growing secularized multitude who fell under Haeckel's spell:

> *I found Haeckel's history of creation one day and read it with burning eyes and soul. It seemed that all problems of heaven and earth were solved simply and convincingly; there was an answer to every question which troubled the young mind. Evolution was the key to everything and could replace all the beliefs and creeds which one was discarding. There were no creation, no God, no heaven and hell, only evolution and the wonderful law of recapitulation which demonstrated the fact of evolution to the most stubborn believer in [a divine] creation.*[5]

Haeckel's effort to advance the scientific "enlightenment" of Christendom provided intellectual encouragement to Germany's new drive to acquire overseas colonies. His evolutionist anthropology identified ten discrete races of *Homo sapiens*, the highest being what he called Caucasians. All of these had origins separate from one another, making them more like separate species. It was the destiny of the Caucasian race, he claimed, to rise above and dominate the others. Using data from meticulous field research, he concluded that "lower races . . . are psychologically nearer to the mammals (apes and dogs) than civilized Europeans." It therefore followed that "we must . . . assign a totally different value to their lives."[6]

More directly than any other evolutionist, Haeckel declared the values of traditional Christianity to be null and void. The human being was not only not *Imago dei*, the image of God—he was, as *Homo sapiens*, divided into levels of worth determined by natural selection. Because human life is a ceaseless struggle, the progress of civilization necessitated violence. A nationalist who strongly supported Bismarck's wars of unification, Haeckel urged the German public to maintain its commitment to both national progress and racial purity.

---

5 Quoted in Robert J. Richards, *The Tragic Sense of Life: Ernst Haeckel and the Struggle over Evolutionary Thought* (Chicago: University of Chicago, 2008), 3.

6 Quoted in De Marco and Wiker, *Architects*, 114.

As Kaiser Wilhelm II lurched toward war during the first decade of the twentieth century, the mood in Germany's capital grew ever more belligerent. Berlin was a booming city in the decades following unification. Its population nearly tripled by the turn of the century. Factories, roads, and parks multiplied. But what was most striking was its display of the future. Nationalism had become the leading agent of progress, leaving old values forever behind. A visitor noted that

> *what Berlin displays to its visitors is modern and absolutely new. . . . When you've explored these straight streets and for ten hours seen nothing but sabers, helmets, and feathers, then you understand why Berlin, in spite of the reputation that events of the last years have bestowed on it, will never be a capital like Vienna, Paris, or London.*[7]

But if the city lacked and did not even desire remnants of an old Christendom in its midst, it welcomed the marks of a secular civilization. Its character had been established at the height of Prussian military strength during the reign of Frederick the Great. That character was expressed soon afterward in the construction of the famous Brandenburg Gate (1791) at the head of the boulevard Unter den Linden. Then, at the opposite end of the boulevard, a Frederick the Great monument (1851) was erected. Once the wars of unification got under way, other monuments arose to supplement it. A Victory Column (1873), for instance, was placed near the site of the future Reichstag Building.

Also located there was a Bismarck Monument (1901). It was one of dozens that had begun to go up even during the Iron Chancellor's lifetime, so enthusiastic was the public about his military victories. In fact, many of these monuments tied into the nationalism of Germany's most famous contemporary composer, Richard Wagner. Perhaps this was due to an effort to counter Austria's claim to musical leadership. Bismarck was commemorated with a network of Götterdämmerung Towers, named for the last opera of

7 Quoted in Modris Eksteins, *Rites of Spring: The Great War and the Birth of the Modern Age* (New York: Doubleday, 1989), 75.

the epic cycle *The Ring of the Nibelung*. Wagner was a notorious nationalist, and linking his music to Bismarck's political legacy seemed completely natural, even if the composer had expressed reserve about Prussian militarism by the end of his life. The Berlin monument itself was not of the Götterdämmerung type, but it was unique in featuring among its lower figures a sculpture of the Wagnerian hero Siegfried forging his famous sword with which to slay the giant Fafner, a symbol of Germany's enemies. Those drawing near to meditate on the monument during the reign of Wilhelm II would have been able to name quite a few such enemies.

Otto von Bismarck Monument with detail of Siegfried, Berlin

The Final Milestone

ALONG THE ROAD OF NATIONALISM, a final milestone marked Christendom's advance beyond the age of utopia. Among the great powers, the Russian Empire was becoming an ambivalent partner in the march of progress. True, her intelligentsia was more radical in its values than revolutionaries in other lands. But her government never recovered its progressive resolve after the assassination of Alexander II.

Ever since the French Revolution, the westernized values of the court and its supporting nobility had become increasingly difficult to sustain. The invasion of Napoleon Bonaparte revealed that the Petrine Reforms and Catherine's wholesale infusion of secular culture were a subversive legacy. Thus, national monuments of the Patriotic War of 1812, as it was known, were by definition ambiguous. An Alexander Column (1834) erected in the capital's Palace Square to commemorate the tsar who led the resistance to the French was one sign of this. It was magnificent in its own way, being the largest victory column in Europe and topped by an angel with a face resembling Alexander's. However, it was thoroughly Western in style and awkwardly matched in many details the Vendôme Column in Paris commemorating Napoleon's defeat of the Russians at the Battle of Austerlitz.

More dramatic was the construction of Christ the Savior Cathedral in Moscow. It was not built in the westernized style that had prevailed since the time of Peter the Great. Instead, it employed Byzantine motifs inspired by Hagia Sophia in Constantinople. What is more, to mark its consecration, the composer Tchaikovsky was commissioned to produce what became one of his most famous compositions.

The *1812 Overture* declared Russia's new attitude toward westernization. It used two Russian melodies: the imperial anthem, "God Keep the Tsar," and the Orthodox hymn for the Elevation of the Cross, "O Lord, Save Thy People." The latter had been the long-lost Byzantine Empire's equivalent of a modern national anthem. It speaks of God protecting His people from their enemies. Tchaikovsky introduces the work with this melody, reminding the audience that Russia's origin is in Eastern Christendom. He then introduces a rival melody from the West: the Marseillaise, national anthem of the French. Accompanied by a martial snare drum, it throws the melodic flow of the composition into confusion. By the end of the work, the Marseillaise looms again. But as it gathers strength, suddenly the other Russian melody intervenes—the imperial anthem. The two national melodies lock in mortal combat, but just as the Marseillaise seems to gain the upper hand in the coda, it is literally blown to pieces by "God Keep the Tsar" as cannons begin to fire. The composer, arranging the premier performance in the exterior courtyard of Christ the Savior Cathedral, actually orchestrated the work to make use of field artillery. A more dramatic statement of Russia's ambiguous (or in this case not so ambiguous) attitude toward westernization would be hard to find.

This is not to say that the Russian Empire forsook Western Christendom and completely reoriented her national identity during this time. Just as Tchaikovsky was composing his famous overture, another composer named Alexander Borodin (d. 1887) was generating a work with a very different message. Borodin was a chemist by profession and fully embraced utopian Christendom's cult of progress. Had he lived long enough, he probably would have welcomed the English poet Rudyard Kipling's *White Man's Burden*, celebrating secular transformation through colonial expansion. Borodin's contribution to Russian nationalism was a charming tone poem entitled *On the Steppes of Central Asia*. Like Tchaikovsky, he uses national melodies to define the empire. In this case, the work opens with a Russian military melody rising above an opening phrase of violins suggesting the empire's guard over the endless plains joining Russia with Asia. Then a musical phrase suggesting the waddling motion of camels is heard, and after it a Turkic melody. The idea conveyed by Borodin's written program is that Russian arms benevolently protect the growing prosperity of the empire's numerous Asiatic peoples. Here there is no conflict, as had been the case with Tchaikovsky's picture of Russia's relations with Western Europe. Instead, the two melodies intermingle and by the end of the composition merge together in harmony.

When Nicholas II (r. 1894–1917) came to power, however, the Russian Empire was faltering in its march toward a progressive future. Only two years earlier, half a million people had starved to death from famine and disease—something that was not supposed to happen in modern societies. Then, on the occasion of the coronation ceremonies in 1896, a stampede erupted when free entertainment and food were offered on the Khodynka Field outside Moscow. Unbelievably, more than a thousand were killed. Nicholas only learned of the disaster hours after the fact. When he hesitated to attend a ball at the French embassy out of grief and respect for the dead, he was talked out of it by his advisors. Like his predecessors, he had been greeted at his coronation by the peasants as Tsar-Batyushka—"Little Father Tsar." In the

Tsar Nicholas II

years following the Khodynka disaster, revolutionaries were able to subvert this image and present him instead as a callous tyrant.

Nicholas was from the first strongly opposed to most liberal definitions of progress. When letters of welcome reached him from loyal noblemen hoping to contribute to government policy, he delivered a speech rebuffing their "senseless dreams" of representative government. During the 1905 revolution he was finally compelled to create a parliamentary Duma, but he soon backpedaled in his promise of a meaningful constitution. In the meantime, an event dubbed Bloody Sunday occurred in that year. It was depressingly similar to the Khodynka disaster. A large group of workers led by a progressive priest named Georgy Gapon filed through the capital on its way to the Winter Palace with patriotic and loyal appeals for improved working conditions. This time the police opened fire on the demonstrators, killing about a thousand of them. Again, Nicholas had little knowledge of the circumstances until after the fact. But as before, he was widely blamed and condemned by the revolutionaries. The Tsar-Batyushka had become in their propaganda the Tsar-Bloodletter.

As the political conditions of a westernized Russia deteriorated, Nicholas turned increasingly to the culture of the old Christendom. Westernization had long been questioned by the time he ascended the throne, and not just in musical monuments like the *1812 Overture*. There was in fact an ideological alternative known as Slavophilism. This movement had emerged in the 1830s in reaction to Chaadaev's condemnation of Russian culture. Whereas Westernizers like Belinsky had called on Russians to reject Orthodox Christianity and embrace utopian values, the Slavophiles had in an equally maximalistic way called into question the society in which secularization had arisen.

Their visionary revival of traditional Christianity caught the attention of contemporaries in England. Leaders of the Oxford Movement, disillusioned as we have seen with utopian Christianity, discovered in Orthodoxy many of the virtues they hoped to reinstill in Western Christendom. Some began to correspond with Slavophiles like Alexey Khomyakov (d. 1860), whose short treatise *The Church Is One* laid out an Orthodox solution to the problems of post-reformational Christianity.

The Slavophiles were not reactionary conservatives like Burke or Maistre. Much of what appeared to be wrong with the West—whether in liberal or socialist forms—was creatively addressed in a blending of nationalism and traditional Christianity. Ivan Kireevsky (d. 1856) was particularly critical of capitalism and the rise of individualism in the new Christendom. Against this, he held up what he called "communality" (*sobornost*), a way of organizing society for the benefit of all without compromising the spiritual freedom of the individual. He looked for inspiration to an ancient institution in Russian rural society known as the *mir* (or *obshchina*), in which land was periodically redistributed among peasants for the greater good.

However, as much as the Slavophiles railed against the Westernizers and their progressive values, they were themselves very much a product of modernity. Inspired by German idealism as much as by Orthodox Christianity, their ideals for Russia were no less utopian than those of their ideological adversaries. Nevertheless, Kireevsky went further than contemporaries in living out his traditional Christian ideals by visiting monasteries such as Optina Pustyn, where hesychasm had again taken root after centuries of neglect.

So did a later heir to the Slavophiles, Fyodor Dostoevsky. The penitent progressive and author of *Demons* had, as we saw in the previous chapter, broken free of the revolutionary intelligentsia. After release from his Siberian imprisonment, he became Russia's most eloquent advocate for a restoration of the old Christendom. However, unlike the Slavophiles he was not utopian in his vision of this. It is true that he was an idealist, and at times fictional characters that most directly speak for him seem to hold an optimism about the future. But he was also an ascetic in that he understood the irreparable degradation of the human condition in this world and the need for salvific suffering in healing it. This insight was cultivated through the study of mystical church fathers like Isaac of Syria as well as by occasional visits to Optina Pustyn.

Tsar Nicholas II was not a mystic. But the accumulating doubt about building utopia was part of the air he breathed as Russia entered the twentieth century. He had proven more than once to be administratively ill equipped to lead Russia away from the abyss. One critic observed that he had no political convictions of his own—to which another critic sarcastically rejoined that he did have strong convictions, but they happened to be those of the last advisor with whom he had happened to speak.

Regardless of administrative talent, Nicholas's vision of Christendom was teeming with spiritual vitality. He set an example early in his reign by making pilgrimages with the royal family to the holy sites of the Orthodox Church. Saint Sergius Monastery north of Moscow was the most well known. He also grew to love Seraphim of Sarov and led the way in the saint's canonization in 1903. By traveling to central Russia in order to participate in the canonization ceremonies at sites such as the glade in which Motovilov beheld the transfiguration of the world, Nicholas linked himself inseparably to the old Christendom's paradisiacal culture.

This is perhaps most memorably demonstrated by his support for the recovery of authentic Orthodox architectural and iconographic styles. He patronized a society for the restoration of traditional iconography. Since the time of Simon Ushakov, naturalism had flooded the iconography of Russian churches. Even the Byzantine revivalist Christ the Savior Cathedral had been decorated with totally incongruous examples of "liturgical" painting by realist artists such as Ivan Kramskoy—a founder, along with the anticlerical Perov, of the Itinerants. Nicholas lent his ear to artists who instead advocated a return to traditional approaches to iconography.

The last tsar was even more active in advancing a return to traditional temple architecture. During his reign, the Window on the West became progressively easternized. Kireevsky had accused Peter the Great of being Russia's first revolutionary nihilist by westernizing the nation. Nicholas did much to atone for his predecessor's sin. In 1903, for instance, the bicentennial celebration of the founding of Petersburg was marked by a costume ball in which Nicholas dressed not as the city's progressive founder but as the pious Tsar Alexey Mikhailovich (r. 1645–1676).

More importantly, under Nicholas, Orthodox churches were erected at a phenomenal rate. In St. Petersburg the majority of them were in styles drawn from the pre-Petrine past. The most famous of these was the Temple of the Resurrection (1907), popularly known as the Church of Christ the Savior on the Spilled Blood. It was built on the place where Alexander II had been assassinated. Equal to Moscow's St. Basil's Cathedral in its joyful colors, textures, and shapes, it declared that Russia's submission to Western values was drawing to an end.

Other churches reinforced this architectural statement. One built to commemorate the victims of Japan's surprise attack on Port Arthur in 1905 looked to the Cathedral of St. Dmitry in twelfth-century Vladimir. It was known as the Church of the Savior on the Waters (1909) and featured a single dome sitting atop an elongated drum. Another, built in the suburban town of Tsarskoe Selo (site of one of the eighteenth century's most splendid palaces), self-consciously brought St. Seraphim to mind. Known as the Feodorovsky Cathedral (1912), it housed an icon of the recently canonized national saint as well as one of the Virgin Mary dating to the twelfth century. It too

Feodorovsky Church, Tsarskoe Selo, Russia

had a tall single dome and featured a roofline resembling sequences of *kokoshniky*, the pointed headdresses of Russian peasant women. The church served as a chapel for the tsar's elite guards regiment, and it was here that the royal family most frequently attended divine services and received Holy Communion when in town.

It seems that for the politically unmotivated and reclusive Nicholas, building churches and celebrating Russia's national culture would have been much more rewarding than beating the drums of secular progress.

Christmas in No-Man's Land

BUT THE RESPONSIBILITIES OF AUTOCRACY would not allow for that. Like it or not, Nicholas II was heir to a powerful state whose predecessors, beginning with Peter the Great, had used modern bureaucracy to transform Russia and make her a leader of the West. The empire now found herself in an alliance of survival with the Third French Republic.

That most politically progressive great power of the new Christendom had a foreign policy that was reducible to a single goal: revenge on Germany. What is more, Austria had set her diplomacy against Russia. In 1849 Russia had saved the Habsburgs by putting down the Hungarian Uprising. Only six years later, Austria did not raise a finger to help her deliverer when France and Britain invaded the Crimean Peninsula. Now Austria was pressing into the Balkan Peninsula to expand her territories at Russian expense. In 1908 she annexed the territory of Bosnia-Herzegovina, populated by a mixture of Croatians and Serbs. The former shared Austria's Roman Catholic faith, but the latter were Orthodox and looked to Russia for support.

Serbia was herself seeking territorial expansion in the region. Ethnic nationalism—inflamed throughout the West by a century of secularization—was the most effective means of advancing this policy. After the annexation of Bosnia-Herzegovina, a terrorist organization called the Black Hand began to organize resistance to the Austrians. Its founder expressed the organization's ideology and goals thus:

> *The war between Serbia and Austria . . . is inevitable. If Serbia wants to live in honour, she can only do this by war. This war is determined by our obligation to our traditions and the world of culture. This war must bring about the eternal freedom of Serbia, of the South Slavs, of the Balkan peoples. Our whole race must stand together to halt the onslaught of these aliens from the north.*[1]

On June 28, 1914, in the streets of Sarajevo, one of the Black Hand's members fatally shot Archduke Franz Ferdinand, the heir to the Austrian throne. This event set in motion the events that would lead to the most destructive war to date in the history of Christendom.

Back in Vienna, news of the assassination provoked an ultimatum to Serbia that she allow for an Austrian investigation to come to the capital of Belgrade to investigate the Black Hand. Serbia balked, encouraged by her close relations with Russia. Austria might have hesitated to follow through on her threat to attack the Balkan nation in light of the possibility of intervention by Russia. Her ambassador to Germany therefore needed first to inquire about the attitude to war there.

In Berlin, as we have seen, the public mood had been growing more and more bellicose. A meeting between the Austrian ambassador and Kaiser Wilhelm produced a "blank check" offering unlimited military support for

---

1 Quoted in James Joll, *The Origins of the First World War* (London: Longman, 1992), 90.

a war against Serbia—and, if necessary, Russia. With this and the refusal of the Serbian government to capitulate, Austrian shelling of Belgrade began on July 29.

Now all eyes turned to St. Petersburg. There, under pressure from his nationalistic foreign minister Sergey Sazonov, Nicholas had reluctantly agreed to a partial mobilization of the armed forces along the Austrian border, but he had stopped short of ordering an attack. He still desperately hoped for peace. A deceptive telegram from Wilhelm on July 29 appeared to support him in this hope. But Sazonov was relentless. He confronted the tsar with a series of terrible and sequentially related facts. After consulting with the generals, he had determined that a partial mobilization against only Austria was logistically impossible; the opening conflict that had now begun between Austria and Serbia prevented Russia from canceling partial mobilization; the tsar therefore must immediately order general mobilization against Germany as well.

Always lacking political resolve, Nicholas looked in vain for advice to the contrary. With a shaking hand, he finally signed the order for general mobilization. However, the document required countersignatures from several ministers, and by the time they were obtained that evening, the tsar's desire to avoid war had reasserted itself. He therefore phoned army headquarters and withdrew the order before it could be put into effect. Sazonov was beside himself. The following day, July 30, he marched into Nicholas's office and demanded, in the name of Russia's national honor, the reissuance of the order.

"Think of the responsibility you are asking me to take," cried Nicholas. "Think of thousands and thousands of men who will be sent to their death!"[2] Sazonov remained resolute, and again Nicholas relented. After the tsar had reissued the order for general mobilization, the pugnacious foreign minister phoned army headquarters and told them to smash their phones to prevent them from receiving further communications from Nicholas. Russia now mobilized against both Austria and Germany.

---

2 Quoted in Joachim Remak, *The Origins of World War I* (New York: Holt, Rinehart, and Winston, 1967), 124.

In Paris, no such hesitation as that which tortured Nicholas occurred. French nationalists had been waiting more than a generation to take back Alsace-Lorraine in a war of revenge against Germany. Before they could act, however, Germany launched an invasion across her western frontier. Germany's generals had dreaded the thought of a two-front war. But one of them, Alfred von Schlieffen, argued that a swift defeat of France would free the army to turn to the east before a slow-moving Russia could fully mobilize. According to this Schlieffen Plan, conquest of France required passage through Belgium, whose neutrality was guaranteed by Britain.

And this brings us to the last of Christendom's national capitals, London. There repugnance at the spectacle of another continental war was strong. Britain's trade within her overseas empire was as lucrative as ever and promised yet more progress at home and abroad. However, nationalism was as strong an ideology as liberalism, and the public could not be expected to watch as the country's treaty obligations were trampled underfoot by an upstart naval power now calling into question the national slogan "Britannia rules the waves." When Germany declared war on Belgium on August 3, Britain responded with a declaration of war the following day.

With all five great powers now embroiled in conflict, the deadliest war in the history of Christendom had begun. Eventually it would draw into its maw non-European powers like Ottoman Turkey, Japan, and the United States. This would earn it the name of the First World War. But for now, it was known simply as the Great War.

Nothing went as planned. As the Germans poured into France according to the Schlieffen Plan, the Russians swiftly invaded from the east. As a result, German troops had to be redeployed, weakening the western advance. By early September, the First Battle of the Marne in northern France had effectively halted the Germans. They and their Anglo-French enemies formed defensive lines. Trench warfare became the mode of combat on the western front. Between opposing lines, an area some hundred yards or more in distance became known as no-man's land, due to the deadly conditions there. As armies attacked and counterattacked across the area, bomb craters appeared and gradually filled with water. The bodies of fallen soldiers accumulated. Eventually the "corpse rats" appeared. Men who fell wounded could not be rescued without risk of falling prey to snipers. Soldiers dug in on either side were therefore forced to listen to their comrades cry out in agony as they slowly succumbed to their wounds.

On either side of the hellish landscape, entrenched defenders scanned the horizon interminably, looking for signs of an impending infantry charge. Each side was equipped in its defenses with the fruits of technological progress. The most advanced was the machine gun. It fired so many rounds in such a short space of time that attackers were quickly reduced to piles of corpses. The only military skill needed for an effective warrior was enough sustained finger pressure to keep the trigger engaged and arm strength to track the weapon back and forth across the landscape. Modern science did the rest.

To supplement this dreadful weapon, other means of killing were invented. One was the result of the burst in electrical engineering that had occurred during recent decades. By installing an electrical motor within a watertight hull, an underwater boat (or U-boat) was able to travel long distances undetected. Armed with torpedoes (which also depended on electronic propulsion), a U-boat could approach enemy shipping and sink it without warning. Another technological breakthrough was poison gas. Scientists like Fritz Haber—whom we met in chapter nine as the father of nitrogen fertilizer—used chemistry to develop ways of killing large numbers of enemy soldiers in a single act. Once mustard gas was delivered by artillery shells, masses of the enemy unprotected by gas masks were killed through paralysis and asphyxiation.

Several months of this brought millions of soldiers to the breaking point. By the end of the first year of fighting, some three hundred thousand Germans and an equal number of Frenchmen were dead. The British suffered a similar toll. The number of wounded mounted to twice these numbers. The secular causes of the horror were not lost on the combatants, especially within the lower ranks.

Having been led by modern Christendom's elite to abandon traditional Christianity for secular humanism, the men on the front lines had soon

The Christmas Truce on the Western Front, 1914

discovered the limits of utopia. In the case of nationalism, they had been encouraged to look on ancestry as a source of transcendence. The monuments scattered across Western capitals had provided a pseudo-sacramental means toward communion with something greater than the present. Now the mythos of progress had become vacant of meaning. And if liberals and socialists preferred to find transcendence in posterity, both had succumbed to the lure of nationalism and supported the war. On the Champs-Élysée in Paris; on Trafalgar Square in London; on the Ringstrasse in Vienna; on the Unter den Linden in Berlin; and on Palace Square in St. Petersburg, modern Christendom cheered the opportunity to transform the world through warfare. After five months of carnage in the name of utopia, however, many were prepared to exchange secular transformation for at least a recollection of heavenly transformation.

And so, on Christmas morning, fighting came to a stop on much of the western and some of the eastern fronts. Soldiers declined to fire at their erstwhile enemy. Slowly, some began to appear above the cover of their trenches and, as the morning advanced, make their way cautiously out into the center of no-man's land. Meeting fellow Christians there, looking into the eyes not of a German or a Frenchman or a Briton but of the image and likeness of God, they exchanged greetings. Many exchanged souvenirs and rations. Some began to sing Christmas hymns. A few even skirmished in soccer matches. One Scottish soldier reported in a letter the collective effort among both sides of his sector to capture a rabbit that ventured onto the battlefield. The Germans prevailed. "But more was secured than the hare," he noted. "A sudden friendship had been struck up, the truce of God had been called, and for the rest of Christmas day not a shot was fired along our section."[3]

The Christmas Truce of 1914 was a judgment upon a civilization with a supporting culture that no longer directed its members toward the heavenly transformation of the world. But as soon as it was delivered, post-Christian Christendom's utopian project revived. On the day following, the thundering of cannon and cracking of machine guns quickly drowned out the memory of paradise.

The Great War only came to an end four years later. And when it did, some twenty million people had been killed. What is more, the representative governments that had declared war and sustained it with propaganda were no longer trustworthy. The capitalist economies that had built the munitions were exhausted. The socialist parties that had called on their members to fight were ashamed. The liberal intellectuals that had endorsed the carnage—among them Germany's most renowned utopian Christian, the Lutheran theologian Adolf von Harnack—were discredited.

In Germany, military collapse resulted in a revolution that brought into being the Weimar Republic, complete with voting rights for women and unemployment rights for workers. This "most progressive state in Europe" soon descended into the chaos from which emerged the Nazi regime. That story, however, belongs to the age of nihilism.

For its part, the age of utopia had but one final chapter, and it was written by Russia.

3 Quoted in Eksteins, *Rites of Spring*, 123.

CHAPTER TWELVE

"Building Socialism"

PERHAPS IT WAS ONLY IN Russia that an event like the Great War could release, among revolutionaries, messianic hopes of progress. For most of Christendom and the majority of Russians, total warfare—as it came to be known—was horrific and demoralizing. As it dragged on beyond the Christmas Truce of 1914, an unprecedented death toll mounted. Commerce, industry, and transportation were disrupted. Hunger overtook the civilian population. And all the representative governments of national states—a showcase of progress—engaged in mendacity and manipulation in an effort to feed yet more young men into the meat grinder of no-man's land.

In Russia, two years of this was enough to bring the government to its knees. Everywhere, Nicholas II was confronted by the disturbing consequences of his agonized decision to go to war. Hostility was especially concentrated in the Duma. There the radically liberal Kadet party turned parliamentary debates into indictments of the regime. In the fall of 1916 the party's leader, Paul Milyukov, issued a scathing review of military performance following the tsar's decision to take personal command. After relating every setback the army had recently suffered, he asked rhetorically, "Is this stupidity, or is this treason?" Nicholas, on the eastern front far from the capital, could make no effective reply.

On February 28, 1917, autocracy came to a sudden end. A strike on

International Women's Day in Petrograd (the new Slavic-derived name for German-sounding Petersburg) precipitated a shutdown of the entire economy. Russia became paralyzed, as in October of 1905. But now, the tsar could not respond. His effort to return to the capital was foiled by strikers who refused to let the imperial train pass. Politically paralyzed and realizing the army needed leadership, Nicholas II abdicated. After a century of conspiracies and assassinations, monarchy thus fell without a single casualty and almost on the initiative of the dispirited and reclusive tsar himself.

Yet chaos soon ensued. A Provisional Government headed by Milyukov was formed by drawing deputies from the Duma, but it lacked popular support. When the liberal revolutionary leader came out onto a balcony to greet the masses, a cry was heard, "Who elected you!" Soon a Socialist Revolutionary named Alexander Kerensky was in charge, but he foolishly (though honorably) insisted that Russia fulfill her obligations to her allies and continue to fight the war to a victorious conclusion. This is not what the masses wanted to hear. For them revolution meant peace. It also meant worker control of factories, land to the peasants, and independence for national minorities. The Provisional Government declared that all of these ideals could be fulfilled only when a democratic "constituent assembly" was elected and met to formulate a republican constitution. But with the war raging, this had to be postponed indefinitely.

In the meantime, the authority of the Provisional Government dissolved. In its place, democratically elected soviets, or "councils," sprang up throughout the land. Then in April Lenin returned to Russia from foreign exile. Appearing in the city he had fled after the unsuccessful 1905 revolution, he was Rienzo redivivus. Alighting at the Finland Station in northern Petrograd, he was greeted by a delegation of revolutionaries who appraised him of the great progress achieved by the fall of autocracy and the formation of a revolutionary Provisional Government. His response, formalized soon after, was that the Bolsheviks would support the Provisional Government "as a noose supports a dying criminal."

On October 24, with the help of Leon Trotsky and Joseph Stalin, he arranged the government's arrest at the Winter Palace (though without Kerensky, who had escaped). Then, appearing at Petrograd's Smolny Institute early on October 25 before a previously scheduled Congress of Soviets, he declared that all power had passed into the hands of the soviets.

Vladimir Lenin before the October Revolution

In fact, it had only passed into the hands of Lenin and his fellow Bolsheviks. It was clear to all that a dictatorship was in the making. When a crowd of revolutionaries protested this by marching out of the hall, Trotsky jumped to his feet and howled, "That's right, get out of here! Your role is played out. You are worthless individuals. Off you go, into the dustbin of history!"

This outburst said everything about the age of utopia. If one was not with historical progress—defined here by revolutionary transformation—he belonged to the past and therefore had no value as a human being.

"Rivers of Blood"

SINCE ITS APPEARANCE IN THE fourteenth century, secular humanism had grown ever more contemptuous of the new Christendom that had given illegitimate birth to it. We have now traced this utopianism over the course of six centuries. Petrarch looked on the millennium that preceded his generation as a time of despicable darkness. Rienzo embraced this prejudice and used it to justify a bloody assault on the Roman aristocracy. Thomas More dreamed of a civilization yet to be established and was later joined in this by Francis Bacon. Philosophes like Voltaire pledged to do everything in their power to "crush infamy," and the Jacobins translated this hatred into political action. The romantics viewed the world through the lens of misunderstood genius and agonized accordingly—to the point of rebellion in some cases and despondency in others.

Then, six centuries after the death of Petrarch, revolutionary ideologies appeared that promised what the father of humanism had never even imagined: a transformation of the saeculum so complete that Christianity, with its virtue of deifying love, would simply vanish from the culture of Christendom altogether.

The Russian Revolution brought this story to completion. It was the outcome of an age in which indignation, once regulated by humility and subjected to sacrificial love, became completely untethered to any greater virtues.

Following in the footsteps of Marx, the Bolsheviks did not typically express concern for proletarian persons as such, just the ideological abstraction called the proletariat. This enabled them, again with Marx, to classify whole sections of humanity as good or evil—valuable or worthless—based on class affiliation. This meant that members of the historically unprogressive bourgeoisie were subject to the most extreme measures of repression and violence. What is more, virtually anyone who stood in the way of Lenin and his party were labeled "agents of the bourgeoisie" and therefore subject to the same treatment. Landowners, peasants, and clergy—though occupying very different places in society from capitalists—all found themselves in this situation.

The ideological redefinition of humanity also meant that members of the progressive proletariat were not of any value in and of themselves. Again, the standard of human value was future-oriented, that is, linked to progress. If workers should ever presume to raise objections to the revolution and therefore obstruct the march of progress, then the Bolsheviks—the only truly progressive force according to Trotsky's dustbin speech—were justified in destroying them.

These were the anthropological circumstances that accompanied the outbreak of the deadliest domestic conflict in the history of Christendom. The Russian Civil War would kill more people than even the religion-induced French civil wars of the sixteenth century. It was that earlier conflict and the broader wars of Western religion generally that marked the fall of Christendom's paradisiacal culture. As we have seen, advocates of utopia such as Voltaire had long afterward blamed Christianity for the bloodshed. Now a perfectly secular force was the cause of even greater suffering.

And for this reason the Russian Revolution represents a crisis of secular humanism. As a system of beliefs and values, the latter had promised to the new Christendom that emerged from the Great Schism relief from penitential pessimism and a celebration of man's place in the cosmos. It convinced adherents from Ficino to Kant that all human beings possess an innate dignity that deserves recognition. Secular humanism was, however, a counterfeit of the anthropology of traditional Christianity. As the romantics who followed Kant began to see, when humanity is separated from a transcendent source of being, it eventually disintegrates. The nineteenth century had witnessed this process. During its course, liberals and socialists looked beyond real persons to a transcendent posterity. To this nationalists added a transcendent ancestry. Both were inventions. Both were abstractions. And both failed to transform the West on a truly transcendent rather than merely immanent level.

In 1917, the Bolsheviks made one final heroic effort to redeem secular humanism by locating a transcendent anchor for it in a "proletarian dictatorship." And though they would eventually fail, plunging their movement into the depths of nihilism, for about a decade they claimed to have the key to utopia.

As October approached, Lenin wrote one of many harrowing statements about the need for class violence and its inevitability. Analyzing the revolution's course since February, he claimed the country was moving ever more decisively toward a cataclysmic contest between the bourgeoisie and the proletariat. But the approaching "proletarian civil war" would be liberating when seen against the backdrop of the Great War. "No rivers of blood in an internal civil war," he declared, "can ever approximately equal those seas of blood which the Russian imperialists have shed."[4] In point of fact, the civil war unleashed by the Bolshevik seizure of power would kill more than twice as many Russians as the one from which it sprang. But Lenin and his party were willing to pay that price.

Murderous indignation now took possession of utopia's proponents. Having arrested the Provisional Government and driven rival revolutionaries into the opposition, the Bolsheviks formed the framework for the world's first totalitarian system.

It contained four important features. The first was political dictatorship. After renaming themselves the Communist Party, they banned the legal existence of all rivals. When the long-awaited constituent assembly finally convened, instead of allowing its democratically elected members to write a new constitution, the party dissolved it after a single day of deliberations. The second feature of the totalitarian system was police terror. Within months of October, a body called the Cheka was created. Its head, Felix Dzerzhinsky, was a fanatic made all the more effective by his extreme asceticism. A third feature was control over the economy. Lenin endorsed the violent seizure of landed estates by the impoverished peasantry and the establishment of worker control over factories. Both were intermediate steps toward direct control over the economy. Lenin followed these measures with a declaration that those who withhold grain from the government are to be treated as "enemies of the people."[5]The final feature of the Communist system was ideological uniformity. The government did everything within its formidable power to bring Russian culture into conformity with the beliefs and values of Communism. The single most effective means of accomplishing this was the founding of an official Communist newspaper named *Pravda*, or in English *The Truth*. One of its earliest editors was Joseph Stalin.

The goal of Communist totalitarianism from the start was what the

---

4 V. I. Lenin, "The Russian Revolution and Civil War," in *Collected Works*, vol. 26, ed. George Hanna, trans. Yuri Sdobnikov and George Hanna (Moscow: Progress Publishers, 1972), 28–42.

5 W. Bruce Lincoln, *Red Victory* (New York: Simon and Schuster, 1989), 65.

Bolsheviks called "building socialism," the creation of a truly progressive civilization with a supporting culture that would direct its members toward the socialist transformation of the world. Less than a year after seizing power, they found an opportunity in the Russian Civil War.

The causes of this ghastly conflict were largely of their own making. Since the Communists had so brazenly betrayed the democratic aspirations of revolutionary Russia, they had come to be hated by many. In March 1918, they were forced by political circumstances to negotiate a defeatist peace with Germany, but this estranged both conservatives linked with the old military leadership and radicals who looked on imperial Germany as a target for revolutionary warfare.

Then, on July 17 (July 4 according to the old calendar the Communists replaced), the imperial family of Nicholas, Alexandra, and their five children—Olga, Tatiana, Maria, Anastasia, and Alexey—were executed on Lenin's orders in Yekaterinburg, where they were living in detention. This provoked the already growing opposition to the Communists by a so-called White Army consisting of everyone from monarchists to Socialist revolutionaries. In August a representative of the latter named Fanny Kaplan tried to assassinate Lenin by shooting him on the street. After the Cheka had tortured her, executed her, and burned her body to ashes in a trash can, it eagerly launched what came to be known as the Red Terror.

It was during the Civil War that the rivers of blood Lenin anticipated began to widen expansively. For the Communists the conflict was reduced to a dynamic often articulated by Lenin: "who-over-whom" (*kto-kogo*), that is, who will annihilate whom in the revolutionary struggle? Needless to say, in their scientific understanding of things, harmony, forgiveness, and sacrificial love were bourgeois sentiments and totally out of the question. As Marxists, they believed wholeheartedly in the evolutionist principle that progress occurs through a violent struggle for existence. As history's most progressive class, the proletariat can advance only through class warfare against the bourgeoisie (which itself will fight back with equal violence). This dialectic of annihilation creates the need for an all-powerful totalitarian state.

"The transition from capitalist society . . . to communist society," Lenin declared in *State and Revolution* (published on the eve of the October Revolution), "is impossible without a political transition period, and the state in this period can only be the revolutionary dictatorship of the proletariat."[6] As the self-declared agent of historical progress, the Communist government was chosen by a kind of transcendent historical reason to wage a merciless war against the class enemies of the proletariat.

The Cheka led the way. During its first year of existence—that is, before the Civil War really got underway—it succeeded in shooting more than six thousand "class enemies." These figures demonstrate how the Communists, who like other revolutionaries had indignantly condemned political repression under the old regime, soon exceeded it beyond any comparison. One Communist newspaper reacted to the assassination attempt on Lenin (which, it should be remembered, was the act of a fellow socialist) with the following declaration:

> *Without mercy, without sparing, we will kill our enemies in scores of hundreds. Let them be thousands, let them drown themselves in their own blood. For the blood of Lenin . . . let there be floods of blood of the bourgeoisie—more blood, as much as possible.*[7]

In Dzerzhinsky, the Cheka had a leader both fanatical and unscrupulous. Among his subordinates he was likened to "a monk in soldier's clothing." When in the early days one questioned the Cheka's indifference to the law, Dzerzhinsky, with burning eyes, would reply, "We don't want justice; we want to settle accounts."[8]

But for that an army was needed, and Trotsky provided it. Though he had no military training of any significance, the sheer power of his oratory and capacity for organization resulted in an effective force known as the Red Army. It fought on all sides of Moscow, to which the capital had been

6 "State and Revolution," in *The Lenin Anthology*, edited by Robert C. Tucker (New York: W. W. Norton, 1975), 311–98.
7 Quoted in Anne Applebaum, *Gulag* (New York: Doubleday, 2003), 9.
8 Quoted in Lincoln, *Red Victory*, 136.

Leon Trotsky as Commissar of War

relocated. Racing from one front to another in his personal military train, Trotsky established a strong sense of unity and purpose among his soldiers. This is something the White Armies lacked. He also recruited much-needed officers with experience in the old regime. For this he was criticized by Stalin, but the results justified the decision. By 1921, the last of the Whites evacuated the Crimea and sailed into the oblivion of exile.

During the course of the Civil War, the Communists had matched a ruthless struggle against the White Armies with a policy in lands they controled called War Communism. It was an effort to turn Russia into a socialist utopia overnight. While all Communists endorsed the policy, Nikolay Bukharin (d. 1938) was its most eloquent advocate. He coauthored a work entitled *The ABC of Communism* that was the fullest account of what Communism stood for at the time. While the work had much to say about all aspects of the utopia then being realized, Bukharin's contribution was mainly economic. "The dictatorship of the proletariat," he wrote, "is not only an instrument for the crushing of enemies; it is likewise a lever for effecting economic transformation."[9]

---

9 N. Bukharin and E. Preobrazhensky, *The ABC of Communism*, trans, Eden and Cedar Paul (Baltimore: Penguin, 1969), 127.

During the Civil War the economy was in shambles. Fighting and famine had left many factory towns almost void of industrial workers, who had been a tiny minority of the population even before the revolution. Now they were streaming back into the countryside, leaving their Marxist rulers with even less legitimacy. War Communism sparked a resolve to build a proper working class. It was becoming clear that if the Soviet Union was to have a respectably large working class, equal in size to her capitalist rivals in Germany or America, she would need to extract wealth from agriculture, the only significant source of capital for industrialization.

"One of the fundamental tasks of Soviet power," Bukharin claimed, "was and is that of uniting all the economic activities of the country in accordance with a general plan of direction by the state."[10] As for the peasants, they were on notice that the proletarian dictatorship would not tolerate continued resistance to what it defined as progress. In standard Marxist fashion, Bukharin presented the matter in terms of class conflict.

> *As long as this class of rich peasants continues to exist, its members will inevitably prove to be the irreconcilable enemies of the proletarian State and its agrarian policy. In its turn it can expect nothing from the Soviet Power but a pitiless struggle against its counter-revolutionary activities.*

And then, ominously:

> *The Soviet Power may eventually be compelled to undertake a deliberately planned expropriation of the rich peasants, mobilizing them for social work, and above all for the task of improving peasant land and the land of soviet farms. . . . The system of petty agriculture is in any case doomed. It must inevitably be replaced by a more advantageous and more productive system, by the system of large-scale cooperative agriculture.*[11]

In other words, the seeds of Stalinist collectivization were being sown.

---

10 Ibid, 319.

11 Ibid, 372.

In 1921, as the Civil War was coming to an end with a Red victory, War Communism was suddenly abandoned as a policy. The reason was in no way a reassessment of the long-term goals of the socialist utopia. A rebellion of sailors and workers on the naval island of Kronstadt in the Gulf of Finland forced Lenin to order a "strategic retreat." Realizing that the government had gone too far, that it was losing the hard core of its political constituency, a New Economic Policy (often abbreviated as NEP) was introduced. It withdrew the former draconian requisitions of grain from the peasants and forced labor from the workers. It freed agriculture to return to profit-based principles. In other words, it was a compromise with the government's class enemy.

This provoked indignation within the Communist party. A debate about how long such a compromise should be in place arose and dominated the party for the remainder of the decade. As long as Lenin remained in power, NEP prevailed. But in 1924 he died, the victim of a stroke. Among his successors were Trotsky and Stalin, and each realized power would belong to the Old Bolshevik (named for party membership dating before the Revolution) who successfully returned the party to the policies of true progress—economic transformation.

The New Martyrdom Begins

IN THE MEANTIME, THE COMMUNISTS were busy building socialism through other means. One was the annihilation of Christianity. Communists were not mere atheists. They did not take the position, as a Comte or Mill had, that religion limits human reason and will disappear as science progresses. They were preoccupied with the corollary to Marx's statement that it is the "opium of the masses."

Marx had claimed that religion—and especially Christianity—was an instrument of class oppression. It was used by capitalists to induce workers to seek a paradise beyond this world so that their immiseration would not become revolutionary in this one. That traditional Christianity in its prereformational form revealed the kingdom of heaven *in* this world and not just beyond it was more or less irrelevant, insofar as secular humanists knew little or nothing about Eastern Christendom, even when contemplating a revolution in Russia. Marx's claim meant that the very presence of religion in a society was a sign that class oppression was still formidable within it. The Communists, having created a socialist utopia, had a vested interest in eliminating Christianity from the lands they ruled. This became part of the new transformational imperative, and it assumed existential proportions.

Even in the *ABC*, Bukharin had prophesied excitedly that "the transition from socialism to communism, the transition from the society which makes an end of capitalism to the society which is completely freed from all traces of class division and class struggle, will bring about the natural death of all religion and all superstition." He then continued: "It is essential at the present time to wage with the utmost vigour the war against religious prejudices, for the church has now definitely become a counter-revolutionary organization, and endeavors to use its religious influence over the masses in order to marshal them for the political struggle against the dictatorship of the proletariat."[12] Lenin could not have agreed more.

So from the start—from 1917 on—the party of Lenin waged a merciless war against all manifestations of religion and against Orthodox Christians in particular. Before the revolutionary year was over, a priest named Ivan Kochurov had been brutally put to death by a Bolshevik mob in Tsarskoe Selo. Then, during the following year, what came to be known as the New Martyrdom began in earnest. In their effort to find class enemies everywhere, the Communists looked on the Orthodox as inseparable from the bourgeoisie, even if they were peasants or nobility.

One of the earliest assaults occurred in Kiev at the ancient Caves Monastery. There Metropolitan Vladimir had taken a stand against Ukrainian nationalists who demanded a separate Orthodox jurisdiction for their country, as well as against the Bolsheviks, who were fomenting civil war. On February 7 (January 25 on the old calendar) a group of Bolsheviks entered the monastery and, after beating Vladimir, marched him outside the gates and

12 Ibid, 307.

shot him to death. Bystanders reported that his last action was to make the sign of the cross over his executioners.

Attacks on Orthodox clergy also took place in Petrograd. When a priest blocked armed Communists from pushing their way into the Alexander Nevsky Cathedral, he was shot through the head. Soon the government expropriated the property, and more clergy were shot. Far to the east, in the Ural town of Merkushino, a priest named Constantine Bogoyavlensky was executed after his parishioners refused to cancel an outdoor icon procession. After gunning down many of the laity during the event, officials arrested the young priest and marched him into the woods for execution. Locals remembered how along the way he sang his own funeral service, knowing that no one would be left to bury him properly.

The year 1918 also marks the martyrdom of one of the most beloved saints of the time, Grand Duchess Elizabeth. She had been born in Germany, the daughter of a Lutheran prince. She married into the Russian royal family (as did her younger sister, Empress Alexandra) and, though she was not required to do so, ultimately converted to Orthodoxy. She had always been a deeply pious Christian. Yet her social status exposed her to opulent balls, gourmet feasts, and other comforts of palace life.

Grand Duchess Elizabeth

In 1905, her husband, Grand Duke Sergey, left their home within the Moscow Kremlin and moments later was brutally killed by a terrorist's bomb. Elizabeth ran into the street to see the ghastly results. Yet she visited the killer in jail and implored him to repent. She even went so far as to intercede for him before the tsar. On the site of the assassination she erected a monument consisting of a cross bearing the words, "Forgive them Father, for they know not what they do."

Elizabeth then gave away much of her wealth and built a monastery to which she retired for the rest of her life. Her main occupation apart from prayer became care of the poor. The aristocratic woman who had been accustomed to sleeping on feather mattresses now slept on wooden planks. She who had been privileged to eat fine foods now ate the spare rations of the monastery refectory. And having formerly passed gay nights in dancing and sociability, she now kept prayerful vigils over the deathbeds of Moscow's industrial workers.

Then, in 1918, the Communists came for her. In addition to her German ancestry and ties with the imperial family, her face-to-face compassion and care for the working class was too much of a challenge to the Communists' aloofness to the personal lives of their people. They transported her to the Ural Mountains and eventually to Yekaterinburg. The night after executioners gunned down the imperial family in nearby Tobolsk, Elizabeth and several companions were marched through the woods to an abandoned mineshaft and hurled to their death below. Many of the martyrs survived the fall, however. One of the Bolshevik executioners later reported hearing the Orthodox hymn of the cross, "O Lord, Save Thy People," rising out of the dark abyss. A hand grenade was then dropped into the mineshaft, and the singing came to an end.

During the Civil War the Communists put thousands of Orthodox clergy and innumerable laypeople to death. Some of the clergy were drowned, some were buried alive, and some were crucified on the royal gates of their parish churches. When the laity rose up in protest, they were arrested, and in many cases executed, as agents of the bourgeoisie. Frequently those who resisted the murder of clergy were in fact from the working class. The initial wave of persecution was simply the religious parallel to the regime's draconian economic policies during the period. It was part of the project to build socialism in a short time with great violence, an approach to utopia based on the apocalyptic circumstances of the Civil War.

The decision of the Communist Party to moderate its utopianism in 1921 by introducing the New Economic Policy meant that religious persecution would also assume new and less direct forms. One was a policy to blame the Church for a famine that resulted from the Civil War. In 1917, the Orthodox had reestablished the Moscow patriarchate and elected a bishop named Tikhon as their head. One of his first actions was to excommunicate those in the government who were persecuting believers and causing fratricidal conflict. Then, when the famine came, he called on parish communities to offer their valuables to be used in the relief effort. The Communists could not allow such socially beneficial acts from an "historically primitive" source, and certainly not when that source was not assimilated within the totalitarian system. They therefore resolved to push the church leadership to the point where they could attack it.

This they did by ordering the involuntary surrender not only of all church valuables but of consecrated objects such as eucharistic chalices. This directly violated the canons of the Church, and Tikhon refused to bless it. When in 1922 a local group of believers in a town called Shuya resisted the forcible expropriation of such objects, the regime had its excuse to attack the church leadership. "It is precisely now," a secret document attributed to Lenin declares, "that we must wage a merciless battle against the reactionary clergy and suppress its resistance with such cruelty that it will remember it for several decades." The memorandum recommends that at Shuya and "other spiritual centers of the country" (such as Moscow) mass arrests of the faithful be made and that "the maximum possible number of executions" occur.[13]

Nevertheless, the church leadership remained firm in denying the regime unrestricted control over valuables. Given the role played by the Communists in causing the famine and their patent indifference to human suffering, it was apparent to many that such donations would not be used for famine relief in any case. In Petrograd, Metropolitan Benjamin cooperated with the government to a large degree but did not fully surrender to its demands. In 1922 a schismatic priest named Alexander Vvedensky met with the local

13 Quoted in Dimitry Pospielovsky, *The Russian Church under the Soviet Regime*, vol. 1 (Crestwood, NY: Saint Vladimir's Seminary, 1984), 95.

The trial of Metropolitan Benjamin of Petrograd

head of the Cheka to arrange for Benjamin's arrest, and after a trial the hierarch was executed with a group of other Orthodox. In the months that followed, more than ten thousand clergy and laity were put to death in connection with the valuables campaign. Lenin's policy of linking persecution to famine relief had appeared to work.

A second alternative to direct attacks on the Church was a policy of encouraging schism. The grave condition of Orthodoxy after centuries of westernization and state domination cannot be overstated. By the time of the revolution, church governance, parish worship, and theological training had in many cases fallen to unprecedented lows. The reign of Nicholas II had seen conscious efforts at improvement, but a spiritual malaise continued to grip much of the Church. This provoked in some would-be leaders a desire for the wholesale reformation of Orthodoxy.

Whereas the majority of the Church did not fall into this tendency, finding in the restored patriarchate the path toward spiritual renewal, a group calling itself the Living Church advanced significant changes. These "renovationists" called for things like the introduction of a married episcopate, the abolition of fasting practices, and incorporation of secular ideologies. They also embraced utopia in the form the Communists were giving to it. At a council held in 1923, they sang "Many Years" for the government and praised its progressive commitment to "social truth."[14] The Communists therefore bestowed favor on the schism.

This proved to be a sort of kiss of death, however, and the vast majority of Orthodox refused to accept renovationism. Vvedensky and his supporters tried to counter this by forcing Patriarch Tikhon's resignation. They even collaborated with the secret police in having him arrested. However, their

14 Ibid, 56.

Patriarch Tikhon of Moscow

lack of unity and the fact that Tikhon soon obtained release resulted in their failure to gain control of the patriarchate. In subsequent years, Vvedensky receded in influence, and the renovationist movement died out.

Patriarch Tikhon thus led the Church through a perilous period in her history. The New Martyrdom had begun, and it would continue for decades to come. Without reliable records, we will never know how many Orthodox gave their lives for Christ during this time. The number certainly surpassed one hundred thousand. What is more, innumerable churches and monasteries were desecrated, deserted, or destroyed. One figure puts the number at fifteen thousand.[15] Optina Pustyn, where hesychasm had once again cultivated Russian Christendom's experience of the kingdom of heaven, was shut down. The relics of Seraphim of Sarov were seized by the government and hidden away in a museum storeroom. In 1922 Solovetsky Monastery in the White Sea was converted into a prison camp to which tens of thousands of victims of the Red Terror became, as one historian has put it, "unwilling pilgrims."[16]

When in 1925 Tikhon finally died from the effects of continual arrests, interrogations, and tortures, it was clear that in the socialist utopia envisioned by the Communists, traditional Christianity would have no place.

15 Paul Froese, *The Plot to Kill God: Findings from the Soviet Experiment in Secularization* (Berkeley: University of California, 2008), 53.

16 Roy Robson, *Solovki* (New Haven: Yale University, 2004), 205.

Tikhon's cryptic but ominous final words suggested as much. "The night will be long," he murmured on his deathbed, "and very dark."

God-building

LENIN'S DEATH IN 1924 HAD created its own sense of crisis, at least for the Communists. The creators of a socialist utopia lost their creator. They were left to figure out on their own the way to continue building socialism. The New Economic Policy was in full swing, and no one within the party could abide it very long. But the personal genius of Communism, who himself had insisted on adopting the compromise policy, ceased to be present to them in this world. Utopia was again threatened by an agonizing loss of transcendence.

As Trotsky, Stalin, and other Old Bolsheviks began to turn on one another, Lenin—even in death—became a necessary presence. Since the father of Communism spent the last year of his life partially paralyzed and nearly mute, the struggle for succession commenced before he breathed his last. Trotsky was seen by all as the most charismatic candidate. He was a phenomenal orator and the mastermind of the Red victory in the Civil War. But he was also something of a loose cannon. He was one of the last to join the Bolsheviks on the eve of the October Revolution. He was also contemptuous of other party leaders. As Lenin lay on his deathbed, Trotsky issued a broadside on the Old Bolsheviks in the form of a collection of essays entitled *The New Course*. In it he accused them of deviating from Leninism through a process of "bureaucratic degeneration."

For his part, Stalin had assumed control of the party as its general secretary and had every intention of using the growing bureaucracy to his advantage. When Lenin died, Trotsky happened to be in the Crimea, far from Moscow. Stalin intentionally misled his rival about the date of the funeral, resulting in Trotsky's conspicuous absence from the political ceremonies. Then, later in the year of mourning, Stalin penned a work entitled *The Foundations of Leninism* to establish his authority as the true interpreter of the leader's vision. Though Trotsky continued to challenge Stalin (he later ridiculed *Foundations* as "ideological rubbish"), he found himself increasingly outwitted by his rival.

Yet the passing of Lenin was an event with far more than political significance. It endowed the nascent utopia with a much-needed source of transcendence. Until 1924, the Communists had simply been Russia's most effective revolutionaries. Now they were endowed with a creator whose presence lived on in the culture of Communism. As the end approached, *Pravda* printed a statement on the sixth anniversary of the October Revolution defining the personal source of this culture.

> *Lenin is not only the name of a beloved leader; it is a program and a tactic . . . and a philosophical world view . . . Lenin is the hatred, the ardent hatred of oppression and the exploitation of man by man. . . . Lenin is the rule of pure reason . . . Lenin is the limitless enthusiasm for science and technology. . . . All problems find a solution in him. . . . Lenin has the greatest beauty in the world, because he is the incarnation of a seeming contradiction, because Lenin—is the dynamic and the dialectic of the proletariat. . . . Lenin is the suffering for an idea; it is a bleeding for the proletariat . . . Lenin . . . is the one Communist Party of the Red Globe. Long live Comrade Lenin!*[17]

Lenin did not live long, at least in the body. In spirit, however, he seemed immortal. As a popular poem proclaimed following his death, "Lenin lived, Lenin lives, Lenin shall always live!"

The author of this poem was the famous Vladimir Mayakovsky (d. 1930), eventually dubbed the "poet of the Revolution." He had been a leading force in an artistic movement known as futurism, which, in a perfectly utopian way, rejected all values associated with the past. One of his devices was to insult his audience at public recitations, sometimes by hurling objects at them. Personally, he lived out his contempt for moral traditions by seducing married women, abandoning the children he sired by them, and, in the end, committing suicide.

---

17 Quoted in Nina Tumarkin, *Lenin Lives! The Lenin Cult in Soviet Russia* (Cambridge, MA: Harvard University, 1997), 132.

In the aftermath of the leader's death, Mayakovsky put the finishing touches on an epic entitled simply *Vladimir Ilich Lenin*. It opens with a paradox: "There's no one more alive than Lenin in the world." This is so because all of human history finds its fulfillment in the events surrounding the proletarian revolution he created. Indeed, he is presented as the mystical point of union between history and the working class. Like Christ, in whom two realities—the divine and the human—were joined in hypostatic union, so in Lenin the cosmos and man become one. And this happens through the agency of the party he created. "The party embodies the immortality of our cause," the poet writes. And as the father of Communism ascends, as it were, into the heavenly realm of collective memory, he leaves behind—as did Christ—a communion of believers whose ministry is the continuous transformation of the world.

> *What a joy it is to be part of this union,*
> *Even tears from the eyes to be shared en masse,*
> *In this—the purest, most potent communion*
> *With that glorious feeling*
> *Whose name is Class.*[18]

Completely immanent in a materialistic world, Communist culture could thus inspire a "glorious feeling" of transcendence through the person of Lenin.

Mayakovsky's intentional mystification of Lenin was an example of what contemporaries called "god-building" (*bogostroitelstvo*). As a philosophical movement before the revolution, it attracted Marxist literary figures like Maxim Gorky. Its most accomplished advocate was Anatoly Lunacharsky (d. 1933), who would go on to become the Soviet Union's first "commissar of enlightenment." On the one hand, god-builders were atheists. However, like Comte, they believed the thoroughly secular civilization of the future should offer its members a mystical participation in something that transcends

18 Vladimir Mayakovsky, "Vladimir Ilyich Lenin," in *Lenin 150* (New Delhi: LeftWord Books, 2020), 15–118.

themselves. They did not reject outright the rituals and myths of Christianity, but sought to reconstitute them in a scientifically acceptable Marxist form. For them the proletarian revolution promised to create a truly progressive religion. As one historian has noted, such "Promethean rhetoric and deification of humanity, with its stress on a future harmony as a surrogate of transcendence for the individual, was in effect a repetition of Feuerbach's philosophy."[19]

Philosophically redundant it may have been, but in the context of early Soviet culture, god-building became an urgent task. This can be seen in the creation of a pseudo-religion of Communism. Again, Christianity offered its pattern. For instance, in the place of holidays like Pascha (Easter) and Christmas, the Communists established, respectively, the Day of Workers' International Solidarity and the Day of Industrialization. They even tried to abolish the weekly Lord's Day (stubbornly known in Russian as Voskresene—"Resurrection Day"). But this failed to take hold. In the place of baptism, the state offered a civil "octobering," in which the newborn child would be given a name like Traktor (if a boy) or Elektrifikatsiya (if a girl). Children of either sex might be pseudo-christened Ninel—that is, Lenin spelled backward. Young couples were encouraged to forgo the primitive Orthodox rite of crowning and instead were offered a civil "red wedding." For the end of life, burial was discouraged and cremation made available in one of many new facilities with transformational names like Phoenix.[20]

Cremation was not an option in the case of Lenin, however. Within hours of his death, the Communist leadership had resolved to embalm his body for public veneration. They could not resist the god-building impulse. A Commission for the Immortalization of the Memory of V. I. Ulianov (Lenin) was formed. It summoned a leading engineer to the Moscow Kremlin to present, in very short order, a plan for the devout undertaking.

The man chosen was Leonid Krasin (d. 1926), himself an advocate of

---

19 Leszek Kolakowski, *Main Currents of Marxism*, vol. 2, trans. P. S. Falla (Oxford: Oxford University, 1978), 447.

20 Some of these Communist practices of ritualizing the cycles of life are described in Richard Stites, *Revolutionary Dreams: Utopian Vision and Experimental Life in the Russian Revolution* (Oxford: Oxford University, 1989), 109–14.

god-building. He had been a close associate of Alexander Bogdanov, who, as the most influential philosopher of the movement, had become convinced that a mystical participation in the entire working class was possible through blood transfusions with its members (the philosopher was technically a member of the bourgeoisie and lacked proletarian blood). This, he believed, would provide the key to physical immortality. Before he could become a god himself, however, an experimental transfusion caused him to contract a fatal case of tuberculosis. For his part, Krasin seems to have seen the embalming of Lenin as a related case of human deification through science. Only three years before the commission's founding, he optimistically declared:

> *I am certain that the time will come when science will become all-powerful, that it will be able to recreate a deceased organism. . . . And I am certain that when that time will come, when the liberation of mankind, using all the might of science and technology, the strength and capacity of which we cannot now imagine, will be able to resurrect great historical figures.*[21]

He did his best in the case of Lenin. And once the right combination of chemicals was injected into the leader's corpse, his immortality became visible.

All that remained was to build a proper mausoleum in which to enshrine the relics. The architectural style would need to be properly modernistic but at the same time suggest the piety (if not actual faith) of the old Christendom. In the person of Alexey Shchusev (d. 1949) the Immortalization Commission found its man. He had distinguished himself as one of the leading architects in efforts to easternize St. Petersburg before the Great War. It was he whom Grand Duchess Elizabeth had commissioned to design the Martha-Mary Convent in Moscow, using pre-Petrine liturgical themes. Shchusev showed himself eminently adaptable to the tastes of his patrons and now produced the mausoleum by employing a style called contructivism. In this case, it was based on the square, which avant-garde artists claimed was the symbol of eternity.

21 Quoted in ibid., 181.

Lenin's Tomb in Red Square in Moscow became the center of a veritable Lenin cult during the years following the leader's death. Other expressions of the cult appeared, to be sure. The city that witnessed the October Revolution was renamed Leningrad. The Finland Station, where the leader famously alighted in 1917 to call for the overthrow of the Provisional Government, became the site of an archetypal Lenin statue that was reproduced in nearly every city and town throughout the Soviet Union. "Lenin corners" even began to appear in piously Communist homes to replace the traditional Orthodox icon corner.

But Lenin's Tomb was the most explicit example of how utopia, though quite secularistic, had failed to defy Christendom's need for transcendence. The body, although chemically preserved, was the obvious counterfeit of saintly relics kept incorrupt miraculously. The pilgrims who passed by it, despite holding totally different beliefs and values, were little different from the pious Christians who journeyed to monastic shrines. Secular humanism may thus have completely displaced traditional Christianity, but it could not eliminate the new Christendom's pattern of transformation.

Visitors queuing up to venerate Lenin's Tomb. A desecrated St. Basil's Cathedral stands in the distance.

At the summit of Lenin's Tomb, during the tenth anniversary celebration of the October Revolution, leaders of the Communist Party assembled to watch a victory parade on Red Square below. Their experience must have been something like that of Petrarch atop Mount Ventoux six centuries earlier. Then the father of humanism had contemplated the dawn of utopia. And now that vision had been fulfilled.

As the Communist leadership looked down from the heights of Lenin's Tomb, they had much of which to be proud. As a parade of faithful party members marched past them below, they would have thought about the victorious march of progress. The event was but the culmination of a year celebrating the building of socialism. Throughout 1927 numerous cultural projects had been commissioned by the government. The authors of *Pravda* had done their part. So had intellectuals. The Soviet Union's leading cinematographer, Sergey Eisenstein, produced his most famous film to commemorate the moment, ten years earlier, when utopia was born. The film *October* culminates in the storming of the Winter Palace (which he famously reenacted on a scale grotesquely inaccurate) and the proclamation of victory by Lenin. At the moment of Bolshevik victory, the film presents a montage of clocks throughout the world, brilliantly indicating that a turning point in history has been reached and that Russia, under Lenin, was responsible for uniting the present with posterity. There was, indeed, much for the party members standing atop the mausoleum to celebrate.

But for one of them the occasion was especially triumphant. As Joseph Stalin looked down on the rows of soldiers, workers, peasants, and representatives of various nationalities filing beneath him, he would have brought to mind the genius of his predecessor in marshaling them all into the revolutionary force that inaugurated the socialist utopia. He would surely have identified with the genius whose embalmed body lay in perpetual state beneath him. But even more, Stalin would have gloated that no other Old Bolshevik could enjoy such communion with Lenin.

For in that very year, his only rival had been irrecoverably cast out of government and, Stalin was sure, would soon be expelled from the party itself. Leon Trotsky, ruthless master of the Red Army, had been outmaneuvered and defeated. The orator who had cast non-Bolshevik revolutionaries into the dustbin of history a decade earlier was now lying in it himself. Within a year he would be exiled from the Soviet Union. Eventually, he would be hunted down in Mexico by the Communist terror machine and murdered with an ice pick. But Stalinism itself belongs to another story—one shaped by nihilism.

For now, the age of utopia seemed to those standing atop Lenin's Tomb to have reached its completion.

EPILOGUE

A Great Deception

THE RUSSIAN REVOLUTION BROUGHT TO completion Western Christendom's centuries-long project of transforming the world. It was in a way the outcome of a process begun in the aftermath of the Great Division. Like the Papal Reformation, the Russian Revolution appropriated the same condescending model of a bifurcated society in which a self-appointed elite indignantly challenges the untransformed saeculum. Lenin's confrontational model of "who-over-whom" gave expression to this. Claiming enlightenment (in this case the "scientific socialism" of Marx), the Bolsheviks led the way to perfection, forcing the unenlightened masses to be free. The difference between the two transformational movements was to be found, of course, in the motivation. In the eleventh century the motivation had been reformational Christianity. In the twentieth century it was secular humanism.

It is often stated that humanism need not be secular—that it is fully compatible with Christianity. Many historians speak of "Christian humanism," seeing in the work of a man like Erasmus the union of Christian faith and classical wisdom.

Jens Zimmermann is one such historian. He has argued that the early church fathers were humanists, even citing Augustine. As late as the so-called Enlightenment, he claims, an "incarnational humanism" animated

Christendom's vision of man and the world. Only in the work of Kant, when the Incarnation ceased to be real and became only idealistic, did humanism become truly secular.[22]

Zimmermann's purpose is to point to ways in which modern Christians might again lay claim to the culture of the West. Since so much of that culture was shaped by secularists during the age of utopia, it is understandable that he would point to earlier, first-millennium expressions of anthropology and cosmology. He emphasizes, of course, the glorified status Christianity assigns to man in the world. As he correctly notes, pagandom never came close to such dignification. And in this his work is a refreshing contrast to that of postmodernists and new atheists, who so often set the terms for discussions about culture and civilization in our times. But even his philosophical defense of Christian culture concedes rather more to the secularists than seems necessary or warranted.

For as the present book has tried to show, humanism is a system of beliefs and values about man in the world that originated not with Pentecost or the early fathers but with the pagan rebirth of Christendom during the Italian quattrocento. It appeared at a time in which the gospel's dignification of man and its affirmation of the world suffered from a neglect stretching back at least to the eleventh century. Humanism was not an extension of earlier, first-millennium patterns of culture. It was a departure from them. It was concocted by Petrarch as a balm to heal the wounds caused by his penitential despair. And for centuries it proved to be effective.

But the elixir also produced a kind of narcosis. It caused forgetfulness. As the first millennium slipped ever further from Western memory, humanism began to take the place of Christianity. In this its rise provides evidence to support Charles Taylor's dismissal of a "subtraction narrative" about the origin of secularism.[23] Christianity did not cease to answer the life questions of modern man, leaving secularism to fill the gap. It was not simply subtracted out of the equation. In its reformational form, it answered those life

22 Jens Zimmermann, *Incarnational Humanism: A Philosophy of Culture for the Church in the World* (Downers Grove, IL: InterVarsity Press, 2012).

23 Charles Taylor, *Secular Age*, 26.

questions incorrectly, or at least in an unsatisfactory way. Humanism provided the alternative.

At first it did so as a defense of man and the world against accusations like that of Pope Innocent III, whose twelfth-century *Misery of the Human Condition* characterized Western culture during the age of division. Then, in the wake of the wars of Western religion, both governments and intellectuals turned to humanism for relief from the divisions and hypocrisy of reformational Christianity. By the time the French Revolution arrived, the philosophes, who mostly renounced their baptisms, had forgotten that enlightenment was a Christian concept. Their anti-evangelical reorientation of the West not only deprived Western civilization of the culture that had made it great. Their project actually disoriented it, establishing in the place of Christianity a counterfeit vision that sought human fulfillment in a desecrated world. The romantics momentarily awoke from humanism's spell after being jolted by Robespierre and Napoleon, but without the means of authentic transcendence. (One suspects that none of them in good conscience could ever have seriously embraced something as ludicrous as Emerson's Over-Soul.) So, like Lamennais's laughing madman, many of the romantics plummeted into an abyss of self-destruction.

By the middle of the nineteenth century, as humanists looked to various ideologies to sustain them in secularism, an essayist named Jules-Antoine Castagnary gave them a voice. Castagnary was himself a secularist and a devoted advocate of Gustave Courbet, the pioneer of realist painting and sometime anarchist. Indeed, as the creator of the *Stone Breakers* rendered a portrait of Castagnary, the latter worked on a biography of Courbet.

In 1858 Castagnary was reviewing the paintings of the Paris Salon, an avant-garde exhibition with lineage through figures like David and Boucher all the way back to the artists of the Renaissance. His review provided the occasion for a comment he placed in the mouth of what he considered modern man. It was noteworthy in that even then, in an atmosphere of atheism and revolution, the review could not advance utopia without the imagery of traditional Christianity: "Beside the divine garden from which I have been driven away," he wrote,

> *I will build a New Eden for myself which I will populate with mine own kind. I will station the invisible sentinel Progress at its entrance, and place a flaming sword into his hands. And he will say to God, "Thou shalt not enter here!"*

Such was the outcome of humanism a half-millennium after Petrarch. Though idealism had given way to realism and deference to rebellion, the promethean sentiment was not a great deal different from that of Petrarch's successors, such as Ficino or Pico. With or without God, man is autonomous and will find his fulfillment in a spiritually untransformed world. Traditional Christianity had been displaced by a humanism that was all too secular.

And because it was secular, it was deceptive. A spiritually neutral space known as the saeculum had not been part of the early Church's cosmology. According to the gospel, the Creator of the world was present on earth within the body of Christ, and through the Holy Spirit He promised to dwell among men until the end of time. An expansive doctrine of secularity only subverted this.

This is not because the world and its Christian culture became the kingdom of heaven. It could never do that, because the kingdom of heaven is not of this world. But the world and its culture were subjected to heavenly immanence through the sacramental life of the Church. The saeculum, formulated first by St. Augustine in his effort to counter the heresy of Donatism, was distorted into becoming—after a full millennium had elapsed—the means by which humanists escaped the misery of the human condition. According to traditional Christianity, however, human fulfillment could never be realized in a spiritually neutral condition. Instead of a saeculum, it preached a world spiritually transformed by the kingdom of heaven and leading toward it. From this point of view, secular humanism was a deceptive substitute for the gospel.

This is not to deny the profound achievements of utopia. The secular transformation of the world proved to be not only possible but phenomenally prolific. The benefits of humanism, perceived only dimly by its father, Petrarch, accumulated on a grand scale during the centuries that followed his ascent of Mount Ventoux. From philosophy to statecraft to music to technology—the West during the age of utopia surged ahead of all other civilizations on earth. By the beginning of the twentieth century, a European colonist in Asia or an American missionary in Africa could not divest himself of this fact; he applied it to form what, to a more sensitive generation a century later, may seem like unjustified condescension. Be that as it may, global civilization was ultimately drawn toward and forever altered by the utopian civilization of the West.

Nevertheless, many of its effects were soon to appear anything but progressive. This was due in part to the fraudulent promises of utopia.

The path from humanism to nihilism, it turned out, was a swift one. Only a few prescient intellectuals had seen what was coming. Among them were Friedrich Nietzsche and Fyodor Dostoevsky. The first, an atheist, had mocked liberalism as a form of crypto-Christianity certain to bind rather than loose humanity. For this German philosopher, the ideologies of socialism and nationalism were no better. Instead, he prophesied the coming end of morality altogether. The Russian novelist was no less cynical about ideological substitutes for Christendom's lost primordial values. He was also no less prophetic in his vision of what they would bring. But as a Christian, he warned that atheism would only make the looming disaster worse. "Without God," one of his characters declares, "anything is permissible."

Indeed. But the catastrophic reckoning that accompanied secularization took many by surprise. It began in earnest with the First World War. Following the hesitation of the Christmas Truce of 1914, total warfare caused the death of twenty million men. The new methods of killing it employed were the cause of almost apocalyptic despair. Factory-produced munitions kept cannon and other weapons firing so relentlessly that soldiers were driven into their trenches like cowering children. Rarely was the enemy seen face to face. Rifles and the recently invented machine gun made sure of that, chewing up human life whenever it dared appear above the lines. Electrical engineering enabled the design of underwater boats that put thousands of unsuspecting sailors and civilians to death within the brief minutes that followed a torpedo strike. Then there was mustard gas. The fruit of modern chemistry, it became the most disturbing weapon in industrial Christendom's burgeoning arsenal. In many ways it became the most infamous token of total warfare—until, that is, the atom bomb took its place.

World War I subverted faith in utopia. And when it was over, so was the age of utopia. Only in revolutionary Russia was there a strong conviction that the promises of the past six centuries might still be fulfilled. But the ferocious violence of the Bolsheviks suggested that here, too, secular humanism would fail. It certainly did so under Stalin. Bringing about the chilling but fictional prophecy of Dostoevsky's *Demons,* the heir to Lenin murdered some of his own supporters in order to create a bond of fear among those remaining. The Old Bolsheviks like Bukharin—visionary author of the *ABC of Communism*—were killed off after being placed on bizarre show trials in which they confessed to completely implausible crimes. Even the most ruthless among them, Trotsky, could not escape Stalin's terror. As we have seen, the former commissar of war and Lenin's right-hand man was hunted down and put to death in Mexico City on the orders of Stalin.

And as the spectacle of Stalinism was unfolding, an even more nihilistic process was being directed by Adolf Hitler. It too was inspired by the promise of utopia. Granted, Nazi Germany was a racist utopia, but it was still a utopia. It sprang up from the indignation of German nationalists following the defeat of 1918 and the economic depression that followed. It was an answer to the promise that modern Christendom should transform the saeculum in order to provide happy lives in an economy of abundance. By the millions, German men and women used their republican voting rights in 1932 to make the Nazis the most powerful political party of the most progressive democracy in history. The head of that party, Hitler, was then quickly and inevitably appointed head of state.

Once Hitler had suspended the Weimar constitution and created a dictatorship, he unleashed his genocidal plan to enslave the Russians and annihilate the Jews. To do so he drew heavily on social Darwinism and the racial "science" of Haeckel. World War II and the Holocaust were the outcome of an ethnic nationalism empowered by modernity. As twenty-seven million Soviets and six million Jews were murdered through blitzkrieg and

Zyklon-B—a poison gas more advanced than previous chemicals—utopia became dystopia. What, an educated Soviet war prisoner building bombs in Germany or an assimilated Jew awaiting the gas chamber at Auschwitz might bitterly have asked, deluded humanists so long ago into thinking man could be autonomous?

But as I noted in the introduction to the first volume of this narrative, history, in the words of Georges Florovsky, is a creative tragedy. The catastrophe that was the twentieth century provided correction for a benighted vision of man and the world. And if it exposed secular humanism as a great deception, it did little to undermine the heavenly promises of traditional Christianity. In fact, the coming age of nihilism would serve as a reminder that not utopia but paradise had once defined what the West once was.

Index

Illustrations indicated by page numbers in italics

D

T

Z

About the Author

JOHN STRICKLAND IS AN ORTHODOX priest and former college professor. His first book, *The Making of Holy Russia,* is a study of the resilience of Christianity in the modern world. An active blogger and podcaster, he brings to the present work a lifetime of reflection on the religious background of the West. He lives in western Puget Sound with his wife and five children.